STUDIES IN ANTIQUITY AND CHRISTIANITY

3/29/02

The Roots of Egyptian Christianity
Birger A. Pearson and James E. Goehring, editors

Gnosticism, Judaism, and Egyptian Christianity
Birger A. Pearson

Ascetic Behavior in Greco-Roman Antiquity: A Sourcebook
Vincent L. Wimbush, editor

*Elijah in Upper Egypt: "The Apocalypse of Elijah"
and Early Egyptian Christianity*
David Frankfurter

The Letters of St. Antony: Monasticism and the Making of a Saint
Samuel Rubenson

Women and Goddess Traditions: In Antiquity and Today
Karen L. King, editor

*Ascetics, Society, and the Desert:
Studies in Early Egyptian Monasticism*
James E. Goehring

The Formation of Q: Trajectories in Ancient Wisdom Collections
John S. Kloppenborg

Reading the Hebrew Bible for a New Millennium
Volume 1: *Theological and Hermeneutical Studies*
Wonil Kim, Deborah Ellens, Michael Floyd,
and Marvin A. Sweeney, editors

STUDIES IN ANTIQUITY AND CHRISTIANITY

The Institute for Antiquity and Christianity
Claremont Graduate University
Claremont, California

STUDIES IN ANTIQUITY & CHRISTIANITY

Reading the Hebrew Bible for a New Millennium

Form, Concept, and Theological Perspective

Volume 1: Theological and Hermeneutical Studies

Edited by
Wonil Kim, Deborah Ellens,
Michael Floyd, and Marvin A. Sweeney

TRINITY PRESS
INTERNATIONAL
HARRISBURG, PA

Trinity Press International, P.O. Box 1321, Harrisburg, PA 17105
Trinity Press International is a division of the Morehouse Group.

Cover art: *Isaiah*, James Jacques Joseph Tissot. Photographer: Joseph Parnell.
The Jewish Museum, New York/Art Resource, New York.

Cover design: Jim Booth

Library of Congress Cataloging-in-Publication Data

Reading the Hebrew Bible for a new millennium : form, concept, and theological
perspective / edited by Deborah Ellens ... [et al.].
    p.   cm. – (Studies in antiquity & Christianity)
   Includes bibliographical references and index.
   ISBN 1-56338-314-4 (pa : alk. paper)
   1. Bible. O.T. – Theology. I. Ellens, Deborah H. II. Studies in antiquity and
Christianity.
BS1192.5.A1 R43 2000
230'.0411 – dc21   00–021124

Printed in the United States of America

00   01   02   03   04   05   06   10   9   8   7   6   5   4   3   2   1

Contents

Abbreviations

AB	Anchor Bible
ABD	*Anchor Bible Dictionary*. Ed. D. N. Freedman. 6 vols. New York, 1992
ACNT	Augsburg Commentaries on the New Testament
AnBib	Analecta biblica
ANET	*Ancient Near Eastern Texts Relating to the Old Testament*. Ed. J. B. Pritchard. 3rd ed. Princeton, 1969
BA	*Biblical Archaeologist*
BBB	Bonner biblische Beiträge
BBR	*Bulletin for Biblical Research*
BN	*Biblische Notizen*
BSac	*Bibliotheca sacra*
BTZ	*Berliner Theologische Zeitschrift*
BWANT	Beiträge zur Wissenschaft vom Alten und Neuen Testament
BZAW	Beihefte zur Zeitschrift für die alttestamentliche Wissenschaft
CBQ	*Catholic Biblical Quarterly*
CTJ	*Calvin Theological Journal*
DMOA	Documenta et monumenta Orientis antiqui
EDNT	*Exegetical Dictionary of the New Testament*. Ed. H. Balz and G. Schneider. ET. Grand Rapids, 1990–93
EKKNT	Evangelisch-katholischer Kommentar zum Neuen Testament
ETL	*Ephemerides theologicae lovaniensis*
EvT	*Evangelische Theologie*
ExpTim	*Expository Times*
EZ	Exegese in unserer Zeit
FCB	Feminist Companion to the Bible
FOTL	Forms of the Old Testament Literature
GAT	*Grundrisse zum Alten Testament*

HBT	*Horizons in Biblical Theology*
HDR	Harvard Dissertations in Religion
HTR	*Harvard Theological Review*
Int	*Interpretation*
JBL	*Journal of Biblical Literature*
JES	*Journal of Ecumenical Studies*
JNES	*Journal of Near Eastern Studies*
JR	*Journal of Religion*
JRE	*Journal of Religious Ethics*
JSJ	*Journal for the Study of Judaism in the Persian, Hellenistic, and Roman Periods*
JSOTSup	Journal for the Study of the Old Testament: Supplement Series
LCC	Library of Christian Classics
NICNT	New International Commentary on the New Testament
NICOT	New International Commentary on the Old Testament
NIDNTT	*New International Dictionary of New Testament Theology.* Ed. C. Brown. 4 vols. Grand Rapids, 1975–85
NIDOTTE	*New International Dictionary of Old Testament Theology and Exegesis.* Ed. W. A. VanGemeren. 5 vols. Grand Rapids, 1997
OBO	Orbis biblicus et orientalis
OBT	Overtures to Biblical Theology
OTL	Old Testament Library
RB	*Revue biblique*
RelSRev	*Religious Studies Review*
SBLDS	Society of Biblical Literature Dissertation Series
SJOT	*Scandinavian Journal of the Old Testament*
SJT	*Scottish Journal of Theology*
SNTSMS	Society for New Testament Studies Monograph Series
TB	Theologische Bücherei: Neudrucke und Berichte aus dem 20. Jahrhundert
TDNT	*Theological Dictionary of the New Testament.* Ed. G. Kittel and G. Friedrich. Trans. G. W. Bromiley. 10 vols. Grand Rapids, 1964–76

TDOT	*Theological Dictionary of the Old Testament.* Ed. G. J. Botterweck and H. Ringgren. Trans. J. T. Willis, G. W. Bromiley, and D. E. Green. 10 vols. Grand Rapids, 1974–
THAT	*Theologisches Handwörterbuch zum Alten Testament.* Ed. E. Jenni, with assistance from C. Westermann. 2 vols. Stuttgart, 1971–76
ThTo	*Theology Today*
ThWAT	*Theologisches Wörterbuch zum Alten Testament.* Ed. G. J. Botterweck and H. Ringgren. Stuttgart, 1970–
TLOT	*Theological Lexicon of the Old Testament.* Ed. E. Jenni, with assistance from C. Westermann. Trans. M. E. Biddle. 3 vols. Peabody, Mass., 1997
TS	*Theological Studies*
TWOT	*Theological Wordbook of the Old Testament.* Ed. R. L. Harris, G. L. Archer, and B. K. Waltke. 2 vols. Chicago, 1980
TZ	*Theologische Zeitschrift*
VT	*Vetus Testamentum*
VTSup	Supplements to Vetus Testamentum
WBC	Word Biblical Commentary
WUNT	Wissenschaftliche Untersuchungen zum Neuen Testament
ZAW	*Zeitschrift für die alttestamentliche Wissenschaft*

Introduction

Wonil Kim

This collection of essays is the first of two volumes consisting mostly of articles by Rolf P. Knierim's former students now engaged in their professions around the world. Other contributors include panelists who participated in reviewing Knierim's latest book, *The Task of Old Testament Theology: Substance, Method, and Cases* (Grand Rapids: Eerdmans, 1995), at the 1997 Society of Biblical Literature (SBL) meeting in San Francisco. Within a short time and as no surprise to the editors, the majority of those invited sent articles, making it necessary to turn the project into a two-volume work instead of the originally planned single volume. The editors are grateful to the contributors for their excellent essays as well as for their patience while the volumes were taking shape.

A *Festschrift* was published in Rolf Knierim's honor in 1997, *Problems in Biblical Theology* (Grand Rapids: Eerdmans). We therefore do not consider this and the subsequent volume *Festschriften*. In fact, that cannot be, since we have invited Rolf Knierim himself to contribute to the project. Six of his recent articles appear in this first volume.

Our main intention in these volumes is to carry forward Knierim's legacy by focusing on the implementation of various aspects of his methodology. The majority of the contributors have had first-hand experience with Knierim's method, and we solicited a diversity of essays that would demonstrate ways of implementing the method particularly as proposed by Knierim in recent works such as *Text and Concept in Leviticus 1:1–9* (Tübingen: J. C. B. Mohr [Paul Siebeck], 1992) and *The Task of Old Testament Theology*.

Knierim is perhaps best known for his contributions to exegesis and theology of the Hebrew Bible/Old Testament texts. Far from being only a descriptive exegete of the literary and theological concepts of texts, however, he is in the end a systematician. His ultimate concern is the hermeneutical encounter at the substance level between the texts and the world — the world populated by the people whose lives are affected by those texts *in actu*. His *Task of Old Testament Theology* is nothing other than a programmatic statement, a prolegomenon to his system of doing Hebrew Bible/Old Testament theology.

Implementing Knierim's methodology of exegesis, theology, and hermeneutic as proposed in that prolegomenon would, in the words of a

1

perceptive reviewer, "be massive and involve the reconceptualization of basic interpretive paradigms" (Katrina Larkin, *Theological Book Review* [U.K.], June 1996). We do not presume even to have begun that massive task in this volume. Instead, the present volume offers "showcases" by those who understand his method together with Knierim's own recent essays as well as those of some of his critics.

Rolf Knierim's opening essay in this volume, "On Biblical Theology," addresses the problem arising from the relationship between the two Testaments in the Christian Bible. He argues that even Gabler did not overcome the traditional view, which considers the Old Testament inferior or penultimate to the New Testament, and that this situation has not changed in the post-Gabler period to the present. Here Knierim lays out a methodological ground on which the two Testaments can maintain their "fundamentally different theological concepts" and at the same time be mutually open to each other in equal status, in "mutual critical complementarity."

A second essay, "On the Task of Old Testament Theology," originated as a lecture at the annual meetings of the Korean Society of Old Testament Studies and the Japanese Society of Old Testament Studies, both in May 1994. In this essay Knierim provides a synopsis of his methodology, with particular attention to the task of biblical exegesis and biblical theology. Exegesis, he says, examines hierarchical semantic systems, the infratextual and subtextual concepts operative in the text, theology that by definition is not external but intrinsic to the text, and finally, the truth claim that is also intrinsic to the text. A theology of the Bible, on the other hand, interprets the *relationship* of the various theologies in the Bible, a task sui generis that neither the writers nor the canonizers of the Bible have carried out. This task yields a systematic relationship of plural and diverse theologies built on "a hierarchy of values, and hence, the degree of validity or truth of each concept in its relation to all others." The criterion for this degree of validity is the universality of God. Knierim compares numerous theological concepts (justice, liberation, election, etc.) in order to illustrate his method.

Knierim's third essay, "Comments on the Task of Old Testament Theology," began as introductory remarks at the 1997 SBL panel review of his *Task of Old Testament Theology*. This essay is a response not to "legitimate agreements, disagreements, or differing positions," but to "disagreements [that] rest on...what [Knierim has] neither said nor meant." It is the author's attempt to clarify misunderstandings regarding the nature of his book as well as specific methodological issues such as diversity, systematization, text and concept, theology of individual texts vis-à-vis Old Testament theology, truth claim, validity, tradition history, recontextualization, meaning, intrabiblical criteria, and others.

The essay is also a defense of his methodological proposal for Old Testament theology that is to be fundamentally distinguished from methodology for phenomenology of the texts, their isolated theologies, and their developments.

The fourth essay by Knierim, "On the View of Reality and Public Human Ethos in the Bible," focuses on what he calls *Geistesbeschäftigung,* public ethos that not only belongs to the common human mentality but is also shared by the religious communities that produced the Jewish and Christian Bibles. After arguing that this *Geistesbeschäftigung* intensively involves systems of gradation between values and antivalues, the author turns his attention to "the distinctly divided views of reality in the two Testaments [that] have led to two distinctly different foundations for evaluation." For the Hebrew Bible, "the view of the indefinitely ongoing world is fundamental," and its ethos is "determined by the experience of this world" and is characterized by the process of "seeking" values that are "found in degrees." The view of reality in the New Testament, on the other hand, is based "on the mythology of a new creation beyond any human experience . . . on truth known rather than truth to be sought and found." Knierim concludes that "in view of the defunct mythological eschatology, ethos as search for truth rather than ethos from a possession of truth is the human lot."

In his fifth essay, "On Two Cases of the Biblical Hermeneutic of Justice," Knierim compares two relatively recent events with basic aspects in the biblical theology of justice: the jury's verdict in the trial of O. J. Simpson in Los Angeles and the assassination of Israeli prime minister Yitzhak Rabin in Tel Aviv. Discussion of the first event focuses on the difference between the concerns for societal justice and decisions about specific cases in courts. He argues that this difference is suspect of having been set aside by the jury, in contrast to biblical ethos and law, where such an action is not allowed. Discussion of the second event focuses on a conflict within the Old Testament itself and its influence on the law and ethos in contemporary politics: the conflict between especially the Pentateuch's theology of Israel's exclusive possession of the promised land — the position of Yigal Amir — and a principle of peace between Israel and other nations in the land.[1]

Knierim's final essay in this volume, "On the Subject of War in Old Testament and Biblical Theology," is a response to Hans Eberhard von Waldow's 1984 article, "The Concept of War in the Old Testament." While agreeing with von Waldow on many methodological points, Knierim argues against von Waldow that there are different concepts of

---

1. This summary is nearly a direct quotation from the author's own summary that accompanied his original manuscript.

war in the Old Testament that reflect markedly different assumptions. With this observation he examines von Waldow's basic statement that war is sin because it violates God's order of creation and his distinction between "sacred" and "secular" wars. He contends that while von Waldow's criterion for this distinction is seemingly based on the question of the agents (Yahweh or humans) of war, his real, predominant criterion for valid and invalid war betrays the substantive question (violation or defense of creation). Knierim concludes that the question is not one of "God and war" but of "creation and war" regardless of the agents (divine or human) involved, and that the question applies to all nations and peoples, including Israel. With this premise he asks, "What is the function of Israel in Yahweh's wars?" and concludes that in the Priestly concept "God's order of creation and Yahweh's wars in history function for the sake of Israel's election." Knierim concludes his essay by noting the New Testament's programmatic (!) lack of attention to the question of the pervasiveness of war in history, which he critically attributes to "the fundamental difference between the Old and the New Testament's view of reality."

James Brenneman, "Debating Ahab: Characterization in Biblical Theology," compares the Ahab story as it appears in the Masoretic Text and in the Septuagint, noting the conspicuous difference between the two in the plot line. He moves beyond the traditional question of "originality," "priority," or "authenticity" to ask, "What hermeneutic may be at work in *both* accounts that would make sense of the discrepancies?" He finds an answer to this question, traces its trajectory in the postbiblical literature using the methodology of comparative midrash, and searches for "a more complex, fully modulated characterization of Ahab." Included in the survey are pseudepigrapha, Josephus, *Targum Jonathan, Midrash Rabbah,* Babylonian Talmud, Jerusalem Talmud, and interestingly, history and archaeology. While concluding that "the Deuteronomists sought rhetorical purity over full-fledged characterization," Brenneman moves beyond the question of characterization to respond to Knierim's call for the task of adjudication among conflicting theologies and renders his verdict.

Mary Deeley, "Memory and Theology: Ordering the World for the Community of Faith," explores the function of memory as a constitutive element of Old Testament theology. Capitalizing on the contemporary understanding of memory, she contends that memory is not only mental image or the basis of knowledge but is the strategic construction of the sense of one's past. Deeley then examines how memory — both Israel's and God's — plays a constitutive role in the shaping of the theological thinking in the early chapters of Deuteronomy (7–10) as it is operative in reflection, prayer, and storytelling. On the basis of this exegetical and theological observation she concludes that "memory provides the means to order chaotic events of life," and that God, too, uses her memory to act in accord with the divine worldview. Deeley then suggests that memory has a central function for a community that orders itself as a participant in the divine worldview of justice and righteousness. For her, "to participate in God's memory is to make sense of the world according to God's understanding."

Simon DeVries, "Rapprochement with Rolf Knierim," sees his approach to the Old Testament essentially congenial with Rolf Knierim's. DeVries's article is a detailed delineation of this similarity as he sees it. After identifying the areas in which he defines the task of Old Testament theology in terms similar to Knierim's, DeVries gives a synopsis of the relevant points from his 1983 book, *Achievements of Biblical Religion: A Prolegomenon to Old Testament Theology*. He believes that this work particularly fits well Knierim's description of *Sachkritik* and further develops the same line of analysis that he believes significantly contributes to Knierim's discussion of *Sachkritik*. DeVries's proposal for what is normative in the Old Testament, however, is his own: monotheistic personalism (or personalistic monotheism).

Michael Floyd, "Can God's Name Change? A Biblical Theological Perspective on the Feminist Critique of Trinitarian Nomenclature," attempts to "follow Knierim's general approach in order to clarify how the Bible might speak to a specific issue in the contemporary [feminist] debate" on Trinitarian language. After critically engaging the current hermeneutical and biblical-theological discourses (Sallie McFague, Elizabeth Achtemeier, Elizabeth Johnson, Alvin Kimel, Ruth Duck, and others), Floyd exegetes Exod. 3:1 to 6:13 as a pericope in order to delineate "an obvious intertextual connection" between Exod. 3:1–15 and 6:1–13. The outcome is an exegetical, biblical-theological, and hermeneutical case for divine name change that does not violate "the fundamental continuity in God's personal and historical identity," a name change that still meets the Trinitarian criteria of "the radically interpersonal nature of God's love toward all creation and the radically egalitarian nature of God's shared responsibility for the world."

John Goldingay's essay, "Justice and Salvation for Israel and Canaan," developed from his paper at the 1997 SBL panel review. Goldingay presents a counterargument to Knierim's critique of election-conquest theology, which he based on the inner-biblical criteria of universal justice and righteousness. Engaging several relevant discussions on the topic (Levenson, Soulen, Plaskow, Wyschogrod, and others), Goldingay argues that election theology is so central to both Testaments of the Bible that no biblical theology is conceivable without taking it into full account. He also presents an exegetical argument that in the original

Hebrew "justice" and "righteousness" are not abstract nouns but carry concrete connotations such as societal relationships (for "justice") and personal right living (for "righteousness"). As such, they do not denote "universalizable principles" but authoritative, decisive action in specific historical situations. On the basis of these arguments Goldingay draws a conclusion regarding the "annihilated" Canaanites, a conclusion that some readers (Knierim, at least!) may find astonishing.

Robert Hubbard, "The Divine Redeemer: Toward a Biblical Theology of Redemption," presents an exegetical survey of the redemption motif in its longitudinal trajectory throughout the Old and the New Testaments. His aim is to showcase Knierim's call for "mutual critical complementarity" of the two Testaments. Hubbard limits his investigation to the texts that "invoke the vocabulary of redemption but which involve God, either as lawgiver or as redeemer." After thoroughly accounting for the contours of the subject in both Testaments, the author establishes not only the dominance of the divine redeemer motif as a central biblical theme but also the wide variety of its function, especially with different nuances and foci in the separate Testaments. He then suggests the ways in which each Testament can complement the other, bringing together into a synthesis the differing chronological and spatial aspects of redemption, such as its regional versus universal or temporal versus eternal scope.

Mignon Jacobs's essay, "Toward an Old Testament Theology of Concern for the Underprivileged," is an exhaustive exegetical study of the concept of the underprivileged in the Hebrew Bible/Old Testament. The author examines the "semantic indicators and conceptual formulations" of the relevant texts in order to reconstruct the "inherent pluralism" of the concept under investigation. The work is thus a conceptual-critical analysis of the diverse meanings that "underprivileged" denotes and connotes. She limits the task of her essay to critically reconstructing the diverse meanings of "underprivileged" as they occur in the texts and systematically examining the relationship among the diverse meanings. Jacobs notes, however, that a theology of the underprivileged emerging from such an investigation ultimately needs to be analyzed in its relationship to the other theologies in the same canonical corpus. She also acknowledges that the theology of the underprivileged so reconstructed may have its limitations, and calls attention to the hermeneutical challenge faced by the underprivileged of today's world that may differ in nature from the one faced by the underprivileged of the biblical texts she investigates.

Isaac Kalimi's essay, "The Task of Hebrew Bible/Old Testament Theology — Between Judaism and Christianity," likewise originated from a response given at the 1997 SBL panel review. Kalimi shares many of

Knierim's methodological premises for the task of Hebrew Bible/Old Testament theology as he sees them: a comprehensive canonical and historical purview as an essential methodological framework; the plurality of theologies that constitutes a fundamental and central problem; rejection of criteriological superiority of the New Testament; and so forth. The author is critical of Knierim, however, on several accounts. While recognizing Knierim's record of fairness to the Hebrew Bible as an entity in its own right, he believes Knierim sometimes slides back into the mode of a Protestant theologian. He also finds Knierim's nomenclature "Old Testament" and "Jewish Bible" problematic. Perhaps most importantly, he disagrees with Knierim's theological assessment of election theology and argues that "there is no [tension] between the election theology and the Bible's 'claim to Yahweh's universal justice.' "

Joel S. Kaminsky, "Wrestling with Israel's Election: A Jewish Reaction to Rolf Knierim's Biblical Theology," is another contributor whose essay comes from a presentation at the 1997 SBL panel review, bringing an additional criticism of Knierim's work as it pertains to the theology of election. While acknowledging that "Knierim has taken the first giant step by arguing that [the] plurality constitutes a problem [forcing the reader] to make hard choices," he flatly rejects one of Knierim's solutions as it is spelled out in his critique of the election theology. Kaminsky knows that Knierim does not want to reject but expand the idea of Israel's election to accommodate humanity in its entirety. For Kaminsky, however, "such a theological move is tantamount to denying the concept as it has been put forward within the Hebrew Bible" and in subsequent Jewish and Christian interpretations. Although such jettisoning has "the noblest" motivation, Kaminsky sees it as another form of supersessionism based on "a modern set of preferences to redefine what the biblical text should mean," supersessionism that Kaminsky finds less desirable even than that of Christian readings which retain "exegetical integrity."

Hyun Chul Paul Kim, "Gender Complementarity in the Hebrew Bible," examines the ancient texts in Exodus 15 and Judges 4 and 5 and finds "subtle" and "hidden" conceptual "signifiers" for gender complementarity. Kim investigates these texts within the framework of "Knierim's interpretive tools" of exegesis, theology, and hermeneutics and compares both the complementing and the contending conceptualities in their complex of intratextual and intertextual relations. Comparing the Song of Moses/the Sea and the Song of Miriam in Exodus 15, the author finds not only a reduction and marginalization of women's role but also the texts' hidden efforts to elevate it, thus balancing the gender relation with an implicit "concept of complementarity of Moses and Miriam." The relation between Deborah and Barak in

Judges 4 and 5 displays, perhaps in less subtle ways yet still with hidden signifiers, the concept of balance toward equality, forming a conceptual "chiasm" with Exodus 15. At the end of his essay Kim proposes hermeneutical ramifications of these conceptual exegeses within the horizons of the Hebrew Bible, the Christian canon, and contemporary settings.

Wonil Kim's essay, "Liberation Theology and the Bible: A Methodological Consideration," is a response to the methodology of J. Severino Croatto, a liberationist and Hebrew Bible/Old Testament scholar. Kim examines Croatto's approach as developed in its Gadamer-Ricoeur axis of hermeneutics as well as in the context of the "history of salvation" school, which Kim characterizes as "anti-conceptual." Using Knierim's conceptual analysis of Exodus 3, Kim challenges Croatto's semiotically drawn conclusion that the exodus is completed by the narratological closure of "entry" into Canaan. Kim then calls for biblical theological and hermeneutical reexamination of the relationship between liberation theology and conquest theology within the methodological framework proposed by Knierim.

Charles Mabee, "A New Approach to the Christian-Jewish Dialogue," proposes that the prophetic tradition of the Hebrew Bible/Old Testament — the "Mosaic prophetic tradition," as he calls it — moved from its preexilic peripheral existence to the mainstream of religious thinking during the exilic period. Mabee attributes this move to the Deuteronomists, who used the strategy of "co-opting" the mainstream traditions (Zionist, priestly, wisdom, etc.) by allowing them to remain only as textually based entities in the newly founded textually based religion. The author maintains that "Judaism and Christianity represent variant forms" of this move that put Mosaic prophetic tradition at the center of the postexilic community. Within this interpretive framework, Mabee sees the Pentateuch as a "prologue" to "the Mosaic prophetic tradition," the "Torah tradition" as an "attempt to democratize" this tradition, and the New Testament as its continuation. The author then concludes that the central issue is the Mosaic prophetic tradition "not as Jewish or Christian, but as a movement in its own right," forming a common axis for both religions with the particular attention to the question of violence within each.

Stephen A. Reed's essay, "Human Dominion of Animals," is an exhaustive survey of the texts that either directly deal with or shed light on the question of human dominion over animals in the Hebrew Bible. While recognizing that "the language of 'dominion' remains problematic in today's world," Reed takes a cautious approach to the relevant texts in order to render an honest exegetical result, then to raise serious and realistic hermeneutical questions. The author emphasizes that the issue is not merely an ethical concern but also a theological problem, because the texts often directly involve God's position in the matter. He argues that the issue needs to be addressed in terms of "relative priorities of values" examined "in light of divine dominion." After the exegetical survey of the texts (Genesis 1, the flood, Psalm 8, etc.) and the theological critique, Reed tackles the difficult hermeneutical questions, such as the conflict between predators and prey, the threat of dangerous animals, including bacterium and virus, and the limits on dominion over animals, all within the changing contexts of our times, where our actions affect the world in a way different from biblical times.

Janet Weathers, "The Value of Rolf Knierim's Old Testament Theology for Practical Theology," considers how Knierim's methodology can contribute to practical theology in an essential and significant way — essential because the problem Knierim addresses in the Hebrew Bible/Old Testament is analogous to the problem practical theology faces; significant because the way (method) Knierim addresses the problem of biblical theology and the criteriological argument (method) he presents can make a salient contribution to the discourse of practical theology. One value she finds in Knierim's work is "[his refusal to bring] the diverse theological understandings in the Old Testament into a harmonious whole." Weathers finds this phenomenon (not only of different but also) of differing voices with contradictory truth claims closely analogous to the discourse of practical theology, "in which pluralism and a diversity of perspectives is a major topic." But for her, the true value of Knierim's method is that "he does not merely let the diversity stand [but demands] the hard work of thinking through the relationships among the diverse theologies and making a case for which theological understanding is most fundamental." Weathers believes that Knierim's approach provides a particular value to "the traditions that honor the doctrine of *sola scriptura*" because he insists that intrabiblical criteria can be used to adjudicate the diverse theologies. But on a broader horizon of hermeneutical discourse, she finds in Knierim's approach to theological negotiating an excellent analogy to the postmodern need for dialogue such as the one proposed by philosopher Richard Bernstein. In presenting her case throughout her essay, Weathers also gives an excellent synopsis of Knierim's argument of method and substance.

The editors are most grateful to Hal Rast of Trinity Press International for his kind guidance during the initial stages of the project, and to the Institute for Antiquity and Christianity of Claremont Graduate University for adopting this project as part of its Studies in Antiquity and Christianity Series. They would also like to express deep appreciation to Henry Carrigan and Laura Hudson of Trinity Press

International for the invaluable help they offered and for their patience while the volume was taking shape. A word of special thanks also goes to J. Harold Ellens for the role he played in the conception of the project and to Professor Roy F. Melugin for reading the manuscripts and responding with valuable and encouraging observations.

Last but not least, the editors would like to thank Robert Maccini for his meticulous and superb copy editing skills, from which the volume has benefited greatly; John Eagleson, the typesetter, for his extraordinary help, particularly with the indices; Tony Kaspereen and Jessica Kim of La Sierra University for creating the database for the indices as well as for doing other sundries of filing work; and John Jones and Suzy Kaspereen of La Sierra University for their administrative support.

1

On Biblical Theology

Rolf P. Knierim

In the so-called Western civilization and in the parts of those civilizations that are influenced by or in dialogue with it, the Bible is today read for three main reasons: for its contribution to our knowledge of ancient history, for being part of the body of classical world literature, and for its role in the Jewish and Christian religions.

It is important that the Bible is read not only for religious reasons. As a source for historical knowledge and as a document of world literature it represents a significant contribution to the total body of human knowledge, and already for this reason belongs not only to the Jewish and Christian communities but also to the entire human race.

The Bible is, however, essentially a religious book. Even where it informs us about history, literature, and much more, its information functions for the religious purposes of its writers. Without these purposes, the biblical books would not have been written.

The fact of its religious purposes does not mean that the Bible belongs only to those communities who produced it. The Bible is not esoteric literature for esoteric religious sects. It is also the religious contribution of its respective communities to all societies and cultures and to all human beings. In this contribution the biblically based communities have expressed their understanding of reality as the basis for the way of life for all and therefore also for themselves. This understanding is religious, and because its religiosity focuses on God, it is essentially theological. And the Jewish and Christian communities read their respective Bibles today because they are the original sources for the theological shape of their religions.

The Jewish and the Christian communities do not have the same Bible. Whereas the Jewish community has the Hebrew Bible, the Tanak, followed by Talmud and Midrash but not the Christian New Testament,

This essay is dedicated to professor James Sanders, my colleague at Claremont since 1976, on the occasion of his seventieth birthday, with best wishes for a long and healthy life. The essay was originally read at the Methodist Seminary in Seoul, Korea, on May 17, 1994, and at the Tokyo United Theological Seminary (TUTS) on May 27, 1994. It is published in Japanese in the *TUTS Annual*. The English version was previously published in *The Quest for Context and Meaning: Studies in Biblical Intertextuality in Honor of James A. Sanders*, ed. C. A. Evans and S. Talmon. Reprinted by permission of Brill Academic Publishers.

the Christian community has one Bible of two parts, the Christian New Testament and also the Jewish Bible as its Old Testament.

The origin of the Christian Bible of two Testaments dates back to the second century when the church decided, against Marcion, to continue to recognize the Jewish Bible as a part of its total Bible rather than reject it as the document of an evil religion. The rejection of Marcion was justified because the Jewish Scriptures had already in the original Christian writings been recognized as Holy Scriptures inspired by the same God who had ultimately revealed himself in Jesus Christ.

Nevertheless, the juxtaposition of the two Testaments in the Christian Bible generated a problem with which the church has had to live throughout its history, and which is, in my opinion, not sufficiently diagnosed, let alone answered, to this day. It is the problem of how the two Testaments are related. We have no consensus on what each Testament means for the other, especially on whether or not the two Testaments are mutually open to each other.

In the tradition of Christian theology, the relationship of the two Testaments has scarcely ever been one of mutually equal openness. From the earliest Christian writings of the first century, it was the Christian theology of the ultimate revelation of God in Jesus Christ that determined the validity of everything else. The principles for theological validity were controlled by Christology, and this Christology also predetermined the sense in which the Jewish Bible could still have a function for humanity from the perspective of the Christian faith.

The original and basic paradigms for this function are contained in the New Testament:

- The Old Testament is prophecy, whereas the Christian faith teaches the fulfillment of this prophecy — so especially in Matthew.

- Moses gave the law, but "grace and truth came through Jesus Christ" — so in John (1:17). It is the truth of the living water and bread, of light rather than darkness, and of resurrection as eternal life rather than eternal death.

- According to Luke, "the law and the prophets were until John [the Baptist]; since then the gospel of the kingdom of God is preached" (16:16), and in Acts the Holy Spirit is poured out.

- For Paul, the gospel and life in the Spirit reveal that every way of life, religious or not, including the way revealed by God to Israel, is the way under the law rather than the liberty of existence. It is under judgment because it is not reconciled through God's work in Jesus Christ. The original creation under the law belongs to the past because the new creation has come.

- According to the Letter to the Hebrews, Israel's believing community only foreshadows the final believing community of those by now once and for all times atoned by Christ's sacrifice.

The decisive ground for these definitions is the Christian belief in the ultimacy of God's revelation in Jesus Christ. In view of this ultimacy, everything said in the Old Testament is at best penultimate. Prophecy is surpassed and replaced by fulfillment; Moses' law by grace and truth; the time of law and the prophets by the time of the gospel; existence as sinner by liberation from death, sin, and law; the old by the new believing community; and in toto the old by the new creation.

The Christian belief in the ultimacy of God's revelation in Jesus Christ is, of course, based on the affirmation of God's resurrection of the crucified Jesus from the dead. Unlike other resurrections, God's resurrection of Jesus was understood as the decisive watershed in the history of the universe, as the replacement of the validity of the first creation by the breaking-in of the new creation into the still existing yet soon ending old creation. It is the root for the affirmation that Jesus is, ultimately, the Messiah, the only Son of the living God, the only Logos, who was with God before creation, and the *kyrios,* the only Lord over heaven and earth. Hence, the eschatological event happened. The new creation has arrived, exists, and will therefore soon be fully revealed in the second coming of Christ. This second coming may be delayed, but it is nevertheless always close and the disciples must therefore always be prepared for it. The temporal eschatology of the second coming of Christ was not an incidental, discardable shell. It was essential for the christologically based worldview of the early Christians. Since the new creation is present only in signs but has not yet subsumed the old creation, the completion of the replacement of the old by the new creation had to be expected. Only in the Gospel of John does the temporal eschatology step back in favor of the ultimacy of life in Christ in terms of eternal life in both life and death.

From this Christian theology of religion, the theology of the Jewish Bible has from the earliest Christian writings appeared to be at best preliminary, preparatory, penultimate, relative, an example for how not, or no longer, to believe, and at worst irrelevant, negligible, or to be rejected. The relationship between these writings and the Old Testament was not one of mutually equal openness, an openness in which the Old Testament and these writings could jointly determine the scope of the religious understanding of reality. This relationship was unilaterally predetermined by the Christians and their Christian agenda.

This situation was reinforced by the canonization of the early Christian writings in the New Testament. Ever since this canonization, the relationship between the two Testaments has meant not only that the

Christian Bible consists of two Testaments, but also, especially, that the judgment of the New over the Old Testament, and with it the judgment of the Christians over Israel, has canonical authority and is a canonical requirement.

This understanding was basic for the churches of the Protestant Reformation, for Protestant orthodoxy, for the periods of rationalism and the Enlightenment, for the religious concepts of romanticism and idealism and the religio-historical school, and for virtually all New and Old Testament theologies in the twentieth century from Karl Barth to Walther Eichrodt, Rudolf Bultmann, Gerhard von Rad, Walther Zimmerli, Claus Westermann, Brevard Childs, and many others.

Despite varying emphases, all Christian interpreters of the Old or the New Testament reflect the essential position that Johann Philipp Gabler presented in his 1787 inaugural lecture, "About the Just Discrimination of Biblical and Dogmatic Theology and the Correctly Governing Boundaries of Each," in which he programmatically declared that biblical theology is a discipline independent of dogmatics.

Gabler's demand for the liberation of biblical theology from its subservience to dogmatic theology was not new. This demand rested on the Protestant principle that the Bible is the basis and criterion for the doctrine of the church rather than dependent on or intertwined with this doctrine. This principle had to be clearly restored in his own time. Also, he succeeded, in my analysis, in demonstrating that the criteria for biblical theology are found within the Bible, without dogmatics, even as the criteria for dogmatics are the same as those found in the Bible, just as they should be as long as dogmatics claims to rest on the Bible.

However, Gabler's concept for the biblical theology of both Testaments is decisively derived from those passages and concepts in the New Testament that most clearly express the criterion for the theological evaluation of all other passages in the New as well as especially in the Old Testament. Those passages and concepts contain the one doctrine that is the most important doctrine in the entire Bible. This one doctrine belongs, first of all, to those doctrines in the Bible that are not restricted to passing times but are valid for all places and times. And of those it is the one doctrine that is most decisive and therefore the most specifically Christian, namely, the doctrine of our eternal salvation. Only this doctrine represents the true foundation of the Christian religion.

This doctrine is only found in the New Testament. Compared to it, other doctrines or opinions found even in the New Testament are relative or irrelevant, whereas the Old Testament does not have this doctrine at all. The Old Testament as a whole is, therefore, not only less important than this fundamental Christian doctrine, but also less important than the New Testament as a whole because even the time-restricted opinions in the New Testament evolved from their Christian foundation, which is nowhere the case in the Old Testament. Not even truly universal doctrines (which are for all places and times) found in the Old Testament — the doctrines of creation, the fall, the ten commandments, and monotheism, for example — represent truly Christian doctrines, let alone the pure Christian doctrine of our salvation. The Old Testament as a whole is, however preparatory and divinely inspired, inferior, old, not as important as the newer and better Testament.

It has been said that Gabler did not develop a program for a separate Old Testament theology — as if he might have done so had he wanted it. In fact, he quite clearly outlined the method for an Old Testament theology. More important is that he saw no reason for two separate theologies, one of the Old and another of the New Testament. It was programmatic that he spoke of two testamentally distinct theologies within one united biblical theology. For him, biblical theology had to include the total Christian Bible, with only one decisive distinction: while the Old Testament is not Christian but for the Christians, the New Testament is not only Christian but also by the Christians. In whatever way the Old Testament must be understood as divinely inspired and written by sacred writers, it can, precisely by being juxtaposed to and compared with the New Testament, only simultaneously reveal two things: its own inferiority and the superiority of the New Testament.

Contrary to a long-held opinion, Gabler did not propose that biblical theology be worked out as the history of the biblical religion. He proposed the precise definition and comparison of all biblical doctrines, including those within the New Testament, even those written by Paul in his very same letters. The comparison of these doctrines shows their relative and decisive differences, and above all the one pure doctrine of the Christian religion that is the criterion for the critical evaluation of all other theologies in the total Bible. His biblical theology is a method by which the biblical doctrine of the pure Christian religion can be worked out, a purpose that can be clearly fulfilled only if all doctrines of the Christian Bible are included and compared. This clarification had in his time become extremely necessary. To prove the result of this goal, a biblical theology was necessary rather than two separate theologies of the two Testaments as we have had them for a long time.

Nevertheless, the theological difference between the two Testaments remained fundamental for Gabler, and remains so to this day, notwithstanding aspects common to both, such as word of God, inspiration, monotheism, history, canonicity, authority, and so on. This basic difference is the reason why the separation of the theologies of the two Testaments has been stronger than a united biblical theology and why biblical theology is and has never been anything but in crisis.

When considering a biblical theology, we must realize that in view of their basic difference, the search for a theological unity of the two Testaments is futile. For whatever reason a biblical theology is required, it can be based only on the recognition of the fundamentally different theological concepts of the two Testaments rather than on what both have in common despite that difference. A biblical theology must at its outset interpret this difference.

In order to confront the issue of biblical theology, more is then necessary than the two-thousand-year-old reading of the Old Testament from the New Testament and from the perspective of its specifically christological theology. Attention is necessary to the difference between the Bible's doctrine of the kingdom of God, its theology proper, and the New Testament's focus on Christology. The difference between theology and Christology is clearly attested also in the New Testament, where the reign of Jesus Christ is never regarded as having replaced the reign of God.

The New Testament's perspective is decisively determined by its eschatologically based Christology, and the pneumatology and ecclesiology resulting from this Christology. The eschatological reality of the new creation has begun with Christ, and the church is the new, eschatological humanity on earth. The lifestyle of the church is guided by the Holy Spirit, and is marked by the eschatological sign of the sacraments of baptism and the Eucharist, by being crucified with Christ, by agape in this world, all based on faith in and hope for the new world. The church's members are assured of eternal salvation, in death as well as already in all hardships of this earthly life.

But as much as these eschatological signs are already experienced, the full realization of the new creation has not yet happened in the sense that the old creation no longer exists. The expectation of this full realization in the second coming of Christ is therefore both intrinsic to the eschatological Christology of the new creation and the indispensable condition for the existence of the Christians in this old world. Except for the Gospel of John, the entire extant New Testament makes it clear that the Christians await, for very decisive reasons, Christ's second coming, because they already belong to the new creation while they still have to endure the old one. Their ethos is totally determined by this expectation and their preparation for the second coming, and it is for this reason neither controlled by nor even interested in the structures of this ongoing old and especially sinful world. Even for the Gospel of John, in which the expectation of the second coming is peripheral at most, the separation of the disciples from the structures of this old world is fundamental.

To be sure, the Jesus of the Gospels, as retrospectively understood decades after his resurrection, did good works of various sorts and also challenged the religious authorities. And the Christian disciples did and were called to do the same in their non-Christian environment. They even developed strategies of communal, including economic, life within the Christian congregations and among the congregations of the wider church, as in the case of their support for the church in, but not for the city of, Jerusalem.

Neither Jesus nor the early churches, however, were involved in the structures that are constitutive for the affairs of this ongoing world. They did not intend to establish the kingdom of God, let alone the reign of Christ, in it. The policies of the Roman Empire were for them of no concern, such as its subjection of other countries by military force, its tax system, its social stratification and economic organization. The field of public law, embodied in the historically famous Roman law, a field central in all ancient societies, is not challenged by the criteria of God's or Christ's reign. Indeed, the Christians have to observe it as it is — as God given. Thus, the slaves had to remain slaves, and the women had no place in public life, not even a place in the church equal to that of men. Also absent in the New Testament is, except for the discipline of ancient rhetoric, the entire breadth of the state of science in the Roman Empire, and so on.

It is very clear that the early Christian movement was focusing on the salvation of individuals from the world, on joining them to the new humanity that prepares for the arrival of the new world in the second coming of Christ, rather than on the transformation of the structures of the indefinitely ongoing old world through God's constant presence and involvement everywhere in these structures. The old world had to be left aside and behind. This theological position was not incidental but programmatic. It was the logical consequence from the eschatologically based Christology and ecclesiology.

In the meantime, some two thousand years, Jesus Christ has not come again, and it is undeniable that the temporal eschatological expectation of the early Christians was not only unfulfilled, but was also — next to John's theology of eschatological ultimacy — the reason for their neglect of God's presence in this indefinitely ongoing world with all its sinfulness. And while many essential doctrines of the New Testament — especially those of justification by grace, of ultimate salvation and freedom in life and death, of agape and life guided by the Holy Spirit — represent unsurpassable truth quite independently of the temporal eschatology, it is obvious that the eschatologically determined and restricted early Christian worldview has amounted to a significant limitation of the vision of the presence and involvement of God in the totality of this world in all places and at all times. Instead of saying that

God will always come because God is always and everywhere present, one said that God is present because, and where, and in the sense that, God comes. The vision of the reign of God, and of Jesus Christ as well, has been deprived of its true universality. And the New Testament's legacy consists not only of its unsurpassable advantages but also of the deprivation of the vision of God's presence and involvement in the totality of reality by neglecting this presence and involvement in God's indefinitely ongoing old and imperfect world.

At any rate, the delay of the parousia for two thousand years means that its expectation was an insufficient ground for the worldview of the early Christians, and is even more insufficient for us today. When Christ comes again, or whether or not he ever comes again, is at best a question of relative validity, and a shaky foundation for biblical theology and human faith in the reign of God and Jesus Christ. Indeed, this theology and faith stand in the way of the much more urgent reason for the human openness to God's radical call to conversion, today rather than tomorrow, because God is present today and an answer tomorrow means that today will forever be lost.

By contrast, where the New Testament has its deficiency, the Old Testament enters the stage with full legitimacy. For its most part by far, it focuses on what the New Testament ignores: on the presence and involvement of God in this world in both space and time, in its cosmic order as well as in the order of this earth, in the midst of sinful human history and in imperfect human existence. Heaven and earth may "wear out like a garment" and "pass away" (Ps 102:26), but they are the original creation that continues to be upheld by the deity despite the sinful human history.

In the primeval history of the Pentateuch, the deity is seen as constantly at work in preventing humanity from total self-destruction. The election of Israel from the patriarchs throughout the Pentateuch is a history of God's people in the midst of the ongoing human history in this indefinitely ongoing world, with its focus on the realities of this world: land, food, population growth, social and political liberation, international relations, the organization of public justice, law and ethos, and on the cult, especially for the constant opportunity for the liberation from the always reoccurring destructive influences of guilt.

The Deuteronomistic and Chronicler's history works, as well as the prophets and many psalms, focus on Israel's existence in this world, its sociopolitical structure and international relations, all involving the deity's critical presence. Other psalms and the books of Proverbs, Ecclesiastes, and Job focus on the basic kinds of experience lived by all human beings. The issue of war and peace is addressed everywhere, and the international state of scientific knowledge and practice has directly influenced many texts.

Compared to this overwhelming focus — throughout a thousand years — on the realities of this ongoing world, including the many prophetic announcements of Israel's restoration after the judgment, the texts about the otherworldly new creation, as in Trito-Isaiah and Daniel, are minimal. Those few texts in particular have not replaced the vast majority of texts that focus on the realities in this ongoing old and imperfect world and on God's presence and involvement in it. The assumption that the history of Israel's religion developed over the centuries from an inner-worldly to an apocalyptic-eschatological worldview represents at best a very one-sided, and lastly a false, construct of that development. The composition of the tripartite Hebrew Bible in the late postexilic period proves Israel's overwhelming preoccupation with the affairs of this indefinitely ongoing world, both in that period and beyond it.

It has always been pointed out that the Old Testament's focus on this world, when compared to the New Testament's focus, reveals its theological deficiency, because Israel's election in the Old Testament is considered in terms of a political system; in terms of hierocracy rather than theocracy; of ethnic nationality; a particular land and the oppression, expulsion, and even extinction of the original inhabitants of that land and of their culture — none of which belongs to the ideal doctrine of the *ekklēsia*. It has been said that the Old Testament speaks of liberation only socially and politically rather than in terms of ultimacy, and of forgiveness of sins only from case to case rather than once and for all.

Some of these arguments are valid, while others are one-sided. It is true that the concept of God's elected people in terms of national and territorial identity is invalid when compared to the concept of a people internationally and at all places on earth. It is especially true that Israel's election is in the Old Testament very often — not always — depicted preferentially and at the expense of humanity rather than as a model for God's presence in humanity equally. In these respects, the Christian doctrine — though often not the history of Christianity! — is better than the particularistic notion of Israel's election.

It is also true, however, that Israel's participation in all affairs of humanity testifies to a presence of God in this ongoing world that has no parallel in the New Testament, and that is as important today as it was for Israel and would have been for the early Christians. After all, the Christian expectation of the impending end of the world through the coming of the kingdom remains not only unfulfilled to this day, but was wrong in its own time and was the main reason for their unjustifiable neglect of God's presence in the totality of this ongoing world, its human history, and the earthly existence of all humans.

Through Christ, the humans are assured of forgiveness ultimately. Nevertheless, this forgiveness must still be reappropriated from case to case, from day to day. Israel must be forgiven from case to case, but it can always be assured of God's unshakeable loyalty and willingness to forgive. The difference between the two concepts is relative. These and other comparisons show that each Testament has advantages as well as disadvantages, that each complements as well as corrects the other, and that it is one-sided and unjustifiable if we only read the Old Testament from the vantage point of the New Testament and not also the New Testament from the vantage point of the Old Testament.

Fundamentally, the two Testaments differ in that the Old Testament focuses on God's presence in the totality of this ongoing creation, whereas the New Testament focuses on the new creation. Within these respective foci, each Testament has, when compared to the other, theological advantages but also disadvantages. The difference between the Testaments, in their mutual critical complementarity, is not a weakness but a strength. It amounts to the strength of a biblical theology. The New Testament, with its focus on the ultimate meaning of the reign of God, says unsurpassable things. The Old Testament, with its focus on the reality of this world, makes sure that God is not absent from its imperfection. This aspect is especially relevant for us. Just as our world has lasted indefinitely, so it may continue to last — unless we humans destroy it ourselves, a possibility that neither Testament ever thought possible.

What I am saying amounts to a program for a biblical theology of the Christian Bible in which the two Testaments are mutually and equally open for each other. Such a theology must rest on a vision of the total reality rather than of one of its aspects at the expense of the other. It must include the aspect of ultimacy in the world's penultimacy, but also the aspect of the world's penultimacy itself. God is not only the God of the new but also the God of the original creation, not only the God from afar but also the God who is near, or else God is not the God of the whole world. When one considers the whole world as the realm of God's presence, penultimately and ultimately, in terms of the world's imperfection and its realistic utopia, it is especially the Old Testament in the Christian tradition that must be upgraded to a status equal to that of the New Testament. Whenever the new world comes and whether or not it will ever come as originally expected, the Old Testament says that God's salvation is at work in this ongoing world, with nothing in it excepted, everywhere, at all times, and for everyone, as long as this world lasts.*

---

*I am indebted to Brenda Hahn and Mignon R. Jacobs for editorial assistance during the evolution of this essay.

2

On the Task of Old Testament Theology

Rolf P. Knierim

INTRODUCTION

This essay will focus on a method for doing Old Testament theology. In order to see this focus in its proper perspective, I will first discuss what I perceive to be the necessary distinctions between the disciplines of biblical exegesis, biblical theology, and biblical hermeneutics. In the process of interpretation, these three disciplines are closely related. Nonetheless, they must be distinguished because each confronts us with a different set of problems.

We first need to understand the individual texts to be examined, each on its own terms and in its own right; this is the process of exegesis. But since the Bible consists of many texts, small and large, we need to explain the meaning of each text in the light of all texts. This task presupposes but goes beyond exegesis. *Biblical exegesis* explains what the texts themselves say. In contrast, *biblical theology* must explain what is not, at least not sufficiently, said by the texts of the Bible, namely, the relationship among the different theologies of the texts. And *biblical hermeneutics* then needs to explain what the encounter between the worldview of the Bible and our modern worldview means for us today.

Each of these tasks is distinct. But since we cannot interpret the encounter of the biblical worldview and our own worldview without understanding each, the task of biblical theology is not only distinct from but also precedes the task of biblical hermeneutics, just as it follows the task of biblical exegesis. Hence, biblical interpretation moves from the exegesis of the texts to biblical theology and then to a biblical hermeneutic.

In light of my topic, I leave aside discussing the question of the relationship between ancient and modern worldviews. But I will elaborate

This essay is dedicated to Professor George Coats, a scholar totally committed to Old Testament scholarship and a good personal friend, on the occasion of his retirement, with heartfelt good wishes. The essay represents a slightly revised version of a lecture given at the annual meeting of the Korean Society of Old Testament Studies in Seoul on May 21, 1994, and at the annual meeting of the Japanese Society of Old Testament Studies in Tokyo on May 25, 1994. It was previously published in *A Biblical Itinerary: In Search of Method, Form, and Context: Essays in Honor of George W. Coats,* ed. Eugene Carpenter. Reprinted by permission of Sheffield Academic Press Limited.

on some specific issues that are important for the distinction between biblical exegesis and biblical theology. These issues concern first of all the task of exegesis. The methods of exegesis are well known and need no reiteration at this point. I need only to highlight four aspects that are intrinsic to exegetical work because they are also intrinsic to the nature of the biblical texts.

First, the texts are not quarries of words or sentences but entities (*Ganzheiten*) within which all elements are related in hierarchical semantic systems. These text systems must be explained holistically rather than solely, as is often done, verse by verse, sentence by sentence, or word by word. Without a holistic explanation of a text's overall system, the meaning of a text cannot be understood properly.

Second, and in particular need of attention, is that in each text, its story or message and its concept, idea, or doctrine are indissolubly connected and interdependent. While a text's story or message is explicit in what it says, its concept is basically inexplicit, infratextual or subtextual, but nevertheless operative in the text. It is presupposed and only coincidentally signaled by a word or phrase in the text itself as, for example, in "Let my people go!" (e.g., Exod. 5:1). In this sentence, the possessive pronoun "my" is vital and reveals the conceptual presupposition for the liberation theology of the story: Yahweh liberates the oppressed because they are Yahweh's own people. Yahweh does not liberate all people who are oppressed. There is a theology of liberation in this text, but this theology is based on and controlled by the theological concept of Israel's exclusive election. Where this concept is overlooked in exegesis, the story and its concept of liberation are not correctly understood. The *concept* of a text controls its story, while the story actualizes its concept or idea. Sometimes, of course, the concepts are expressed directly in particular nominal phrases, as in the statement "God is gracious."

The recognition of the concepts or ideas of the texts has nothing to do either with a withdrawal from the texts into a world of abstract ideas or with an abstraction of the ideas from the texts. On the contrary, this recognition is exegetically indispensable because the ideas are the ideas of the texts themselves. Ideas and thoughts are just as real as stories in human history and existence, and the fact that they may be considered as abstract ideas does not mean that the idea of a text is abstract. There is no text without an idea. Its idea as well as its story belongs to the concreteness of a text. Both are to be exegeted together. In a text both language and thought, or its story and its concept, belong together, and the emphasis on the need to interpret the text's thought and concept has nothing to do with removing thought and concept from language and story or with replacing narrative by abstract concept. What is called for is the interpretation of the *conceptualized* narrative, not just narrative. It is in this sense that the focus on concept is understood in this essay. It is important, however, that we distinguish between the ideas of texts and the ideas of the biblical worldviews. Many texts share the same worldview, such as, for example, the dynamistic ontology (Klaus Koch's *Tatsphäredenken* or my own category of the concept of the holistic dynamic). While by and large sharing such a common worldview, many texts nevertheless have different conceptual foci, such as justice, judgment, liberation, forgiveness, election, corporateness, individuality, and so on. And while it is necessary for us to be aware of their common ancient worldview, this awareness interprets only what is common among them and not yet those varying concepts that are directly operative in them. The exegesis of the individual texts must interpret their specific concepts, or these texts cannot be distinguished from each other.

Third, the exegesis of texts includes each text's theology. The biblical texts are essentially theological in nature. Without this nature they would not exist. Exegesis that fails to include a text's theology is not exegesis in its proper sense. The interpretation of the theology of the texts is not something done in addition to exegesis. We exegete each text's own inherent theology. We do not theologize the texts. Were the texts not theological, exegesis should not say more about them than what they are. Inasmuch as exegesis may be called theological exegesis, it may be so called because of the theological nature of the texts themselves, and not because of our interest in theology. Yet precisely because of that nature of the texts, the attribute "theological" added to "exegesis" is pleonastic and should be avoided.

Attention to the theology of the texts is especially important because the theological task starts already with exegesis and is not reserved for biblical theology. Biblical theology is not theological because it is a discipline distinct from exegesis but because it evolves from the results of the exegesis of the theological nature of the texts. Whereas the theological task is common to both disciplines, the two differ in that exegesis interprets the theologies of the texts while biblical theology interprets the relationship of these theologies.

Fourth, exegesis not only describes the texts and their theologies, but also includes in its descriptions the fact that the texts claim to be true, valid, and authoritative. The Bible does not understand itself as a lexicon of science, history, or sociology, but as a collection of books that may in any of these aspects refer to what it claims to be divine truth that is therefore valid and authoritative for the world and certainly for its readers. We may use the Bible for all sorts of purposes, but if we ignore this claim, we certainly ignore its own raison d'être.

Thus, we exegete the theologies and truth claims of the Pentateuch, the Deuteronomistic and Chronicler's history works, of Job, each of the

Psalms, the Proverbs, and so on, and of each of the prophets, just as
we exegete the theologies and truth claims of the Synoptic Gospels, of
John, Paul, and the rest of the New Testament books. And the more we
do careful exegesis, the more we learn that the Bible is a compendium
of many theological concepts and their stories, of theologies that sometimes agree, sometimes differ even as they complement each other, and
sometimes disagree. Every good student of the Bible is familiar with
this fact. This situation is true not only for the relationship of the two
Testaments, but also for the various theologies within each Testament.

After we have done our exegetical work, we write books in which
we describe each theology or selected theological aspects, juxtapose our
descriptions in anthologies of theologies, each bound in one volume,
and call such a volume an Old or New Testament theology.

It is clear, however, that a theology of the Old or New Testament,
let alone a biblical theology in the singular form, must be more than a
collection of juxtaposed theologies derived from exegesis, a collection
analogous to the collection of the juxtaposed biblical books, even where
those juxtapositions rest to some extent on organizing principles such
as the tripartite Tanak, or the distinction between the Gospels, Luke's
Acts, and the letters in the New Testament. A theology in the singular
must do what neither the biblical writers nor those who canonized the
Bible have done: it must *interpret the relationship of the various theologies
in the Bible.* This task presupposes the totality of exegetical work. But it
involves *more* than the sum total of exegesis. Indeed, it is not solved but
generated by that sum total. It is a task sui generis. The sum total of
exegesis shows the diversity and even the divisiveness of the theologies
in the canon. It reflects the theological pluralism of the biblical canon
and the pluralism of its truth claims.

THE OLD TESTAMENT DEFINES ITS OWN AGENDA

In the Christian tradition the reading of the Old Testament has in one
way or another always been controlled by the theological criteria expressed in the New Testament. Whether these criteria contributed to
keeping both Testaments together in the one Christian Bible, or whether
they contributed to separating the theology of each Testament from that
of the other, they were in either case the basis for the judgment of the
Christian movement that the Old Testament, whatever it may mean for
Christians and humanity, is fundamentally different from and less important than the New Testament. And in whatever sense one may want
to speak of a *biblical* theology, the burden for such an advocacy lies
always on the shoulders of Old Testament scholars.

Of course, for at least the last two hundred years all biblical scholars have asserted that the Old Testament must be afforded the right to speak on its own terms. It especially must not be forced to speak against what its exegesis reveals. Still, the validity or truth of such exegetical results has always been adjudicated by the Christian perspective. Whether you say with Bultmann that the Old Testament, precisely when exegeted correctly, reveals how Christians or humans must not believe, or with von Rad or any similar interpreter that the kerygmatic axis of the Old Testament's salvation history leads to Jesus Christ, the Old Testament is in either case exegetically said to be theologically irrelevant without the decisive Christian perspective. It must have the right to its own position, but only as long as it defines its position in response to the predetermined Christian agenda. This situation amounts to a double standard for the Old Testament's freedom, a standard, both unconditional and conditional, which has no integrity. Instead, what is necessary is an Old Testament theology in which the Old Testament itself may define its own agenda vis-à-vis the New Testament rather than be dependent on it, a theology that would precisely for this reason also be of benefit for the Christian faith.

THE OLD TESTAMENT IS ONE

The Old Testament is one not only because it is the first part of the bipartite Christian Bible but also because it is the only Bible of the Jewish people. Its oneness is especially constituted by the fact that it is the original compendium of ancient Israel's Yahweh religion. Take Yahweh out of it, and it collapses. The Tanak represents ancient Israel's wisdom as reverence for and knowledge of God Yahweh.

The oneness of the Old Testament does not mean that its Yahweh wisdom is conceptually uniform and that everything in it has the same degree of validity. Just as it is a collection of many literary works, so it is also a collection of diverse theologies. Exegesis has long since established that Israel's Yahweh religion is theologically pluralistic. This pluralism became decisively established in the final juxtaposition of the theologies of the Yahweh religion at the same historical level during the late postexilic period. The theological traditions put together in this period had emerged diachronically, in the course of Israel's historical process, and to a large extent separately. But once they were juxtaposed, the meaning of the traditions was no longer determined by the diachronic but by the synchronic order of their relationship. What had formerly had a certain meaning because of its distinct time came to have a different meaning as it was placed side by side (i.e., synchronically) with traditions of earlier times. This synchronization of the traditions amounted to the canonization of theological diversity. For the heirs of the Tanak or the Old Testament, be they Jewish or Christian, this pluralism is its inevitable legacy.

What is generally recognized to be the case in the New Testament is also true for the Old Testament. Its theological diversity, like the New Testament's diversity, is inherently connected to the Old Testament's claim to truth and validity and, hence, with the quest for truth and validity in Old Testament theology. This quest amounts to more than merely describing the Old Testament's texts and their theological concepts. Also, it is something different from a type of interpretation based on a confessional stance. It must explain why and in what sense any of its theologies are true and should be affirmed or confessed as true. Only this kind of explanation qualifies the discipline as theology. Otherwise it represents a phenomenology, history, or sociology of Israel's religion, or our confession of truth regardless of what is said.

In the history of the discipline, one has for too long attempted to overcome the Old Testament's theological diversity by focusing on its unifying aspects, on the unity in diversity. Thus, one has emphasized that the Old Testament is Yahwistic, monotheistic, word of God, inspired, revealed, the religion of holiness, covenantal, of the believing community, and so on.

All of these aspects exist, whereby some represent unifying factors while others, such as the aspects of holiness, covenant, or even — strictly speaking — word of God, do not, as we have learned. Decisive, however, is that none of the evidently unifying factors solves the problem of the theological diversity within each of them. The Old Testament is monotheistic, but its monotheism is theologically diverse and even divisive. It is divinely inspired and revealed, but the contents and concepts of inspiration and revelation (including theophany and epiphany) are diverse. It is altogether the witness of the believing community, but the beliefs of this community are diverse and the community itself has from its beginning been divided precisely because of its different beliefs.

The unifying aspects of these theologies belong to the Old Testament's oneness and must be interpreted in this respect. However, if we want to know in what sense the Old Testament is true and valid, even with respect to its unifying aspects, it is imperative that the discipline of Old Testament theology shift from its focus on the Old Testament's theological diversity. Rather than focus on unity in diversity, we must explain the diversity within the unity, indeed, the diversity within each unifying concept. This shift is basic, and amounts to a change in direction compared to the direction of many approaches during the last two centuries.

This approach is not completely new. Gabler proposed in 1787 that we should describe the biblical books, interpret each of their concepts, compare them, and arrange the results of their comparison in a system of biblical theology in which the validity of each can be determined precisely in its relationship to the others. Gabler thought of a biblical theology conceived from the doctrine of salvation expressed in the New Testament alone. Yet his method remains valid, indeed the best, for an Old Testament theology on its own terms. This method accounts for the relativity of each theological concept in its relation to all others. While none is irrelevant, the degree of validity of each is discerned in its relation to all others.

The basic approach to Old Testament theology is guided by our need to identify the Old Testament's theological concepts individually, to compare them, and thus to arrive at an integrated theological value system of the Old Testament. In what follows I give some examples.

No system of positive values can exist without its opposite, a system of antivalues. In Old Testament studies, the system of antivalues is basically established through Old Testament hamartiology, the doctrine of sin and guilt. The Old Testament speaks neither only of what is good nor only of what is evil, but of both as opposites. When it speaks of what is valid, it is always aware of what is destructive and, hence, invalid. Indeed, it essentially derives its judgments about evil from its knowledge of what is good. Evil is what is not good. The distinction between good and evil, even terminologically, is widespread and fundamental. For this reason, Old Testament hamartiology is an indispensable part of Old Testament theology, even though it is subservient to the positive side of Old Testament theology.

Within Old Testament hamartiology both the diverse terminology and the many texts have one uniting feature: no matter how diverse, the aspects always point to what is destructive. And this also shows that all aspects are not equally destructive. Someone who steals is not a murderer. Someone who holds a grudge against a neighbor or covets a neighbor's property does not publicly slander or rob that neighbor. Someone who inadvertently causes damage does not commit a crime. The murder of a person by an individual is a severe crime, but it is not as severe as genocide or the destruction of the whole earth by humanity's all-pervasive violence.

When we come to the theology of the positive concepts in the texts, we encounter concepts such as liberation, justice, blessing, mercy, goodness, holiness, peace, and so on. Each of these concepts is indicated by its own word field, and all word fields signal an already conceptualized understanding of the constructive side of reality.

It is clear that these words and the concepts they signal do not all mean the same thing. Each has a distinct meaning. These meanings, including where they overlap, are interpreted in commentaries, dictionaries, monographs, and articles. But Old Testament theology must interpret the relationship of these concepts and discern their degrees of validity within this relationship.

For example, the semantic fields and concepts of liberation, or salvation, and justice and righteousness are related but not identical. When compared, liberation appears as an element of justice, namely, as liberation either from injustice suffered by others or from self-inflicted sin. Justice is distinct in that it involves more than liberation alone. Justice also means that the liberated are freed in order to do what is just. It is not only more inclusive than liberation, but is also the criterion for the truth of liberation because it is both the reason for and the purpose of liberation.

When applied to the story of the Pentateuch, the result of this distinction becomes painfully clear. Israel's liberation from Pharaoh's oppression is an act of justice. But Israel, at Yahweh's and Moses' command, is to subjugate or ban the free Canaanites. Those liberated from oppression are commanded to use their freedom for the oppression of others. The reason for Israel's transition from being the liberated to becoming the oppressors is well known: it is the theology of Israel's exclusive election for its possession of and multiplication in the promised land. Also clear, however, is that in this kind of liberation theology, the principle of indivisible justice is destroyed. Justice, especially God's justice, cannot mean both liberation and oppression at the same time. And other Old Testament traditions, especially in the wisdom traditions, disagree with this concept in the Pentateuch.

It is known that the Old Testament does not represent a religion of judgment compared to a religion of grace in the New Testament. It is also known that the concept of judgment, present everywhere and not only in the prophetic literature, is an inevitable element of the concept of justice. No justice can do without judgment. But judgment itself must be valid. And the criterion for its truth is not emotional, irrational, or based on the mood of a tyrant. Rather, the criterion for judgment is the rationality of justice to which even the freedom of God is bound. The Old Testament texts demonstrate this rationality very clearly.

Is there also a criterion for the truth of justice itself, even for the truth of its rationales? I have in mind many texts that in various ways speak about judgment on the one hand, and about mercy or pardon on the other hand. The relationship of these two concepts pervades the entire Old Testament and the history of Israel's theology. Where there is judgment, there is no forgiveness. And where there is mercy, pardon, or forgiveness, judgment is replaced. And just as judgment must be justifiable, so can mercy not be unjustifiable. The Yahweh of Hos. 11:1–9 is caught in the tension between the justice of judgment and the justice of mercy, and is forced to replace his just judgment by just mercy because mercy is the better justice. Why is it better? Because allowing his people to live is better than destroying them. Justice itself is relative. A similar conceptual dynamic is also found, among others, in the primeval history and in the Joseph novella.

The Old Testament speaks about peace (šālôm) and war, especially Yahweh's wars, which are perceived to be just wars. And while it is obvious that the notion of war is in need of theological evaluation, it is also obvious that no war, not even Yahweh's just wars, has the same validity as the condition of peace. The fact that there is "a time for war, and time for peace" (Eccl. 3:8) does not mean that the times of war are as good as the times of peace. The Old Testament theology of war is, at any rate, subject to the distinction between just and unjust war. Even so, no war is as just as peace; nor is war ever considered just when compared with peace. The theology of war is evaluated sufficiently only when compared to the theology of peace.

What is the relationship between justice and peace? This question is important not only today; its importance is also reflected in the Old Testament itself. The texts speak about both peace and justice. God fashions justice (Jer. 9:24) and also peace (Ps. 147:14). Humans are to seek both. The world is in good shape when "righteousness and peace will kiss each other" (Ps. 85:10). But peace and justice are not the same, and they do not always kiss each other. The two realities differ and often conflict. What is their relationship? Is peace a precondition for justice, so that justice depends on peace, and there can be no justice unless there is peace? Or is justice a precondition for peace because there can be no peace without justice? Is the theology of peace subordinate to or the criterion for the theology of justice, or are both related on the assumption that justice and peace rotate about each other in a bipolar tension and complementation?

The evidence seems to support the view that, at best, there may be false but no true peace where there is no justice, whereas there can be a degree of justice even where there is no peace. Justice appears to be the criterion for true peace, whereas peace is not the criterion for justice, and it does not necessarily create justice. But more important than my opinion is the need for us to clarify their relationship in the horizon of Old Testament theology.

Finally, in this series of examples, which can be expanded almost ad infinitum, what is the relationship between justice, liberation, mercy, or peace on the one hand, and blessing (běrākâ) on the other? The importance of the reality of blessing, and the difference between blessing and liberation, have especially been emphasized in the work of Claus

Westermann. Blessing is the perpetual presence of the goodness of life, or of life as goodness, for all living beings and in everything that belongs to their earthly welfare.

Rather than merely being the *fact* of life, blessing is what we call the *quality* of life, as good rather than bad life, or life without any quality at all. And it is a gift because we have not created life but are sustained by it. The reality of blessing not only differs from the reality of liberation, but is also more fundamental than that reality. Whereas the event, or the events, of liberation presuppose conditions of oppression, fallenness, or sin, the goodness of blessing is the original condition of life. Whereas liberation may or may not be experienced by all and at all times, blessing is the basic experience of all at all times. Blessing can be absent, as in the case of hunger. Such absence amounts to the threat to, or loss of, created life itself. The absence of blessing, as in the lack of food, represents an attack against the order of creation. And liberation from hunger amounts to the restoration of the blessing of food.

Blessing belongs to the theology of creation, whereas liberation belongs to the biblical soteriology that is connected with the theology of history fallen out of the order of creation. The theology of creation is not replaced by soteriology. Rather, it is the reason for soteriology. Liberation is necessary only where the order of creation has been corrupted. The restoration of the old or the vision of the new creation is the reason for the need for and truth of salvation.

Finally, Genesis 1, important psalms, the deity's speeches in Job, and other texts say that the created world is good, or very good. These qualifying judgments are themselves acts of justice. They confirm that the creation of the world out of chaos and its sustenance above chaos are acts of God's universal justice. It has been said that creation theology is soteriology. It is more appropriate to say that the Old Testament's creation theology represents the first, and fundamental, chapter in the theology of universal justice, whereas its soteriology represents that theology of justice which deals with the restoration of creation.

The comparison of the biblical concepts involves a heuristic process through which we can establish their relationship systematically. We can discern the place of each concept in a hierarchy of values and, hence, the degree of validity or truth of each concept in its relation to all others. This heuristic process is systematizing in nature, and its results amount to a systematic Old Testament theology in which the relationship of the concepts is the basis for the evaluation of all that is said and presupposed, and also for the evaluation of all other kinds of systematization, such as, for instance, tradition history or sociology.

Thus far, all the concepts mentioned are qualitative in nature. The texts show, however, that correlated to the qualitative aspect of each concept is also a quantitative aspect. Mercy, justice, blessing, liberation, and peace apply to individuals, to groups, to Israel, to humanity, and even to nature on earth and the cosmos. Each of these aspects is everywhere evident in the Old Testament. They range from the narrowest to the widest situations. Their varying boundaries indicate the Old Testament's differentiating awareness of reality. None of the qualities is important only for the world and not also for each individual and every quantity in between.

The problem arises, however, of whether, for example, justice and liberation are considered valid for individuals regardless of, or because of, their validity for all. If they are true for all, they are therefore also true for each person. If they are true only for one person, justice and liberation are divided, and what is justice for one party is injustice for another. The widest boundary, which includes all equally, is the quantitative criterion for the validity of the positive qualities, just as the widest boundary is the quantitative criterion for the antivalue of the negative aspects in Old Testament hamartiology.

The most inclusive aspect is directly important theologically. If God's peace is only for me, such a god is only my God and not the God of all. This god is my idol. If God's peace is for all, it is therefore also for me, and God is the God for me because God is the God of all. God is the deity of the total world, or god is not God. The universality of God is the criterion for the truth of God's presence in each particular situation.

This criterion is critically important for the evaluation of those texts in the Old Testament in which Israel's election is not seen as functioning for God's universal justice equally for all but at the expense of the other nations, or in which even the creation is seen as serving the purpose of Israel's election. Nothing is said against anyone's election. But in a particularistic theology of election, Israel subjects the nations to the interest of its own benefit rather than serving God's universal goodness for the benefit of all nations. This theology of Yahwism represents the opposite of a theology according to which God works out the same justice for all. It amounts to a nationalistic religious idolatry.

The Old Testament does not simply speak about God. From its first page to its last, it speaks about the relationship between God and world. Its focus on this relationship lies at the heart of its understanding of reality. In this understanding, the deity is considered as the ground of the truth of the world's existence, and the world is therefore considered as created and sustained by, and dependent on, this ground. If the world, including especially the humans, remains in accord with this ground, it actualizes it in its existence. The actualization of the ground of the truth of existence is represented especially in human ethos.

When speaking of ethos theologically, we normally use words such as "response" or "reaction" to God's word or action. God acts and we "*re*-act"; God speaks and we "*re*-spond." This language is questionable. It means that by responding or reacting, we do on our part something that God does not do. I know that the Old Testament itself very often says that humans responded to Yahweh's speeches. Even so, the problem is deeper. It is clear that when responding properly, humans accept what God says or does. They then transmit this content into, or actualize it in, their own existence and, hence, carry on God's own work and word. Rather than doing what God does not do, they continue God's own work by actualizing it. The actualization of God's own work in the world is both the matrix of and the criterion for the Old Testament's ethos.

Finally, the Old Testament focuses overwhelmingly on the affairs of this existing and ongoing world. With this focus it speaks about God's presence in the originally created world, whereas its passages about the new creation are not only minimal but also textured in the sense of the restoration of the depraved world to the shape of its original creation. All of this is clearly distinct from the New Testament. The New Testament considers the original creation from the vantage point of its replacement by the new creation and the expectation that this replacement is impending.

Thus far, the new creation — though considered as already arrived in Christ's resurrection — has not replaced the old creation. Regardless of when, or whether, this will happen, the millennia of the ongoing original creation teach us that we must pay attention to the presence of God in this original creation as long as it lasts. They teach us that the corruption in, and even the fallenness of, the original creation are no longer sufficient reasons for a theology of the *absence* of God from the structures of this creation, whether original or fallen. Indeed, if God were not present also in these structures, the deity would not be the God of the total reality, both new and old.

Thus, we realize that the total Bible teaches us this: God is not present because God comes out of the future, but God comes out of the future as well as out of the past because God is always present. When we come to these fundamental theological realizations, we will have to realize that the Old Testament, with its focus on the ongoing presence of God in this ongoing creation, original or fallen, represents in its totality an independent and critical complement to the worldview of the New Testament. This function constitutes the legitimacy of the Old Testament theology in its own right in a truly bipolar theology of the Christian Bible.*

---

*I am indebted to Brenda Hahn and Mignon R. Jacobs for editorial assistance.

3

Comments on the Task
of Old Testament Theology

Rolf P. Knierim

I am grateful to the Committee for the Theology of the Hebrew Scriptures Section for putting my book on the agenda of this annual meeting of the Society, and especially to the members of the panel for their willingness to discuss it.

Since I am scheduled to introduce the discussion rather than to respond to it, my remarks must be confined to highlighting what in my opinion is essential for understanding the task of the theology of the Old, or First, Testament — Hebrew or Greek and taken in whatever boundaries — or of the Tanak.

To some extent, the following remarks imply reactions to reviews thus far, either of the book as a whole or of the original 1983–84 methodological essay[1] on the task, beyond those to which I already have directly responded. I am thereby not concerned with expressed legitimate agreements, disagreements, or differing positions. But if disagreements, especially, rest on readings that I have neither said nor meant, they stand in the way of advancing the discussion. I realize that my thoughts and their expressions sometimes appear different in readers' eyes than in my own, and in such cases that I need not to defend but to clarify them.

The book has a number of editorial deficiencies, the responsibility for which I cannot escape and for which I am sorry.

The book consists of a collection of methodological and case studies. They are diverse in kind and represent the history of a part of my work that began to set me consciously on my own course almost thirty years ago with the essay on Revelation in the Old Testament.[2] (Indeed, this

---

This essay represents my presentation of November 22, 1997, at the Society of Biblical Literature meeting in San Francisco.

1. See the edition of this essay found in *The Task of Old Testament Theology: Substance, Method, and Cases* (Grand Rapids: Eerdmans, 1995) 1–20.
2. R. P. Knierim, "Offenbarung im Alten Testament," in H. W. Wolff, ed., *Probleme Biblischer Theologie: Gerhard von Rad zum 70. Geburtstag* (Munich: C. Kaiser, 1971) 206–35.

course began already with my 1958 dissertation[3] and my 1963 habilitation,[4] both on some Hebrew words for "sin," a fact the consequences
of which I became only years later fully aware and that finds its latest
fruition in the articles on *Strafe* and *Sünde*, to be published in vol. 31 of
Theologische Realenzyklopädie.

Everyone has seen that the volume is a collection of articles and not
an Old Testament theology. But while in reviews published thus far
some have seen nothing more than that, others have seen a bit more —
with more or less engagement in what that "more" may be — while a
few have correctly seen in it a new definition of the task of Old Testament theology and a new design for doing it. (There is now also, in
the Ph.D. dissertation of Wonil Kim, the extensive analysis of the book
in the horizon of the history of the discipline from the beginnings of
the German salvation-history school up to the wide spectrum of recent
programs.[5])

The book, in both its thesis and design, claims to represent a program. In order to highlight its programmatic nature, I quote a statement
from my original 1983–84 essay on the task, and comment on what is
meant by it. The statement says,

> I wonder what would have happened in Jerusalem around 612 B.C.E. had
> an encounter taken place between the deuteronomic theologians, the je-
> hovist, the priestly temple theologians, sages, and Jeremiah, Zephanajah,
> Nahum, and Habakkuk; or a hundred years later, around 515 B.C.E., how a
> theological encounter would have looked with all of those (or their voices)
> just mentioned, but now also with the addition of Ezekiel and his school,
> the deuteronomistic school, Deutero- and Trito-Isaiah and their disciples,
> and Haggai and Zechariah as well. Unfortunately, we are only left with
> their juxtaposition in the canon but not with any discussion about their
> relationship, neither their own discussion nor a discussion by those who
> juxtaposed them canonically. At this point the theological problem of their
> plurality [sic! meant is their diversity] appears.[6]

This statement focuses on method. The method is formulated with
respect to the texts — those mentioned and more — from which it
is derived, not regardless of those texts. When I publicized the statement fourteen years ago, I had for twenty-five years taught classes on

---

3. *Studien zur israelitischen Rechts- und Kultusgeschichte I* (Theolog. Dissertation, University of Heidelberg, 1958) appearing subsequently in *Die Hauptbegriffe für Sünde im Alten
Testament* (Gütersloh: Gütersloher, 1965; 2nd ed., 1967).

4. R. P. Knierim, *Studien zur israelitischen Rechts- und Kultusgeschichte II* (Theolog. Habilitation; University of Heidelberg, 1963) appearing subsequently in *Die Hauptbegriffe für
Sünde im Alten Testament* (Gütersloh: Gütersloher, 1965; 2nd ed., 1967).

5. W. Kim, "Toward a Substance-Critical Task of Old Testament Theology" (Ph.D.
diss., Claremont Graduate School, 1996).

6. See the edition of this essay found in Knierim, *Task of Old Testament Theology*, 5.

virtually all Old Testament texts, and had the experience of that research and teaching on my mind. Off and on, I have implemented this text-encounter method in classes for students and lay people.

The following methodological comments revolve above all around the issues of diversity, the systematization of the diverse theologies by comparison and their relativity to each other, the relationship of text and concept in the individual texts, and Old Testament theology as a genre sui generis.

First, then, the issue of diversity. That the First Testament is theologically diverse has not only always been known in both the Jewish and Christian history of its interpretation, but was also known among those responsible for the history of its production in their own times. Also known has been that this diversity has always constituted an essential problem in view of the coexistence of the diverse positions in the history of ancient Israel's society and lastly in one and the same body of its original foundational literature. Whereas many of the diverse theologies have been complementary, others have been mutually contradictory and even divisive. Because of that history of coexisting voices, the question of their relationship has to this day been inevitable — unless we want to ignore the reality of that coexistence and to present all voices in the form of a lexicon of theological anatomy. Of course, the problem is not solved with reference to the unifying notions, such as Yahwism above all, because the diversity has always existed within Yahwism and within all other unifying notions.

Second, the issue of systematization by comparison. Relating the diverse theologies amounts to what I have called their systematization, by which I mean their comparison. (On the point of the method of comparison, Gabler was correct, although he was neither the first nor the last to call for and do it. My essay on Gabler, however, should make clear that I disagree with the substance of his conceptual presupposition and of his objective for which he wants his method to be employed.) In the history of the discipline, the method of comparison has often been submerged under other kinds of systematization, although it is everywhere and inevitably discernible and has its beginnings in the organization of the texts themselves and in their own value systems. Moreover, almost thirty years ago, Roland E. Murphy's discussion of the genre of *better-sayings*, afterwards published in his monograph on the Wisdom literature,[7] began to open my eyes to the fundamental importance of the method of comparative thinking among the ancients for prioritizing or arriving at gradated value judgments. The term "systematization" is ambiguous, but I know of no biblical theology, nor of a biblical text it-

---

7. R. E. Murphy, *Wisdom Literature* (FOTL 13; Grand Rapids: Eerdmans, 1981).

self small or large, that is not the product of systematized comparisons one way or another.

Comparison is not done by criteria external to the texts; it rests on what I have called the different quantitative and qualitative aspects everywhere in the texts themselves that range from the most particular to the most universal. These aspects keep each other in check. I have thereby distinguished between the terms for universality and universalism and those for particularity and particularism. It is often assumed that once a universal aspect appears in the Old Testament, it points to truth. What is not recognized is that universalism may also be despotic and represent a particularistic ideology designed to subject all others to one's own interests and goals. The concept of monotheism is a prominent case in point. It denotes by definition a universalistic worldview. Whether it is universally inclusive or divisive, good or evil, depends always on the criteria by which it is controlled.

The method of comparison pursues the discernment of priorities of positive values, and that vis-à-vis the Old Testament's strong consciousness of antivalues or nonvalues and the gradation of their own different weights. These value judgments are everywhere operative in the texts. If in exegesis one has done the structure analysis of about a thousand texts, this fact is indelibly impressed on one's mind, in addition to the principal fact that the Old Testament does not present itself as a quarry of value-neutral data. Even in multivalency, all is by itself not considered to be equivalent! These values were defined in relation to, and relative to, each other. They include an endless line of aspects, among which the relationship of past, present, and future; of creation, history, and eschatology; of salvation/liberation and justice, the nations and Israel, righteousness and sin, the individual and community are only the most prominent. Therefore, to compare the diverse theologies of the body of the Old Testament literature, to do what in the composition of the literary works of this body, including its tripartite composition to begin with, was done but never fully executed, means only that we follow the methodological precedent set by the First Testament itself by discerning the degrees of validity of its theologies in their relativity to each other.

Third, the issue of text and concept in the individual texts. Naturally, the comparison of the diverse theologies presupposes the identification of the theologies of the individual texts, which is an intrinsic part of exegesis. This identification focuses, to begin with, on the substantive aspects of the texts. Especially, however, it includes the methodologically focused study of the relationship between the surface of the texts and their — mostly infratextual, only implied — conceptuality or conceptual substance on which the texts rest. The discovery of this infratextual conceptual substance and, hence, the interpretation of the relationship between a text and its concept, are indispensable requirements for exegesis. In this regard, our exegetical methodology is not sufficiently developed, and our commentaries prove this lack. I am speaking of the concepts which are operative in and controlling the texts themselves, not of the well-known exegetical taboo of using concrete texts as springboards for creating a world of abstract ideas. Even if the concepts or ideas can become abstracted from their texts, they are intrinsic to any text in the first place. The issue of the genre of story is a case in point. I am all for story and stories. But any story represents first of all the narrative by its narrator about an event, not that event itself. An assumption that stories, by virtue of being stories, reflect their events most realistically and truly is not defensible. Especially, and quite apart from their propagandistic functions and intentions, they are basically controlled by and serve the infratextual concepts of their narrators. Tell me the concept of a story, and I may see whether the story or history is true or not. What is the concept of the Pentateuch, or the concept of any of its strata, not just their contents and plots, and themes, but the concepts of those contents, plots and themes? As long as we have not clearly defined these concepts, how can we define the Pentateuch's theology and proceed to compare it with other theologies in the Psalms, the prophets, the Wisdom books?

A widespread misunderstanding must be addressed. The discussion of the theology of an individual text has as yet nothing to do with the discussion of its place in the discipline of Old Testament theology. The theology of any text can be discussed in isolation from the theologies of all others. Its discussion belongs to the discipline of Old Testament theology only when its individual theology is compared with the other theologies in the Old Testament.

And fourth, the issue of Old Testament theology as a genre sui generis. What, then, constitutes Old Testament theology as a genre sui generis? My answer is simple: it is the interpretation of its claim to the validity or truth of its own theologically based worldviews.

This definition applies to all other approaches to the study of the Old/First Testament, but its objective, and the method proposed for it, distinguishes Old Testament theology from them all. It is, for example, distinct from the method of tradition history or the history of resignification or the dynamically forward-moving history of recontextualization in which inherited contextual meanings are transcended by new contextual meanings. Has any history ever been characterized by anything but these truisms? Since when may reinterpretation or recontextualization or resignification, the emergence of new meanings in new contexts, be considered as true and valid for any of their stages, and even for the dynamic process of the whole, by virtue of the fact that they take place obviously in their respective contexts? As with all other approaches in research, I am all for transmission/tradition history, including its usage for an approach to Old Testament theology. But no tradition history is true by virtue of the fact that it happens, be that in terms of continuity or discontinuity. It is not true as such, but subject to criteria for truth. The traditio-historical model of Gerhard von Rad (my forever venerable teacher) for his Old Testament theology did not succeed for a variety of reasons, but he certainly was concerned with the truth of the Old Testament and knew that this truth was not constituted by the fact of its tradition history but that the truth of its tradition history was constituted by and depended on the truth criterion of what he interpreted as the revelatory salvation-historical axis in that history. Of course, I take it that, for example, a history of Christian or Jewish thought does not yet amount to a Christian or Jewish theology or philosophy, much as the former must be considered in the latter. Tell me why and how anything in the Bible is true in light of the whole Bible, and you give me a biblical-theological argument.

I distinguish truth or validity from the much used notion of meaning. Meaning is always intratextual, contextual, and intertextual, for individuals as well as for societies. It may appear to be new or reflect tradition. But is it therefore true? A lot of what Hitler and Goebbels said in the context of post-1918 Germany was for many, increasingly most of the Germans, meaningful, even for Heidegger for some time on the ground of his ontology, but it was not true, as was already realized by some in its own time and not only in retrospect.

That the notion of truth or validity is intrinsic to, indeed decisive for, the theological endeavor is inescapable. How can one affirm the deity and a theologically based worldview without claiming it to be true? Which is what the entire Bible does to begin with. That absolute truth is hidden from our knowledge should be known by any reader of the Bible itself, long before any philosophical critique teaches us so. Our knowledge of truth is relative, just as truth claims themselves are relative — which, of course, has nothing to do with irrelevance. It depends on our recognition of the weight that individual truth claims have when compared to others. Such recognition can be achieved by their critical comparison in terms of both the texts and their conceptual substance.

We may object to the word system, but what evolves is certainly an understanding of gradated values, of priorities and subordinate values, and also of antivalues and nonvalues. By pursuing this one-and-the-same method for finding the relative truths through any and all approaches, we do nothing but what any historian does. In this regard, and confined to the body of the Old Testament literature, the discipline of Old Testament theology belongs to the field of historical research in which the past is studied, critically studied with particular regard to the question as to what was true, more or less true, or untrue in its own time, and regardless whether anything from that time should be considered as passed away or not.

That Old/First Testament theology must rest on this Testament's internal criteria alone, and not on external, such as Christian criteria or those of postbiblical Judaism or those based on the worldviews of modern cultures, has at least by Christian theologians often been claimed but scarcely ever executed. It may be done by people of any persuasion, but is neither Christian nor Jewish nor modernist. It is thereby self-evident that trajectories from the First Testament evolved into, and are everywhere found, in both early Christianity and postbiblical Judaism. However, these developments prove neither that they are true because they developed the way they did, nor that they were not diverse, even contradictory, and essentially represent the continuation of the diversity of the First Testament's own theologies and, thus, of the problem of its own theology in the first place. Diversity did not begin after the canonization of the Scriptures; it began in their very roots. At any rate, the theologies of the Bible of the ancient Israelites existed before and without these subsequent developments, and should already for that reason be considered in their own right, on their own terms and criteria.

The description of the method of Old Testament theology governed by the criteria for the discernment of the Old Testament's own claims to truth discussed here, as often in the book, is, in my opinion, distinguished from the conceptualization of a biblical theology of the bipartite Christian Bible, which has to rest on a critical comparison of the essentially different worldviews of the two Testaments. And the task of biblical hermeneutic rests, in my opinion, on the critical comparison of the biblical worldviews with our own worldviews. In recent months I published another version of my understanding of the task of Old Testament theology in the *Festschrift* for George Coats,[8] and an essay on the task of biblical theology in the *Festschrift* for James Sanders,[9] and an essay on the task of biblical hermeneutic, demonstrated on the two cases of the jury verdict in the first trial of O. J. Simpson and on the assassi-

---

8. "On the Task of Old Testament Theology," in E. E. Carpenter, ed., *A Biblical Itinerary: In Search of Method, Form and Content: Essays in Honor of George W. Coats* (JSOTSup 240; Sheffield: Sheffield Academic Press, 1997) 153–66.

9. "On Biblical Theology," in C. A. Evans and S. Talmon, eds., *The Quest for Context and Meaning: Studies in Biblical Intertextuality in Honor of James A. Sanders* (Leiden, New York, Cologne: Brill, 1997) 117–28.

nation of Prime Minister Rabin — written just after the two events — in the *Festschrift* for Erhard Gerstenberger[10] at the University of Marburg.

This program can be executed. In the conclusion of the 1983–84 essay I emphasized the wide-open possibility for many different approaches, as long as they are subject to one and the same method. This method can be applied, and yields a new type of results. The problem is that our inherited paradigms for interpretation have not taught us to pursue this method as a matter of principle. The disciplined application of the method does not depend on the production of comprehensive volumes. Indeed, it seems to me that comprehensiveness presupposes a great number and variety of case studies. That is what I have had in mind with this collection of essays, which by no means claims to address all issues.

And last but not least, I do believe that the number of aspects to be studied is endless, and that in this regard no volume will ever be able to say it all. I also believe that the process of systematization by comparison will always be heuristic, one of finding, and continue to finding ever clearer, what we do not yet know, rather than one that becomes fixed let alone one that would be externally predetermined by fixed doctrines. Does this method for the search of the truth in the historical sources of the Old Testament lend itself to making a contribution to our discussions in our modern or so-called postmodern world? Who am I, or who is anyone, to decide that in advance?

BIBLIOGRAPHY

Kim, Wonil. "Toward A Substance-Critical Task of Old Testament Theology." Ph.D. dissertation, Claremont Graduate School, 1996.

Knierim, Rolf P. "Offenbarung im Alten Testament." In *Probleme Biblischer Theologie: Gerhard von Rad zum 70. Geburtstag.* Edited by H. W. Wolff. Munich: C. Kaiser, 1971.

———. "On Biblical Theology." In *The Quest for Context and Meaning: Studies in Biblical Intertextuality in Honor of James A. Sanders.* Ed. C. A. Evans and S. Talmon. Leiden and New York: Brill, 1997.

———. "On the Task of Old Testament Theology." In *A Biblical Itinerary: In Search of Method, Form and Content: Essays in Honor of George W. Coats.* Ed. E. E. Carpenter. JSOTSup 240. Sheffield: Sheffield Academic Press, 1997.

———. "On Two Cases of the Biblical Hermeneutic of Justice (O. J. Simpson and Prime Minister Rabin)." In *"Ihr Völker alle, klatscht in die Hände!" Festschrift für Erhard S. Gerstenberger zum 65. Geburtstag.* Exegese in unserer Zeit; Band 3. Ed. R. Kessler, et al. Münster: LIT Verlag, 1997.

---

10. "On Two Cases of the Biblical Hermeneutic of Justice (O. J. Simpson and Prime Minister Rabin)," in R. Kessler et al., eds., *"Ihr Völker alle, klatscht in die Hände!" Festschrift für Erhard S. Gerstenberger zum 65. Geburtstag* (EZ 3; Münster: LIT, 1997) 238–55.

————. *Studien zur israelitischen Rechts-und Kultusgeschichte* II (Theolog. Habilitation; Heidelberg, 1963) appearing subsequently in *Die Hauptbegriffe für Sünde im Alten Testament*. Gütersloh: Gütersloher, 1st. ed., 1965; 2nd ed., 1967.

————. *The Task of Old Testament Theology: Substance, Method, and Cases*. Grand Rapids: Eerdmans, 1995.

Murphy, R. E. *Wisdom Literature*. FOTL 13. Grand Rapids: Eerdmans, 1981.

4

On the View of Reality and Public Human Ethos in the Bible

Rolf P. Knierim

INTRODUCTION

Let me explain what I mean by this topic. My perspectives are drawn from a particular kind of observations on the biblical texts and answers to questions prompted by these observations.

By *ethos* I refer to the structuring and structured mentality of the people of the Bible in which the concepts for their behavior are rooted. This mentality is basically not explicitly systematized, but nevertheless is structured or systemic, that is, coherent rather than chaotic. Its systemic shape depends on two things: a certain view, quite articulate, of what I call *reality*, and a heuristic process for discerning and ranking or gradating or stratifying or prioritizing qualitative differences in real observations and experiences.

By *public ethos* I refer to the roots that guide the public behavior of the biblical people, the behavior that affects their public arena rather than their private sphere only; whereby the public arena includes the ethos of politics by governing institutions but is not confined to it.

In the sense of public ethos, virtually everything discussed in the Bible is public. I distinguish between public ethos and private ethos practiced away from the public eye in privacy or even secrecy. With few exceptions, the biblical texts narrate nothing about the private lives of the masses of the individuals in their communities. However, by *speaking* about all kinds of thoughts, words, actions, and behavior committed not only in the public eye but also in the individuals' private lives, they do so publicly. They publicly discuss the affairs of private life as a matter of public ethos. This fact is especially and widely documented in the laws, the proverbs, the prophetic books, and in psalms of the Hebrew Bible, and also in the parenetic texts of the Second Testament. The public ethos in the Bible reaches much more into the private sphere than the private sphere reaches into the public ethos.

By *view of reality* I refer to the Bible's view of both God and the world, a view in which each is related to but distinct from the other. Because of the Bible's concept of deity, I distinguish between the terms for *real-*

ity and *world.* In its view of reality, the world, expressed in the bipolar perception of heaven and earth, is understood as created and sustained by God. As in the Bible, the concept of deity also belongs to the views of reality among most of the ancients. Yet, whereas the distinction between deities and the world in the polytheistic religions is at least fluid, it is decisive for the three monotheistic religions. For them, the deity is perceived as related to and present in the world as a whole, but neither as an element of or as the whole world itself nor as a divine world. The deity belongs for them to reality, and first of all but in contradistinction to its world. The biblical view of reality is wider than and encompasses its view of the world.

Of course, language has distinguished between the words for deity as such, for example, "God," a generic word; for names by which deities are individually identified and distinguished, such as Asherah, Baal, Yahweh; and by titles that denote their position and function, such as Lord and Ruler. The meanings of these words are not interchangeable.

By *Bible* I refer to both the Hebrew Bible, the Tanak of Judaism and the First Testament of Christianity, and, distinct from it, the Second or New Testament of Christianity alone. Although the Hebrew Bible and the New Testament have many things in common, they rest for their most part, at least in their extant texts, on fundamentally different assumptions.

The texts of the two Bibles that we read were progressively produced and composed in blocks during a period of some 650 years, from the beginning of the Persian period around 540 B.C.E. until about 100 C.E. in the Roman era. This history of their production and composition has traversed the Persian and Hellenistic eras. Of course, I am aware of the so-called intertestamental literature and its partly canonical and partly extracanonical recognition in the various Jewish and Christian communities.

What does my topic have to do with the conditions of the Jewish and Christian communities under the rules of the Persian, Diadochan, and Roman empires, during which they established their Bibles? It has to do with the problem of their cultural, especially religious, identity between the two poles of assimilation and isolation as they coexisted with the communities of different indigenous cultures under the ruling umbrellas of these empires.

The aspect of assimilation is real, but its dynamics have throughout all historical eras until today been multifaceted. Save the outright extinction of an indigenous community by a totalitarian regime — which did not and does not permit assimilation at all — it becomes critical, and a cause for fighting for survival, where it is forced by the powers in control upon such communities for whom the preservation of its unique identity is so decisive that assimilation would amount to the loss of this very identity, regardless of its ability to accommodate those powers otherwise. However, the Jewish community, with its especially religious identity, as long as it paid its taxes, did not rise against Persian, Diadochan, and Roman rule outright, and was not seen as destabilizing, partly through its own internal strife or as challenging one of these empires' claimed legitimacy, was in principle just as much tolerated by the policies of these empires as those of other communities embraced by them. And when repression or persecution or war against this community on occasion happened, it would be difficult to say that the essential reason lay in the intention to erase its indigenous identity — as convenient as the disappearance of such identity might have been for the ruling powers — and that forced assimilation for that purpose had replaced the policies of tolerance. What has been said about the Jewish community can also be said about the earliest Christian communities living under controlling powers, especially Rome, as long as they did not challenge those powers' claimed legitimacy, specifically through their Christology.

The aspect of isolation must also be considered. It is not identical with the aspect of the tolerance by the empires of the insistence by the Jewish and Christian communities in their distinct religious identities. Nor has it been the inevitable alternative to imposed or expected assimilation. Rather, it amounts to the difference between the will of a community to protect its distinct identity through self-isolation, and its coexistence with all either in spite of its distinct identity or because of it as its unique beneficial contribution to all. The difference becomes acute in light of the claim of both religions that their doctrines and faith are not meant to be relevant for them alone but for all humanity. Those claims have never represented isolationist ideologies. To retreat in practice from them while at the same time making them would amount to the self-contradiction of that very community, and of its ethos or nonethos of a split existence, without integrity. However fundamentally each Bible emphasizes the decisive importance of its distinct views of reality, none of them represents an isolationist view of reality, and none allows for an isolationist ethos of its communities. The Pentateuch alone depicts Moses as the apex of all human history, past and future, because in his mission in and for Israel he mirrors not only what Israel is and should be but also, above all, for humanity the alternative to its own failing of its own history. In the New Testament, Christ instead of Moses is said to be the Savior and Lord of all humanity, and the fulfillment of all divine purposes for all creation. The eschatologies of both the Hebrew Bible and the New Testament were by no means meant only to strengthen the loyalty of their respective communities to their identity and perseverance. As they aimed at these effects, they did so by announcing the judgment over their oppressors especially, and increasingly over the entire sinful world. As much as the books of the Bibles were written to be read by, and even in part directly addressed to, their own communities, their messages were not restricted to these communities but intended to be heard and read by those about whom they spoke.

The Bibles intend to shape and defend the distinct identities of their communities, but they represent no isolationist religions and support no isolationism of their so-called believing communities. And as they speak about humanity, its nations and individuals, the question is of how all those others see themselves considered in these messages, how they are affected by and react to them. The purpose and function of the texts as comfort for their own communities and as call to resist pressure toward unjustifiable assimilation are perfectly legitimate. But this purpose and function cannot predetermine the reactions of the nations themselves to what these texts and their communities say about them. These reactions are beyond the control of the texts and their communities. They depend decisively on whether or not the texts and their communities reveal a view of reality and an ethos that the nations can accept for themselves because such a view and its ethos appear to be good, true, and valid for them also and, hence, for all. Otherwise, the nations will at best leave these texts and their believing communities alone, and certainly want to be left alone and go their own way. To be sure, the nations, too, have their own selfish interests. But the yardstick for the credibility of the texts and their communities is not the reaction of the nations, even at their best; it is the common credibility of the texts and their communities themselves in the first place. One need not depend on the reactions of the nations. One needs to be concerned about the common credibility of one's own view of reality and its ethos.

FOCUS

In a significant regard, the structure of the mentality of the biblical people reflects the structure of the mentality of the people of their environment, and by and large of the human species. Its study belongs to the wider field of anthropology. Specifically, I am focusing on the question of how their experience of reality functions in their *Geistesbeschäftigung*, that is, the intellectual activity that is intrinsic to any ethos.

This kind of activity can often be observed in the surface of the texts themselves, for example, in many narratives about dialogues or disputes in which the substantive arguments confront each other as the issue under discussion is driven forward (see Abraham's dispute with the deity about the deity's decision to destroy Sodom [Gen. 18:22–33]). But more is at stake. While the intellectual activity is often explicit in the forms of the texts themselves, it is always implicit behind or beneath them, infratextually or subtextually, as the prestage for their compositions and for what they say.

Our reconstruction of the infratextual intellectual activities of the biblical people therefore deserves special attention. It is there, where the roots can be discerned for what humans experience, think, and say, for their observations of different factors in reality, their recognition of the relationship of these factors and of their different weights or values, and for their modus operandi and their guidelines for it through which they seek and arrive at coherent, that is, systemic, understandings and value judgments about what is not only real but also true and valid. It is there, where the ethos of the biblical people is a part of the ethos of the *Geistesbeschäftigung* that pervades all cultures of antiquity and also human history until — at least in part — today.

A large volume would not suffice for discussing the entire evidence. The issue of biblical ethics has gained increasing attention, as publications during the last generation indicate. I have to confine myself to examples, mainly from the Hebrew Bible and with a view at the New Testament.

To begin with the most obvious, all biblical texts are full of — besides other grammatical indicators — verbs, nouns, and adjectives, which denote the aspect of quality outright. At the same time, their meaning stands in contrast to the meaning of others, their opposites. Thus, value is contrasted to antivalue: good versus bad or evil, war versus peace, blessing versus curse, truth versus falsehood, liberation versus oppression, love versus hate, grace versus revenge, just versus unjust, righteousness versus sin. Beside the qualifying words stand quantifying words, which also, like the former, either presuppose opposite perspectives or are even directly used as opposites, such as big versus small, high versus low, strong versus weak, fast versus slow, and so on. Depending on their sentences and contexts, these quantifying words, too, frequently connote the aspects of value and antivalue.

Furthermore, the individual words among each of the two groups of opposing words are netted together in word fields or clusters of words in which the aspects of value and antivalue are opposed to each other comprehensively, in the sense of opposite value systems. As systems, they point to the aspect of the total, all-encompassing breadth and weight of value versus antivalue, which is more than the particular aspect of any single word. However, notwithstanding the meaning of a word field as a totality, each word field consists of individual words that by and large point to different aspects, meanings, and weights. I am aware, of course, that the meanings of words vary, that they function within their sentences and especially their immediate literary or oral units and also larger contexts, and that we often coin the meanings of texts by words while the texts themselves do not do the same. In what follows I elaborate on this rudimentary discussion of semantics by focusing on each of the two contrasting value systems.

The value system proper consists of the cluster of the *positive values*. The values within this system are related synthetically, not antithetically. Important, therefore, is the question whether all of them were considered equally valid, or equivalent — a possibility — or as valid in degrees in their relation to each other.

For example, the texts show that liberation from oppression, or salvation from sin, do not mean the same as justice. They are forms of, and valid because of, justice. Hence, liberation is not the criterion for the validity of justice, but justice is the criterion for the legitimacy of liberation. Israel was not liberated from Egypt in order to do what they wanted, but to be a just and righteous community. In the total process of justice as opposed to injustice, liberation from injustice is no end in itself; it is the beginning of this process that is to be followed by the life of the liberated themselves in justice. To understand the liberation of oppressed as their chance for becoming oppressors is unacceptable, at least for the understanding of the righteousness of justice in the Bible. The same kind of understanding is true also for the relationship between the forgiveness of sin and the new life in the New Testament. The freedom of Christians is not only freedom from sin, but also the freedom for the new life.

Or, how are justice and peace related, in private as well as in political affairs? They may coincide, but they are not the same. Thus, is peace the condition for justice, or justice the condition for peace? Or do they rotate around each other in a sort of bipolar balance? Clearly, neither is unrelated to the other. Or, how are justice and blessing related? Again, both are not the same. Blessed persons are at least also those with health and a secure livelihood. Are they thereby also just and righteous persons? These and other questions are directly addressed in the Bible or arise from its reading.

Let me give an example from the story about the beginning of the monarchy in Israel. In 1 Samuel 9–11 we read a conceptually structured story about Saul's secret anointment as the (messianic) king, followed by his public election, that is, the public confirmation of his secret anointment, and finally by the confirmation of his anointment and election in his defensive war against the Ammonites. This confirmation demonstrates, typically, the successful functioning of the king's charisma: he unites the twelve tribes, is victorious in war, and pardons the base fellows who had earlier publicly dispised him. The last aspect in the part about his public confirmation is revealing: When he was publicly elected, some base fellows despised him and brought him no present, and he had kept his peace. (Ethos?) Now, after the public confirmation of his divine selection and public election, the people wanted those base fellows put to death. They did not want revenge for an insult, but the capital punishment for a capital crime, the blasphemy of God and God's anointed. How does Saul react? "No one shall be put to death this day, for today Yahweh has brought deliverance to Israel" (11:13). Is that nothing more than an act of Saul's magnanimity? Or is it an act of quite a different kind, namely, an act of pardon, however magnanimous? In a tension between two legitimate kinds of justice, the justice of judgment and the justice of pardon, Saul overrode the legitimate judgment of his own people by resorting to the right of heads of state to apply the law of pardon. On what ground? On a day of salvation, a day in which the nation is well, the law of pardon represents the higher value of justice in law, because it corresponds to the quality of the nation's salvation. (Ethos as value judgment?)

Opposed to the system of positive values functions the system of *antivalues*. For this system, too, one cannot presume that all antivalues are equally grave. The texts clearly point out that the various antivalues are of different degrees of gravity.

The violations belong to the side of ethos that focuses on what is destructive and therefore prohibited or to be avoided. The differentiation of the degrees of gravity of violations is the background on which the law corpora in our texts were organized. Their organization reflects the value stratifications of the society. I can refer only to the oldest layer of the so-called Covenant Book, Exod. 21:2–22:17, in which the individual prescriptions are successively placed according to the descending order of the weight of violations. The same is true for the order of the so-called Ten Commandments: The rules for the deity's prerogatives come first. They are followed by the focus on the inviolability of the parents, and then by the focus on human and neighborly relations, which themselves follow an order of graded values: murder, adultery, theft, false witness, and — finally and distinct from the preceding actions — covetousness, which may only take place in someone's mind. Words and actions are public and prosecutable; thoughts, as long as they remain hidden and separate from words or actions, are private and not prosecutable. Their hiddenness may only be hinted by the curse. Even so, public ethos reaches into the sphere of private thoughts as well as of private words and actions. The book of Proverbs contains innumerable examples for this fact. And as with the laws, so do the prohibitions and commands and exhortations and admonitions not replace but presuppose and implement public ethos.

The terminology for what we call sin is also a major case in point for the ranking of antivalues. Its word field in the Hebrew Bible easily comprises some seventy different words. With differing respects, all either denote disqualification directly, as so-called abstracts that disqualify otherwise unnamed concrete violations, or they connote disqualification by directly naming such concrete actions that are presumed as wrong. But the weights of what is disqualified differ. In words for actions, for example, theft is not murder; mass murder weighs heavier than the murder of one person (see quantifiers, below); violence includes more than murder alone and is most heavy if it fills and ruins the earth. Examples are endless. Furthermore, terms for thoughts, words, and actions point in their contexts to the different weights of thoughts, words, and actions. They are used on the basis of value differentiations. Cain is jealous — which is only a state of his mind (even if observed by God on Cain's falling face) — and only warned (Gen. 4:3–7); when he kills his brother, he is cursed (Gen. 4:8–16). The terms for or the aspect of actions point to the gravest kind of violations in this ethos. Not quite as grave, but still more weighty than thoughts alone, are spoken words, because they, like actions, turn outside what is inside and adversely affect the community directly.

If in those days, and not only in them, somebody did not care about the different degrees of severity of violations, he or she was in for an uncomfortable surprise when subjected by the community to the consequence for a committed violation. The weights of these consequences are meant to be equivalent to the different weights of the violations. Thus, the stipulations for these consequences differ between bodily punishment, nonbodily penalties of various sorts and degrees, including fines and imprisonment, and compensation for damages with or without various degrees of fines. The bodily punishment itself consists of the death penalty and, of course, the less grave infliction of bodily injury, which itself distinguished between mutilation (such as removal of hand, ear, eye, toe, penis) and chastisement (such as flogging) — the latter also for educational purposes because there was hope for better behavior without the necessity of permanent damage to the body. The prescriptions of these consequences belong to the realm of public law for the judiciary. They are systematically stratified with respect to a value system that reflects the different degrees of violation. In them, law does not replace public ethos but implements it.

The view of the qualitatively different weights of thoughts, words, and actions is intensified quantitatively by the view of their varying extent. The widest dimensions of those quantitative aspects are those of creation and human history. Among many places, they are programmatically addressed in Genesis 1–11. The narrative about the creation of the world out of chaos in Gen. 1:1–2:4a is structured according to the view of a universal cosmic system within which each part has its solid place and depends on others just as others depend on it. The creation of this stratified order is from day to day called "good," and in its totality after six days, in the superlative sense, "very good." If one asks what the combination of the qualitative and quantitative aspects in this order has to do with ethos, one needs only to read the novel of Jonah, at the end of which the deity teaches his rebellious prophet that not only are animals more weighty than plants, and humans more weighty than animals, but also that 120,000 people and many animals are immeasurably more weighty than one plant. That qualifying and quantifying gradation is found in Genesis 1 and 9, and it is the criterion for the deity's own ethos of change of mind, from planning to destroy to saving even Nineveh, the most wicked city on earth, from destruction — after Nineveh, reacting to the threat, acted (!) by turning from their evil ways (Jon. 3:10). As far as the picture of human history in Genesis 3–11 is concerned, it has long been recognized that this picture is characterized especially by the ever expanding spread of violence until the whole earth is filled with, and itself corrupted by, violence, and — so we have to understand — by this permanently continuing kind of history after the flood, including the predisposition of the human mind for evil and the human hubris. In light of this destructive tendency of human history, the reason why it does not self-destruct is seen in an amazing fact, also present in history, by which this history is nevertheless undeservedly upheld: the deity's patience with this history, which lies in the deity's own ethos.

One has to distinguish between the ethical positions and their maxims in the Bible, and the ethos leading to these decisions and maxims. I am focusing on the latter, because it is the presupposition for the former. How, then, do the ancients arrive at their value judgments? Basically, by comparing and distinguishing. The texts give us clues.

We know something about the judicial proceedings in what is called "justice in the gate." Confronted with a case, civil or criminal, normally of two opposing parties, the community, or its judges, has to obtain and analyze and evaluate the evidence and arrive at a judgment. The judgment can be made only after this complex process is completed. Then it can be pronounced and even written down. What guides the judges who are involved in such procedures? Precedence provides a guiding framework. But more is at stake. Exod. 23:1–9 appeals to the ethos of the judges. They must not be corrupt, favoring some parties and oppressing others. Deut. 16:18–20 reinforces: You must not distort judgment (*mišpāṭ*), but in rendering judgment, it is — emphatically! — righteousness, righteousness (*ṣedeq, ṣedeq*) that you must pursue! A judgment is as such not yet self-evidently righteous. It must be equally true for all. The truth equally for all is called *ṣedeq*, righteousness. The ethos of righteousness is the yardstick for truth in judgment. Amos complements: "*Seek* good and not evil.... *Hate* evil and *love* good, and establish (just) justice in the gate" (Amos 5:14–15).

But what is it that is righteous or just judgment and good? Surely, it consists of a web of known positive values, which can be applied as basis and framework in the search for judgments from case to case. But within such frameworks, each judgment requires specific justifications that must be sought and found from case to case. It is the result of a process of searching. No result is known before that process is concluded. What is righteous, *just* justice, and good, must be sought and found out in an ever new process of seeking and finding. No wonder that the prophet says: *Seek* justice! The process of seeking and finding what is good is heuristic in nature. It is the condition for justice that is as righteous as possible. And even that righteousness is only approximate. The procedure itself of the search for truth is the ethos that is presupposed for any value judgment, also in judiciary law.

What is true for the legal and prophetic texts is equally true for each of hundreds of proverbs, especially in the Wisdom literature. These proverbial statements are the end result of intensive processes of discriminating thought. Any of these statements can be read in a second. But just think about what it had to take for a sage or popular wisdom to produce one. "Hatred stirs up strife, but love covers all offenses" (Prov. 10:12); "The beginning of strife is like letting out water; so stop before the quarrel breaks out" (Prov. 17:14). The so-called *better-sayings* are especially significant. They compare what is better to what is less good. These comparative statements are the result of the process of comparing the values in experiences. "A good name is better than riches, and favor is better than silver or gold" (Prov. 22:1); which presupposes Prov. 16:8: "Better is a little with righteousness than large income with injustice." Two things are important: One is that the expressed or implied value judgments in Proverbs are not only derived from real experiences and observations but that the values themselves are seen as happening in the differing and contrasting realities of the events themselves. The ethos of the mentality of the sages or of sage communities, which consists of heuristic processes for arriving at discriminating value judgments about real conditions or events, is rooted in and derived from their experience of reality which is not univalent, let alone devoid of value, but multivalent itself. Their ethos is rooted in and derived from their view of reality itself. The other thing is that the heuristic method for finding truth is just as important as the truthful aspect in, or the truth of, each judgment. No proverb says it all. Each needs to be, and many are, complemented, or even contradicted, by opposite judgments. This ethos knows that no value judgment is final or ultimate but, while not irrelevant, always relative. To seek truth is its trademark; to possess it would be untrue.

This ethos, then, reveals the sharp difference between the seeking and the possession of truth. This difference applies to all value judgments in all realms of public and private life, in ideologies and religions, and also in the Bible of both Testaments itself. There should be no doubt that the two Bibles claim both, the search for and the possession of truth. When we come to the sharp difference between these two claims in them, it should for very serious reasons become clear that their positions of truth are relative to and subject to the critical scrutiny by their own search for truth.

Interestingly, the heuristic mode of searching for truth is not confined to the generations of the Bible. It is international, as especially the Wisdom literature documents. It belongs to the best across human cultures, and is the impetus for the ongoing critique of all cultures and the self-critique within each culture as well. It amounts to the critical presence of human ethos in the ethics of each society, also of the theologies of the biblical people.

The aspect of an indefinitely ongoing world and its history brings me, finally, to a comparison of the view of reality of the Hebrew Bible with that of the New Testament. I am focusing neither on what both have in common nor on their differences nor on their historical connections, but on their views of reality themselves by which they have become separated.

As far as I can see, the decisive reason for their separate views lies in the kind of eschatology expressed in the New Testament's texts. This kind of eschatology is their conceptual basis, without which the New Testament could not exist as it does. To be sure, while eschatology in it is not new, its kind of eschatology separates it from the eschatologies preceding it. It is the vision not of inner-historical revolutions but of the end of all historical eras; not of the return of failed history to its beginning in the original creation but of the replacement of the original creation itself by the new creation of a new cosmos; not of an *Endzeit* mirroring the *Urzeit* but of the end of the *Urzeit* of both, original cosmic order and paradise, when the new world comes; not of the coming of the kingdom when history has fulfilled its true meaning but of the end of failed history when the kingdom comes; and not by anything that humans, believers or unbelievers, do but by the act of God alone. This new creation lies not only in the future, but the expectation of its future consummation is inseparably connected with the belief that the eschaton has already arrived in its forerunner, Jesus Christ (so virtually exclusively in the Gospel of John), who is not *another* messiah, prophet, teacher, sacrificial lamb but once and for all *the* Messiah, *the* Son of God, *the* Kyrios of and *the* lamb of God for the sins of the world. The passages for this view are countless. Some say it most radically: "In accordance with his promise, we wait [not just for a new earth but] for new heavens and a new earth, where righteousness is at home" (2 Pet. 3:13). Note that the eschatological view is often defined in the genre of hope. In fact, it is knowledge, the knowledge of the eschaton, not the hope for it. It is waiting for what through and in the promises is known. Whatever hope has to do with it, it rests on "the *assurance* of things hoped for, the *conviction* of things not seen" (Heb. 11:1). It rests on predictions that are to be taken for granted, not hoped for. This eschatological knowledge is most radically expressed by Paul, for whom even the new creation will not be a distinct world but absorbed into God, who will be "all in all" (1 Cor. 15:28). (Such a word allows even for the speculation that the primordial chaos is not absorbed into God but extinguished.) There is no precedent in the pre-Christian traditions for this kind of cosmic, new creation worldview, let alone for one where God is the only reality that counts. And since this eschaton is already present, the *ekklēsia* of Christ already exists in this new creation in accordance with its order, no longer under the law of the old world even as it still lives in it for a short while, and this precisely because it is assured of the universal, and imminent, parousia of this new creation. Never mind the aspect of the delay of the parousia. It amounts just to that: its delay, not its nonfulfillment.

The consequences of this worldview and view of reality set the ethos of the *ekklēsia* apart from the ethos of the worldview in the Hebrew Bible, including the ethos from its own eschatologies, which are by far inner-historical. A major case in point: The Hebrew Bible draws, also for its theologies, extensively on the state of the sciences internationally available at its time, the sciences of ethnography, geography and topography, economy, law, biology, medicine, administration of government, organization of warfare, architecture, metallurgy, medicine, cosmology, and more. It is deeply connected with the state of knowledge in many ancient cultures.

Compare the narrative about the deity's instruction to Moses for the building of the desert sanctuary and the organization of its priesthood in Exodus 25–31, or the instruction for the registration and induction of the Israelite militia and the organization of its hierocracy as preparation for the impending epiphanic sanctuary campaign toward the promised land in Num. 1:1–10:10. These verbalized blueprints belong

to the ancient science of administration. They are thoroughly systematized. Their expressions represent the results of preceding intensive
intellectual efforts in the planning stages, and the bases for the following executions of operations, which are then also narrated. According to
these and other texts, a total operation consists of the consecutive steps
of its planning stage, itself proceeding from deliberation to decision; of
the stage of its publication in words and/or, for example, architectural
blueprint, a stage represented by our texts; and of the stage of execution. In the texts mentioned, the deity itself is understood as a thinking
and planning deity, not only as a speaking and acting one. Just as the
texts speak about the plans of persons and the nations, so do they speak
about the plan or thoughts of Yahweh, who says that "they execute a
plan, but not mine" (Isa. 30:1).

Nothing of all this plays a role in the New Testament. Why? Because the things that inevitably belong to the structure of the ongoing
human history, even its inner-historical eschatologies (see the architectural blueprint for the building of the second temple in Ezekiel's
eschatology [Ezekiel 40–43]) play no role for a community that exists no
longer according to the structure of the old but according to the order of
the new world. And even if one lives in the old world while expecting
the impending consummation of the new, one has every reason, even
ethical obligation, to ignore what belongs to the old and to structure
one's life in view of the new so rapidly approaching. The aspect of the
temporal nearness of the new intensifies the abandonment of an ethos
oriented on the view of an indefinitely ongoing, and imperfect, world.
Of course, the ethos based on this vision of the new world also explains,
at least, either the indifference of the texts to, or, by the same token, the
unqualified rejection of, all worldly politics, and to programs for the
social organization of societies nationally and internationally as well.

The contrast between the views of an eschatologically ending and
an indefinitely, however imperfectly, ongoing world is obvious. The latter view is based on and limited by human experience. It is the view
of a forever penultimate world. In the former view, the aspect of the
penultimate world is subordinate to that of the ultimacy of a new and
different world in light of which the penultimate world is at least relative, certainly qualified negatively, if not irrelevant altogether. As such,
the aspect of ultimacy cannot be ignored inasmuch as it signals that no
experience of the penultimate world may claim ultimate truth. Its effect
on all penultimate experience is that it reveals the ground for the ethos
of human self-relativization radically, and the need, ultimately, for the
acknowledgment that in their view of the world and of themselves, all
humans are interdependent and no one possesses, let alone controls, absolute truth. Nevertheless, the awareness of the humans' relativity and

of the need for their self-relativization, if their behavior is to be constructive rather than destructive, is also derived from their experience of a penultimate world. In view of the idea of the ultimate nature of their relativity, however, the experience of that relativity can itself not be relativized. It is final.

The valid idea of ultimacy, however, is not the problem in the contrast between the eschatologically ultimate and the penultimate worldviews in the Bibles. The eschatologically ultimate worldview in the New Testament is different from a radical idea of ultimacy by which the relative or irrelevant nature of the penultimate world may be adjudged. It is based on the view that the concept of the imminent and, for that reason, already present new creation is *die Sache selbst,* the issue itself, substantially. This view is decidedly mythological. Rather than being nothing more than a discardable shell for a different concept, it is the concept itself on which the claim to its validity depends. This concept is not rooted in the experience of the ongoing world, just as the myth of the *Urzeit* is not rooted in such experience, but derived from a view of reality beyond any possible human experience. And as the judgment over this imperfect world is considered to be fulfilled by this mythical execution itself, this claim has never materialized as promised and expected. Its failure to materialize deprives this mythological view of the credibility of its claim to be the ultimate judge for the validity or invalidity of, and of validity and truth in, the penultimate world.

The ethos based on the mythology of eschatological ultimacy in either Bible/Testament has proved to be relative if not irrelevant and even an obstacle, when compared to the ethos based on the experience of this indefinitely ongoing world, imperfect as it is. The so-called delay of the parousia has at least become indefinite, defunct, and, hence, relative or irrelevant or an obstacle to the focus on the ongoing world. An intelligent person objected saying that the kingdom may come in a million years. Good enough. Until then, we better attend to the things at hand for the next 999,999 years, and a few things for today, tomorrow, and the next generation, regardless of the date 2000.

What has been said about the two Bibles has decisively to do with their consciousness and speaking of God. They used the God-language because they had inherited it from the ancient history to which they belonged. Even we today use this vocabulary primarily, if, unfortunately, not exclusively, because we have inherited it from that millennia-old vocabulary. Would we coin the word "God" de novo, had we not inherited it, or would we use a different terminology from our own vocabulary? This legacy is as such not insignificant. However, were we to use the God-language only because we inherited it, we would do so without asking what it meant and means. What, then, did it mean for the biblical people to say "God"? It may be safe to say that they meant someone who incomparably is involved in everything they experience and envision ultimately. In the contents and concepts of all their texts about events and conditions, they speak in endlessly manifold ways about the presence of an influence on everything in this world that they call God. And although in distinct respects, their own understandings in and messages of these texts are clearly set apart from those of their environment, they could not have generated these understandings and messages without presupposing the presence of the influence of God. I think we would speak about the experience of a presence in the world, which should be circumscribed with what appears to be true, more true, and ultimately true in everything that can be qualified and quantified, and the experience that truth is always independent of us but never ceases to confront us, pulling us forward, affirming some of our steps and saying no to others, all the while being out of our final reach and control. It is always to be sought rather than to be possessed. As far as I can see, the consciousness of God in the biblical writings as quest for truth and its heuristic approach represents the best foundation of their ethos. And in whatever way their documents appear to represent a possession of the truth of God, those appearances are not God but subject to the search for the truth of God in and beyond them.

CONCLUSION

I have attempted to describe a kind of ethos in which value stratifications are sought and found from the human experience of the differences in an indefinitely ongoing imperfect world. This kind is in many respects found in the Hebrew Bible, and represents the presence of international human wisdom in and its influence on the Bible. I have also pointed to the kind of ethos which is derived from the professed knowledge of a perfect — new — world and, hence, from an understanding of absolute truth that is a priori known for the world rather than always to be found through the experience of it. This kind represents the basis for the New Testament. I am far from ignoring or underestimating the importance of many aspects in the New Testament for a basic human ethos, even and precisely as they point to the criterion of ultimacy, which remains valid apart from its imbeddedness in the mythological eschatology of a new creation. Also, I do not mean to say that in light of an ethos of the search for the truth of God, everything said in the Hebrew Bible appears to be true or equally true simply because it is said. I am saying that that mentality of the biblical generations which finds human beings in the position of being called to seek rather than to possess the truth of God appears to be the most fundamental basis for human ethos, and for this reason even more for the ethos of the biblical communities themselves. Lastly, the validity of the ethos in the Bible depends on that view of reality by the generations who produced the Bible, in which the truth in the world is sought and found for their own good and also for the good of all. The recognition of this kind of ethos marks the difference between a human and a literalistically biblicistic reading of the Bible. The convergence of the best in the Bible and the best in what has come to be called humanism represents, from the times of its emergence in its own times until today, the legacy of its communities to the presence and future of the human race.

5

On Two Cases of the
Biblical Hermeneutic of Justice

Rolf P. Knierim

Biblical hermeneutic discusses the encounter of the biblical worldview and our own. This discussion requires hermeneutical theory. Its proper subject, however, is not its theory but the reality of the encounter itself. The laboratory in which hermeneutical theories are tested is not a classroom but this encounter. And short of being directly involved in encounters, the first hermeneutical way is to discuss that reality.

The encounter is not abstract. It happens in concrete cases. By definition these cases involve the encounter of diverse persons and their positions and, as in the case of biblical hermeneutic, the encounter of positions, in which the biblical traditions in some ways play a role, with positions today.

The meeting of diverse positions becomes most critical when diversity becomes divisive and destructive instead of becoming supportive and constructive. In what follows I discuss two cases of divisive nature in light of the biblical hermeneutic of justice: the recently decided trial of O. J. Simpson in Los Angeles, and the death, shortly thereafter, of Prime Minister Yitzhak Rabin in Tel Aviv.

By the time this essay is published and read, these two events will have been long left behind in the public discussion. Nevertheless, their aspects must not be passed because the events belong to the past. Indeed, each of these past events is respectively part of a wider range of ongoing developments.

THE VERDICT IN THE SIMPSON TRIAL

A Particular Aspect of the Verdict

While this criminal trial is in itself relevant in a biblical hermeneutic of justice, the following discussion specifically focuses on the verdict

This essay is dedicated to Erhard Gerstenberger, whose life and work have been a testimony to the open encounter of cultures and especially to the support of the marginalized everywhere, with the expression of my admiration and friendship. This essay was previously published in *"Ihr Völker alle, klatscht in die Hände!" Festschrift für Erhard S. Gerstenberger zum 65. Geburtstag,* ed. Rainer Kessler, Kerstin Ulrich, Milton Schwantes, and Gary Stansell. Reprinted by permission of LIT Verlag.

of the jury. Whereas this verdict has been applauded by a smaller part of the population, it has been condemned as a miscarriage of justice by the great majority of Americans. It has certainly not diminished the divisions in the society.

The Problem of the Deliberation

After many months of trial the jury, despite the judge's recommendation not to start with straw votes, did exactly that. In less than four hours the jury of twelve arrived at its verdict, acquitting Simpson after three votes, starting with ten to acquit and two to convict and ending unanimously to acquit. The jury was composed of nine African-Americans, two Caucasians, and one Latino. The two members who originally voted in favor of conviction had the right to change that vote, however rapidly, and must have had their own reasons for doing so. This quick unanimous verdict in a trial as complex and complicated as this murder case can by no means be understood as the result of a careful deliberation of the massive amount of argumentation presented by the prosecution and defense.

To be sure, the condition for conviction in criminal cases is a judgment "beyond reasonable doubt." The opinions, even among legal experts, are divided on whether or not this condition was met in this trial. Interestingly, after months of following the televised trial and reading the published arguments, the great majority of Americans considered the condition clearly met. By contrast, the tiny group of jury members — lay persons and supposedly representative of the society at large — was sharply at odds with that majority.

It is clear that a majority may be wrong and a minority right, and also that the majority is not beyond suspicion of being racially prejudiced even though no one would admit to such prejudice. The case was decided by the jury, however, not by the majority in the streets and their homes. The case is, at any rate, closed, and accepted as closed by society.

Group Solidarity and the Verdict: The Issue of Suspicion

Is the jury itself beyond suspicion because it is the jury? Does its rapidly determined verdict signal its own certainty of reasonable doubt? Or does its verdict signal a different reason quite apart from the question of whether or not there was reason for doubt? Is the jury beyond the suspicion of having acquitted Simpson regardless of the kind and degree of evidence and short of Simpson's own confession for the murder?

This suspicion is reinforced by defense lawyer Cochran's blatant use of the "race card," his appeals to the ethnic self-awareness of the predominantly African-American members of the jury; by the fist of one such member triumphantly raised toward Simpson after the trial's adjournment; by the almost unanimous outbreak of celebration in the African-American communities in Los Angeles and across the nation; by the enthusiastic and congratulatory reception of such members in their local ethnic neighborhoods; and, next to other indicators, by the televised outbreak of "Thank you, Jesus...Hallelujah...Praise the Lord" among those gathered in the sanctuary of the African Methodist Episcopal Church in Los Angeles. What was the triumph for? That evidence for conviction was insufficient? Why triumph and praise to Jesus for that reason? Would there have been praise to Jesus had there been a conviction for that horrible double murder?

It is officially accepted, including by the U.S. Supreme Court, that a jury may neglect even irrefutable evidence if it was obtained through objectionable or reprehensible procedures, especially by the police. If a messenger is not clean, the message may be discounted. The reasons for this allowance in trials are well known and well justified.

These reasons particularly take into account that side of American judicial history in which especially African-American people, when involved with the police and the courts, have been treated in violation of common legal and just standards. To this day, legitimate complaints about mistreatment and miscarriage of justice, based on reports verified by white people, are on record and continue to be reported.

Societal Ethos and the Verdict

As these lines are being written (December 4, 1995), *Los Angeles Times* staff writer Edward J. Boyer, with whom I spoke on the telephone, reports that a (white) woman who participated in convicting a former Black Panther leader, Elmer Pratt, of murder in 1972 is now seeking a new trial for exonerating him and freeing him from prison. After that trial, new evidence emerged that "a key witness had lied, and that the eyewitness [a second, different witness] had earlier identified someone else," and that "retired FBI agent M. Wesley Swearingen says the bureau knows that because Pratt was under constant surveillance" and at the time of the murder was four hundred miles away from its location.

Particularly disturbing is that the judiciary has thus far repeatedly refused to reopen Pratt's trial, despite support for him by "Amnesty International, the American Civil Liberties Union, members of Congress, and a virtual Who's Who of local politicians and clergy." By now, one wonders if the O. J. Simpson case has freshly hurt Pratt's chances for a new trial, especially since Pratt had also been defended by the leading and successful defender of Simpson, Johnnie L. Cochran.

What does it mean, however, if a jury's reference to either insufficient evidence or its bungled acquisition is a rationalized front for a quite different motive, namely, its group solidarity with a defendant and its own group constituency by which its members are bound and to which they will return after the trial?

In such a scenario the court, rather than being the system's setting for adjudicating specific cases, becomes the instrument for a different strategy: "beating the society's system" by "turning the table around" in the perpetual group warfare within the society. Any group using the system for this purpose is just as bad as any other group that did, does, or may use the system in this way. It is certainly not better and more trustworthy, and cannot function as a signal in its own right for a better societal justice or for alliances of people across all groups who strive for a better justice. And in undermining the court system for this purpose, a group beats the very institution that, for all its weaknesses — and despite the progress made and being made — is more than any other societal agency obligated to protect everyone's rights equally. Of course, whoever has no money for lawyers does not have the better chances, which is true regardless of ethnicity and gender.

The American jury system is for many reasons highly controversial. For its improvement, one emphasizes, among other things, locations of trials in communities more appropriate for them, and compositions of juries that are balanced ethnically, intellectually, socioeconomically, and in terms of gender. Whatever cross section is more representative of the society is what should be done. But one must in all such considerations not forget the overriding goal: that juries decide a case on the merits and conditions of that case. This is the goal regardless of the person on trial, where the case is tried and by whom, and the composition of the jury — whether exclusively white or black or Latino or Asian, or of men or women only. Surely, this criterion is the ideal. But this ideal is demanded of everyone, even constitutionally. Abandoning it under the pressures of group-based partiality would amount to the depressing conclusion that no justice for a case can be expected and that each group is just as bad as any other. We are speaking about the relationship of group solidarity and law in a just societal system, and especially about the role of the Christians in these respects.[1]

The Verdict in Light of the Biblical Hermeneutic of Justice

Old Testament Ethos

In the Old Testament ancient Israel's ethos pervaded all areas of public and private life, including those of social justice, of substantive laws

---

1. According to the California state law of "jury nullification," a jury is prohibited to nullify evidence for a case with reference, for example, to the higher purpose of the larger good. In his closing arguments, defense lawyer Cochran had appealed to the jury to take that prohibited road. The prosecution objected but was overruled by Judge Ito.

and the proceedings for cases in trials. This ethos, particularly as ethos sanctioned by the Yahweh religion, was binding not only in spite of but especially with respect to its actual violations.

For the ethos itself, it was clear that the righteous condemnation of society-wide social injustice and its prosecution also in trials was not the same as the adjudication of a specific criminal case in which, for instance, an individual was accused of having murdered a neighbor. Such cases were decided from case to case solely on the basis of what contributed to ascertaining whether or not the accused had committed the murder.

It was inconceivable that either the prosecution or the defense or a communal jury would be considered as operating legally or ethically were it to attempt to instrumentalize any such case for a different kind of problem, such as the rectification of patterns of social injustice or for class, clan, or tribal warfare. A trial for the murder of a fellow Israelite by an individual was a trial for that murder — nothing else. No one accused, whether acquitted or convicted, would be shielded from the decision on that question — that question alone — by the solidarity of the members of his or her clan and class, whether privileged or marginalized. In reality, this principle was certainly violated, as especially the prophetic literature shows. But its violation was never sanctioned ethically or legally. It was always violation of justice.

The solidarity of any group with one of its members ended where the question of murder by that member was at issue. The same would have been true for the solidarity of any judge, or group of judges, with their own social constituencies in such cases. Not even the suspicion of the prevalence of such solidarity over a case of that nature would have been acceptable. Had this not been so, not only would the fact and crime of a murder have lost its severity, but the diversion from the focus on it to the focus on a different sort of injustice — for a purpose other than that case — would have meant the destruction of the instrument for adjudicating any criminal case. It would have corrupted not only the court system but also the ethos of societal justice itself to which the court system is responsible.

New Testament Ethos

In the New Testament the disciples of Jesus or the early Christians are generally presumed to be subject to the public courts, except in conflicts of conscience, in which case they "must obey God rather than men" (Acts 5:29). Unlike the Old Testament, the New Testament with few exceptions pays no explicit attention to the public laws themselves and — save the cases of Jesus, the apostles, and Paul — to trials in public courts. Even the issue of justice in the Roman Empire is of no interest.

Nevertheless, it is equally clear that the ethos of the disciples, pervading the entire New Testament, would not permit the perversion of conditions specifically germane to the adjudication of a murder case either for the purpose of advancing a different cause or for the purpose of shielding an accused for the sake of personal or Christian solidarity. No party functioning that way in a murder trial would be considered to have integrity and not to violate the law. Any such consideration would distract from the trial's purpose or be suspect of doing so. This position is so fundamental to the general ethos of the New Testament that to observe it one need not even resort to the ethos of the Sermon on the Mount.

Summary

When one considers the basic position in both the Old and the New Testament on the particular aspect discussed, one has to realize the biblical contribution to the distinction between the necessary concern for social justice and the adjudication of specific individual cases on their own merits in public courts today. That the distinctiveness of each process is manipulated in the interest of the solidarity of groups is too often a fact perpetrated not only by one but by any kind of group; and that solidarity itself can be unethical, even criminal, as much as it can be ethical and legal.

True ethical standards are expected by everyone, but certainly by those claiming to adhere to biblical standards. Which Jesus, then, is to be praised? The Jesus who, for the sake of adjudicating cases, supports what Deut. 16:18–20 says, that the judgments of the judges must be "righteous," that the judges "shall not show partiality" but follow "justice, and only justice," the justice of a case; and who wants to overcome the group divisiveness by ending the perpetual turning of the table? (Has any turning the table around kept the table from ever turning?) Or is a Jesus to be praised who uses murder cases for keeping the table being turned around?

Are we Christians beyond suspicion of using Jesus for the justification of our divided and divisive interests, all the while claiming that we follow him? As long as the criteria for understanding Jesus are convoluted by whomever, Jesus functions in a pluralistic society and humanity just as much for the authorization of its divisiveness and the perpetration of evil as he may function for what in their diversity is good, or better, for all.

Lastly, on trial are not only social justice and justice in the courts today, but the integrity of the biblical religion including the integrity of Jesus Christ himself in these realms. That affects all of us, regardless of race or gender. Group identity is important, but group separatism not only defeats constructive intergroup allegiance, it increases the isolation of a group — any group.

THE DEATH OF PRIME MINISTER RABIN

The Question of Ethos

Present

On October 26, 1995, the top Palestinian of the Islamic Dshihad, Fathi Shalaki, was shot to death on the island of Malta by a commando of Israel's Mossad — with the knowledge if not by order of Israel's prime minister, Yitzhak Rabin. The Islamic Dshihad swore bloody revenge. Nine days later, the prime minister was shot to death, not by a Palestinian but by an Israeli, Yigal Amir, a student of both secular and biblical Israeli law. He said, "I acted alone on God's orders and I have no regrets." He apparently was referring to his understanding of the written biblical Torah rather than an impromptu, personal divine audition.

The prime minister's death at the hands of an Israeli citizen affects not only Israel's citizenry and the Jewish people in the Diaspora, though by far these are most affected. In various ways it affects all nations and their governments, the three monotheistic religions, Jews and Muslims but also Christians, because the Old Testament and its meaning for today belong especially to the roots of their faith.

Historical

The debate in the Israeli-Jewish community is intensely soul-searching as well as controversial. One must very much remain aware that this inner-Jewish debate cannot be separated from the massive concern for the state of Israel's struggle for its existence and permanent security. Whatever is under dispute, whatever injustice was done by any party, and whatever progress has been and is being made, one must acknowledge that more than compartmentalized compromises with the Palestinians and its neighbors are at stake for the state of Israel. All is at stake as long as not only Hamas, Islamic Dshihad, and similar groups, but also Arabic and especially Islamic states, including Saudi Arabia, reject Israel's existence. In principle such a rejection may at any opportune moment shift into acute and deadly confrontation.

Modern Challenges

With these serious perspectives a reflection is necessary on the part of those who, though not Jewish, are involved in a biblical hermeneutic that includes the Old Testament. The reflection has to focus on two questions: the Old Testament's position on the concept of trading land for peace, and the death penalty for an Israeli(te) leader who implements such a concept. Both questions are prompted by Amir's reasons for his act, and by the roots of these reasons.

One must assume that Amir committed his act as the legitimate execution of a perceived death penalty verdict, not as an assassination or murder, and that he believed to be personally called to execute this verdict. It is also clear that he would not have committed his act had the prime minister and his government (Amir had intended to shoot the foreign minister, Shimon Peres, too!) not entered a process that had already led to the level of official treaty forms, a process about trading parts of the land of Israel for peace, at least with the Palestinians. Finally, it seems clear that the specific biblical Torah, that is, the Pentateuch, represents above everything else the framework and most authoritative basis for Amir's outlook, action, and even his self-defense without a lawyer in court.

The Pentateuch's Concept of Trading Land for Peace

The entire Pentateuch rests on the concept of Israel's election as Yahweh's special nation for the purpose of permanent existence in the land of Israel. Without this basic concept, neither the Pentateuch as a whole nor any of its parts can on its own terms be correctly understood. Thus, it is the epos of Israel's migration in many stages toward the borders of this land, a migration caused by the divine promise of it and the divine order to take and possess it. The book of Joshua narrates Israel's conquest and the distribution of the promised land among the tribes.

The Pentateuch says that this land has been the land of the Canaanite nations, and in Genesis calls it the land of Canaan. But it especially says that this land will be given to, taken by, and belong to Israel. The promise and the order are the basis for the change of title from "the land of Canaan" to "the land of Israel."

The program in the Pentateuch for executing this promise and order is the divine command to conquer the land by war, including the deity's own leading part in the war, and to disinherit the Canaanites of it. In many texts the order of conquest and disinheritance is positively commanded by the deity and then by Moses; and disobedience is, under threat of divine punishment, strictly prohibited. In both, its commands and prohibitions, this order is apodictic, irrevocable, and nonnegotiable. This aspect in the covenant between Yahweh and Israel focuses on the initial stage in Israel's possession of the land, on the conditions for taking possession of it.

Once the land is taken and Israel lives in it permanently, Israel will be obligated to continue keeping the covenant. This entails fulfilling those covenant stipulations that refer to permanent life in the land so that Israel's blessing and peace in the land and uninterrupted possession of it will be preserved. The meaning of this second aspect differs distinctly from that about the initial conquest and settlement.

Both aspects belong to the same covenant theology. Fundamental for this theology in both these aspects is the unity of "one God — one people of this God — one land." This unity is indivisible. Its conceptuality governs first the Sinai narrative, expressed in the form of divine revelation, and subsequently the book of Deuteronomy, expressed in the form of Moses' testament. In both narratives the covenant concept is therefore concerned not only with Israel's life in the land after the initial conquest and settlement, but is already concerned with the distinct phase of the conquest and settlement themselves as the presupposition for Israel's life in the land following them.

Also, the triune concept of the covenant theology is already fundamental for the divine promise to the patriarchs. And like the covenant, this promise distinguishes between the gift of the land to the descendants of the patriarchs and their subsequent possession of and multiplication in it. This promise is unilaterally valid. It is unconditional and forever irrevocable, regardless of Israel's obedience or disobedience. Three aspects need clarification.

Fulfillment of the Promise of the Land

Whereas the divine promise of the land is unconditional, its fulfillment is conditional, in the Pentateuch said to depend on Israel's obedience to the command to conquer the land and to the law for permanently possessing it. These requirements for the implementation of the promise do not become relative or obsolete when, as long as, or because Israel does not fulfill them. On the contrary, they themselves are absolute and irrevocable. That the promise depends on its implementation does not mean that the divine command depends on Israel's obedience.

Indeed, precisely because the condition for implementing the promise is Israel's obedience, this obedience is absolutely expected, and as long as the promise is valid. And, the unfulfilled promise is no reason for letting the command and the laws go unfulfilled, but a compelling reason for fulfilling them.

Decisive for the Pentateuch is not that the implementation of the promise is conditional, but that this condition must be fulfilled. To be fulfilled is the content of the command: take the land completely and observe the laws in order to preserve its possession. All else amounts to disobedience to Yahweh and Moses. Lastly, the intention of the absolute necessity to fulfill these stipulations is to finally assure the promised goal: the sole and total possession of the land.

The Land of Israel as Yahweh's Gift

The Pentateuch says that the land of Israel will be the gift of Yahweh. Seen from its perspective before its actual event, the announcement that the gift will happen in the impending future is understood as a declaration of Yahweh's will and decision. Like Yahweh's promise, this decision to give the land to Israel is unconditional. The gift will happen in the conquest and distribution of the land, including Yahweh's own leading role in the war against the Canaanites and in Yahweh's abiding loyalty to Israel's permanent inheritance.

Israel is required to accept this gift by fulfilling the conditions for its acceptance. Inasmuch as the gift is not fully realized, responsibility for this shortfall is seen in Israel's own failure rather than in Yahweh's. Yet this failure neither compromises Yahweh's will nor relativizes Israel's obligation to accept it. It reinforces both.

Again, precisely because the condition for realizing Yahweh's gift lies in Israel's obedience, this obedience to Yahweh's decision and orders for realizing the conquest and the possession of the land is absolutely commanded as long as the decision is valid.

Distinction between Conquest/distribution and Possession of the Land

The distinction in the Pentateuch's instructions between the two aspects of the original conquest and distribution of the land — the latter especially also in the book of Joshua — and its subsequent possession are important not so much because of their chronological order but because the aspect of the original event is the conceptual presupposition for Israel's subsequent life in the land.

According to this perspective, Israel's required observance of the laws for life in the already possessed land is not the condition for the original conquest and distribution of it. The condition for conquest and distribution is obedience to the command to conquer and distribute the land itself.

The land is not the land of Israel because the Israelites lived in the land of the Canaanites and together with them but because of the transfer of title that is to happen, according to the Pentateuch, through the impending conquest, the dispossession of the Canaanites, and the settlement of the Israelites. From the Pentateuch's perspective before these events, the decisive texts are therefore, and most fundamentally, those that focus on the immediately impending events, that is, texts in which the transfer of title through these events is ordered by divine and Mosaic authority, and to which Israel's obedience is first of all committed.

Summary

These texts are known. Their evidence is extensive, conceptually homogeneous, and, for all their diverse aspects and expressions, unambiguous. Concerning the issue under discussion, they represent the Torah proper, the most authoritative divine as well as Mosaic commands and prohibitions and the parenesis reinforcing them.

The land of the Canaanite nations is to be conquered by war. These nations will be blotted out by Yahweh himself. They are to be subjected to the ban, dispossessed of their land, and driven out. The prohibition "you shall make no *bĕrît* [formally a treaty whose content is peace] with them or with their gods" (Exod. 23:32; cf. 34:15) and "they shall not dwell in your land" (Exod. 23:33) is basic and most probably from the oldest layers in the tradition-history of this concept. Furthermore, it is valid throughout all its stages including the latest layers of the extant Torah. You must make no peace treaty with the inhabitants of the land! — said on Mount Sinai by Yahweh himself, and only secondarily reinforced by the Deuteronomic Moses.[2]

True, strangers and sojourners are not to be oppressed. Perhaps they include remnants of the original Canaanite population. But they are no more than that — strangers and sojourners. They are cohabitants in the land of Israel but neither co-owners of it nor owners of a land divided among themselves and Israelites, let alone owners of a land of Canaan.

True, the texts say that not all happened that way, and historical research has shown that it did not happen that way at all except for a few local instances. Does the Torah therefore mean that Yahweh's and Israel's policies were fortunately not meant for what they said, that history revealed the divine will correctly and the word of the Torah incorrectly? Does it mean that these instructions have a different, spiritual rather than a literal, meaning? Or does it mean what is also said, that the historical unfulfillment of these policies was sinful and that their implementation at the earliest possible occasion, as originally commanded, had to be awaited?

That these policies reflected the customs of war at their time is as half true as it is irrelevant. Not all wars were waged that way in antiquity, and wars in our century have been equally barbaric. The claim that this war should be taken as a symbol of its nation being a light to the nations is a self-contradiction. The conclusion is inevitable that this theological

---

2. For a comprehensive treatment of this issue see G. Schmitt, *Du sollst keinen Frieden schließen mit den Bewohnern des Landes: Die Weisungen gegen d. Kanaanäer in Israels Geschichte u. Geschichtsschreibung* (BWANT 5.11 [91]; Stuttgart: Kohlhammer, 1970); see also E. Otto, *Das Mazzotfest in Gilgal* (BWANT 6.7 [107]; Stuttgart: Kohlhammer, 1975); R. P. Knierim, "Israel and the Nations in the Land of Palestine in the Old Testament," in *The Task of Old Testament Theology: Substance, Method, and Cases* (Grand Rapids: Eerdmans, 1995) 309–21.

ideology was rooted in and generated by the radical concept of the indissoluble unity of one God — one people of this God — in one land, according to which everyone different was to be subjected or destroyed.

As long as this Torah is sacrosanct, should anybody, especially a member of the people of Israel, be exempt from divine judgment who does not obey these instructions? Should anybody who considers the authority of this Torah as exceeding the authority of any other law, worldly or religious, not read in it the word of God when rejecting any authority that is prepared to conclude a peace treaty with the inhabitants of the land by means of trading parts of the land of Israel for that peace? Is such a person not obedient to the most decisive of all divine orders? No land of Israel for peace! And no peace for that price!

Violation and Penalty on Israelite Leaders

Does a person, especially a leader of Israel, who violates this fundamental norm, stand under the judgment of the God of this Torah? How can this not be the case? Has he or she lost the right to live, not to be murdered or assassinated but to be executed in consequence of a legal, divinely sanctioned verdict of death penalty?

It is clear that the prohibition of murder in the Decalogue — be it murder in general or of a fellow Israelite or of a parent — does not apply to the kind of case discussed. Murder and assassination are prohibited; the execution of persons condemned to death by trial, even divine judgment, for capital crimes is not prohibited.

There are no texts in the Old Testament that would directly speak about a death verdict or execution of a leader who trades away Israel's land for peace with non-Israelite inhabitants or neighbors. The first reason for the absence of such evidence may be that such a trade would have been considered impossible in the first place. That it would not have been considered — at least by the representatives of the inheritance of the land theology — as anything less than high treason is scarcely imaginable. An opinion, however, on this question can be derived only circumstantially, if conclusively at all.

A prophet "who speaks in the name of other gods...that same prophet shall die" (Deut. 18:20). The kings, especially Ahab and Jeroboam II, of the northern kingdom are condemned to death for their apostasy. More could be said along these lines. Could any leader violating the norm of no land of Israel for peace have expected not to belong to such condemnable persons?

Yet, who renders and executes the verdict? The people, a government, a religious party, a democratic majority, religious "extremists" and "fanatics"? Or is an individual, any individual, called to obey divine law if all other agents fail? An Elijah or Jehu or Amos? One of the minor judges in early Israel, and with the same claim to divine authorization by which an American "executed" a doctor performing abortions?

Can these questions be resolved as long as the basic norm for religious loyalty to a religious taboo remains untouchable, in our case not only because of the justifiable and necessary consideration for the nation's future security but because it is a taboo beyond all allowable consideration, a taboo that appears to be the heart of Amir's position?

Whether or not the messianic expectation, too, plays a role in Amir's motive is currently unknown to me. This expectation says that the Messiah will not come unless and until Israel will have taken complete possession of the land. It does not say only that Israel must perfectly observe the Torah everywhere, especially in the land in which Israel already lives, but also that Israel must take the land into sole possession in the first place. Just as in the Torah, or because of the Torah, the taking of the whole land into sole possession appears to be the first and fundamental requirement before the requirements that focus on life in this land. The structure of the conditions for the coming of the Messiah appears to be the same as the structure of the conditions for the fulfillment of the promise to the patriarchs. In both cases Israel must take exclusive possession of the land and keep the laws concerning its subsequent permanent possession.

Summary

It is undeniable that in our generation the incitement to violent action by "responsible" individuals, including killing, and sometimes the direct call to it and its legitimation in the name of God have been inflamed by politicized hate rhetoric, particularly of influential religious leaders in Christianity (especially in the United States), in the state of Israel, and in Islam.

For extreme Christian fundamentalists, homosexuals — and abortionists, along with others labeled as "perverts" — are "Satanists" whose movements must be eradicated because "God hates homosexuality."

The basic philosophy of Israel's Irgun, currently the extreme right wing of the Likud party, had decreed the existence of the Jewish nation on both sides of the Jordan River, and that any who gave away even a handful of Israel's soil, for whatever reason, did so at their peril.

Unfortunately, one does not go far enough as long as one protests against this reality solely on the ground of a civilized morality with which these appalling eruptions of hatred, its violent rhetoric and actions, are incompatible — a protest that is true at any rate — and as long as one explains it with nothing more than the arguments about the degeneration or breakdown in our time of an ethos whose original roots are assumed to be clean and unblemished. All religious extremists justify themselves precisely with reference to these original and absolutely authoritative religious roots.

Thus, Christians maintain that the New Testament does not only say that God forgives sinners but also that they — the sinners themselves, and their sin — are condemned unless they repent and turn from their vices. In Jewish perspective, the theology of the land of Israel is not the result of a degenerate development in postbiblical Judaism but of a nonnegotiable radical stance in its original biblical roots themselves. Lastly, all modern religious radicalisms, extremisms, fanaticisms, and those who offer justifications of hatred and its consequences, draw their legitimation and "ethical" imperatives from those roots in parts of the biblical texts themselves.

The so-called[3] assassination of Prime Minister Rabin confronts all with the inevitable fact of the irreconcilable conflict between two politics of religion or public religious policies. It is about more than the conflict between secular and religious law, or tolerant and fanatical people, or even about the alternative between democracy and theocracy. It is about the root concepts and ideologies beneath any of these surface formations.

This event forces into the open the question of whether, as in this case, there will under no circumstances be any peace at the price of parts of Israel's land; or whether this norm will have to be relativized or reconceptualized, also in the name of a God whose priority is peace at such a price — if peace for it can be secured. The theology of the Torah makes no such allowance.

The reversal of the Torah's theological taboo would amount to the recourse to such theological concepts — be it in other parts of the Old Testament or in the rabbinical or the Christian tradition — in which for the sake of universal justice equally for all, the pursuit and process of peace, including the secure coexistence of diverse populations and neighbors even at the expense of traditionally sacrosanct positions, is more important and true than the defense of nonnegotiable positions. At stake is not a sell out of religious principles for the sake of secular ones, but the very substance of religious identity itself by pursuing the better truth, also in the secular realms.

From both the Old and New Testament, there is much to be directly derived for a biblical hermeneutic of a balance between justice and peace universally. However, we all are in our respective traditions

---

3. My usage of the adjective "so-called" is meant from the assassin's own perspective, with which I disagree. More essential than my disagreement with Amir's standpoint, however, is my disagreement with its roots.

also traumatized when the reasons for the discord in our seemingly irreconcilable positions and strategies are found in the very roots of even
our most authoritative traditions. We are traumatized when we cannot
repress this fact and the fact that our way into the future to an essential
and perhaps decisive extent depends on how we confront those roots.*

BIBLIOGRAPHY

Knierim, Rolf P. "Israel and the Nations in the Land of Palestine in the Old Tes-
    tament." In *The Task of Old Testament Theology: Substance, Method, and Cases.*
    Grand Rapids: Eerdmans, 1995.
Otto, Eckart. *Das Mazzotfest in Gilgal.* BWANT 7/107. Stuttgart: W. Kohlhammer,
    1975.
Schmidt, Götz. *Du sollst keinen Frieden schliessen mit den Bewohnern des Landes.*
    BWANT 11/91. Stuttgart: W. Kohlhammer, 1970.

*I am indebted to Mignon R. Jacobs for editorial assistance.

6

On the Subject of War in Old Testament and Biblical Theology

Rolf P. Knierim

INTRODUCTION

In an important article, "The Concept of War in the Old Testament,"[1] H. Eberhard von Waldow writes in his conclusion that three statements appear to be important for further study:

1. "All Old Testament accounts of war...are subordinate to the basic concept of order and the understanding of life."[2]

2. "The discussion of peace in the Old Testament must take into account what the Old Testament believes about war." War is "the most effective means to destroy šālôm," whereas peace "is a matter of faith in the fact that God is in charge who wants peace on earth."[3]

3. "Today's binding Christian teaching...must be based on the unequivocal and clear biblical message: 'War is sin,'" whereby the choice for us today is not "between good and evil" but "between evil and the lesser evil."[4]

The following thoughts are belatedly written in honor of my wonderful colleague and trusted friend on the occasion of his seventieth birthday in December 1993. When taking up von Waldow's invitation to further study, I am confident that he will permit me to discuss issues addressed in his entire article rather than only those in his conclusions.

No apology is necessary for addressing the issue of war. Even apart from the nuclear threat, there were at the time of von Waldow's seventieth birthday in 1993 some forty wars raging on this planet. And one cannot say that religion, any religion, has the power to contain, let alone prevent, war. In fact, religion is all too often one of the forces reinforc-

---

This essay is in honor of Hans Eberhard von Waldow. It was originally published in German ("Zum alttestamentlichen Verständnis von Strafe") and is reprinted here by permission of Institut für Alttestamentliche Wissenschaft und Biblische Archäologie, Universität Wien.

1. H. Eberhard von Waldow, "The Concept of War in the Old Testament," *HBT* 6, no. 2 (1984) 27–48.
2. von Waldow, "Concept of War," 45.
3. von Waldow, "Concept of War," 45.
4. von Waldow, "Concept of War," 45.

ing and legitimizing war. And the Bible of both Testaments remains one of the sources for supporting these forces.

Our discussion of war in biblical theology should not be kept separate from our personal biographies, which contribute not only to our outlook on reality but also to what we are looking for when studying the Bible. For years von Waldow was a soldier on the German side of WWII, as I was too, five years younger, as a fifteen-year-old air defense artillerist (*Luftwaffenhelfer*) during the war's last fifteen months on the western front. When speaking about war in the Bible, we, as many, encounter the biblical texts about war as references to the destructive side of reality that resonate with our own experiences in life. Of course, we belonged to the losing side, which, in this case, for very good reasons also turned out to have been the wrong side. These experiences, followed by the impact of the Holocaust, or Shoah, profoundly influenced the direction of our lives, including our commitment to Old Testament studies. These decisions were not based on market research.

Still, that was only WWII in Europe. It was not Hiroshima, Korea, Vietnam, or any of the other barbaric wars during the past decades. And today one reads and sees (without personal experience) how among all involved parties in the former Yugoslavia, women are warriors more fierce in battle than men, and that for those parties this war is the only thing in their lives that matters at all, ethically, ethnically, religiously, beyond which no future is of interest. When one reads these things, one must ask who of us not directly involved in this or similar situations has any access to a mentality for which totally destructive war has become the ultimate value and reason for living or dying. Compared to this kind of experience, our WWII experiences are outdated. Nevertheless, they still remind us that writing about war or studying war in the Bible is different from experiencing it, and that no judgment about the nature of war can afford to reflect a judgmental moralism, even where one disagrees, especially with the Bible.

REVIEW OF VON WALDOW'S ARTICLE

Von Waldow's article is especially important because it focuses on the theological problem of war in the Old Testament, rather than on the exegetical description of Old Testament texts about war. At issue is "God and war."[5] For this focus he correctly demands a compass by which the various concepts may be correlated, so that one can discern what is basic and what is subordinate. His attempt amounts to a design for the systematization of the Old Testament's concepts, or theologies, of war in an Old Testament theology of war. I could not agree more with this intention.

---

5. von Waldow, "Concept of War," 28.

The article deals in three sections with God's order of creation, the sacredness of war in ancient Israel, and the secularization of the concept of war. Based on Genesis 1 and the primeval history, he says that,

> in the Old Testament understanding of the world, war is a violation of God's order of creation and as such war is sin. . . . *Christian* theology has to say clearly, unequivocally and without any qualifications: War is sin.[6]

All other references to war in the Old Testament are subordinate to this basic concept.

Nevertheless, war in premonarchic Israel is considered sacred because "God was at work"; "God exercises his lordship by acting in the fallen world," and is "using sinful people for his purposes."[7] "Whenever God decides for a war, he has his purpose."[8] War as such is something sacred because "the decision to go to war was made by Yahveh the God of Israel."[9] Of course, the concept of divine war is not confined to Israel: "It reflects the general belief that war is always something sacred because in a war God is at work."[10] But this sacredness is true only for the time before the establishment of the state order.

With the formation of the state, Israel's kings became subject to the policies of human kingdoms in which kings take "God's prerogative to decide over war and peace . . . into their own hands." Thereby, "what used to be a sacred instrument of God would be turned into a tool of sinful people."[11] Deuteronomy takes Israel back to Sinai and tries to revive the concept of war "as an instrument of God" for "the occupation of the land" on the one hand, and as "Yahveh's punitive action against the deprivation [i.e., depravity] of the Canaanites" on the other.[12] The prophets reverse Deuteronomy's focus on war against foreign peoples and announce Yahweh's deployment of foreign nations for punishment over Israel. They "developed the old concept of Yahveh as the supreme war-lord, and in conjunction with this the idea of the sacredness of war to the concept of Yahveh, the God of Israel, as the universal lord of history."[13] Even so, some of the prophets (e.g., Isaiah and Micah) look forward to the restoration of "the old order of creation of Gen 1 with one undivided human race in unity under God."[14]

---

6. von Waldow, "Concept of War," 33 (italics added).
7. von Waldow, "Concept of War," 36, 34.
8. von Waldow, "Concept of War," 36.
9. von Waldow, "Concept of War," 37.
10. von Waldow, "Concept of War," 37.
11. von Waldow, "Concept of War," 38.
12. von Waldow, "Concept of War," 39.
13. von Waldow, "Concept of War," 39–40.
14. von Waldow, "Concept of War," 40.

ANALYSIS

It is clear that any analysis of von Waldow's interpretation must not be caught up in quibbling about exegetical details. His is an attempt at integrating the Old Testament's statements about war within a system of Old Testament theology in which the notions of war, sin, justice, and peace are interrelated and understood in terms of conceptual priorities. This attempt proceeds with regard to the relationship between God, humanity, and the world. Any discussion can only acknowledge the level on which von Waldow works and the direction in which he pursues the problem, and continue thence.

There are at least six methodological aspects in need of attention.

1. Von Waldow's critical assessment that the discussion of the topic of war is very often "narrowed down to the war accounts or to related passages"[15] is correct. War accounts and related passages must be considered in light of the larger corpora, or macrounits, of which they are part, as well as in light of the concepts of those macrounits. We shall return to this point later.

2. Additionally, we must address the issue of whether all concepts of war essentially complement each other or whether some disagree with others. Von Waldow's interpretation gives the impression that the differences reflect the same basic assumption, only from different conditions, even when Deuteronomy is compared to the prophets. After all, Deuteronomy knows about Yahweh's war against Israel just as much as the prophets know about it, and the prophets know about Yahweh's wars against the nations just as much as Deuteronomy. The problem must lie somewhere else.

Especially in the case of the theology of war against the Canaanites, von Waldow fortunately does not evade the problem arising from the texts. He does not approach the problem of Yahweh's war against the Canaanites by referring to the historical argument. This argument says, as also stated in Judges, that it was not that bad because it did not happen as Yahweh and Moses had commanded. Is history an excuse for Israel's disobedience? And do the texts and their theology, especially when adopted canonically, have the authority to be actualized whenever the occasion arrives? We must focus on the concepts of the texts, not on what happened in history.

3. When discussing the ban (ḥērem) and its cruelty, von Waldow says that "modern categories should not be applied here," because the original theological thrust says that everything of possible use to the winning side "must be dedicated to Yahveh the war-lord who gave

---

15. von Waldow, "Concept of War," 28.

victory."[16] The ground for this kind of argument, however, is as indefensible as it is common. Not even in its historical context was this concept unequivocally valid, let alone when one considers alternatives from other contexts. Even though Yahweh, just as any other deity in the ancient Near East, was believed to be at work in war, one cannot defend the idea or practice of the ban on the ground that this was the sole form of honoring the deity's victory in a universal religious policy of warfare. Compared to alternatives, also in the Old Testament, the ban is subject to the same kind of inner-biblical theological critique that von Waldow himself employs when saying that war is sin. This judgment rests on why war is sin, not on where, when, or by whom it was said. The Yahweh of the primeval history is involved in preserving the nations through restraining the evil in their history, and not in warring against them and banning them because they are sinful.

4. The argument that the establishment of the state amounts to Israel's apostasy from Yahweh's own sacred wars, or to the secularization of the concept of war,[17] appears to be one-sided. Surely, the texts speak about this secularization. But they also speak about the even cultically celebrated theology of Yahweh's election of the Davidic monarchy and Yahweh's sacred wars through the institution of the monarchy.

Modern ideology-criticism criticizes this royal theology as a symptom of the usurpation of religious legitimacy by the autonomous state. We, the scholars, say that the concept of sacred war became secularized in the system of Israel's statehood. But while some texts substantiate this claim, other royal texts support the opposite claim. These texts say that the king's wars are Yahweh's wars. Hence, we must distinguish between the royal theologies of the texts and our critique of those theologies, whether this critique is justifiable or not. It is only our critique that sees war as secularized in the royal theology texts. This is not uniformly the case in those texts. At any rate, when doing exegesis, we cannot afford to employ conflicting methods by describing and defending what the texts say on the one hand (e.g., the ḥērem texts), while on the other hand criticizing what they say elsewhere. Our method of interpretation must be the same for all texts.

It is very doubtful that the difference between sacred and secularized wars can be equated with the difference between the periods before and during Israel's statehood. The texts claim that Yahweh was Israel's warrior throughout its history. When Yahweh went to war against Israel, it was not because Israel had become a state but because the state had emancipated itself from Yahweh's reign. Therefore, the criterion for the

---

16. von Waldow, "Concept of War," 36.
17. von Waldow, "Concept of War," 37–40.

Old Testament's perception of just war does not lie in the antinomy between Yahweh and the king but in those theological aspects that point to the substance and intention of Yahweh's own kingship, in view of which the kings were either approved or rejected.

In ancient Israel's theology, peace, rest (měnûḥâ), or safety (beṭaḥ) is, of course, considered the normal state for ongoing history and not only for the eschatological end time. War and other kinds of catastrophes are considered abnormal. But since the structure of human history is not in the state of the order of creation, as von Waldow emphasizes, and since God/Yahweh is involved in human history, including its wars (von Waldow's "God and war"), the issue of war in Old Testament theology involves more than the stated fact of Yahweh's involvement. We must focus on the question of the reasons for and purposes of this involvement. We must equally focus on what it means that the Old Testament considers just war to be generated by the deity rather than by humanity.

5. I do not believe that the discussion of war in Old Testament theology can be based on the tradition history of ancient Israel's theologies. The study of the history of these traditions, as far as we can reconstruct it (and we should do so more adequately than has been the case), is important in its own right. But no history of theology or of any of its subjects can be a substitute for the theologies of those subjects themselves. One need not be a canon theologian concerned with the extant canonical text in order to know that the growth of the traditions created from step to step their simultaneous coexistence and, hence, the problem of the variety, diversity, and differing meanings for each new situation, each all the while affirming the one and same God, Yahweh.

We may reconstruct, however correctly, the Old Testament's concepts of war before, during, and after the monarchy. The Old Testament does not say, however, at least not in principle, that each of these concepts was valid only for its own time. Increasingly, it juxtaposed the different conceptual legacies as potentials for present and future times.

The Deuteronomic priests of Josiah's generation went back, for understandable reasons, to the ideal — not Sinaitic — in the fields of Moab. The Priestly narrators did the same during the exilic time, going back to Sinai itself. Sinai is the place where the plan for Yahweh's sanctuary campaign toward the promised land is given. Here Yahweh is to be accompanied by the host of Israel's militia encamped around the sanctuary in defensive order during stays, and marching in linear order in front of and behind the sanctuary on the march. The arrangement of the camp in Numbers 1–2 accounts only for the males capable of bearing arms. More than any other Old Testament text, and comparable only to a generically similar description in Homer's *Iliad*, Numbers 1–2 represents the program for the registration and mobilization of Israel's militia for the purpose of Yahweh's sacred (what else!) sanctuary campaign. Traditio-historically speaking, neither the Deuteronomic nor the Priestly concept of sacred war was replaced by the other existing concepts for Israel's new beginning, whether for the monarchy or for postmonarchic society. Indeed, the sacred war traditions continued to be included in the forward-moving growth of the traditions, alongside the royal messianic theology.

6. Lastly, the tradition history of Israel's concepts of war inevitably points to two questions: What do these concepts contribute to a theology of divine war in the Old Testament, including its extant level? How do these concepts look when they are compared with each other? The answers to these questions demand future research. In the meantime, I want to return to the substance of von Waldow's thesis.

Von Waldow's basic statement, to which everything else is subordinate — or to be subordinated! — is that war is sin because it is a violation of God's order of creation. For this order, the understanding of life is fundamental.

In light of the preceding methodological discussion, it is clear that von Waldow's judgment results from the comparison of substantive arguments — regardless whether it is derived from Genesis 1 or any other passage; whether other passages agree with it or not; whether Israel's history honored or violated it; whether the concept of Yahweh's wars or the history of the concepts of war affirms it or not; whether it belonged to the theology of the monarchy or any other institution, group of theologians, or individual, regardless of its place in Israel's theological tradition history; and even regardless of whether or not the Old Testament has anywhere a declaratory statement categorically saying that "war is sin."

The judgment represents the interpreter's systematization of his or her arguments. These arguments are drawn out of Genesis 1 even though that chapter does not speak about war. It is, of all others, the most fundamental argument. In a sense, I agree with the essence of von Waldow's argument.

Of course, we are subject to suspicion. Creation theology has become a trend, and even a yardstick for professorial legitimacy these days. Thus, we become suspect of being trendy rather than substantively on target. In order to substantiate von Waldow's categorical statement, we need to further the discussion with some considerations so that his statement may stand "without any qualifications."[18]

In light of the fact that Yahweh is said to be involved in war and that Yahweh's own wars are considered sacred wars, the most obvious

---

18. von Waldow, "Concept of War," 33.

conclusion from the statement that "war is sin" is that the primary sinner is none other than Yahweh. Of course, nowhere does, or would, the
Bible speculate about such a conclusion. Is the categorical statement itself wrong, or at least in need of further clarification? If war is sin, even
Yahweh's sacred wars are not exempt from being sinful wars.

Von Waldow's argument that only human, "secularized" war is sinful seems to rest on two presuppositions. First, Yahweh's wars cannot be
sinful because God is always just, regardless of what God does. Second,
only human war is considered a violation of the order of creation; hence,
Yahweh's wars have nothing to do with the violation of that order. They
are always in defense of creation. While it appears in von Waldow's
article that the criterion for the difference between sacred and secular
war is the difference between Yahweh and humans, the actually dominant criterion for the difference between valid and invalid war in his
article is whether war, human or divine, is in violation of or in defense
of creation.

In order to uphold von Waldow's categorical statement, one qualification must be added: war, be it divine, semidivine, or human, is not
sin as long as it happens in defense of creation and all life. Either all
war is sin, including war in defense of creation, or only the kind of
war through which the order of creation is violated is sin. When one
compares these two conflicting maxims, the question arises as to which
of them has the priority over the other. In any case, the question is no
longer one of "God and war," but of creation, or life, and war, whereby
God as well as humanity is involved in both creation and war.

While the protection of life as the fundamental aspect in the meaning
of creation is an end in itself, the same cannot be said about war. War is
only a means toward an end. Where it is an end in itself, the destruction
of life becomes a means toward that end. In such a scenario, war would
be the basic law of the order of creation. Nowhere in the Bible would
such a maxim find support. Moreover, war is sinful not only when considered an end in itself, but is sinful also when conducted in the interest
of the order of creation. After all, even in that interest, war, also God's
war, kills life, especially human life. The only sinless rationale for the
defense of creation and life would be no war at all, even if God is the
defender. In the Bible that option does not exist, because the Bible faces
war as an inevitable fact in history. When conducting sacred war, God,
too, kills life.

To be sure, the Old Testament's theology of creation must be considered as the criterion for the difference between the truth and sinfulness
of history. And this criterion leaves little doubt that history basically
does not represent the original order of creation, with its priority on the
blessing, the protection of life, not even where the deity is considered

the God of universal history. One can say that the deity's involvement in history serves the defense of the order of creation against the always lurking chaos, as especially in war. Even so, and precisely so, the deity is drawn into war, into killing life, and into contradiction with the intention of sustaining life. As the skepticism in the Old Testament's wisdom tradition indicates, theodicy becomes submerged in the conflict between God's presence in the order of creation and God's presence in the structure of history. And while the protection of life remains the blueprint, or ideal, the deity's practice cannot but compromise that ideal, even when such practice is executed for the ideal's sake. If there is a defense for the justice of the Creator, it has to be found in the Creator's involvement in the imbroglio of history — not the idea but the reality of history — in which the ideal of the protection of life is compromised by the killing of life, especially through war. It is found in the deity's selfless sacrificial involvement rather than in an abstract ideal of sinlessness.

When we come to the aspect of history, the question is not whether God is or is not involved in war, or whether war is or is not sin. In the face of the reality of war as an inevitable evil rather than a constructive element of the historical process, the primary question is whether the evil of war is limited or unlimited, or more or less limited.

In light of this question, the Old Testament points in certain directions. While not justifying war, Eccl. 3:8 says that the time of war is limited, not unlimited: "There is a time for war, and a time for peace."[19] Amos 1 and 2 condemn the barbarisms of warfare. The Yahweh of Isaiah says this about Assyria:

> Against a godless nation I send him . . . to take spoil and seize plunder, and to tread them down like the mire of the streets. But this is not what he intends . . . ; but it is in his heart to destroy and to cut off nations not a few. (Isa. 10:6–7)

And the farmer has taught the prophet the counsel and wisdom of Yahweh; the prophet realizes that plowing and sowing do not happen continually, and that,

> Dill is not threshed with a threshing sledge, nor is a cart wheel rolled over cummin; but dill is beaten out with a stick, and cummin with a rod. Grain is crushed for bread, but one does not thresh it forever. . . . (Isa. 28:27–29)

This line of thinking in the Old Testament would have to be pursued further.

Another aspect of the theology of war in history that needs to be addressed is whether or not the reasons and criteria for war are the

---

19. Biblical quotations are from the New Revised Standard Version.

same for all humanity and for all nations. This aspect brings into sharp focus all the Old Testament texts in which Israel serves in Yahweh's wars. That Israel almost always serves in these wars is a truism. The question that remains unaddressed is, What is the function of Israel in Yahweh's wars?

We have to ask whether God/Yahweh, the creator of the world and lord of universal history, acts in these wars through Israel on behalf of life for all nations, or whether Yahweh, the God of Israel, acts as the God of all nations on behalf of Yahweh's elected people. In the first case, the election of Israel stands in the service of humanity. The welfare of humanity is the objective and criterion for Israel's role, even in war. In the second case, the election of humanity and the meaning of its life would stand in the service of Yahweh's people, Israel. Here, the welfare of Israel would be the criterion for the meaning and function of the existence of humanity, regardless of the cost to, indeed at the expense of, the life of humanity.

For the sake of the heart of any credible theological quest, this distinction is inevitable. No interpretation of the texts, beginning on the strictly exegetical level, that ignores this question can be regarded as meeting exegetical or theological standards.

Genesis 1 can provide a basis for the universal validity of the thesis "war is sin" only with serious qualification. It is not an isolated chapter, but a part of the total Priestly narrative. Therefore, it must be considered in light of the theological concept of that total narrative. Already the pattern of seven days is a decisive signal. Without this pattern Genesis 1 would not exist as it does. This pattern points to Israel's Sabbath week as the most fundamental sign of Israel's existential identity, quite before and independent of history. This sign is implanted in the structure of creation and is even more fundamental than circumcision. It has been said that this creation belongs to the etiology of Israel (G. von Rad). It aims not only at Sinai, with its establishment of the cult and the holy community, but through Sinai and via the military campaign toward the conquest of the promised land, in which both cult and the holy community are to be permanently established. The Priestly work not only aims at this goal, but conceptualizes it at the outset, from Genesis 1 on, from this final vantage point of the writers' setting in life.

The Priestly writers were probably not soldiers. But the assumption that they were pacifists is an illusion. Likewise illusory is the assumption that their theology of creation had to do only with peaceful cultic purity and the social ethos of the community, and had nothing to do with the concept of the epiphanic military conquest of the promised land. These writers spoke most programmatically about Yahweh's sacred war on behalf of Yahweh's elected people. From a strictly exegetical perspective, the view that the Priestly concept of Israel's life in the promised land stands in the service of God's care for creation and all humanity equally remains incomprehensible. Unless exegesis can prove that Israel functions in the priestly concept for the care of God's creation and all nations everywhere equally, one must say the opposite: God's order of creation and Yahweh's wars in history function for the sake of Israel's election. Nothing is being said here against the notion of anyone's election. The problem is for whose sake election functions.

When speaking about the Deuteronomic theology, von Waldow says that "the wars of Israel in the context of the occupation of the land are interpreted as typical wars of Yahveh for the benefit of his covenant people," and "this conquest is seen as Yahveh's punitive action against the deprivation [i.e., depravity] of the Canaanites."[20] He states the obvious. One may even add that the Yahweh of the Deuteronomic theology is just as much the creator God and universal lord of history as the Yahweh of the Priestly theology. Does not this God, then, when acting "for the benefit of his covenant people" and when punishing the Canaanites, use the military power of the creator and lord of universal history — so already before the prophets — for the benefit of God's elect at the expense of the nonelect? Are Israel's sacred wars examples or paradigms for the Creator's protection of the life of all nations equally, in accordance with the principle of the sanctity of life drawn out from the order of creation? Or are they at least universally applicable paradigms for less destructive, more limited, kinds of historical warfare? Are these sacred Yahweh wars in Israel wars for the benefit *solely* of Israel? Or are they wars in which Yahweh uses Israel for the benefit of all humanity?

And where is the Canaanites' right to life considered in the name of the sanctity and protection of all life by God, the Creator? Why are they "punished"? They had not even known Yahweh. And if they were punished because they belonged to the sinful nations of the primeval history, why were they alone to be wiped out, or at least to be subjugated, and not all other nations likewise? Is not the reason for their exceptional punishment from among all other nations — save Amalek, Midian, Moab, Ammon, and Edom — that they stood in the way of the possession of the land of Canaan by Yahweh's elect? Is this a theology of creation and legitimate divine war in defense of all life in creation? Does this creation theology serve the purpose of creation or the purpose of an exclusionary election? Where in it is the judge of the earth for whom justice is indivisible universally? Does this judge hear the cries of all afflicted, of all of sinful humanity, of all destroyed by war and dispossessed? Or does this judge only hear the cries of the judge's own

---

20. von Waldow, "Concept of War," 39.

people because they know this judge and this judge knows them, and they are in covenant together? How should the Canaanites ever have been persuaded to praise and bless Yahweh and become Yahweh devotees? They were not told, "If you worship Yahweh, your land is yours and there will be no war." They were told nothing. Their expropriation was a foregone conclusion. They had to be expropriated of their land because Yahweh had promised their land to Yahweh's own people. Yahweh was going to fulfill this promise to make the land Yahweh's own land, but not because of the Canaanites' "depravity." Had their "depravity" been the legitimate and basic reason for their expropriation, all nations existing in the same sinful condition should have been expropriated, and Yahweh's people could have settled anywhere rather than only in the land of Canaan. They could have possessed the earth.

More could be said in this regard about the Yahwist and the Pentateuch, as well as about the function of the exodus liberation, Sinai, and the desert theology in the total concept of the Pentateuch. More could also be said about the Deuteronomistic and Chronicler's works, the prophetic books and the Psalms. Yet much of the Wisdom literature is very different. The problem discussed here cannot be avoided. It is an intrinsic part of exegetical responsibility, which not only has to renarrate, critically paraphrase, or describe what the texts say, but also has to interpret the conceptual presuppositions on which the texts rest and by which they are controlled, regardless of whether these presuppositions are infratextual or intertextual.

From its beginning, the Pentateuch is the story of Israel's election out of the nations to be Yahweh's own people, through the mediation of Moses during the last, internationally public, forty years of his life. The purpose of their election is their conquest of and permanent settlement in the land of Canaan. This concept controls what is meant and said in the Pentateuch about war.

Genesis 1 and the primeval history imply that the destruction of human life by war in and through humanity is sinful, and Genesis 12–50 does depict the life of the few patriarchal families basically in terms of peaceful coexistence with the Canaanites in the promised land of Canaan. By contrast, the establishment of the covenant nation of Israel includes, explicitly, programmatically, and completely apart from the role of the monarchy, the sanctioning of war on Israel's behalf against the enemies of its election history. The establishment of the covenant nation is also the basis for both Yahweh's punishment of Israel (Num. 14:28–29; 26:63–65) and the threat of war and defeat (Lev. 26:17; Deut. 28:25–26) if Israel breaks the covenant.

In light of the original condition of humanity, although the wars in human history are evil, they are also an inevitable fact of that history. The same inevitable fact also pertains to the history of Yahweh's covenant with Israel, with two basic differences: the possibility of war is specifically defined by this exclusive covenant, and within this covenant war is sanctioned and not evil. It should be evident that the theology of war that is subject to the conditions of the covenant cannot function for the condemnation of the wars of the nations, because the covenant is not interested in war among the nations in the first place. In covenant war theology, the nations are either the victims of the covenant or the legitimate tools for the covenant's enforcement. Furthermore, this theology cannot function for the justification of war among the nations themselves. It contributes nothing to the problem of international warfare in human history as such. Indeed, it diverts attention away from that subject. Unless the specific nature of Israel's covenant war theology is explained, this theology is not sufficiently interpreted; rather, it is being reconceptualized on grounds other than those evident in the Pentateuch.

Warfare among the nations themselves is acknowledged in the Old Testament as a fact of human existence, alongside Israel's covenant history and basically surrounding it. Evil as it is, this fact in human history, rather than the original condition of humanity in the order of creation, is the arena in which the deity is ongoingly involved. In light of the ideal, every war is sin, even and especially the wars in the name of the covenant. More fundamental than evaluation in light of the ideal is the ongoing resistance against sinful reality. The reminder of the ideal is one thing; existence in a world where the ideal is unavailable is a quite different thing. It is in this world where the ideal does not exist that the deity is found after creation.

There is an eschatological hope for a world without war in some prophetic traditions. By and large, this outlook awaits the restoration of the order of creation. Compared to Yahweh's involvement in war in history, this perspective points to the ideal, which is fundamentally different from historical reality, just as much as the picture of the original creation does.

There are two problems with this eschatological outlook. First, it never was the sole theology on the subject; and in view of the final outcome of the growth of the Old Testament's tradition history, it is not the only theological program for the future of humanity — certainly neither in the Pentateuch nor in the Wisdom literature. Second, its temporally determined aspects have not materialized to this day. The delay of that parousia after millennia, and with it the delay of the restoration of the original ideal, is evidence enough that, whether or not that parousia ever materializes, the history of humanity with its wars continues indefinitely.

Whatever the critical function is of our awareness of the ideal, as both reminder and expectation, war is inevitably encountered indefinitely in sinful human history. In view of this indefinitely open future, we have to focus on the present times as long as they last. And one can only concur with the theology of the primeval history that looks at the self-destructive human forces in history and wonders why history has not yet self-destructed. One can only see in it the constant laboring and suffering of God for the sake not only of the cosmic order of the earth but especially for the protection of the life of all humanity, despite its self-destructive dynamics. Those texts in the Old Testament in which God appears involved for the sake of saving humanity from itself may be understood, as von Waldow says, as "the lesser evil,"[21] because the totality of human history does not allow for more. This means again that the less destructive wars are, the less they are evil. They point to the alien work of God, hidden in the process of evil so that greater evil may be prevented.

Even so, the validity of this alien work of God is restricted, because war, not compared to creation but to what is better in history, does not save. It is no equivalent to constructive justice and the balance of peace. In the genre of the *better-sayings*, Eccl. 9:18 says, "Wisdom is better than weapons of war."

Compared to the Old Testament's and our own awareness of the pervasive presence of war in human history, the New Testament pays little attention to this fact. In the New Testament there are a few references concerning war among members of the church (James 4:1), war between the law of sin and the law of the mind (Rom. 7:23), and Christ's war against the church of Pergamum (Rev. 2:16). Yet the New Testament speaks about literal war only in reference to the warriors of old (Heb. 11:34), as a simile for discipleship (Luke 11:21; 14:31–32) and, most importantly, in relation to the end time in terms either of its dawning (Matt. 24:6; Mark 13:7; Luke 21:9) or of its arrival (Rev. 11:7; 12:7, 17; 13:7; 19:11, 19). Finally, of course, Revelation 16 narrates the cataclysmic consummation of human history in the most horrific blood bath of all biblical scenarios: Christ's battle at Armageddon.

The absence in the New Testament of attention to war among the nations can scarcely be explained as a result of the *pax Augustana*, as if the issue of war were nonexistent at that time in the Roman Empire. Rather, one has to presuppose that the writers of the New Testament were very much aware of war in their time but ignored it nonetheless, just as much as they basically ignored all other aspects pertaining to the policies of the nations, such as political and economic structures both domestic and international, and so on. The reason for their neglect of these issues

---

21. von Waldow, "Concept of War," 45.

is programmatic and points to the fundamental difference between the Old and the New Testament's view of reality, including war.

Whereas the reality of war belongs to the Old Testament's perception of ongoing human history, for the New Testament this history is no longer an essential issue. It is no longer an essential issue because the end of history is already determined by the eschatological presence of Jesus Christ and the eschatological existence of his church. The church awaits the complete unveiling of the already existing new creation, and with it, the end not only of human history but of the original creation altogether through the impending second coming of Christ. In light of this worldview and the intensity of its future-oriented temporal-eschatological expectation, the affairs of this world, including its wars, had become irrelevant — except the wars of the end time itself. Attention to wars in history, and the nature of God's involvement in such wars, was at best marginal. Indeed, it was better to ignore these issues, because they had nothing to do with the reign of God through Jesus Christ in the new creation. Such attention could only detract from full concentration on what was decisive for the fulfillment of salvation. Now, creation and history had in principle become the old world.

The neglect of the nations' wars does not, therefore, mean that the New Testament is indifferent to this issue. It means, on the contrary, that war is now, to use von Waldow's words again, "unequivocally and without any qualifications" considered as sin in its most radical sense. It belongs not only to history, which is full of sin, but also to the old, sinful history and the old rather than the new creation. It is again judged against the ideal of creation, this time radically: against the ideal of the new creation.

Apart from the temporal aspect in this eschatology, the concept of the new creation is important because it points to *the* criterion in light of which no war, not even the relative truth of divine war in history, is just in an ultimate sense. The notion of ultimacy is an essential ideal. It amounts to the irrevocable rejection of any claim, by anyone, at any place and time, by victor or vanquished, that any war would unquestionably represent the revelation of the full truth of and in this world.

The temporal aspect in the New Testament's eschatology, with its focus on the wars of the end time, is more than a discardable shell or an inessential chronological formula; it is an intrinsic element of that eschatology. Had the New Testament writers had to anticipate an indefinite delay of the parousia — by now of at least two millennia — it is impossible that they would have spoken about the impending parousia the way they did. It is also extremely unlikely that they would have ignored the fact of war as well as other such factors in the ongoing history of humanity and the world. The fact that this history has continued means that any temporal eschatology is at least relative, if not irrelevant, when compared to the openness of the existing worldly history. And save the New Testament's aspect of eschatological ultimacy, it means that the Old Testament's full attention to war as the most destructive element in human history reflects, as it has for the last two millennia, at any rate, our reality as long as this history lasts. For this reason, it is primary for any theological agenda. It is neither overcome nor replaced by the New Testament's agenda, not even by Johannine theology.

There is one aspect most exemplified by war that neither the Old nor the New Testament could have envisioned: by now the end of this earth may not be determined by God. We can determine and create it ourselves.

BIBLIOGRAPHY

von Waldow, H. Eberhard. "The Concept of War in the Old Testament." *HBT* 6, no. 2 (1984).

7

Debating Ahab:
Characterization in Biblical Theology

James E. Brenneman

Bible characters offer intriguing resources for doing biblical theology. Whatever else one says of biblical characterization, it is no longer tenable to suggest that biblical narratives portray characters merely as "flat," "static" and "opaque."[1] With the emergence of literary criticism and its other methodological offshoots, such negative claims about the art of biblical narratives are fast disappearing.[2] True, there is any number of characters within the Bible who fall flat, functioning merely as ciphers for larger theopolitical biases. Of such characters we know little or nothing. It is also true that in order to discover complex character types of "real people" in Scripture, one may have to cull from its narration the "real person" buried beneath and between the contradictory accounts of a given character, piecing together a portrait from fragments and odd juxtapositions. Unfortunately, the compressed histories of biblical narratives have led scholars using the standard historical-critical methods, with their penchant for dissection and atomization, away from the narrative art of characterization. This has been a loss to biblical theology. The programmatic essay by Rolf Knierim that views the Pentateuch as a biography of Moses stands as a dramatic example of the Bible's ability to portray a "full-fledged character" with a broad range of traits about whom we know more than is necessary for the plot.[3] By reading for so long only the fractures within the Pentateuch, we may

---

1. R. Scholes and R. Kellogg, *The Nature of Narrative* (New York: Oxford University Press, 1966) 164.

2. In *Poetics and Interpretation of Biblical Narrative* (Winona Lake, Ind.: Eisenbrauns, 1994) Adele Berlin argues convincingly against these earlier generalizations about the "primitive stories" found in Hebraic and Hellenic literature and their "dull, flattened" characterizations.

3. Rolf Knierim, "The Composition of the Pentateuch," in *The Task of Old Testament Theology: Substance, Method, and Cases* (Grand Rapids: Eerdmans, 1995) 351–79 (an updated version of his essay originally published in 1985). Jonathan Kirsch's *Moses: A Life* (New York: Ballantine, 1998) confirms Knierim's earlier instincts. One might also suggest as formidable examples the multilayered characterization of David in Walter Brueggemann's *David's Truth in Israel's Imagination and Memory* (Minneapolis: Fortress, 1985) and the characterization of God in the Pulitzer Prize-winning book by Jack Miles, *God: A Biography* (New York: Alfred A. Knopf, 1995).

have missed the overall characterization of Moses as portrayed by its macrostructure and literary genius.

Debating Ahab, that wily, wicked, manipulated king of Jezebel fame, offers opportunities for further appreciating the art of biblical characterization and provides possibilities for the task of biblical theology. We turn now to uncovering Ahab amidst the gaps, the fragments, and the contradictory characterizations of him in Scripture and beyond.

AHAB BOUND BY LITERATURE

One can hardly discuss character without first referencing the point of view of the narrator(s). For understanding Ahab, herein is the literary rub.[4] The stories about Ahab (1 Kings 20–22), especially Naboth's vineyard (1 Kings 21), viewed through the eyes of the early Greek-speaking Jewish communities and recorded in the Septuagint (LXX), contrast materially with the characterization of Ahab by the Hebrew Masoretic text (MT) accounts. There is a notorious difference in the order (structure) of the events unfolding around Ahab and consequential variations in content between the LXX and MT versions of the Ahab stories in 1 Kings 20–22. For whatever reasons, scholars have neglected to discuss at length these discrepancies, except to argue for genetic priority of one version over the other.[5] From a text-critical or historical-critical stance such arguments are valid. Still, no consensus has emerged on what constitutes the original unit(s) or on the history of composition and redaction of these stories.[6] Perhaps the time has come to look again at

---

4. I will not spend time arguing for historicity of these accounts, especially the Naboth story, along the lines proffered by the historical "minimalists." As Baruch Halpern argues of these texts in *The First Historians: The Hebrew Bible and History* (University Park: Pennsylvania State University Press, 1996), "Their form is historical. The author takes them as historical. The author presents them as historical." Deciding this question need not diminish the mostly literary and canonical point of view that I am undertaking here.

5. D. W. Gooding provides a rundown of scholars arguing for the priority of the LXX over that of the MT and vice versa ("Ahab According to the Septuagint," *ZAW* 76 [1964] 270–71). In two more recent studies S. J. DeVries (*1 Kings* [WBC 12; Waco: Word, 1985] 247, 243–44, 253–54, 261–66) cites all the variants in his textual notes. He suggests that 1 Kings 22 originally followed chapter 20 and that chapter 21 originally followed chapter 19. In siding with the LXX's order of the narratives, he appears to conclude implicitly that the LXX version was original, although he does not elaborate. J. Gray (*1 & 2 Kings: A Commentary* [Philadelphia: Westminster, 1963] 386, 369–71) does note the change in order. He suggests that the LXX grouped the accounts of the Syrian wars together, chapter 21 being a later insertion. Here, too, Gray seems to side with DeVries in granting to the LXX order the label "original." Variants are referred to in the textual notes, but are not elaborated on.

6. B. O. Long (*1 Kings* [FOTL 9; Grand Rapids: Eerdmans, 1984] 224) notes this disarray among scholars with respect to the history of composition and redaction of 1 Kings

these variant stories in light of the gains made in literary and canonical criticism.

The Ordering of the Ahab Stories[7]

The sequence of events in the MT is:

- The Two Victories against Syria (chap. 20)
- Naboth's Vineyard (chap. 21)
- Defeat of Syria: Death of Ahab (chap. 22)

The sequence of events in the LXX is:

- Naboth's Vineyard (chap. 20)
- The Two Victories against Syria (chap. 21)
- Defeat of Syria: Death of Ahab (chap. 22)

It is at once obvious that the LXX interchanges the first and second stories. In reading the stories carefully, it is clear enough that in either version Ahab's fate (chap. 22) is sealed by a prophecy of doom (20:17ff. LXX; 21:17ff. MT). A rereading of each version, however, suggests that there is a more logical progression of events in the LXX account than in the MT version. The sequence of events in the MT goes like this: Ahab sins, is sentenced, is unrepentant, and no delay in the execution of the sentence is mentioned. Ahab sins again, is sentenced, repents, and a delay in the execution is promised, but execution follows immediately. Contrast that order of events with the seemingly more logical sequence of the LXX: Ahab sins, is sentenced, repents, and delay of the execution is promised. Ahab sins again, is sentenced, is unrepentant, and no delay in the execution is promised. Execution then follows immediately. The logical order of events in the LXX, coupled with the added logic of grouping the Syrian wars together and linking the Naboth story more closely with the Elijah cycle, provides an internal coherence lacking in the MT.

In noting these variations of structure, commentators have followed the temptation to label this or that account as "original," or "prior to"

---

21. One might just as well generalize such an assessment to include chapters 20 and 22 also. Long summarizes, "A clear understanding of the prior history of the text eludes us" (225).

7. Here summarizing the earlier work of Gooding, "Ahab According to the Septuagint." Although Gooding's purpose in assessing the differences between the MT and LXX is meant to trace a non-MT Hebrew text as the urtext for the LXX, Gooding is also concerned with discovering the more original account of the two versions and concludes that it is not that of the LXX (271). My task in the present essay is not to isolate an earlier text per se, but to discover the hermeneutics and conceptual field in the MT in distinction to the LXX version.

or "more authentic than" the tradition accounted for by the LXX version, using the criteria of logical coherence as the norm for making these assessments. A more important question for the purposes of this study, however, is to ask, What hermeneutic may be at work in both accounts that would make sense of the discrepancies in the ordering of the material? Discovering the answer to this question is invited precisely because of the conflict between these two canonical accounts. Questions regarding differing hermeneutics that may underlie these variant accounts need not be limited to completely separate bodies of work such as those of the LXX and MT. Likewise, differing hermeneutics may be unearthed with respect to conflicts within a single canonical tradition. Identifying the underlying (unwritten) hermeneutic is helped, not hindered, by having contrasting accounts from which to work. To ignore the differences between the structures or to resolve the tension between the versions too readily by subordinating one version to the other through historical-critical means may be to lose valuable insight that might be gained in analyzing each side of the debate more fully. Before attempting to identify the respective hermeneutics at play in either version, it is important to understand the apparent message of each in its given structure. The *why* of these differences (i.e., the hermeneutics and conceptual presuppositions) is undertaken below.

Ahab: Weak or Wicked?

The differences in how Ahab is portrayed in both versions are remarkable.[8] The LXX preserves a tradition in which Ahab is seen as more impotent than depraved. In contrast, the MT vilifies Ahab relentlessly. The comparisons in the table on the following page underscore these varying assessments.

Ahab's reaction to the news of Naboth's death is told quite differently by the LXX (20:16) from the way it is told in the MT (21:16). The LXX describes Ahab as being deeply grieved over the news of Naboth's death. Furthermore, he takes over the vineyard only after an interval of genuine mourning. In its deliberate use of the first aorist passive indicative (20:25), the LXX implies that Ahab was a passive pawn to Jezebel's checkmate.

Lest one see in Ahab's remorse mere hypocrisy, repenting only because Elijah confronted him, the LXX underscores through expansion how sorry he truly was (20:27). In addition to the acts of repentance listed in the MT (21:27), Ahab's inner sorrow is revealed by the LXX: he is "pierced with sorrow" and goes forth "weeping." More emphatically still, we are told that he put on sackcloth on the very day that Naboth

---

8. Here, I confine the discussion to the Naboth story (chap. 21 MT; chap. 20 LXX).

MT *chapter 21*	LXX *chapter 20*
(21:16) "And it came to pass, when Ahab heard that Naboth was dead, that Ahab rose up to go down to the vineyard of Naboth the Jezreelite, to take possession of it."	(20:16) "And it came to pass, when Ahab heard that Naboth the Jezreelite was dead, *that he rent his garments, and put on sackcloth. And it came to pass afterward,* that Ahab arose and went down to the vineyard of Naboth the Jezreelite, to inherit it."
(21:25) "There was none who *sold himself* [active verb] to do what was evil in the sight of the Lord like Ahab, whom Jezebel, his wife, incited."	(20:25) "But Ahab did wickedly in that *he was sold* [passive verb] to do evil in the sight of the Lord, as his wife Jezebel led him astray."
(21:27) "And it came to pass when Ahab heard those words,	(20:27) "And because of these words, Ahab *was pierced with sorrow before the face of the Lord, and he both went weeping,*
that he rent his clothes, and put sackcloth upon his flesh, and fasted, and lay in sackcloth, and went softly.	and rent his garment, and girded sackcloth upon his body, and fasted; *he put on sackcloth also in the day that he smote Naboth the Jezreelite,* and went his way.
(21:28) "And the word of the Lord came to Elijah the Tishbite, saying,	(20:28) "And the word of the Lord came by the hand of his servant Eliu concerning Ahab, and the Lord said,
(21:29) 'Have you seen how Ahab humbled himself before me? Because he humbled himself before me, I will not bring the evil in his days; but in his son's days, I will bring the evil *upon his house.'* "	(20:29) 'Have you not seen how Ahab has been pricked to the heart before me? I will not bring on the evil in his days, but in his son's days will I bring on the evil.' "

was slain, suggesting that his sorrow was more than mere drama upon being caught, as the MT seems to imply.[9] However one might want to explain these variants, it is clear that the LXX is deliberate in its attempt to emphasize Ahab's repentance, providing an angle of vision for

---

9. Gooding ("Ahab According to the Septuagint," 274) suggests that the time note in 20:27 LXX transfers at least the "lying in sackcloth" episode, if not all the other penitential acts, to the time of Naboth's death.

understanding the motive behind its version of the order of events as outlined in its structure.

The contrasts between the MT and the LXX accounts of Ahab are striking enough to suggest different suppositions and conceptual motives for the two accounts. Do these interpretative differences reflect differing, but acceptable, traditions about Ahab? How do these differences reflect the different hermeneutics of the narrators and their audiences in the telling of these stories? Prior to addressing these questions, an additional methodological inquiry is in order, that of comparative midrash.

AHAB ACROSS TIME AND SPACE

The history of the use of the Ahab tradition within and outside the biblical corpus provides a hermeneutical continuum on how this particular tradition functions across time. Methodologically, such analysis has been called "tradition history" within the biblical canon and "comparative midrash" when done outside the biblical corpus. Whereas such a diachronic reading does not address the theological task of adjudication between differing points of views, it does validate, through modeling, the need to advocate for a particular tradition against the alternatives. Furthermore, in the quest for truth, that is, for a more complete fully contextual characterization, it is epistemologically more advantageous to put to the test more not less conflicting points of view. Ironically, it lies in the self-interest of one's theological argument for the better reading to have that reading contested. A comparative approach across time can offer a constructive gain through such contestation. Furthermore, such a comparison of traditions across time underscores the gaps left in the text about Ahab that provide the basis for a more complete and "full-fledged" characterization of Ahab the man. As such, this discussion will center only on those texts and contexts that differ to a greater or lesser degree with either the MT or LXX versions.[10]

Intrabiblical Uses

The Ahab story is limited to 1 Kings 16–22 MT and the fulfillment passages of the Elijah prophecy against the house of Ahab in 2 Kings 8–10 MT (see also 2 Kings 22:7–8). In these passages Ahab is viewed, as one might expect, in an extremely negative light. The rhetorical purity and

---

10. Since, for example, the Syriac and the Vulgate stand solidly behind one version or the other, they are not considered for analysis here. The Qumran fragments of Kings offer no additional information for consideration. For a history of use of the Ahab tradition see also Nahum Waldman, "Ahab in the Bible and Talmud," *Judaism* 37 (winter 1988) 41–47.

power of the Deuteronomic theologians assures the reader that Ahab is the epitome of Israel's sin, as Manasseh will be for Judah.

Other biblical references include 2 Chronicles 18 and 21. Here, references to Ahab are only in connection with his alliances with the southern Judahite king Jehoshaphat. The Micaiah story is repeated without elaboration. No mention of Naboth's vineyard or other more elaborate conflicts between Ahab and Elijah are found. Since the Chronicler's interest lies mainly in the south, this omission is not unexpected. Space given to Ahab is minimal and his downfall is simply related to his conflict with Micaiah. By the time of the Chronicler, much of the tradition of Ahab has been shelved.

The only other biblical reference to King Ahab, found in Mic. 6:16, is typical. Micah views Ahab as the negative standard by which Yahweh judges and condemns Israel in the late eighth century. In short, the biblical tradition of Ahab as represented by both the LXX and the MT is consistently negative, except for the 1 Kings 20–22 passages as noted above.

Pseudepigrapha: *Martyrdom and Ascension of Isaiah*[11]

The story line in this early Jewish work, whose earliest recension dates to around 200 B.C.E., recounts the legend of Isaiah's death at the hands of Manasseh. A digression in the narrative (2:12b–16) related to the story of Micaiah, son of Imlah, well noted in the biblical parallel in 1 Kings 22:5–8, does mention Ahab. Here, Ahab is criticized for throwing Micaiah into prison. However, Ahab's son Ahaziah is portrayed as the true villain who actually kills Micaiah, a tradition unknown to the biblical storytellers. In this context, the long-standing negative portrayal of Ahab becomes a cipher linked to the real antagonist of the story, Bilkirah. Guilt by association provides the fodder for judging Bilkirah as a false prophet in contrast to the protagonist, Isaiah. Bilkirah is shown to be a descendent of the false prophet Zedekiah in the Ahab/Micaiah story.

Josephus[12]

Josephus follows the structure of the LXX when recounting his version of the Ahab tradition. Still, he is somewhat ambiguous in his assessment of Ahab. Josephus amplifies the biblical account of Naboth's vineyard and portrays Ahab as having been insulted by Naboth's refusal to sell his vineyard. Indeed, according to Josephus, Ahab had initially

---

11. See J. H. Charlesworth, ed., *The Old Testament Pseudepigrapha* (2 vols.; New York: Doubleday, 1983) 2:140–76.

12. *Ant.* 8.316–418. See L. Feldman, "Josephus's Portrait of Ahab," *ETL* 68, no. 4 (December 1992) 368–84.

approached Naboth warmly, using "mild words in asking Naboth, hardly in keeping with royal authority." Having been refused, Ahab becomes legitimately incensed. One senses that Josephus then transfers the explicit fury of Jezebel, as so graphically portrayed in the biblical accounts, to Ahab. Indeed, upon hearing of Naboth's death, Josephus describes Ahab in stark reversal of the LXX version. Says Josephus, "Ahab was *pleased* at what happened."

If Josephus was dependent on an earlier version of the LXX for his parallel accounts of the books of Samuel through 1 Maccabees, as clearly seems to be the case,[13] his departure from the LXX tradition in this instance is striking. Still, Josephus falls back in line with the LXX when it comes to Ahab's repentance. Josephus portrays Ahab as genuinely sorry for his crimes, even to the degree that Ahab invites the prophet to do to him as the prophet sees fit because of the shameful way he had acted.

Josephus seems to have little invested in being overly harsh or lenient in judging Ahab. Josephus appears to allow for mistakes on Ahab's part that were a combination of wrong choices and fate. He doesn't overly vilify or demonize Ahab's actions. Of interest to Josephus was how Ahab's plight was due simply to his ignoring the prophetic advice given to him (twice), and so suffering ill fate. Josephus, writing to a Hellenized, Greek-speaking audience that included Jews and non-Jews, appears not to have wanted to utterly condemn Ahab, who was, after all, from all secular points of view, a highly successful Israelite king. Josephus was able to draw his moral from a modified retelling of the biblical tradition of Ahab: "Since befell Ahab the fate spoken by two prophets, we ought to acknowledge the greatness of Deity everywhere and everywhere honor and reverence him."[14]

Targum Jonathan to the Prophets[15]

Ahab gains stature in the Aramaic expansion of Zech. 12:11 MT. An oracle has gone out from Zechariah regarding the day of judgment. In the MT account the inhabitants of Jerusalem are spared Yahweh's wrath. They, in turn, lament their rejection of Yahweh's anointed one, "whom they have pierced" (v. 10). From the least to the greatest, all

---

13. On the question of sources in Josephus see L. Feldman, *Josephus and Modern Scholarship, 1937–1980* (Berlin: W. de Gruyter, 1984) 20–27, 121–91, 392–419. A nuanced view of Josephus's sources suggests that for the Pentateuchal parallels Josephus used the MT, whereas for Samuel through 1 Maccabees he used what appears to be a "proto-Lucianic" version of the LXX. He may have also used some Aramaic Targum sources, which might explain his divergence here from the LXX on Ahab. See H. Attridge *The Interpretation of Biblical History in the Antiquitates Judaicae of Flavius Josephus* (HDR 7; Missoula, Mont.: Scholars Press, 1976) 30.

14. *Ant.* 8.418.

15. See A. Sperber, ed., *The Bible in Aramaic* (4 vols. in 5; Leiden: Brill, 1992) 3:495.

the inhabitants mourn "as great as the mourning for Hadad-rimmon in the plain of Megiddo" (v. 11). Because nowhere in the Hebrew Bible is such mourning for Hadad-rimmon mentioned, the Aramaic translator of this passage offers an expanded version by way of explanation. *Targum Jonathan* interprets the mourning of Hadad-rimmon as being, in fact, a weeping on behalf of Ahab, "who was killed by Hadad-rimmon," a clear expansion of 12:11 MT. The Targum explains the MT's ambiguous geographical reference to the plain of Megiddo by suggesting that the mourning of Ahab will be just like that of the "weeping for Josiah who was killed by Pharaoh Neco on the plain of Megiddo."

Here, the Targum provides a remarkable revision to the negative assessment of Ahab. Not only is his death deeply mourned, but it is a sorrow on par with the lament for the death of the deeply pious Josiah, a king only slightly less revered than the great King David. Further still, Ahab's death, alongside that of Josiah, is held up in the same literary breath as a standard by which the reader can begin to understand the great remorse the inhabitants of Jerusalem will have at the end of time ("in that day") over their earlier rejection of the Shepherd Messiah. The Targum describes it as a day of weeping as if mourning the loss of two great kings (Josiah and Ahab), and a day of lament as if over the loss of one's "first-born child," one's "only child." *Targum Jonathan* views Ahab in a variety of ways. It follows the overall negative assessment of the MT in its translation of 1 Kings, but in this instance is remarkably complimentary.

Midrash Rabbah[16]

In *Gen. Rab.* 84:20[17] the mourning of Jacob in sackcloth and ashes over the loss of Joseph (Gen. 37:34) gains paradigmatic force in the midrash. The mourning of Joram (2 Kings 6:30), Mordecai (Esther 4:1) and, surprisingly, Ahab (1 Kings 21:27) are likened to the great lament of Jacob for Joseph. Here, Ahab's remorse is not differentiated in degree from the kind of pain Jacob felt in losing his favored son. From such a point of view, the sincere repentance of Ahab is assumed.

In *Gen. Rab.* 98:8[18] Ahab's legacy is assured. In this midrash a debate ensues over the ancestry of the great Rabbi Hillel. Rabbi Levi describes

---

16. See H. Freedman and M. Simon, eds., *Midrash Rabbah* (10 vols.; London: Soncino Press, 1939). Comprising haggadic narrative literature loosely covering the period from the beginning of the Common Era to its tenth century, this collection contains midrash on the five books of the Torah and the five Megilloth. Its importance here lies in its link to earlier interpretive traditions and its own value as an example of hermeneutical revision.

17. *Midrash Rabbah*, 2:785.

18. *Midrash Rabbah*, 2:956.

a genealogical scroll found in Jerusalem that clearly delineates Hillel's roots. Included in this table of ancestry are noteworthy rabbinic leaders and sages, not least of which is Rabbi ben Kovesim, a direct descendent of Ahab. Ahab poses no threat to the establishment of Hillel's pedigree.

In the midrash for the Song of Songs[19] Ahab's character becomes one example among many for interpreting the lyric "I am black and beautiful" (or "very dark, but comely" [RSV]). According to Rabbi Joshua ben Levi, the fact that Ahab "put on sackcloth and fasted" and then "went down softly" (1 Kings 21:27 MT) provides a testimony of what it means to be both "black" (for R. Levi this means "evil" or "rebellious") and "beautiful" (for R. Levi, "good" and "obedient"). Ahab emerges as typical of most of God's people throughout history, a mixture of good and evil.

In the midrash on Esther 1:5 and 12[20] Ahab's wealth and leadership are glorified. Ahab, alongside David and Solomon, has the distinction of ruling over "the whole world," an apocryphal regency of some 250 kingdoms. The midrash underscores Ahab's great wealth. Expanding on the biblical text that tells of Ahab's seventy sons who were slain en masse by Jehu (2 Kings 10 — Rabbi Hoshaia suggests that Ahab had another seventy sons in Jezreel, his summer home). Furthermore, each of Ahab's 140 sons owned a summer and a winter home, as did their father. Rabbi Simon exaggerates still more, giving four palaces to each son. Other rabbis join in the praise of Ahab, adding still more wealth and palaces to each son. Ahab is held in esteem by these rabbis, at least in light of his amazing wealth, a sign of great blessing.

Babylonian Talmud[21]

Baba Qamma 16b–17a[22] elaborates on the mourning rituals surrounding Ahab's death at Ramoth Gilead. Thirty-six thousand mourners bare their shoulders in mourning to him, a ritual done in Ahab's honor because he was "a righteous man and a scholar."[23] Hezekiah, that great, model king himself, is afforded only thirty-six thousand mourners as well, although in deference he also merits a scroll placed upon his coffin. Naturally, questions arose as to how one such as Ahab could be so honored on par with so great a king as Hezekiah. To such questions the rabbis have a ready reply. In particular, Rabbi Judah explains that whereas both kings were great and worthy of a comparable memorial, Ahab had not fulfilled the law as had Hezekiah, so the scroll represents

---

19. *Midrash Rabbah,* 9:52–53.
20. *Midrash Rabbah,* 9:21.
21. See I. Epstein, ed., *The Babylonian Talmud* (34 vols.; London: Soncino, 1935–59).
22. *Babylonian Talmud,* 4:75.
23. "Mo'ed Paṭan," in *Babylonian Talmud,* 8:188–89.

special honor for Hezekiah. Whatever the case, tradition concluded that whatever Ahab's demerits in life, they were not such as to forbid an honorable burial. Here, an almost total acceptance of Ahab seems to diminish the strong overall negative view of him elsewhere.

In *B. Meṣ.* 59a[24] Jezebel shoulders the blame for Ahab's downfall. Ahab is responsible for listening to her advice. As Rab intones, "He who follows his wife's counsel will fall." The ambiguity of assessing Ahab's responsibility is furthered in the immediate response of Rabbi Papa to Abaye: "If your wife is short, bend down and hear her whisper." That is, there are occasions when one should lean down and take counsel with one's wife, a sentiment countering Rab's own. The tension is resolved by concluding that in important decisions, especially of a religious nature, the advice of one's wife is not appropriate, whereas in matters of the hearth and home, a man should consult his wife. Therein was Ahab's judgment: not that he listened to Jezebel's advice per se, but that he did so in matters religious and public. Using such criteria, the rabbis neither sanctioned Ahab for gross wickedness (cf. 1 Kings 21:21) nor excused his now circumscribed behavior.

More than any other tractate within the Babylonian Talmud, the tractate *Sanhedrin* reuses earlier Ahab traditions.[25] Here also, a mixed review of Ahab is provided. His minor transgressions are said to be worse than the worst sins committed by the notorious King Jeroboam II, an assessment even the Deuteronomic theologians do not make. Ahab is described as one of only three kings who do not have a "portion" in the world to come. Ironically, *Sanhedrin* also counters its own negative portrayal of Ahab. Rabbi Mar, son of Rabina, counsels regarding Ahab and his two cohorts, along with all others who have been excluded from any future kingdom, "Do not use [the biblical passages dealing with these condemned ones] to discredit them, except for Balaam."[26] Only in assessing Balaam can one apparently throw judgmental caution to the wind. Ahab must be given his due, if for no other reason than that he is better than Balaam.

By the standards of *Sanhedrin*, Ahab fares reasonably well. Up to half of his sins were remitted because he provided good financial scholarships to budding divinity students. Furthermore, his merits are said to balance his sins, a zero-sum elimination. His twenty-two-year reign signaled to the rabbis that Ahab must have honored the Torah, which was, after all, written with the twenty-two letters of the Hebrew alphabet. *Sanhedrin's* interpretation of the name Ahab itself indicates its

---

24. *Babylonian Talmud*, 24:351.
25. *Babylonian Talmud*, 28:602, 695–98.
26. *Babylonian Talmud*, 28:106b, 176.

own ambiguous assessment of Ahab himself: *ah* defines him as *"brother* of heaven," and *ab* as *"father* of idolatry." Without any hint of embarrassment for their contradictory claims about Ahab, the rabbis continue to provide a seesaw assessment of Ahab's merits, sometimes favorable, sometimes not.

Jerusalem Talmud[27]

Rabbi Levi's midrash on 1 Kings 21:25 is recounted in the tractate *Sanhedrin* of the Jerusalem Talmud. The rabbi describes an event in which the spirit of Ahab appears to him declaring Ahab's innocence. The ghostly creature defends Ahab like a good lawyer, arguing that the preponderance of the evidence used to prosecute Ahab should more rightly weigh against Jezebel, his consort. It is a tattletale scene reminiscent of Adam trying to blame Eve for his own ill-fated choices. Rabbi Levi seems to give Ahab's ghost the benefit of doubt, not counting Ahab's sins solely against him.

History and Archaeology

The biblical record is primarily interested in Ahab's religious loyalties, particularly his apostasy to Baal. But a fairer reading of Ahab's legacy, using extrabiblical, historical, and archaeological sources, warrants a brief discussion. By nearly any other account, other than his vacillating religious commitments, Ahab appeared to be a successful king, evidenced by his long reign.

His status as a military leader was on par with other great military leaders, not least of which was King David. Among his allies Ahab was given due honor. In a battle not described in the biblical narratives, a battle described in the Assyrian inscription of Shalmanesser III, Ahab's military prowess is noticed.[28] He is listed as third in line of military importance, and said to have brought two thousand chariots, well over half of the chariots making up the coalition forces. In addition he supplied ten thousand conscripts in full armor to assist in battle, a remarkable effort by a relatively small state.

Ahab's political skills are considerable. His marriage to Jezebel was both strategic and pragmatic. Because Jezebel was from the northern coastal land of Tyre, was a royal daughter of its ruler, and was a loyal member of the fertility cult so important in agricultural climates, marriage to her was a wise political choice for Ahab. Elijah suggests her

---

27. See M. Schwab, ed., *Le Talmud de Jerusalem* (11 vols.; Paris: G. P. Maisonneuve, 1977) 11:45.

28. See "Shalmaneser III (858–824): The Fight against the Aramean Coalition," in *ANET*, 278–79.

economic independence as well as her abundant resources by specifying that the 450 prophets of Baal and 400 prophets of Asherah ate not at Ahab's table but "at the table of Jezebel" (1 Kings 18:19). If one compares Jezebel with the description of the "good wife" in Prov. 31:11–12, 16–17, one cannot help but appreciate the skills she brought to Ahab's dominion.[29] The marriage of Ahab and Jezebel prevented frequent incursions into Israel from the north by the growing Syrian military power broker, Ben-hadad. Increased trade with merchants from Tyre and Sidon, Jezebel's homeland, brought new wealth to both countries. It was a nearly perfect union made on earth, if not in heaven.

Archaeological evidence reveals Ahab to have been a master builder. Major efforts were undertaken by Ahab to fortify the cities of Samaria, Jericho, Hazor, Shechem, and Meggido. Huge stables have been uncovered at Megiddo, thought to date to the time of Ahab. Beautiful palaces with ivory inlays and ornamentation (1 Kings 22:39) and quantities of the highly prized "Samaritan" pottery show that trade imported luxury items. Trading chariots and horses between Egypt and Anatolia (1 Kings 10:28–29) had become a booming business for Ahab. Ahab was a king of means.[30]

Extrabiblical evidence offers a quite positive point of view to Ahab's rule, though not without its shadow side. Ahab's assimilation of the gods bode well for religious toleration and the incorporation of a more diverse public, both notable political achievements.

Summary of Diachronic Comparisons

A diachronic study of the use and reuse of the Ahab traditions suggests a lively debate in the formation of an overall characterization of Ahab. Ahab is vilified and glorified, humanized and demonized. The variety of responses to Ahab both mirrors and contrasts to the MT and LXX versions. Those with a more positive portrayal of Ahab pick up, knowingly or not, on the subtler interpretations of the Ahab tradition offered by the LXX. The less accommodating stance of the MT certainly comes through subsequent traditions with much force as well, though often nuanced. The communities of authority passing down these traditions allowed for a variety of viewpoints, leaving the reader to sort, prioritize, and evaluate them for a more complex, fully modulated characterization of Ahab.

---

29. See P. Trible, "Exegesis for Storytellers and Other Strangers," *JBL* 114 (1995) 3–19.

30. See K. M. Kenyon, *Royal Cities of the Old Testament* (London: Barrie and Jenkins, 1971) 81, 83, 104, 106; see also J. W. Jack, *Samaria in Ahab's Time* (Edinburgh: T. & T. Clark, 1929) 106–31.

CHARACTERIZING AHAB

Returning to the structure of the overall story of Ahab in Scripture, Ahab's repentance (1 Kings 21:27–29 MT) stands out in what has been called by form critics a "schema of reprieve."[31] Why here? Why this awkward sequence? As noted, the MT tells it this way: Ahab sins, is unrepentant, and no delay in the execution is mentioned; he sins again, repents, and promise of delay in execution is followed by his immediate execution. The LXX, as noted, seems to provide a more logical account of events: Ahab sins, repents, and execution is delayed; he sins again, does not repent, and so is executed.

Some commentators on the MT sequence have argued that a later redactor inserted the story of Ahab's repentance into the middle of an account that is otherwise quite unflattering and almost wholly negative toward Ahab. Such an assertion was meant to offer an explanation why Ahab went on living for some twenty years in relative prosperity despite the prediction of his impending death.[32] Others see no necessary break in the story as told. The storyteller may have intended to tell the story as it is (no later insertion). Ahab's repentance may have been seen as a means of stemming the tide of judgment against the dynasty of Ahab ("the evil upon his house" in 21:29) for another two generations (2 Kings 9–10). Ahab's subsequent death in 1 Kings 22 would then simply be seen as punishment for his sins unmitigated by his repentance. Certainly, those rabbis in later tradition who argued for Ahab's sins and merits canceling themselves out would have found this explanation lacking and may have provided the very reason for their midrash in the first place.

Ahab is characterized by the MT as either depraved or, at best, an "ineffectual weakling."[33] The striking thing about the Naboth account is its "backstage atmosphere." So much happens in secret. Ahab tries on his own to make a deal with Naboth. When rebuffed, he pouts in his room, whereupon Jezebel secretly promises to get the vineyard. She surreptitiously writes letters in Ahab's name, ordering the elders of Jezreel to arrest Naboth for cursing God and the king, to suborn perjury, and to bribe the jury. Ahab does nothing, knows nothing, except that Naboth died. Halpern fittingly typifies the whole thing as that

---

31. Long, 1 Kings, 224–25.

32. See J. M. Miller, "The Fall of the House of Ahab," VT 17 (July 1967) 307–24.

33. For what follows see Halpern, First Historians, xxix–xxxi. While his concern is to use the Naboth story as a vehicle to elaborate his larger thesis about the nature of history writing in ancient Israel, his descriptions are borrowed here to delineate the two characterizations of Ahab that are within the realm of good "historical" analysis.

of the king being "insulated from responsibility almost as well as an American president." The true villain is Jezebel.[34]

But why blame Jezebel? Halpern concludes that the story may have taken shape in the period when Jezebel survived Ahab, with her sons on the throne, at a time when Ahab's reputation may still have been too high to baldly attack. In other words, it comes from a time when Jehu overthrew the dynasty to justify divesting Ahab's queen of her power. Jehu and his political party must have liked this version of events and preserved it accordingly.

Certainly, as the broader historical and archaeological evidence attests, a more sympathetic version might have been told that could withstand historical scrutiny as well, since so much of the characterization of Ahab in the Kings account is "behind the scenes" (not open to public verifiability). A version of events could have been told from the point of view of Jezebel (so Trible) or, for that matter, from that perspective that would later be argued for by Hosea. Hosea, after all, condemned Jehu's bloody coup d'état in his own Yahweh speech arguing, in effect, against Elijah and Elisha's prophetic Yahweh speeches defending Jehu's action (Hos. 1:4).[35] Though Hosea's account may not have been favorable to any king (Hos. 6:5; 13:9–11), a reasonable person on the other side of the party politics of Jehu might have remembered Ahab as decisive and dignified, and recounted events accordingly.

One might reasonably surmise that the king, having tried to negotiate a property swap "in good faith," was insulted by Naboth. Allowing this version some "behind the scenes" leeway on par with the Kings account, perhaps Naboth went so far as decrying the king's prerogative, or questioning the king's taxation policies, or, even more insultingly, his paternity. The king dispenses his courtiers to convict Naboth of treason and then executes him. As a consequence of his criminality, Naboth's property is forfeited. In this possible version of events Ahab, in effect, mirrors Yahweh's own prerogatives against those who hate him (Yahweh), even to the fourth generation. No need to conjure up despotic or Canaanite influence. It would simply be an open-and-shut case of affront to a king. Since no public meeting of Ahab with Naboth is described in Kings, a reasonable historical alternative story could have been told in which Ahab never even met with Naboth. As Halpern suggests, from a historian's point of view, the Naboth account as told in Kings is "party venom." The claims that stand scrutiny are the public

---

34. See Trible, "Exegesis for Storytellers," for the rhetorical characterization of Jezebel in this story.

35. See J. E. Brenneman, "Prophets in Conflict: Negotiating Truth in Scripture," in L. Johns and T. Grimsrud, eds., *Peace and Justice Shall Embrace: Power and Theopolitics in the Bible* (Telford, Pa.: Pandora, 2000) 49–63.

ones: Naboth was tried; his vineyard was annexed by the state. These elements alone would suffice to elicit from Jezebel's political opponents (the Jehu party) enough data to reconstruct the event to fit their party politics. Furthermore, it would be Jehu's version of events that came down to the Deuteronomists, who included it in their history because it also suited their purposes.

It should be clear by now that from a reasonable historical alternative point of view, a more positive characterization of Ahab would be possible. Coupled with the more nuanced version of the LXX and the subsequent characterizations of Ahab over time, Ahab regains some character complexity. Still, this more positive assessment of Ahab's character could not overwhelm the Deuteronomic theologians' unremitting criteria, no matter how much alternative traditions might have led to a more nuanced account. The theological assessment of the Deuteronomists countered any positive assessment, including the seemingly more logical placing of this passage within its literary context (LXX). For them, theology overshadowed a more nuanced characterization of Ahab. By placing the account of Ahab's repentance next to the story of "false" prophets and the story of Ahab's untimely death, they suggest guilt by association for the pericope as a whole. A truly repentant Ahab, after all, given the rhetorical purity and power of the Deuteronomic point of view, would undermine the very antinorthern bias they were trying to convey. The MT's evaluation of Ahab, less complimentary than that of the LXX, evidences that tradition's difficulty with a more ambiguous reality. The Deuteronomic theologians had found in the story of Ahab (and Jezebel, for that matter) a chance to "feed their passion for polarity": life and death, blessing and curse, good and evil, obedience and disobedience.[36] Given their categories of assessment, Ahab emerged as the epitome of evil. Without the more nuanced account of the LXX, readers throughout the ages would have been persuaded by this static characterization of Ahab. The LXX, however, kept the debate about Ahab alive with its more ambiguous account of Ahab's character, a point of view not lost on the later readers of the Ahab story. Some conclusions are now in order.

CONCLUSIONS

Debating Ahab has challenged the notion of a uniform, authoritative reading of a particular biblical story. The contrasting views of Ahab by two canonically authoritative traditions (MT and LXX) and the ambiguous wake they leave trailing them caution against reading any one

---

36. Trible, "Exegesis for Storytellers," 3.

biblical text univocally. Indeed, when it comes to characterizing Ahab, one wonders, as Rolf Knierim has stated so well elsewhere, what would have happened if an encounter had taken place between the Deuteronomic theologians (MT) and their LXX translators? Or for that matter, between the Deuteronomic theologians, the LXX translators, and those who characterized Ahab down through the ages based upon one or the other Scriptural points of view?[37] It is precisely here, in the theological assessment of a particular biblical character that the "task of Old Testament theology" gains its methodological footing. Scripture readers are compelled to make a hermeneutical decision, about which characterization is more accurate, which is more adequate theologically, which is truer to a more complete understanding of a particular "real" personage. In this case, the Bible, or better said, the bibles, do not make that decision for them.

One can rightly ask of the Deuteronomic theologians' characterization of Ahab, Is it the better account of Ahab? More precisely and theologically, does their understanding of the relationship of Yahweh to this fallible king cohere with a more comprehensive understanding of Yahweh's relationship with any and every other king, or lesser subject, for that matter? If so, what does such an account of Ahab's life mean for assessing our own ambiguous existences?

In making such an assessment, one is cautioned not simply to side with that voice or point of view that holds majority status in Scripture. Were that the case, the Deuteronomic point of view on Ahab would win, hands down. The historiography of the Deuteronomists subsumed centuries of tradition under its theological program. They even locked Yahweh into their polarizing scheme.[38] These compilers and authors shaped the narrative in particular ways, adding glosses here or there, forcing their characters into their plot in such a way that often robbed them of true full-orbed characterization. In this regard, the reminder by the great literary critic M. H. Abrams is worth repeating: "Almost all dramas and narratives, properly enough, have some characters who serve as mere functionaries and are not characterized at all."[39] When it comes to Ahab or many other characters from the northern kingdom of Israel, the Deuteronomists sought rhetorical purity over full-fledged characterization. Certainly, from the point of view of Yahweh's exclusive covenant with "Israel," Ahab's alliances with other gods was seen

---

37. Actually, Knierim asks these questions with regard to the various narrators, writers, redactors, prophets, priests, and sages within the MT, but the questions surely apply here. See Knierim, *Task of Old Testament Theology*, 5.

38. See S. L. McKenzie, "Deuteronomistic History," in *ABD* 2:160–68.

39. M. H. Abrams, *A Glossary of Literary Terms* (4th ed.; New York: Holt, Rinehart and Winston, 1981) 21.

as a grave threat to the Jerusalem cult in the south — so much so, that the authors/redactors of the MT version of events did not seem to care that other stories of reprieve and forgiveness of noted southern kings like David (1 Samuel 12), Hezekiah (2 Kings 20:5–6), or Josiah (2 Kings 22:19–20) would show the inconsistencies in their overall conceptual worldview. If Yahweh honored these acts of repentance, why not that of Ahab?

It is precisely at this juncture, between the Old Testament's universal and particularistic claims about Yahweh's rule, that the criterion for assessing the biblical characterization of Ahab must be negotiated. Is the just and forgiving God of David, Hezekiah, and Josiah the same just and forgiving God of Ahab? Or, as it has been asked elsewhere, "Are justice and righteousness [and forgiveness] in Israel revealed and required because they reflect Yahweh's relationship to the totality of his creation and of humanity, or because they stand for nothing but Yahweh's relationship to his elect regardless of his relationship to the rest of the world?"[40] If the former, Ahab is doomed; if the latter, he too might be redeemed.

Clearly, the LXX account and its midrashic trajectories argue for a God who can resignify and redeem all the Ahabs of life, the Ahabs within. To understand this full-orbed characterization of Ahab is to comprehend the limits of polarized thinking and so alter the theological discourse in the process. In loving the Ahabs within, among and all around us, one is reminded of an enlarged biblical theology that evaluates all lesser options: "You have heard that it was said, 'You shall love your neighbor and hate your enemy.' But I say to you, Love your enemies and pray for those who persecute you, so that you may be children of your Father in heaven; for God makes the sun to rise on the evil and on the good, and sends rain on the righteous and on the unrighteous" (Matt. 5:43–45). May the sun shine and the rain pour over us as it has upon Ahab.

BIBLIOGRAPHY

Alter, Robert. *The Art of Biblical Narrative.* New York: Basic Books, 1981.

Armstrong, Paul B. *Conflicting Readings: Variety and Validity in Interpretation.* Chapel Hill: University of North Carolina Press, 1990.

Berlin, Adele. *Poetics and Interpretation of Biblical Narrative.* Winona Lake, Ind.: Eisenbrauns, 1994.

Bloch, Renée. "Midrash," trans. Mary Howard, in *Approaches to Ancient Judaism: Theory and Practice.* Ed. William S. Green. Missoula, Mont.: Scholars Press, 1978.

---

40. Knierim, *Task of Old Testament Theology,* 14.

Boyarin, Daniel. *Intertextuality and the Reading of Midrash.* Bloomington: Indiana University Press, 1990.

Brenneman, James E. *Canons in Conflict: Negotiating Texts in True and False Prophecy.* New York: Oxford University Press, 1997.

————. "Prophets in Conflict: Negotiating Truth in Scripture." In *Peace and Justice Shall Embrace: Power and Theopolitics in the Bible.* Ed. Loren Johns and Ted Grimsrud. Telford, Pa.: Pandora Press, 2000.

Brueggemann, Walter. *David's Truth in Israel's Imagination and Memory.* Minneapolis: Fortress Press, 1985.

Feldman, Louis. *Josephus's Interpretation of the Bible.* Berkeley: University of California Press, 1998.

Fishbane, Michael. *Biblical Interpretation in Ancient Israel.* Oxford: Clarendon Press, 1985.

Kirsch, Jonathan. *Moses: A Life.* New York: Ballantine, 1998.

Knierim, Rolf. *The Task of Old Testament Theology: Substance, Method, and Cases.* Grand Rapids: Eerdmans, 1995.

McKenzie, Steven L. "Deuteronomistic History. " *ABD* 2. New York: Doubleday, 1992.

McKnight, Edgar. *The Bible and the Reader: An Introduction to Literary Criticism.* Philadelphia: Fortress, 1985.

Miles, Jack. *God: A Biography.* New York: Knopf, 1995.

Patte, Daniel. *Ethics of Biblical Interpretation: A Reevaluation.* Louisville: Westminster John Knox, 1995.

Sanders, James A. *Canon and Community: A Guide to Canonical Criticism.* Philadelphia: Fortress, 1984.

————. "Hermeneutics." *IDB Supplement,* ed. Keith Crim. Nashville: Abingdon, 1976.

Scholes, R., and R. Kellogg. *The Nature of Narrative.* London and New York: Oxford, 1966.

Sternberg, Meir. *The Poetics of Biblical Narrative: Ideological Literature and the Drama of Reading.* Bloomington: Indiana University Press, 1986.

Trible, Phyllis. "Exegesis for Storytellers and Other Strangers." *JBL* 114 (spring 1995).

————. *Rhetorical Criticism: Context, Method and the Book of Jonah.* Minneapolis: Fortress, 1994.

8

Memory and Theology:
Ordering the World for the
Community of Faith

Mary Katharine Deeley

Rolf Knierim suggests that the problem of Old Testament theology lies in the somewhat misguided attempt to find a unifying theme or overarching principle that will incorporate the plurality of theologies present in the biblical text. Rather, the task of Old Testament theology lies in naming and recognizing the relationships among the many theologies. To do this the scholar must determine "how Yahweh and reality are seen as related and how are the various modes of this relationship related to one another and . . . with whom and with what is Yahweh related and how are the various realms with whom and with what Yahweh is related, related among one another."[1] For Knierim, the first set of questions is answered fundamentally by the concept of Yahweh's universal dominion over reality. From this flows God's relationship to the earth, to humankind, to Israel.[2] Justice and righteousness provide the ground for all other notions of the quality or modes of God's relationship with reality. Thus, the "ultimate vantage point from which to coordinate (Old Testament) theologies is *the universal dominion of Yahweh in justice and righteousness.*"[3] All other aspects of biblical theology are valid only as they are understood in their relation to and their reflection of this vantage point.[4]

Knierim's understanding provides a framework from which to view the compelling notion of memory in the biblical text. How are we to understand the place of memory in the theology of Israel? In what way is a theology of memory related to the liberation theology of Exodus, the covenant theologies of the Pentateuch, and the understanding of election, law, and obedience? Where does a theology of memory stand in a systematization of theologies governed by Yahweh's dominion and

---

1. Rolf P. Knierim, *The Task of Old Testament Theology: Substance, Method, and Cases* (Grand Rapids: Eerdmans, 1995) 11.
2. Knierim, *Task of Old Testament Theology*, 14.
3. Knierim, *Task of Old Testament Theology*, 15; emphasis in original.
4. Knierim, *Task of Old Testament Theology*, 15.

the notions of justice and righteousness? To explore this concept we will take a brief look at memory, its function in the community of Israel, and then examine how a theology of memory can inform our understanding of biblical text.

Aristotle maintained that memory is the mental image of the world that is past through which one has moved and that is now contained in the soul.[5] Plato suggested that memory was the knowledge of the truth,[6] and Augustine that it was the knowledge of God.[7] Some twentieth-century philosophers either equate memory with knowledge in general or consider it the basis of all knowledge.[8] Contemporary writers have begun to understand memory as more than mental image and moving beyond knowledge. Memory is

> the strategic construction of the sense of one's past. . . . It is not primarily a matter of making copies of past events. It is primarily a matter of making sense of things. . . . Memory is a personal historical project; a tentative archaeology that tries to establish the sense of our origins so that we may encounter ourselves as temporal beings who are always beginning and ending.[9]

This statement of Alderman and its notion of a personal historical project is echoed by Cox:

> To remember is to conserve an image of the self as existing in time. . . . Arendt reminds us that the image allows citizens in a republic to learn where they "belong" and what they are "living for."[10]

Not only does memory relate individuals to their past, but opens up to them the possibilities that existed at the time of the events they recall:

> Heidegger distinguishes two senses of the past: the heritage and tradition. The heritage is the temporal horizon of past possibilities for authentic existence; tradition, on the other hand, refers to the way in which these possibilities have been interpreted and handed down to us in the (unauthentic) existence of the presence. . . . For Heidegger, the act of repeating

---

5. Aristotle, "De Memoria et Reminiscentia," in W. D. Ross, ed., *The Works of Aristotle* (12 vols.; Oxford: Clarendon, 1963) vol. 3, particularly chapters 1 and 2.

6. Plato, "Phaedrus," in E. Hamilton and H. Cairns, eds., *The Collected Dialogues of Plato* (New York: Pantheon, 1961).

7. Augustine, *The Confessions of St. Augustine* (trans. J. K. Ryan; Garden City, N.Y.: Doubleday, 1960) 253–54.

8. See, for example, the discussions of memory in Bertrand Russell, *Analysis of Mind* (London: Allen and Unwin, 1921) 157; Charles Landesman, "Philosophical Problems with Memory," *Journal of Philosophy* 59 (1961) 61; Norman Malcolm, *Memory and Mind* (Ithaca: Cornell University Press, 1977) 102.

9. H. Alderman, "The Text of Memory," in J. Sallis, ed., *Philosophy and Archaic Experience* (Pittsburgh: Duquesne University Press, 1982) 151.

10. J. Robert Cox, "Against Resignation: Memory and Rhetorical Practice" (paper presented at the meeting of the International Communication Association, May 22, 1986).

is not mere "doing again" or an attempt to recall the actual past; it means rather an attempt to go back to the past and retrieve former possibilities which are thus "explicitly handed down" or "transmitted...." Thus memory preserves the image of past possibilities in spite of and against present forgetting.[11]

Memory, then, is the means by which humankind creates and maintains an image of itself in the world — a worldview. It not only shapes the images that form an individual's worldview, but also enables those images to transform the present situation in accordance with the possibilities presented in the past. Memory creates an environment in which a community can "attend to the voices of the past, present, and future, especially the inaudible ones, and settle their claim."[12] Memory does not explore the past; it allows the past to play itself out in the life of the individual. It is the place where the experiences of the individual and the world intersect. Memory shapes the individual's worldview and enables the individual to name experiences and provide perspective and congruity. It also shows the individual the possibilities for change. Through memory, human beings order and reorder the world so that it makes sense.

In Israel memory plays a critical role in Israel's formulation of its self-identity and its comprehension of the relationship between God and the community. Yousef Yerushalmi, in his excellent monograph on memory and history, points out that Israel understands who it is by remembering its relationship to a God who acts in history. "Israel knows what God is from what he has done..., and if that is so, then memory has become crucial to its faith and, ultimately, to its very existence."[13] Maurice Halbwachs perceives memory as the vehicle by which a group "becomes conscious of its identity through time.... [T]he group, living first and foremost for its own sake, aims to perpetuate the feelings and images forming the substance of its thought."[14] Those who share in the collective memory of any group are able to "gain the group viewpoint, plunge into its milieu and time, and feel in its midst."[15] Those who share in the collective memory of Israel find themselves experiencing a worldview that is shaped by Israel's experience with God. Israel is formed as a people by the creative will of God. Its continued relationship with

---

11. Cox, "Against Resignation," 8, 13.

12. Irving Wohlfaith, "History, Literature, and the Text: The Case of Walter Benjamin," *Modern Language News* 96 (1981) 1005.

13. Yosef Hayim Yerushalmi, *Zakhor: Jewish History and Jewish Memory* (Seattle: University of Washington Press, 1982) 9.

14. Maurice Halbwachs, *The Collective Memory* (trans. F. J. Ditter and V. Y. Ditter; New York: Harper and Row, 1980) 85–86.

15. Halbwachs, *Collective Memory*, 118.

God is the result of God's memory of a promise made to Abraham. In some sense, to participate in the memory of Israel is to participate in God's worldview as well as Israel's. Thus, the command to remember becomes "a religious imperative to an entire people,"[16] because it allows them to enter into God's viewpoint, appropriate it as their own, and then shape their lives as a community of faith around the congruence of God's memory and their own. Memory allows Israel to transcend the chronological limits of time and link present, past, and future with the purpose of evoking some action or attitude.

Brevard Childs touches on the idea that memory is participation or discernment that turns one to God.[17] If one does not remember, one cannot enter into the worldviews of either God or Israel and so loses the possibility of being shaped or formed by them. To forget is to miss the possibilities that were present at the original setting. It is to become ahistorical, time bound, unable to make sense of the world. For Israel it meant not being able to choose what God wanted, because neither God's viewpoint nor Israel's reflection on it were any longer informative through memory.[18]

In the Old Testament, memory becomes the arena in which Israel lives out its creation and covenant relationship with God. A theology of memory is the foundation for Israel's understanding of itself in history and in the world as a people created and chosen by God. Memory allows Israel to encounter the world, to understand it to be ordered by God, and to shape and reshape that order as new revelations are given. In memory Israel participates in God's will and God's worldview by continually placing itself in the moment when that will and worldview (even if imperfectly understood) are made manifest to them. When that happens, Israel is able to choose and choose again the path of right relationship with God. In effect, memory makes it possible for Israel to experience the exodus again at the exile, to see creation as the renewal of covenant or spirit at the end of captivity, to comprehend God's intervention in human history as constitutive of an order not yet entirely grasped. In the place of memory, Israel can allow God's worldview to shape and transform its own, allow God's memory to become the standard by which its own is measured.

Reflection, prayer, and storytelling are the means by which Israel

---

16. Yerushalmi, *Zakhor*, 9.

17. Brevard S. Childs, *Memory and Tradition in Israel* (Naperville, Ill.: A. R. Allenson, 1962) 56–60.

18. Herbert Marcuse, *The Aesthetic Dimension* (Boston: Beacon, 1978) 60–70. Marcuse's discussion of remembering and forgetting in their historical dimensions are particularly illuminating on this point.

enters into memory, and Deut. 7:1–10:11[19] provides a text that shows
the importance of memory.[20] Set in the context of Moses' second great
speech in Deuteronomy 5–11, Moses[21] prepares the people to obey
God's law by remembering for and with them a particular order of
events. Throughout the speech he exhorts them specifically to remember and not forget certain of those events. Commands to remember and
the warnings not to forget are clustered in Deuteronomy 7–9 (7:18; 8:2,
11, 14, 18–19; 9:7), forming a dense center for Deuteronomy 5–11. Moses'
selection and ordering of key memories and commands to remember
forces the Israelites to see the world as Moses does. It is a conscious
apprehension of past events that gives them a worldview in which they
can make the appropriate choice to enter or reenter into covenant as
a people of God. More importantly, Moses understands himself to be
giving to the Israelites what he received from God. His selection of
memories is not haphazard, but driven by what he understands to be
God's own will for Israel. Thus,

> Present Israel . . . encounters the same covenant God through living tradi-
> tion. Memory provides the link between past and present. . . . [T]he divine
> commands as events meet each successive generation through her tradi-
> tion, calling forth a decision, and in obedience Israel shares in the same
> redemption as her forefathers.[22]

Moses prepares for the memory cluster by shaping the memory of
the Sinai covenant and the Ten Commandments in Deuteronomy 5–6.
Moses' account is nearly identical to Exodus 20, with one exception. In
Exod. 20:8 the people are to remember the Sabbath because God worked
six days and rested on the seventh. Deut. 5:12–15 commands the people
to observe the Sabbath and remember that "you were a slave in the
land of Egypt, and the Lord your God brought you out from there with
a mighty hand and an outstretched arm." In Exodus, God is the creator who rests; in Deuteronomy, God is the protector and Lord of Israel
who acts in Israel's history. This memory clearly embraces the covenant notion that God has acted on behalf of the chosen people. Israel
now remembers the Sabbath, not because God rested, but because Israel itself "rested" from bondage and slavery through God's gracious

---

19. All quotations are taken from the New Revised Standard Version
20. Mary Katharine Deeley, "The Rhetoric of Memory: A Study of the Persuasive
Function of the Memory Commands in Deuteronomy 5–26" (Ph.D. diss., Northwestern
University, 1989). A full discussion of rhetoric and memory is included in the first two
chapters. Part of this discussion is a revision of material in chapter 3.
21. For convenience, I will refer to Moses and/or the Deuteronomist as speaker/
author of Deuteronomy. The controversies surrounding the authorship of the Pentateuch
in general and Deuteronomy in particular, though well documented, are not revelatory
for this discussion.
22. Childs, *Memory and Tradition in Israel*, 55–56.

intervention. The memory brings with it the knowledge of the intimate relationship between God and human beings. It links forever the cultic keeping of the Sabbath with the act of remembering the exodus and the divine act of creation, both of the world and of the people.[23]

Deuteronomy 6 opens with Moses boldly proclaiming, "Now this is the commandment...that the Lord your God charged me to teach you." The Israelites are given a promise of prosperity in the "land flowing with milk and honey" if they hear and observe the commandment (6:3). The Shema immediately follows as the first command (6:4). It has traditionally been considered the beginning of a section expanding on the first commandment of the Decalogue. However, like the commandment regarding the Sabbath, the Shema lifts up the old rule and subtly changes it. It is no longer enough to have "no other Gods before me"; rather, "You shall love the Lord your God with all your heart, and with all your soul, and with all your might." This passionate, intimate love dominates the command, setting the mode for the relationship between God and the people. The command to remember in chapter 5 anticipates this relationship by focusing on the God who acts in Israel's history. Remembering makes it possible for Israel to love God.

When the Israelites are asked to summon up their identities for the sake of their children who ask, "What is the meaning of the decrees and the statutes and the ordinances that the Lord our God has commanded you?" memory makes it enough to answer that God has commanded them because "We were Pharaoh's slaves in Egypt, but the Lord brought us out with a mighty hand" (Deut. 6:21). Each time the Israelites remember and reflect on God and on the Sabbath, they also remember and reflect on the exodus event, a new creation for the nation of Israel. All their subsequent actions are a response to that event. If they did not remember it, they could not respond; they could not share in the divine will as they understand it.

From this context of shaped memory Deuteronomy begins its descent into the center section with its memory commands. What the author has done in chapters 5 and 6 is lay down the key memory by which all other actions or events must be measured. God intervened in a critical moment in the history of Israel, and the import of that event was so great that even the content of theological and spiritual reflection was forever changed. For the author of Deuteronomy, keeping the Sabbath because of the memory of enslavement and holding that alongside the memory

---

23. Robert Polzin, *Moses and the Deuteronomist: A Literary Study of the Deuteronomistic History* (New York: Seabury, 1980) 54. Polzin does not include the act of creation as part of the remembered past. I think that Deuteronomy was not meant to replace the exodus account narratively but to appropriate it as part of the canonical understanding of the reader/listener.

of God's rest were crucial in establishing a theological perspective that understood the creation of Israel as a nation to be a new beginning of the world.

The Deuteronomist's theological perspective, his theology of memory, grows out of his understanding of God as creator. God, who created the world, created Israel as a people for himself. Thus, it is not a surprise that the Deuteronomist refers to Israel as a holy people of God almost immediately in the next section, Deut. 7:1–10:11. He does not name them in this way as a collective unit in chapters 5–6. He could not have done so until all shared the same worldview that the exodus was an event, celebrated as the beginning of a nation, and it was as a nation that Israel was so involved with Yahweh. Out of this understanding the Deuteronomist exhorts the people to obey the commands of Yahweh by adding other memories to the memory of the exodus/creation event. His pleas organize themselves around one narrative memory, the oath/covenant God made to the ancestors, and they focus not so much on destroying the occupying nations as on not serving or following foreign gods. Three key memories help Israel construct its worldview in harmony with what Moses understands to be God's worldview. If God's view can shape Israel's, then obedience is the only logical outcome.

Moses gives several commands immediately in Deut. 7:1–5. The Israelites are to destroy utterly the seven occupying nations. They are to show no mercy and make no covenant. They are not to marry a foreigner, because "that would turn away your children from following me, to serve other gods. Then the anger of the Lord would be kindled against you, and he would destroy you quickly" (7:4).

These commands are followed immediately by the reasons for them: "For you are a people holy to the Lord your God" (Deut. 7:6). Moses establishes a common identification that all the people share by virtue of a common memory. Israel was chosen "because the Lord loved you and kept the oath that he swore to your ancestors, that the Lord has brought you out with a mighty hand and redeemed you from the house of slavery" (7:8). Now the memory of the exodus and creation is coupled with the notion of the love and faithfulness of God. The memory yields a firm knowledge that the Lord will keep covenant with all those who love God, while repaying the ones who hate God (7:9–10). This is followed by an exhortation to keep the commandment. These last verses (7:8–11) bring out the importance of the Abrahamic covenant in a book that has the Sinaitic covenant as one of its principle foci. As such, it illustrates what Polzin believes to be an ongoing and necessary tension between the "covenant of the fathers" and the events of Horeb. Polzin points out that there are many patterns that "effect a synthesis of the covenant with the fathers and the covenant at Horeb [making] the latter a precondition of the former."[24] Polzin considers the tension necessary:

> The distinction between the covenant with the fathers and the covenant at Horeb is absolutely basic to the ideological tension within the book. The presence of an utterance in Deuteronomy of a phrase such as "the God of our fathers" or "the covenant made with our fathers" or "the oath which God swore to our fathers" brings with it associations of mercy, grace, and divine election that are at odds with the ultimate viewpoint of the book on the justice of God.[25]

It is significant that ten of the thirteen passages that Polzin cites as places of tension between the covenant of Horeb and the covenant of the fathers are in chapters 5–11, precisely where the memories of the people are being shaped by holding them in context with earlier traditions. It is memory that allows the Israelites to hold and shape their world according to their understanding and experience of God's will for them.

The shift between the memory of God's acts in the past and God's present work is slightly different in Clements's formulation:

> Here (7:7–8) the nation's election is traced to the two basic facets of God's love for Israel and his covenant with the ancestors. In this way the patriarchal covenant is introduced by the Deuteronomist in relation to the covenant at Horeb, and is seen as declaring the election which the latter brought to realization.... This use of the tradition of the covenant with the patriarchs which is the earlier history is centered on Abraham, relates the age of the patriarchs to that of Moses in a scheme of promise and fulfillment.... It is significant, therefore, that when Moses faced the possibility of Israel's destruction by God in the wilderness for its obstinacy, he appealed in his prayer to the knowledge of the patriarchal covenant (9:27).[26]

Clements understands the memories of the patriarchal and Horeb covenants to be two sides of a mystery.[27] While he denies the tension that Polzin sees between the two, his thoughts suggest the combining of two memories to shape the context in which the hearers will hear the law code. Moreover, Clements sees urgency in the command to remember the acts of God toward Israel as well as the command to love God, which is placed in the context of the exodus as creation.[28] Without these

---

24. Polzin, *Moses and the Deuteronomist*, 54.
25. Polzin, *Moses and the Deuteronomist*, 54.
26. R. E. Clements, *God's Chosen People: A Theological Interpretation of the Book of Deuteronomy* (London: SCM, 1968) 48.
27. Clements, *God's Chosen People*, 49.
28. Clements, *God's Chosen People*, 49. See also pp. 82–86.

memories, Israel would not be able to love God or obey the commandments; there would be no worldview that would enable Israel to make sense of doing so. Consequently the people could not participate in the redeeming act of God even if they wanted to do so.

As Moses continues in Deut. 7:12–16, he reiterates the promise that God will keep covenant with those who keep the ordinances of 7:1–11. The reader notes that the covenant is defined as that "which he swore to your ancestors," thus emphasizing the memory of 7:8. Verse 7:16 repeats the command to utterly destroy all the people, but adds the injunction against serving their gods, because "that would be a snare to you." The connection of the two commands indicated that the destruction of foreign peoples is not so that Israel might possess the land, but that it might not be tempted to stray from the Lord. Furthermore, with the emphasis on the memory of the covenant already sworn to Israel's ancestors as a basis for the Lord's actions, the sense of binding relationship between God and Israel is established and the course of events appears inevitable. Moses makes it clear that God initiated the covenantal relationship out of love, as was his right by creation; he makes it equally as clear that the people must now respond with obedience and love, participating in God's worldview by remembering and acting on it as if it were their own.

Having established the appropriate course of action for the people, Moses begins to anticipate possible problems or reactions. The first is logical: fear. It is countered by an appeal to memory. In an intensive form, zākōr tizkōr, the people are told, "Just remember [remember, indeed] what the Lord your God did to Pharaoh and to all Egypt" (Deut. 7:18). The promise is made that all this and more will be done to the nations of whom Israel is afraid. The appeal, then, is to allow this memory of God's power and dominion to guide and direct the actions and emotions of the people; to allow it, in effect, to shape their understanding of the future. The memory of God's action in the past helps mold the perception of the world in the present. The people will undoubtedly remember what has been said before: God is faithful to those who follow the commandments and will destroy those that do not (7:9–10). It is no wonder that Moses should follow this memory with the acknowledgment of the people's dependence on God to effect the conquest and then immediately give the command not only to burn the images of foreign gods but also to shun the very silver and gold of which they are made, "because you could be ensnared by it" (7:25). The utter abhorrence with which the people must treat the images of foreign gods takes the initial command two steps further. The first command banned service to foreign gods. The last one commands that the images first be burned and then that the materials used to make the images be considered a threat. The mention of these injunctions in connection with the memory of God's power sets up the exhortation for what is to follow.

In Deut. 8:1 Moses returns to the general injunction to keep "the entire commandment" that he commands so that the people may "go in and occupy the land that the Lord promised on oath to your ancestors." The common memory of covenant promise returns just before Moses invokes a second memory, "Remember the long way that the Lord your God has led you these forty years in the wilderness," whose purpose is "to humble you, testing you to know what was in your heart, whether or not you would keep his commandments" (8:2). This memory becomes the basis for obeying the commandments of which Moses spoke in 8:1. But how does this memory in this place effectively shape and transform the worldview of the Israelites? How does it give them the opportunity to participate in God's memory?

The answer is not long in coming. After describing the land into which God is leading the people, Moses warns against forgetting God by not keeping the commandments (Deut. 8:11). Now he repeats what was said in 6:10–11, thus intensifying the warning. He identifies God through the memories of the exodus event and the trial in the wilderness, bringing them together in 7:18–19 and 8:2–5. Moses again calls on the memory of the patriarchal covenant as a reason for God's action: "But remember the Lord your God, for it is he that gives you power to get wealth, so that he may confirm his covenant that he swore to your ancestors, as he is doing today" (8:18). Finally, Moses promises that, if the people do forget God and serve other gods, they shall be destroyed as surely as those nations that God delivered into their hand. In this instance the verb *škḥ* is in an intensive form, an imperfect preceded by an infinitive absolute (8:19). This corresponds with the intensive form of *zkr* in 7:18. This, of course, is the very memory that Moses invoked first in the exhortation to destroy the foreign nations. If one forgets the Lord, one is not keeping the commandments, thereby making a mockery of the times in the wilderness when God tested the Israelites to see if his commandments would be obeyed. Furthermore, if one forgets the Lord, one is already serving other gods (8:19), an act that will be punished by the same God who punished Pharaoh and the other nations.[29] The entire pericope intensifies the emphasis on not serving foreign gods. Why is this so important?

In building to his climax, Moses stresses the dependence of Israel on the Lord, who "crosses over before you as a devouring fire" to destroy the nations (Deut. 9:3). Moses also notes again that God acts in order

---

29. Note Deut. 8:20, "because you would not obey the voice of the Lord your God." Compare, for example, Exod. 5:2.

to "fulfill the promise that the Lord made on oath to your ancestors, to Abraham, to Isaac, and to Jacob" (9:5). The memory of that bond points out that the people themselves did nothing to earn this support. On the contrary, they are remarkably "stiff-necked." It is God's memory that continues the relationship.

The single longest passage of the Deuteronomy text begins in 9:7 and ends with 9:29. In it Moses appeals to a third memory: the people made God angry in the wilderness and at Horeb God was angry enough to have destroyed them. The double command "remember and do not forget" (9:7) points to this memory as the important one of the passage. Moses follows the command with an account of the events at Horeb and in the wilderness. It is Moses' memory speaking to the memory of the people as he fills in the details of God's anger and his own response, neither of which the people could have known, much less remembered, since Moses had been alone on the mountain. By telling them, he supplies a memory in order to shape their memories.

In this context, however, the recitation by Moses provides an interesting variation on the same story told in Exodus 32. Specifically, Deut. 9:12 does not supply all the details of the sin described by Exod. 32:8: "They have cast for themselves an image of a calf, and have worshiped it and sacrificed to it, and said 'These are your gods, O Israel, who brought you up out of the land of Egypt.' " In this memory there is explicit reference to the very sin against which Deut. 7–10 has been cautioning the people. The exhortation not to serve other gods is amplified by this memory of a time when Israel did exactly that. By not mentioning anything more than the words "an image of a calf," Moses forces his audience to supply the details of their sin for themselves. The memory of their sin exists alongside the memory of the wilderness testing. Its impact is far greater because of it. God wanted to see if they would follow the commandments, and in this instance they did not. Thus memory leads to memory.

Furthermore, in recounting the Lord's anger, Moses recalls that God wanted to blot out the name of the people from under heaven (Deut. 9:14). In essence, God wanted to make them forgotten, as they had forgotten God. Moses' prayer (9:26–29) implores God to remember Abraham, Isaac, and Jacob, and forgive the stubbornness that caused the people to make a calf in the first place. Moses' plea rests not only on the memory of the patriarchs, but also on the possible memory of the exodus that the Egyptians will have in the future: the Egyptians might say that the Lord "has brought them out to let them die in the wilderness" (9:28). Moses refers to the common memory of the covenant, the same one with which he opened this section, and calls for God's mercy on its account. Moses invokes a memory to persuade God in the context of a memory with which he hopes to persuade the people. Both God and Israel share the covenant memory. Mention of it serves to bring the stories together on a basic level while heightening the tension of the memories of God's power and the rebellion of the people. It is only because of God's memory that the people were not destroyed; their own memories may keep them from rebelling once again.

Together, Moses and the Deuteronomist complete their account in the last small section (Deut. 10:1–11). The listeners are brought full circle to the point where God commands Moses, "Get up, go on your journey at the head of the people, that they may go in and occupy the land that I swore to their ancestors to give them" (Deut. 10:11).

The movement from the memory of Sinai, to the memory of God's covenant with the fathers, to the specific memory of God's deeds in the wilderness and the rebellion of the people enhances the focus on the injunction not to serve other gods. Yahweh's rule is absolute. Without it there would be no covenant, no exodus, no promise. And without Yahweh's memory of a created world ordered by a relationship with its creator and a promise made to a people, Israel would not exist. The common memory of that relationship brings God, Moses, and the people together in an encounter that shapes each of them.

Memory provides the means to order the chaotic events of life in this world. Israel's memory puts the world together around the concept of God who enters into relationship with a people. A theology of memory suggests that God, as well as Israel, remembers, and that God's memory allows God to act in accord with the divine worldview — to offer covenant to Israel again, to free Israel from captivity again, to fashion Israel as a new or renewed people again. If, as Knierim suggests, God's dominion is the theological hub from which all other theologies radiate, God's memory that maintains the worldview is the center from which dominion is made manifest. God's power over creation means that God's purpose is served in time and that God's worldview in its timeless revelation is what makes ultimate order or sense out of chaos. As God remembers the world, God's will is fulfilled in it. Israel's memory is shaped to participate in God's ordering as fully as it is understood. By remembering God's intervention in human history, Israel shapes and transforms its communal memory in accord with it.

God's worldview does not merely include, but has as its ground, justice and righteousness; indeed, it makes them foundational for all other modes of being in relationship. Memory, then, also becomes the place where God orders the world in justice and righteousness. Where Israel does not enter into the memory, where there is discord, there can be no justice, no righteousness. To participate in God's memory is to make sense of the world according to God's understanding. A theology of memory allows the faithful community access to the notion of God's universal dominion, encourages it to enter into a worldview that sees justice and righteousness as the proper order of the world, and persuades the community to adopt God's view as their own personal history.

BIBLIOGRAPHY

Alderman, H. "The Text of Memory." In *Philosophy and Archaic Experience*. Ed. John Sallis. Pittsburgh: Duquesne University Press, 1982.

Aristotle. "De Memoria et Reminiscentia." In *The Works of Aristotle*, Vol. 3. Trans. J. I. Beare. Oxford: Clarendon Press, 1963.

Augustine. *The Confessions of St. Augustine.* Trans. John Ryan. Garden City, N.Y.: Doubleday, 1960.

Childs, Brevard S. *Memory and Tradition in Israel.* Naperville, Ill.: A.R. Allenson, 1962.

Clements, Ronald E. *God's Chosen People: A Theological Interpretation of the Book of Deuteronomy.* London: SCM Press, 1968.

Cox, J. Robert. "Against Resignation: Memory and Rhetorical Practice." Paper presented at the meeting of the International Communication Association, May 22, 1986.

Deeley, Mary Katharine. "The Rhetoric of Memory: A Study of the Persuasive Function of the Memory Commands in Deuteronomy 5–26." Ph.D. dissertation, Northwestern University, 1989.

Halbwachs, Maurice. *The Collective Memory.* Trans. Francis J. Ditter and Vida Yazdi Ditter. New York: Harper and Row, 1980.

Knierem, Rolf P. *The Task of Old Testament Theology: Substance, Method, and Cases.* Grand Rapids: Eerdmans, 1995.

Marcuse, Herbert. *The Aesthetic Dimension.* Boston: Beacon Press, 1978.

Plato. "Phaedrus." In *The Collected Dialogues.* Ed. Edith Hamilton and Huntington Cairns. Trans. R. Hackforth. New York: The Bollingen Foundation, 1961.

Polzin, Robert. *Moses and the Deuteronomist: A Literary Study of the Deuteronomistic History.* New York: Seabury, 1980.

Wohlfaith, Irving. "History, Literature, and the Text: The Case of Walter Benjamin." *Modern Language News* 96 (1981).

Yerushalmi, Yosef. *Zakhor: Jewish History and Jewish Memory.* Seattle: University of Washington, 1982.

9

Rapprochement with Rolf Knierim

Simon J. DeVries

DEFINING THE TASK OF OLD TESTAMENT THEOLOGY

My very dear friend and much admired colleague, Professor Rolf Knierim, is presently facing the widespread and stubborn resistance that he had anticipated, and that was in fact antecedently all but inevitable, considering the disarray into which the science of biblical interpretation has descended in our day. This opposition came to the fore upon the publication of his masterly tome, *The Task of Old Testament Theology.*[1] This work issues a clarion call to all who identify themselves as biblical scholars to give up interpreting the Old Testament either as a Christian book or as a Jewish book. Knierim proposes to interpret it consistently and exclusively on its own terms, foreswearing the attempt to explain it in terms of its function in the Christian Bible, or conversely in the light of the Talmud and similar ancient Jewish works.

Seeking an Inner-Old Testament Standard

Many adherents of either method seem to have strong misgivings about Knierim's elemental claim that the Old Testament contains in itself its own principles for interpretation and validation, and needs neither the New Testament and Christian doctrine nor the teachings of the rabbis to give it meaning and authority.

Certainly Knierim would not invalidate — nor would I — a competently developed New Testament theology, one that would be both exegetically informed and willing to make a place for the New Testament's own implicit concept of scriptural revelation, that which defines the Old Testament as its own holy Scripture, *hē graphē.* Nor would there be any question about the legitimacy of a *biblical* theology as such, that is, one drawn equally from both Testaments, presupposing a principle of unbroken continuity from the one Testament to the other. There is, furthermore, authenticity as well as integrity in Jewish exegetical tradition, from early sources through late, employing Scripture according to its own special hermeneutic. Those who are presently opposing Knierim no doubt stand in one of these traditions — as do we all — but

---

1. Rolf P. Knierim, *The Task of Old Testament Theology: Substance, Method, and Cases* (Grand Rapids: Eerdmans, 1995). See my review in *RelSRev* 24, no. 1 (January 1998) 37–42.

it would be especially wrong to deny the claim of the Old Testament as a literary and spiritual document, independent of the movements that it inspired, to contain its own authentic testimony concerning God and his world.

Identifying the Old Testament's Contemporary Relevance

The questions that this immediately raises are, What is authentic and what is inauthentic testimony with regard to the Old Testament Scripture? and, By what methods are we to elucidate the Old Testament in order to present a clear picture of the processes involved in inner-scriptural self-validation? But we must go beyond the customary methods of historical/philological interpretation if we are to know how we are to answer these questions. We need to know whether the Old Testament's imperatives apply equally to us, living in our own time and place, far removed from those of the Bible itself. And if so, then we need also to know by what analogies this transfer is to be accomplished. One thing is for certain: no one truly understands Scripture — Old Testament or New Testament — unless he or she is willing to respond positively and obediently to its unnuanced demand for contemporary application. The reason is that the Bible cannot be adequately understood or appropriately applied unless treated as God's living word addressed to us and to all humankind, for that is what it claims to be.

Discovering a Distinctively Old Testament Theology

To those who have been trained to interpret the Old Testament out of Christian or out of Jewish precommitments, I have this to say: although both religions have dipped deeply into this fountain, neither of the two individually or separately — or the two of them together — has plumbed the bottom. Apart from the rich tradition that each has borrowed from the Old Testament, there remain profound levels of truth and insight that belong to it alone, and that justify, or rather, demand, attention to what the Old Testament claims entirely on its own concerning the God who created the universe.

I mention a single example by way of illustration: the divine names in the Old Testament. As a whole, the Old Testament adheres faithfully to all that is implied in the proper name of its god, Yahweh.[2] Out of superstition and excessive fastidiousness, this ineffable name was handed

---

2. It is highly significant that the name by which the biblical God reveals himself is unique. To say that the name Yahweh is personal is to say that it is nongeneric. It is not a definition name, intended for identification and classification. Thus it is not like the word "God" (or "god"), which is a generic word that may be used as a proper name. The god of Israel has a proper name, Yahweh, the etiology of which is given in the well-known third chapter of Exodus. There are many Els and many Baals, but only one Yahweh. The gods of the polytheistic religions could be classified and categorized. They were all no more

down by Second Temple Judaism in the form of sterile surrogates, and by early Christianity it was exchanged for quasi-equivalents taken from the refuse heap of empire-age eclecticism.[3]

Identifying and Validating the Competing Voices

Let us understand that Knierim is demanding a venture that far transcends a primitivistic return to undifferentiated origins. There are in fact two parts to his quest. First, he urges that every identifiable voice and viewpoint behind the preserved text of the Old Testament be scrutinized for its own special message, as well as weighed and examined for evidence of its place within the history of transmission as a definable element continuing from one literary unit to others more complex and more sophisticated. This task will be anything but easy, and Knierim is well aware that he cannot accomplish it by himself or in collaboration with his pupils. It will require the participation of Old Testament scholars everywhere, for no scholar or group of scholars is in a position to organize international scholarship to accomplish so vast a task. The best that anyone might expect and hope for is that a significant number of convinced scholars, once they have understood and accepted their obligation as interpreters of the sacred word, will voluntarily and enthusiastically give themselves to this task.

The second part of Knierim's quest is to apply, and to help other scholars apply, a standard method for validation of the individual and often competing voices behind the Old Testament text, once they have been isolated and identified. They will have the task of aligning the passages in question to similar (or even identical) passages elsewhere, and to show how each fits into the evolving structure of the book of which it is a part, and eventually into the Old Testament as a whole. Once this has been done, another task will be to validate it for all ages to come as a divine message concerning the fate and destiny of all humankind.

Knierim has taught us that we must take special pains to carry out this task faithfully. To become a competent and imaginative Bible critic

---

than separate aspects or manifestations of a single, monistic reality; thus they had generic names, representing their function within the cosmos. To know such names was to have a handle on them and a way of controlling them to the worshiper's interest. These gods approached genuine personalism in no more than a tangential way, that is, representatively and analogically, resulting inevitably in schematicism and caricature.

3. It is commonly recognized that in intertestamental Judaism the practice was to pronounce Adonai ("My Lord") wherever the Tetragrammaton (YHWH) was encountered in the biblical text. Besides this, popular piety employed surrogates like "the Glory" or "the Name" whenever God was mentioned. The New Testament no longer remembers that the God of Israel once had the name Yahweh, and refers to God under the Greek equivalents. It is a moot question whether the name *Kyrios* came to Christ as an equivalent for Adonai (thus effectually identifying him as God) or as an honorific name for an entire class of beings populating the world between the earth and heaven.

one must first train painstakingly. He or she is like an opera singer or a virtuoso violinist, practicing the music a thousand times over in order to be able to render it with ease and grace when performing it before an audience. I think that this is a happy and well-suited simile. We biblical scholars must enjoy and come alive in the joyous task of interpreting the Bible, acknowledging by the vitality of our study of it that it is first of all a word from God for ourselves, one that we have listened to often and remembered well.

Knierim has taught his pupils to become adept in the methods of contemporary biblical criticism. They may not hurry through this, for every weighty consideration must be aired and every detail of importance must be examined. Important discoveries in the area of biblical interpretation do not come randomly or by inadvertence; they come through diligence combined with objectivity and impartiality.

The Application of *Sachkritik*

A special term that Knierim has placed before his students in this connection is the German term *Sachkritik*.[4] This means that in the final analysis, the consideration that gives validity and authority to Bible interpretation is whether it is *sachlich*, by which he means appropriate and effective in a realistic and personal way. This requires that the Old Testament be interviewed first of all for its actual, ostensible meaning within its ancient context, and only then put to analogous use in addressing the problems of contemporary human life. In this use *sachlich* means practical and practicable, having an intentionality with regard to high goals of understanding and performance. It also means grounded in actual facts and shaped towards realistic goals.

To the problem of what is truly authoritative in the Old Testament, and in the Bible generally, this concept provides an effective and eminently realizable answer. The choice of the word *Sachkritik*, when ap-

---

4. See Knierim's statement in *Task of Old Testament Theology* (495): "The history of ancient Israel's theology, including the history of the transmission of its theological traditions, belongs to the genre of history writing. In this genre, the question of the validity of each stage or voice or of the total history may or may not be raised and answered. As soon as the question of validity is raised, both a comparative method and substantive criteria for comparison have to be developed by which not only the various theological concepts and messages of each setting but also the total history itself may be evaluated, including the extant 'canonic' level(s) of the Old Testament. In view of this question, an approach via the history of the Old Testament's theologies is relative because every historical observation remains subject to the questions why and how it is theologically valid. The task of Old Testament theology, as of any theology, is constituted by the substance-critical approach." In this connection one should consider the valuable discussion in the doctoral dissertation of Knierim's student Wonil Kim, "Toward a Substance-Critical Task of Old Testament Theology" (Ph.D. diss., Claremont Graduate School, 1996), in particular the section "Question of Substance-Criticism: Confusing Description with Norm."

plied to the interpretation of the Old Testament, immediately commits one to the hermeneutic of practicality and realizability. It is the enemy of fanciful proposals and sloppy methods. It assumes that every discernible voice coming to our attention in the process of biblical study has a reason for being where it is and sounding as it does. It acknowledges that God does not play games in offering holy Scripture. In taking up *Sachkritik,* one is committed to listen as well as one is able, and to take up in all earnestness those things about which the biblical text shows itself to be in earnest.

MY *ACHIEVEMENTS* IN DIALOGUE WITH KNIERIM'S *TASK*

My Search for the Center of Old Testament Authority

I have found that, once I probe deeply enough to think I understand what Knierim is saying, I almost always agree with him. Oftentimes he has new and original insights about which I have not thought. As time has passed, I have found that he has usually agreed as well with most of what I have had to say, and in a certain sense one of my own publications appears to fit well the description of what he means by *Sachkritik,* even though I have not previously thought of it under this rubric. In my book *Achievements of Biblical Religion: A Prolegomenon to Old Testament Theology,*[5] I have done as he now is doing in dealing with the problem of the source of authority in the Old Testament. I wrote there that the Old Testament does not derive its authority from the fact that the New Testament cites it as Scripture, or because it is part of the church's holy book, or because "inspired men" wrote it. For me, both its authority and its power come from its own *sachlich* self-testimony, borne out in the spiritual experience of generations of persons who have benefited from it. Furthermore, I dealt there with this question: Where and in what way does the Old Testament address us as moderns, and in what way does its authority have its effect on us? I ask, Is everything in the Old Testament equally authoritative for us? For instance, are only the Jews expected to keep its so-called ceremonial laws, such as circumcision and Sabbath observance?

When pressed, the adherents of various modern religious groups may admit what the actual source of authority is in their Old Testament. Sunday school pietists are apt to seize upon inspiring sayings and/or examples; perhaps it is this that accounts for the continuing popularity of praiseworthy figures chosen from the Old Testament, as compared with the New Testament. If it is not pious role models that are being sought, it may be amusement and diversion — lively stories to enjoy!

---

5. Lanham, Md.: University Press of America, 1983.

Generally, the biblicistic and fundamentalistic Christian will agree with this use of the Old Testament, but will nevertheless maintain that the entire Bible — Old Testament and New — has to be believed and obeyed because it is "inspired by the Holy Spirit" and is therefore in its totality the veritable "word of God." To maintain this position, they who insist on this put themselves in the difficult position of having to defend absolutely everything the Bible has to say — even when it flatly contradicts itself! Legions of eager apologists search for ever more ingenious ways of getting around the difficult problems presented by individual biblical texts when the events they report are taken as literally historical.

Inadequate and Misleading Proposals

Here, then, are the main apologetic and hermeneutical possibilities: (1) everything in the Bible is God's word and therefore has to be believed and obeyed (the biblicist); (2) whatever supports the rules and mores of "our" movement has to be obeyed — the rest is also God's word but does not pertain to us (the sectarian); and (3) whatever supports and inspires our movement works as God's word for us (the religious liberal). In these definitions, God no longer rules in fact, but is subjected to human rule.

The fault in these definitions of the source and nature of biblical authority is, to be sure, their subjectivism and arbitrariness. There is only one effective way of combating them, and that is to come up with a basis of biblical (and now specifically Old Testament) authority from within the Bible itself. Let the Old Testament be its own judge! Is this possible, and if so, how are we to carry out an interview with it? Harder still, since there are so many different ways of exegeting and expounding the Old Testament, how are we to identify which voices are worth listening to among the diverse and internally multivocal Old Testament witnesses, along with identifying which exegetes are worth listening to among contemporary biblical scholars, and Old Testament specialists in particular?

One good thing to keep in mind is that we have the prerogative of judging Scripture, but Scripture will judge us by how we respond to it. Unmistakably and unavoidably, it speaks to us and calls us to task. Anyone who doubts this has not even begun to understand what Scripture is all about.

Two Converging Lines

In my book I have made a number of observations that seem congenial in scope and spirit to what Rolf Knierim has been writing. At the beginning I proposed two lines for analyzing the content of the Old Testament: (1) that in examining the whole range of biblical witnesses, it is significant and essential continuity among them, illumined and placed in perspective by relevant elements of discontinuity, that promises to be the most revealing of what is most central and essential in the Old Testament; (2) that in examining the cultural context of the Bible, it will be the Old Testament's divergence from the norms of its cultural setting and its distinctiveness in the context of what it shares with its neighbors, illumined and placed in perspective by elements of commonality, that promise to be the most revealing of what is most central and essential.

What follows in the next several pages are extracts from my book that I think are the most evocative in seeking rapprochement with the program that Knierim has set before us, interspersed with comments designed to stimulate dialogue between us, as well as among scholars everywhere who are willing to allow the Old Testament, and the distinctive religion that it reveals, to show us the truths it claims to stand for entirely on its own authority, independently of the sometimes helpful, sometimes irksome, adaptations on the part of those who speak from the allegedly more complete and perfect religious systems that claim the Old Testament as their heritage.

Significant and Essential Continuity

The virtue of employing these two criteria of scriptural authority is that they point away from the subjectivistic and the formalistic viewpoints and allow the Old Testament to have its full effect as the criterion of its own authority.

In mentioning that it is important when "relevant elements of discontinuity" among biblical witnesses serve to illumine the "significant and essential continuity" among elements of commonality, I point to a solution to the problem of seemingly unchecked variety within the Old Testament. To be judged as significant, every element must be subjected to two further criteria: (1) what is held in common amidst divergence, and (2) what is different in the presence of commonality. A way of framing the situation is to ask, What is it that gives the Old Testament its relative cohesiveness in the face of all that is different in it from book to book, from passage to passage, and from verse to verse? We gladly refrain from artificial harmonizing, because it is, after all, the uncensored variety within the Old Testament that brings out to greater significance the surviving elements of commonality. To be judged as significant, the Old Testament's elements of commonness must not be accidental or haphazard, but constitutional, that is, necessarily derived from its essential nature, for only what is constitutionally held in common has the internal cohesiveness and tenacity to remain significant in the face of widely held and persistent variety.

If this is accepted as one criterion of scriptural significance, we readily see why most, if not all, previous proposals have fallen short. Generations of Christians have held that it is the scattered elements of messianic prediction that have made the Old Testament authoritative, yet we soon discover that the passages that have been interpreted as direct references to Christ are actually very few and widely dispersed — certainly anything but significantly common to all witnesses.

Observant Jews point to the Torah as the basis of the Old Testament's authority, and while it may readily be admitted that the Torah became centrally significant in the process of the Old Testament's development, it had not been so from the first. Out of considerable variety in early Israel's cultic tradition, this single symbol eventually emerged as a unifying center, but it is certain that it was not so from the beginning. The people of Israel grew up into Torah observance through the passage of the centuries. The act of choosing the Torah as an external code for Jewish self-definition did in fact impose a certain kind of formal uniformity and conformity upon the Jewish people, but the commonness that was thus created was artificial and not organic. Similarly, Christian sects of various kinds have chosen one or another external code of conduct to become the basis of their own corporate unity, often rendering it highly nomistic and coercive. Social models chosen for this may actually prove to be uncongenial with others that offer themselves. The Amish, for example, adopt more the anticultural models of sectarianism flowing from the fringes of New Testament piety, while the Mormons appeal more to Old Testament models of external morality, but all fall short of a firm grounding in what is genuinely and constitutionally common in scriptural forms of piety.

Everyone ransacks the Old Testament for something that seems to echo what happens to be cherished as of central importance at the moment. Among liberal preachers it is likely to be the courageous independence of the great preexilic prophets, but we see that this trait is not at all centrally common in the Old Testament and is not at all distinctive of it. But things can become still worse. If portions of the Old Testament fail to promote virtues or ideals popular today, then ways will be found to rewrite or reexegete the texts to make them seem to preach the opposite, as, for instance, is done by extreme feminist reconstructionists with the Old Testament's laws and narratives, which are ineradicably patriarchal in their social ideology. The Old Testament is thus bent to what is today called "political correctness."

All this great mischief is occasioned by the failure to detect the true center of Old Testament piety and to apply it to ourselves. In order to avoid such an unhappy outcome, I recommend following my definition. We are searching for the Old Testament's authentic center of authority, and we are searching for it in what shows itself to be constitutionally common in the midst of what is significantly variegated. What else can this authentic center be than God's own being? Not just any god, but the god who was worshiped as "God" in Israel and in the church. Not many gods — one for each and every primeval force — but the one, only God, who relates to his most sensible and most understanding creatures as a person who evokes and nurtures their own existence as persons. Not God therefore as a sublime idea, but as the embodiment of personal power and presence, the God who creates, the God who judges, the God who redeems. Above all, it is the God who cares deeply about his people and commits himself without restraint to their well-being, who is distinctive of biblical religion, Old Testament and New Testament.[6]

We shall discover in following this clue that what is centrally affirmed amidst all the Old Testament's varieties of expression is what I have called "personalistic monotheism."[7] What I mean by this is congenial to what Samuel Terrien calls "the elusive presence," although his choice of words places the emphasis on an epistemological rather than ontological distinction, that is, in the experience of God's ineffable presentness in the midst of all finite phenomena, and particularly in moments and situations in which his worshipers become fully aware of him, but not in such a way that he can be seized and held.[8] I like this concept very much, and I do agree that it is centrally significant for biblical piety, but I do not think that it is as useful in the present discussion as my term, "personalistic monotheism." By "personalistic" I refer to Yahweh as the one, only God, who shows himself to be a caring Person in all his acts and works while treating us as persons. I hold that this definition is a basis of all that the Old Testament witnesses hold in common. This confession is what binds God's followers together as God's people from age to age and forever.

---

6. See my discussion later in this essay under the heading, "A Sin-guilt-punishment Mechanism." One of the most astounding divine self-declarations in the Old Testament is in Hos. 11:7–9, in which Yahweh declares his decision to exercise his sovereign lordship in a refusal to punish blameworthy Israel: "I will not execute my fierce anger; I will not again destroy Ephraim; for I am God and no mortal, the Holy One in your midst, and I will not come to destroy." Other religions suppose that it is the essential duty and prerogative of the world of deity to render judgment on wrongdoing throughout the cosmos. While not denying this, Yahwism refuses to lock God into a mechanism of sin-guilt-punishment. This is, in the last analysis, the foundation of the central biblical concept of divine grace — God's absolute freedom to act according to his will, to punish or to forgive. He retains unto himself the freedom to forgive the sinner quite apart form the normal working of the laws of recompense and retribution.

7. See DeVries, *Achievements of Biblical Religion*, 63–66.

8. Samuel L. Terrien, *The Elusive Presence: Toward a New Biblical Theology* (San Francisco: Harper and Row, 1978).

Divergence and Discontinuity within Israel's Cultural Setting

Perhaps this paragraph should have appeared before the foregoing paragraphs, because the matter with which it deals is by all counts the lesser understood. Be that as it may, it is clear that it complements what has just been said about the significance of common elements in the Old Testament. The condition of discontinuity is equally significant, and it grows in our eyes as we come to learn more about the remarkable resemblances between the ideals of the Old Testament in the context of ancient Near Eastern models of piety and morals. By all means, we must see the Old Testament within the context of its age and the civilization in which it was produced. Here again we discover significant discontinuity amidst the continuity, but it is the continuity between the Old Testament and its environment that provides the disruptive factor in the discussion, because one readily supposes that the Bible is absolutely different from heathen culture. To be sure, if we follow traditional ways of interpreting Bible history, we are bound to assume that the patriarchs of the Genesis story were ethnically distinct from all the peoples whom they encountered. On the whole, however, Abraham, Isaac, and Jacob lived on familiar, if not always friendly, terms with their neighbors. According to the Genesis story, Abram did not leave Ur out of hostility towards his fellow Urians, but because he received a call from Yahweh, a god he had not known before. Reading on through Genesis to its conclusion, we find that the patriarchs and their families live in peace with their neighbors in spite of the fact that they are sojourners in their midst. It is only in the narratives of Exodus through Numbers that an element of ethnic hostility begins to emerge, and this becomes thematic in the entire corpus of settlement stories in Numbers through Joshua. What I am saying is that we have been mistaken in emphasizing elements of hostility between the patriarchs and their environment. On the other hand, as we progress in our reading through the Old Testament, we encounter more and more of the attitude that Israel should be a separate and distinctive people, refusing to tolerate the presence of other ethnic groups within the territory it claimed. Unmistakably, this is erroneously ideological and should be judged accordingly.[9]

For every significant religious practice or theological concept cherished among the Hebrew people there was a corresponding practice or concept among many or all its neighbors. Furthermore, familiar motifs in heathen myth often lie at a nonverbal sublevel in the background of the Old Testament text itself.[10] Not surprisingly, certain of the closest

---

9. See in Knierim, *Task of Old Testament Theology*, "Justice in the Old Testament" (86–122) and "Food, Land, and Justice" (239–43.).

10. For example, the serpent, nakedness, secret tree, knowledge of good and evil, and

apparent parallels are found in the records of the Ugaritic, Syrian, and Palestinian Semites — all ethnic and linguistic cousins of the Hebrews. The genres of prayer, of wisdom, of the love song, of the heroic epic, and so forth are shared by the Hebrews with their neighbors. The Hebrew language is itself a local dialect of Canaanite. Aesthetic elements such as rhythm and poetic lyricism belong to both bodies of literature. I could go on, but enough has been said to make the point that there was widespread similarity throughout the cultural, ethnic, and linguistic group known as West Semitic, to which the Hebrews belonged.

When these things are mentioned, it is easy to understand why the people of the Old Testament are often depicted as being strongly tempted by Canaanite and other heathen cultural and religious practices. There were indeed numerous elements of commonality between them. Nevertheless, when we look for elements of significant discontinuity, we are brought face to face with one of the key elements of that which gives distinctiveness to the Israelite religion, and once again we discover that the most distinctive element of all is the belief in only one God, Yahweh, who reveals himself as a deity who knows, loves, and cares for his people. What is also distinctive and significant is Israel's undeserved prerogative of being Yahweh's chosen and covenanted people.

Let it be added that what is common from one culture to another is not, in the final analysis, as significant as what is different — essentially and constitutionally different. Far less important than what the people of Israel shared with their neighbors was what separated them from those neighbors; and what was most important of all was an awareness that they were not inherently better than their neighbors, but only that Yahweh had chosen them, and had done so through no merit of their own.

THE CONVERGENCE OF TWO LINES OF ANALYSIS

It appears to me that the line of analysis that I have been following contributes significantly to what Knierim calls *Sachkritik*, because it promises to be useful in defining what is essential about Old Testament religion and at the same time helps us identify the source of its authority. When these two lines — the agreement on essentials among relevant biblical witnesses, and the distinctive differences between them and their neighbors — converge, we have every reason to believe that we have arrived at the core of Old Testament religion. Furthermore, while

---

aprons made of leaves in the story of the fall of Genesis — all with well-known fertility religion innuendos.

reviewing every individual detail of commonness and of divergence, in the end we shall discover that we have arrived at the same result as previously: what is most essential and distinctive in the Old Testament is its belief in a God who is one in his being and personalistic in his dealings with humankind.

The Rejection of Alternative Choices

I am willing to defend this conclusion in detail and I am confident that in the end it will prove to be the most satisfying answer to the question of Old Testament authoritativeness. No, it is not the specialness and the chosenness of Yahweh's ancient people, Israel. Nor is it the so-called messianic prophecies. Nor is it instances of prophetic courage or stories of its pious heroes. It is what I call personalistic monotheism that accounts for everything that is true and worthwhile.

Some will ask, "How about the centrality of election and the covenant?" True, these are central, but I subsume them under the concept of God's sublime personalism. On the other hand, others will ask, "How about Jesus Christ and the Trinity? Are they not at the core of biblical faith?" Yes and no: yes if we are talking about New Testament theology or biblical theology as a whole; certainly no if we remain with Old Testament theology.

This is a clear and consistent answer to what many may consider to be a crucial fault, but I consider it to be an advantage rather than a fault. As I have said, I do believe that there is significance in Old Testament piety altogether separately from the Jewish and the Christian forms of piety that have diverged from it. Each adaptation enjoys a relatively complete and consistent system for practicing its own peculiar form of biblical religion. Each is true and satisfying within its special set of presuppositions, but to hold to the one or the other does not render Old Testament religion as antiquated and superseded, and certainly it does not identify it as false or idle. The reason for making this claim is that the God who reveals himself in Old Testament religion is in fact the same God who is adored by Christians and Jews. Among the many things that divide the adherents of the Judeo-Christian tradition from one another, this unifying factor remains firm and unaltered.

Relevance to Modern Concerns

At this juncture, it appears that I have done all that could be asked of me in defining what is central and essential about Old Testament religion. That is what Knierim has also set himself to do. There is, however, the remaining question whether this answer is worthy of acceptance by men and women in the modern world. It was valid and true for the ancient Hebrew, but is it also valid and true in today's world?

When I am faced with this question, the answer I begin to formulate first takes note of such "evidences" as the astounding survivability of the two religious movements having their ground in Old Testament faith and piety: Judaism and Christianity. On the other hand, a very fruitful way to assay the contributions of biblical religion, including specifically Old Testament religion, will be to point to particular benefits that follow from faith in the distinctively personalistic God of the Bible.

Beneficial Effects

I take special note of the rich contribution that Judeo-Christian culture has made toward the improvements taken for granted in modern life — democracy above all. In addition, modern specialists in psychological healing have found that most of their discoveries were already a part of biblical anthropology — for example, a holistic concept of the human personality. Though we in our time cannot claim credit for these blessings, for others before us have achieved them, we certainly need to have unbounded gratitude for them.

Here is where comparing ancient Near Eastern culture and that of the Old Testament can be the most illuminating. Clearly the more helpful and at the same time the more humanly satisfying are the following elements of Old Testament theology: (1) its paradoxical belief in a transcendent God who is also immanent in all of creaturely reality and especially in human life; (2) its concept of a divine image mirrored in human personhood; (3) its promotion of a life of fulfilling integrity within a caring and covenanting community; (4) its understanding of history as responsible dialogue with God; and (5) its sense of meaning and purpose in the evils of finite existence.

These five benefits accrue as well in New Testament theology, and in biblical theology in general, but let it be observed in any case that they were first firmly set forth in Old Testament theology. They affect our understanding of God, humankind, society, history, and existence. This is not the place to do so in detail, but I am prepared to explain at length why they validate Old Testament theology as worthy of acceptance and practice. These elements are not dry and abstract doctrinal propositions, they are specific ways in which Old Testament insights continue to have relevance and usefulness in every age.

A Scarlet Thread

What, then, is normative in the Old Testament, and in the Bible comprehensively? In a broad sense, that which accounts for its continuity amidst all its discontinuity, and at the same time that which accounts for those truly distinctive elements of biblical faith that emerge

out of the midst of a commonality shared with its ancient cultural
environment: monotheistic personalism (or, if you will, personalistic
monotheism). This is the scarlet thread that runs through the entire
biblical heritage while marking it off from ancient and modern rivals.[11]

Another way of putting this is to say that what is normative in the
Old Testament and the entire holy Scripture is (1) what made and makes
biblical religion distinctive; (2) what gave it, and gives it, the vigor
to survive every trial and vicissitude; and (3) what makes it relevant
for all ages of history and for all conditions of human existence. Ultimately, these three tests are the same, for only those elements that were
distinctive in the Old Testament contributed to the survival of biblical
faith, and only those same elements retain relevance for contemporary
human life.

ELEMENTS SHARED BY OLD TESTAMENT RELIGION
WITH OTHER ANCIENT RELIGIONS

What has been stated is not to be taken as a denigration of nondistinctive elements in biblical religion, or of nonauthentic modifications
within the biblical tradition. Each of these has brought to expression
an important concern in humanity's ongoing struggle to cope with the
problems and trials of existence. In the face of contemporary problems,
certain nondistinctive elements may turn out to retain some usefulness,
even though they did represent a blurred or one-sided apprehension of
the truth within their ancient setting.

We moderns need to realize, for instance, that the ancient myths
were, after all, *holy words*, so that, if we can only put ourselves into a
humble and receptive mood, we too may hear some profound and perhaps worthy truth coming to expression in them. All the same, it is
important for us to know where we are to dig our trenches in defending the citadel of biblical truth. When modern understanding comes to
the point of discarding certain previous modes of thought that can no
longer aid authentic human self-understanding, it will be essential that
we learn to distinguish between what the Bible stands for and what it
does not stand for, between what it has borrowed from its culture and
what it has added of distinctive and creative growth to the common
cultural heritage. Contemporary Western civilization is in a very large
degree *biblical* civilization, even though much of it, as it appears in a

---

11. I may be mistaken, but I think that my term "personalistic monotheism" covers
most of what Knierim means in the phrase "God as Yahweh, Yahweh as God." Whatever
its remote origin, the name Yahweh, as it is employed in the Old Testament, is distinctly
personal (as compared with a generic word like "God," which we moderns employ as the
name of a divine person).

modern guise, may prove to be ephemeral, incidental, nonessential, or nondistinctive.

Let us review briefly the main elements shared by ancient biblical religion with the religious cultures of its time, identifying the various points at which it has made a significant modification.

An Awareness of the Holy

It is not just in the Bible that one may encounter the Holy, but in each of its rival contemporary faiths as well. It is found in the Egyptian, Canaanite, and Mesopotamian religions, and also among the Hittites, the Greeks, and so forth. All the faiths and religions of the world are based on an awareness of the Holy. In humankind's confrontation with the supernatural, there are two separate elements: (1) revulsion, a fleeing away and a dread-filled terror; and (2) attraction, a fascination. It is the tension between these two, the revulsion and the attraction together, that furnishes the dynamic of all vital religion.[12]

Yahwism definitely had that quality. It was not just an abstract, intellectual, theoretical system of dogma, but a participation in a deep, vital experience of the ineffable presence of the divine. What makes a difference in the biblical heritage is the element of covenantal integrity, banishing the irrational and the demonic from numinous dread. The God who reveals himself to his people does indeed confront them with his awesome majesty and power, sometimes in wrath rather than with reassuring words of salvation. Yet this God is a god who reveals himself as father to his people, one who cares and one who commits himself irrevocably to his people's well-being. Even while Israel experienced the divine wrath, they continued to receive the assurance that Yahweh was present with them, sharing in their suffering,[13] for their highest and ultimate good.

It is at this point that we observe a clear demarcation between biblical religion and nonbiblical religion. Seen most remarkably in Mesopotamian religion, there was a very high level of anxiety throughout ancient Near Eastern culture. It never succeeded in attaining to a concept of one God in control of all creation, an authentically personal and all-powerful God infinitely committed to the good of his people, acting without ulterior motivation. The God of the Bible is essentially different from the other gods in that he does not seek anything from his people except their responding loyalty and spiritual devotion. He is

---

12. The classic description is in Rudolf Otto's book *The Idea of the Holy* (original edition in German, 1917).

13. We expect next to read that Jesus was the one who demonstrated God's compassionate participation by dying an innocent and efficacious death, but this is already exemplified in Jeremiah and in Job in particular, and the people of Israel in general.

not there to be flattered. He is not there that they might carry on an elaborate cultic institution in his honor. Even though the people of the Bible do adopt cultic and institutional forms as vehicles of their piety, these are, at least in principle, subordinated to the understanding that Yahweh had called and chosen them, graciously accepting their worship as an expression of their gratitude and devotion. The experience of his numinous presence, though it might stun and shock and astound, is nonetheless accompanied by the assurance of Yahweh's beneficent intent.

Anthropomorphic Supernaturalism

Anthropomorphic analogues applied to Yahweh are those exclusively that are compatible with the image of transcendental personalism. These are, specifically, the image of lordship — implying a proprietorship of accepting and belonging — and of parenthood. The fatherhood of God is an especially potent image. Yahweh is a father who is involved in the very life of his people, not in a generative way, but as an infinitely parenting Person. He nurtures, disciplines, and, above all, loves. Although these are themselves anthropomorphic or anthropopathic images — symbols borrowed from the observation of human emotion — they avoid the attribution to deity of every human passion and craving that characterized the polytheistic religions of Israel's neighbors. Biblical anthropomorphism selects only those qualities that accentuate the worthy and are expressive of personhood, those that imply integrity and genuine spiritual concern. These happen to be the very same elements that also lend dignity to human personhood, which explains why biblical piety subsequently remains so deeply concerned with spiritual and intersocial issues in human relationships.

A Sin-guilt-punishment Mechanism

Many interpretations of the Bible go astray in attributing to it the doctrine of a sin-guilt-punishment mechanism, as though this were distinctive of the Bible in comparison with other religions. This is not true. All the religions of the ancient Near East believed in this mechanism. The difference in the biblical view is that it breaks an automatic or dynamistic connection between them. The divine superintendency over cosmic morality is guarded in such a way as to preserve God's sovereign freedom, and at the same time humankind's freedom, which together allow for a turning away from entrapment in this mechanism. It is this that directly makes possible an authentic responsibleness in human beings before God, even while they are in their sin and transgression. In other words, for the Bible — the Old as well as the New Testament — neither God nor humankind is locked into a fatalistic pattern. To be sure, there is a direct connection between sin, punishment, and suffering, but this does not indelibly label God as the judge of man as criminal. Even though biblical humankind is never excused of responsibility for sin and its consequences, Yahweh's sovereign freedom allows the creatively new to emerge as a fresh start with the divine-human relationship. Every day is thus a new day of opportunity, and at the same time, of responsibility to make good use of the opportunity. Even while sinners are experiencing the consequences of their sin, the opportunity of repentance and the promise of restoration are continually being held out to them. This authentically biblical belief is exactly what guilty people need to know and to hear. Pastors and other spiritual advisors must be cautious about telling their parishioners that their suffering is not connected with some fault or transgression of their own, for it may well be that it is.

Sins have consequences — immediate or only eventual — that are certain to come to pass in the normal pattern of things. It does no good to obscure the personal element of responsibility as people suffer the effects of their own or some other person's folly. It is mentally healthful, as a matter of fact, to deal honestly with these realities. Nevertheless, the biblical message is that, while we are in our sin, God's grace is constantly being held out to us — not just once but continually. Every day may be a new day of salvation if we are willing to receive it and use it as such.[14] Although God does not accept our sin, he does accept us as sinners. This is something that the Bible alone has learned to say clearly, and in the New Testament it adds a dramatic emphasis on God's giving of his own Son in order to show that he even takes suffering for human sin upon himself.[15]

Cultic Institutionalism

Another element that biblical religion shares with other religions is cultic institutionalism, involving a professional priesthood or ministry, a pattern of ritual and administration, along with special structures and properties set aside for its interests. The people of the Bible had these as well as the other peoples of their environment. Ancient Israel even had bloody sacrifices.[16] In this connection it is interesting to read Gerhard von Rad's explanation of the probable historical process by which the ancient Israelites, penetrating into the land of Canaan, occupied

---

14. Cf. Ps. 95:7b–8a: "O that today you would hearken to his voice! Harden not your hearts, as at Meribah."

15. See note 13.

16. But see the astounding statement in Ps. 51:16–17, "For thou hast no delight in sacrifice; were I to give a burnt offering, thou wouldst not be pleased. The sacrifice acceptable to God is a broken spirit; a broken and contrite heart, O God, thou wilt not despise."

various shrine sites in the land, taking them over and, as it were, re-baptizing them, turning them into Yahweh shrines. They adopted much of the ritual and perhaps also the actual priestly personnel from these ancient shrines.[17] Thus, the development of an elaborate cultic appara-tus among the ancient Israelites represented an element of significant compromise with a completely different order of religious practice. This became especially prominent with the rise of David's monarchy and the building of Solomon's temple. Ancient Yahwism remained sturdy enough, however, to make this adaptation without committing whole-sale apostasy from its essential principles. True, there was a struggle, but Judahite Yahwism gradually eliminated inimical elements, and the exile to Babylon turned the tide permanently. It became possible to en-rich biblical worship by incorporating sanitized pagan myth and ritual. Traditional cultic patterns and structures became entirely ancillary to the celebration of covenant personalism.

Thus, the people of the Old Testament did not reject formal worship, nor did they repudiate a professional priesthood. On the contrary, these became rigidly fixed in theory and practice, so that only traumatic his-torical forces were able to uproot the old and allow entrance for the new. Eventually, biblical faith did find the means to survive without the tra-ditional cult and priesthood. We who are heirs of the biblical tradition see in this an important lesson concerning the proper place for churchly structures, policies, and personnel. To be authentically biblical, we need to keep these elements in a place of subordination and instrumentality, never allowing them to become an end in themselves. We need to learn especially from the prebiblical and nonbiblical religions how remorse-lessly an institutionalized religious apparatus can quench the spark of an authentically personalistic faith.

A Theological Basis for Morality

Theological ideals undergirding moral sanctions are not something that we find only in the Bible. As we study the documents of faith outside Is-rael, we find that there, too, moral behavior has a theology to support it. The Old and New Testaments, however, place ethics on the firm ground provided by the Bible's distinctive theology, far different from that of Israel's ancient neighbors. The latter were driven to morality chiefly out of fear, while the people of the Old Testament were drawn to morality out of love.

This represents a vast difference in principle between the two. It is especially important for contemporary Christians to understand

---

17. Cf. G. von Rad, "The Crisis Due to the Conquest," in *Old Testament Theology* (2 vols.; Edinburgh: Oliver and Boyd, 1962) 1:15–35.

that biblical ethics cannot therefore be something arbitrary or autonomous, but rather must be based upon biblical theology, with its unique understanding both of God's nature and of humankind's.

The most essential element in biblical theology is its earnest attempt to grapple with the meaning of divine and human personhood, explicated especially in the traditions of the covenant and election. Theologically rooted and socially oriented, biblical morality becomes at last the expression of honor to God and of respect for humankind.

The Bible as a whole is ever committed to the uplifting of humankind in the solidarity of covenantal oneness. Although the successors of the ancient Israelites themselves become particularistic and separatistic, both the Old and the New Testaments cherish a vision of broad universalism, so that in classical Old Testament ideology, the concerns that the Israelites expressed for their fellow Israelites were extended to persons outside their fellowship. There are explicit provisions in biblical law on behalf of the sojourner and the foreigner, the orphan and the widow.[18]

Divine Causation in Historical Event

It is wrong to characterize extrabiblical religion as unconcerned about divine action in historical event. To the extent that they took history seriously at all, the contemporaries of the ancient Hebrews believed that their gods were in fact much involved in history. Nothing happened without the will of the gods; they were present and active in everything that occurred. What is genuinely distinctive about the Old Testament's belief is that divine action in history involves responsible human causation, leading purposefully to the realization of God's greater glory and humankind's greater good. This is, above all else, the surprising achievement of Old Testament historiography, which appeared on the plane of human civilization many centuries prior to the history writing of the Greek classics.

It is important theologically that the biblical writings have taken seriously and handled realistically the element of human participation in historical event. These writings do not see the divine will as something imposed upon humankind from the supernatural world. That is the conception of historical event that prevailed in the extrabiblical religions. True, God was at work, but humankind was also at work as a responsible actor in history's drama. God effectuates his will among humankind through humankind's response and dialogue. God and humankind together interact for God's glory and humankind's good.

---

18. Cf. Exod. 23:9: "You shall not oppress a stranger; you know the heart of a stranger, for you were strangers in the land of Egypt"; Deut. 10:18–19: "He executes justice for the fatherless and the widow, and loves the sojourner, giving him food and clothing. Love the sojourner, therefore; for you were sojourners in the land of Egypt."

These are eschatological goals that remain as constant challenges to greater striving. They can never be regarded as secure accomplishments within the structures of finite existence, but they do define a purpose in human striving and they encourage responsible human interaction with God. When these eschatological goals were grasped and held, they became like a bird squeezed to death in the hand of a careless child. Preserved for their own sake alone, they become idols and drove God away.

SUMMATION

Nondistinctive Elements

Let us now make a list of religious elements in the Old Testament, and in the New Testament as well, that contemporary religious practice and piety seem to regard more highly than they should, because they are at best nondistinctive. As we draw up this list, we see that each element has been borrowed from the culture of the external world and not from the Bible.

Supernaturalism

First of all we mention supernaturalism. It is obvious that the Bible is a supernaturalistic book. People today tend to take sides for or against supernaturalism, and everything stands or falls on this issue. Those who have been strongly influenced by modern science are inclined to dispense with the supernatural, along with the miraculous, and are tempted to reject the Bible because it contains so many of these elements. Others are anxiously committed to guarding it at all costs. The consideration that may make a difference for those who have an open mind is that supernaturalism as such is neither unique to the Bible nor distinctive of biblical religion. But there is an important difference. The element of supernaturalism has been purified and refined within the biblical tradition so as to present the most worthy image possible of God's resplendent holiness; neither the Old nor the New Testament proliferates unrestrainedly the element of the supernatural and the miraculous. This fact is what is truly marvelous about the Bible as an ancient document. It restricts these elements to the specific genres of theophany and sacred legend, which have developed their own special language of spirituality so as to convey a worthy and effective image of God's most awesome presence in the midst of people. I would sum it up by saying that the Bible as a whole reverently presents a very modest element of wonder in order to make it serve the pure vision of God's unique personhood, employing it as an ideological and linguistic vehicle specially designed to express its most unique apprehension of the *mysterium tremendum*. The biblical God is no grandiose actor in a cosmic circus. He refuses to perform his mighty deeds to amuse or astound us.[19]

Cultic Worship

Another nondistinctive element of biblical piety, but again, one that is given great prominence in contemporary religiosity, is a dependence on cultic mechanisms. To the extent that these can be kept instrumental to the expression of a vital and authentic biblical faith, they are useful and necessary, but they are not essential, unique, or distinctive of biblical faith as such.

Apocalypticism

A third element of nonessentiality in contemporary piety is the residue of apocalyptic ideology. Biblical apocalyptic arose in a time when everything was out of joint. Historically conditioned, it spoke a language that was useful in its special situation, but that now has lost all relevance except for those who know how to interpret and retranslate its language. When appropriated literalistically, biblical apocalyptic may become delusive and dangerous. Let us keep in mind that apocalyptic was a mode of religious expression on the fringes of biblical eschatology. Although the New Testament is saturated with elements of apocalyptic ideology, it makes only cautious use of apocalyptic as a literary genre worthy to be treated as Scripture. Both Judaism and Christianity continued to make only sparing use of apocalyptic during the early rabbinic and apostolic era, and it was all but discarded in the church after the rise of catholic Christianity. Once the crisis of high eschatological fervor was past, apocalyptic came to be regarded as presenting far more problems for biblical piety than answers.

Distinctive Elements

Worth defending to the last ditch are those elements that clearly present personalistic monotheism — the recognition of one God in personalistic encounter with his rational and moral creature, humankind. This includes the Bible's — and already the Old Testament's — unique view of divine transcendence in combination with immanent nearness; its insight into human dignity, responsibility, and salvability; its sponsorship of covenant peoplehood; its view of humankind's partnership with God in shaping history; and finally, its grasp of a life that transcends evil

---

19. Cf. Mark 8:11–12: "The Pharisees came and began to argue with him, seeking from him a sign from heaven, to test him. And he sighed deeply in his spirit and said, 'Why does this generation seek a sign? Truly I say to you, no sign shall be given to this generation.'"

and neutralizes death. With regard to God, humankind, society, history, and existence, the Old Testament has worked out a distinctive and consistent stance. At the same time, its distinctive affirmation on each of these questions comes to maximum clarity at precisely those points where it has shared much with the common culture out of which it emerged. The Old Testament has been engaged in a historical dialogue with its environment, and at the same time with itself. The answers that it has held out to posterity, dearly won through agonizing probing and struggle, are those that have not only stood the test of time but also have proven to be of enduring helpfulness in coming to grips with the world's most pressing and persistent problems. While it cannot be claimed that the Old Testament offers final answers — thus making the theological task henceforth unnecessary — it does uncover the ultimate questions, and it does respond to them in a distinctive, consistent, and uniquely satisfying way.

CONCLUSION

Those who hope for future progress cannot go forward without a deep sympathy and appreciation for the past. In the area of common human culture, we value especially those great breakthroughs that have come in the field of technology: first, the use of tools; later, the arts of agriculture and the techniques of animal husbandry; still later, the invention of writing — especially the alphabetic script, which democratized learning; since the Middle Ages, a vast display of mechanical, chemical, and electronic marvels. But all of these would be useless, or worse than useless, without the great achievements of the spirit, and here the heritage of Hebraic faith must receive its due recognition for its unparalleled success in illuminating the meaning of divine and human personhood. The devils have not yet been banished from our universe; indeed, the devils that technology has created are far more frightening than any that were known to primitive humans! We shall treasure, then, the hope that the biblical heritage, promising to bring God and humankind to an ever more effective partnership, may eventually drive back every demon that exists, until the ideal good that the Creator has intended will become a reality.

BIBLIOGRAPHY

DeVries, Simon. *Achievements of Biblical Religion: A Prolegomenon to Old Testament Theology.* Lanham, Md: University Press of America, 1983.
Kim, Wonil. "Toward a Substance-Critical Task of Old Testament Theology." Ph.D. dissertation, Claremont Graduate School, 1996.

Knierim, Rolf P. *The Task of Old Testament Theology: Substance, Method, and Cases.* Grand Rapids: Eerdmans, 1995.

Otto, Rudolph. *The Idea of the Holy.* (Original edition in German, 1917).

Von Rad, G. "The Crisis Dut to the Conquest." In *Old Testament Theology.* 2 Vols. Edinburgh: Oliver and Boyd, 1962.

Terrien, Samuel L. *The Elusive Presence: Toward a New Biblical Theology.* San Francisco: Harper and Row, 1978.

10

Can God's Name Change?
A Biblical-Theological Perspective
on the Feminist Critique
of Trinitarian Nomenclature
Michael H. Floyd

Wilt thou not yet to me reveal
Thy new unutterable name?
— CHARLES WESLEY

Rolf Knierim's programmatic essays suggest that Old Testament theology need not be done in the form of comprehensive works encompassing the whole enterprise. Smaller studies of specific issues can make worthwhile contributions if they are conceived as cases illustrating some definitive aspect of the whole enterprise. According to Knierim, one definitive aspect of the whole enterprise is the dynamic interrelationship between the three closely interrelated but nevertheless distinguishable levels of interpretation: exegesis, theology, and hermeneutic. Exegesis deals with particular biblical texts, seeking to grasp the meaning of the explicitly expressed linguistic forms as well as the implicitly expressed underlying concepts. Biblical theology deals with the wide variety of biblical texts in light of the canon as a whole, adjudicating the diverse truth claims of various texts in favor of those that are most fundamental. Hermeneutic mediates the encounter between different systems of theological meaning, those characteristic of the biblical world and those prevalent in our present world, bringing them into a truth-revealing dialogue. Old Testament theology thus has the responsibility of articulating certain truth claims about God, based on a critical assessment of what the various Old Testament texts are exegetically determined to be saying, so that these truth claims — together with those

An earlier version of this essay was presented at the Southwest Regional Meeting of the Society of Biblical Literature on March 14, 1998, in Dallas, Texas. Revisions have been made in light of the critique given by the respondent, Professor Cynthia Rigby of Austin Presbyterian Theological Seminary, and in response to the helpful questions raised by those in attendance.

similarly derived from the New Testament — can find a hermeneutically mediated voice in contemporary theological debate.[1]

This essay attempts to follow Knierim's general approach in order to clarify how the Bible might speak to a specific issue in the contemporary debate, namely, the sexist implications of God being named Father, Son, and Holy Spirit. In this particular case the discussion will not proceed from exegesis to theology and then to hermeneutic, but will go in reverse order. Our point of departure will be (1) the contemporary debate about the Trinitarian name, after which the discussion will move from (2) critique of biblical theological claims that have figured prominently in this debate to (3) exegesis of a text that provides a crucial basis for any such claims; and to bring the discussion full circle (4) the exegetical results will finally be explored, first on the biblical theological level with respect to their implications for truth claims about the name of God and then on the hermeneutical level with respect to their implications for the contemporary theological debate.

THE CONTEMPORARY DEBATE ABOUT THE TRINITARIAN NAME

In our time we are increasingly aware that Western society has been characterized by an arbitrary and unjust subordination of women to men, and that Christianity has played a major role in the legitimation of this patriarchal social system. On the institutional level the church has uncritically adopted the attitudes and conventions of society at large, thus relegating women to subordinate positions in the organization of the church's common life. On the ideological level Christianity's largely masculine concept of God, particularly as it is expressed in the Trinitarian nomenclature of Father, Son, and Holy Spirit, has provided a basis on which to claim that patriarchy is divinely ordained. There is thus an inevitable tension between the contemporary concern of justice for women and the classically formulated expressions of Christian faith.

One might suppose that the institutional and ideological aspects of the problem are not necessarily connected. Myths are not always a direct reflection of their social context. There are societies that render extravagant devotion to goddesses and yet are just as patriarchal as Western society, if not more so. Although it may be theoretically possible that masculine concepts of God do not inevitably serve to legitimate patriarchy, it is nevertheless true that the concept of God as Father, Son, and Holy Spirit has served this function for most of Christian-

---

1. See in R. Knierim, *The Task of Old Testament Theology: Substance, Method, and Cases* (Grand Rapids: Eerdmans, 1995), "The Task of Old Testament Theology" (1–20) and "The Interpretation of the Old Testament" (57–138).

ity's history. This Trinitarian concept informs a worldview in which the forces that create, sustain, and renew the universe are imagined in primarily masculine terms. Such a worldview has not only implied that patriarchy is natural, but has also provided an authoritative basis from which to derive explicit theological warrants for patriarchy's normativeness. Claims to this effect are already evident in the New Testament, and they have been made repeatedly from ancient times until today.

In view of this long history generally characterized by the subordination of women in the name of the triune God, feminists have rightly questioned whether Christianity is unredeemably patriarchal, provoking a variety of responses. Some feminists have answered yes and have left or distanced themselves from the church. Some Christians have also answered yes and have reaffirmed that the subordination of women in both church and society is indeed divinely ordained. Others, however, have argued that the Christian faith is not inherently sexist, and have in turn raised the question of how Christianity might extricate itself from its long and unholy alliance with patriarchy. The burden of proof is certainly on those who would take this stand, but there is a relatively recent precedent for such change, namely, the transformation of the church's attitude toward slavery.

In the case of slavery the church had similarly taken an uncritical stance toward a conventional but unjust practice of the society at large. Christianity had also described the relationship between humanity and God in terms of the slave-master relationship, implying that slavery was divinely ordained and providing a basis for explicit claims to this effect. And yet, when confronted forcefully with the question of whether slavery was consistent with Christian faith, the church finally managed to renounce and dissociate itself from this institution. Some two centuries later it is evident that the church has not yet obliterated all traces of its long complicity with slavery, but a definite change has nevertheless been made. Could a similar reversal take place with respect to patriarchy? For those who dare to hope that Christianity could break its alliance with patriarchy in much the same way that it has broken its alliance with slavery, the Trinitarian nomenclature of Father, Son, and Holy Spirit poses one of the most pressing issues. In view of how this terminology has functioned ideologically to sanction the subordination of women to men, how should Christians now regard it?

Thanks largely to the work of Sallie McFague, certain insights about the epistemology of theological discourse have now become widely acknowledged. These insights are generally in accord with the great tradition of Christian theology, but they have become somewhat obscured by the turns that theological discourse has taken in modern times. A brief restatement of these classical principles can provide us with a useful point of departure. McFague reminds us that all terms for God are metaphorical in the sense that they relate something that extends beyond our experience of the world to things that lie within our experience of the world. Terms for God thus imply a relationship between God and the world in which God is disclosed as both like and unlike certain things known through our experience. Theological terms must be construed heuristically, and the test of their adequacy is whether they eventually prove to be durable, at which point they become what McFague calls "models" of God.[2]

McFague's restatement of these fundamentals is good as far as it goes, but it begs some important questions. What determines the vocabulary from which metaphorical terms for God may aptly be chosen? And among those terms that may aptly be chosen, what determines their relative importance? McFague describes God relating to the world as Mother, Lover, and Friend, and she justifies these choices in view of what she calls the "new sensibility" of the present "ecological, nuclear age." It is thus not clear whether McFague envisions these terms for God as disclosing something of the nature of reality, or whether she envisions them simply as expressions of our feelings about certain forces that we perceive to be operative in our world.

This difference can be illustrated by comparing theological statements with scientific statements. Scientific worldviews are now also widely acknowledged to be fundamentally metaphorical, and the reality of the universe is regarded as mysteriously exceeding human comprehension, but scientific statements nevertheless purport to disclose something of the nature of reality. In modern times the Copernican worldview, modeled metaphorically on an array of juggled spheres, has given way to the Newtonian worldview, modeled metaphorically on a machine in a room; and this Newtonian worldview has in turn given way to the Einsteinian worldview, modeled metaphorically on the space-time blur created by an ever expanding explosion. From the fact that our knowledge of the world is rooted in such metaphorical models, it does not follow that we can construe statements about the world on the basis of any images that happen to strike the contemporary fancy. There are criteria for the aptness of the language we might use. Nor does it follow that statements framed in terms of an earlier worldview lose their force when a later worldview supersedes it. The law of motion, that for every action there is an equal and opposite reaction, may have been framed in relation to a now outmoded Newtonian model of the

---

2. S. McFague, *Metaphorical Theology: Models of God in Religious Language* (2nd ed.; Philadelphia: Fortress, 1985); idem, *Models of God: Theology for an Ecological, Nuclear Age* (Philadelphia: Fortress, 1987).

universe that no longer appeals to a postmodern sensibility informed by relativity and quantum theory, but we would still do well to reckon with this law in deciding whether to buckle up our seatbelts.[3]

Theological statements are not the same thing as scientific statements, but they are like scientific statements in that they attempt to disclose something of the mystery of reality. This similarity means that there are certain constraints on the admittedly metaphorical terms used for theological statements, and that even though theological models obviously reflect the sensibility of the age in which they originated, they are not necessarily invalidated by a change in social matrix or *Zeitgeist*. In the case of scientific statements, the choice of terms can often be determined either directly or indirectly on the basis of practical experiments. In the case of theological statements, such experiments obviously cannot be done. There is nevertheless an analogous basis for determining the aptness of terms used to describe God in relation to the world, namely, the cumulative experience of the community of faith.[4]

McFague's two main points, that all theological terms are metaphorical and that all concepts or models of God are metaphors that have proved to be durable, are both well taken. Her view of how theological discourse evolves, however, is problematic. As the main criterion for determining the aptness of metaphorical terms, she appears to prefer the sensibility of the contemporary age to the cumulative experience of the community of faith. This leads her to the fallacious claim that models of God reflecting their origin in a past age, such as the ancient royal model of God, tend to loose their signifying force under the changed conditions of a later age. It also leads her to discount the way in which the community of faith has historically weighted the various metaphorical terms in its theological vocabulary, and to treat lightly the fact that the community of faith has traditionally given theological terms derived from Scripture precedence over other terms. In other words, she has minimized the Bible's canonical function.

This critique of McFague suggests that we pay closer attention to the way in which theological discourse evolves. From time to time new models of God have in fact emerged, and later in this essay we will consider the precedents for such changes within the Judeo-Christian tradition. More often, however, theological discourse is renewed when the recontextualization of old terms leads to the realization that they

---

3. See, for example, J. D. Barrow, *The World within the World* (Oxford: Oxford University Press, 1990).

4. See M. Gerhart and A. M. Russell, *Metaphoric Process: The Creation of Scientific and Religious Understanding* (Fort Worth: Texas Christian University Press, 1984); J. M. Soskice, *Metaphor and Religious Language* (Oxford: Clarendon, 1985).

have fresh implications. Figures of speech that had become dead clichés thus resume the function of living metaphors, regaining their capacity to disclose the mystery of the divine reality. In contrast to McFague's quest for new models of God, several theologians have suggested that the feminist critique of patriarchy provides precisely such a recontextualization of the Trinitarian concept of God, a recontextualization that leads to the realization that this ancient figure has fresh implications. Because the feminist struggle puts the Trinity in a new light, it may be transformed from a dead cliché back into a living metaphor, describing a God who relates to the world so as to call forth a radically egalitarian rather than a patriarchal society.[5]

The theologians who take this approach argue that although the Trinity has for so long lent itself to the legitimation of patriarchy, a revisionistic reaffirmation of the Trinity is the most promising means of extricating Christianity from patriarchy. They advocate a return to the creative and formative expressions of Trinitarian doctrine in earlier times. Catherine Mowry LaCugna, for example, harks back to the Cappadocian theologians of the fourth century. She points out that their innovative distinction between the one divine substance (*ousia*) and the three divine persons (*hypostaseis*) entailed a momentous shift in metaphysics, making person rather than substance the primary ontological category. Personhood, defined in terms of being-in-relation-to-another, was thus posited as the ultimate originating principle of all reality. This shift in turn led to a redefinition of God's relation to the world in terms of a shared governance (*monarchē*) that, according to LaCugna, "banished once for all — at least theoretically — the idea that any person can be subordinate to another. This is the kernel of the radical theological and political proposal of the Cappadocians that is relevant to the program of feminism today."[6]

Elizabeth Johnson harks back more to Aquinas than to the Cappadocians, but she similarly proposes that the recovery of a classical notion of the Trinity is conducive to feminist goals.

> As the sustaining ground and ultimate reference point for the human and natural world, the trinitarian symbol for God may function in at least three beneficial ways. The God who is thrice personal signifies that the very essence of God is to be in relation, and thus relatedness rather

---

5. See, for example, Patricia Wilson-Kastner, *Faith, Feminism and the Christ* (Philadelphia: Fortress, 1983); M. Farley, "New Patterns of Relationship: Beginnings of a Moral Revolution," *TS* 36 (1975) 627–46; C. M. LaCugna, *God for Us: The Trinity and Christian Life* (San Francisco: HarperSanFrancisco, 1991).

6. C. M. LaCugna, "God in Communion with Us: The Trinity," in C. M. LaCugna, ed., *Freeing Theology: The Essentials of Theology in Feminist Perspective* (San Francisco: HarperSanFrancisco, 1993) 88.

than the solitary ego is the heart of all reality. Furthermore, this symbol indicates that the particular kind of relatedness than which nothing greater can be conceived is not one of hierarchy involving domination/subordination, but rather one of genuine mutuality in which there is radical equality while distinctions are respected. The trinitarian God, moreover, cannot be spoken about without reference to divine outpouring of compassionate, liberating love in the historical world of beauty, sin, and suffering, thus leading us to envision a God who empowers human praxis in these same directions. With this idea of God we have come just about as far from the isolated patriarchal God of Enlightenment theism as is possible.[7]

A recovery of such classical Trinitarianism seems promising, but those who are promoting it differ with respect to whether the traditional nomenclature of Father, Son, and Holy Spirit should be retained. On the one hand, if it remains clear that the notion of the radically interpersonal three-in-one is basically a metaphorical model of the divine reality, the traditional masculine terminology cannot be taken literally and should thus lose its capacity to suggest that God is masculine or that patriarchy is divinely ordained. On this basis Gregory Nazianzus mocked anyone silly enough to "consider our God to be a male...because he is called God and Father, and that deity is feminine from the gender of the word, and Spirit neuter because it has nothing to do with generation."[8] Along similar lines, Colin Gunton has argued that it is necessary for the traditional nomenclature to be preserved precisely in order for the antipatriarchal implications of classical Trinitarian theology to be realized.[9] On the other hand, the historical tendency of this terminology to be taken literally, so as to imply and thereby legitimate a masculine hierarchy in both church and society, cannot be denied. Johnson therefore argues that alternative feminine nomenclature is necessary to keep Trinitarian language honest. She proposes (1) that the three persons be conceived as united in exercising divine wisdom (ḥokmāh/sophia) rather than divine governance (monarchē); (2) that the three be called Spirit-Sophia, Jesus-Sophia, and Mother-Sophia; and (3) that the unity be called She-Who-Is.[10]

7. E. A. Johnson, *She Who Is: The Mystery of God in Feminist Theological Discourse* (New York: Crossroad, 1992) 215–16.

8. Gregory Nazianzus, *Theological Orations* 5.7, in E. R. Hardy and C. C. Richardson, eds., *Christology of the Later Fathers* (LCC 3; Philadelphia: Westminster, 1954) 198.

9. C. Gunton, "Proteus and Procrustes: A Study in the Dialectic of Language in Disagreement with Sallie McFague," in A. F. Kimel Jr., ed., *Speaking the Christian God: The Holy Trinity and the Challenge of Feminism* (Grand Rapids: Eerdmans, 1992) 65–80; idem, *The Promise of Trinitarian Theology* (Edinburgh: T. & T. Clark, 1991).

10. Johnson, *She Who Is*, 124–223.

CRITIQUE OF PROMINENT BIBLICAL THEOLOGICAL CLAIMS

At this point in the discussion, those who want to deny the possibility of renaming the triune God often resort to a particular argument from Scripture. As we noted in the foregoing critique of McFague, her attempt to develop new feminine and gender-neutral models of God is problematic precisely because she minimizes the canonical function of the Bible as the paradigmatic expression of the faith community's cumulative experience. Some scholars have maintained conversely that if the Bible's canonical function is fully acknowledged, the use of anything other than masculine theological terminology is precluded. Elizabeth Achtemeier, for example, has stridently argued that the Bible abhors feminine terminology for God because such terminology inevitably leads to pantheism and thus erases the distinction between God and creation.

> The basic reason for [the masculine] designation of God is that the God of the Bible will not let himself be identified with his creation, and therefore human beings are to worship not the creation but the Creator. . . . It is precisely the introduction of female language for God that opens the door to such identification of God with the world. . . . If God is portrayed in feminine language, the figures of carrying in the womb, of giving birth, and of suckling immediately come into play. . . . But if the creation has issued forth from the body of the deity, it shares in deity's substance; deity is in, through, and under all things, and therefore everything is divine.[11]

Variations on this view are widely held.[12] It is obvious that the Bible uses relatively little feminine imagery in describing God, but is Achtemeier's explanation an accurate description of why this is the case? Is it true that the Bible particularly associates feminine imagery with the immanence of the divine in the natural world, and is it true that the Bible regards any acknowledgment of God's immanence in nature as necessarily implying an idolatrous kind of pantheism?

Before turning to look at the textual data, it must be noted that a dubious logic underlies Achtemeier's claims. She assumes a priori that feminine terminology necessarily implies immanence to an extent greater than masculine terminology. But are penis and sperm any less caught up in the natural cycle than ova and womb? She arbitrarily presupposes that masculine terminology can only be taken metaphorically

---

11. E. A. Achtemeier, "Exchanging God for 'No Gods': A Discussion of Female Language for God," in Kimel, *Speaking the Christian God*, 8–9.

12. This view is frequently expressed in the various contributions to Kimel, *Speaking the Christian God*. See especially R. M. Frye, "Language for God and Feminist Language: Problems and Principles" (31–41), which is often cited by other contributors in this collection of essays.

so as to connote God's genderless transcendence, but that feminine terminology can only be taken literally so as to connote God's gendered
immanence. This presupposition is nothing more than a patriarchal
prejudice. Actually, masculine terminology has tended to connote the
kind of gendered divine immanence decried by Achtemeier, and feminine terminology has tended to avoid it. Church history is littered with
countless official statements of male clergy and scholars in which masculine terminology is used literally to connote the male immanence
of God. When feminine terminology has been used at all, as in the
unofficial devotional writings of mystics, it has generally been used
metaphorically to connote both the genderless transcendence and the
genderless immanence of God.[13] Achtemeier can attempt to get away
with such prejudicial and illogical assumptions only because she thinks
it self-evident that the Bible shares them. We thus return to the question of whether it is true that the Bible particularly associates feminine
imagery with the immanence of the divine in nature, and whether the
Bible regards any acknowledgment of God's immanence in nature as
necessarily implying an idolatrous kind of pantheism.

The Bible is patriarchal through and through in the sense that it
presupposes everywhere that patriarchal social systems are culturally
normative. Nevertheless, the evidence does not support Achtemeier's
stereotype of a biblical diatribe against the threat of idolatrous pantheism posed by feminine representations of divinity. Biblical Hebrew does
not even have a word for "goddess" as such, and in the New Testament
there is only one episode that explicitly involves a goddess (Artemis
in Acts 19:21–41). In constructing a rough statistical profile for the Old
Testament, let us concede the unlikely possibility that all occurrences
of the feminine noun ʾăšērâ are references to the goddess Asherah, and
that all occurrences of the feminine nouns ʿaštōret and ʿaštārôt are references to the goddess Astarte, regardless of whether these nouns are
modified by the definite article.[14] Even so, there are only some thirty
references to these two goddesses, in contrast with more than three
hundred references to foreign gods in general and some eighty references to the god Baal in particular. In about half of these thirty cases,
Asherah and Astarte are mentioned in conjunction with the cult of Baal
or some other masculine gods rather than independently. In sum, there
are at most only ten to twelve clear-cut descriptions of goddesses as
objects of devotion in their own right. Running throughout the entire
Old Testament there is certainly a polemic against foreign gods, but it is

---

13. See, for example, the cases cited by Caroline Walker Bynum in *Jesus as Mother:
Studies in the Spirituality of the High Middle Ages* (Berkeley: University of California Press,
1982).

14. J. Day, "Asherah," *ABD*, 1:485–86; idem, "Ashtoreth," *ABD*, 1:491–92.

false to claim that this polemic focuses specifically on goddess worship as an especially problematic manifestation of this phenomenon.

It is similarly false to claim that the Old Testament specifically associates natural manifestations of divinity with feminine representations of divinity. In the one case of an extended polemic against the worship of a goddess, Jeremiah's condemnation of Jerusalem's devotion to the Queen of Heaven (Jeremiah 44), the issue has nothing to do with the divine in nature. Rather, it is a question of how to interpret a historical event. Is the Babylonians' first capture of Jerusalem Yahweh's punishment of Judah for their devotion to the Queen of Heaven, or is it her punishment of Judah for King Josiah's suppression of her cult? Conversely, when the issue does concern the divine in nature, there is no association with goddesses. There are two major cases of this sort: Elijah's claim regarding whose power is manifest in the abundance or scarcity of rain (1 Kings 17–18) and Hosea's claim regarding whose power is manifest in the provision of grain, wine, and oil (Hosea 1–3). In both cases the immanence of the divine in nature is associated not with a goddess but with the god Baal. Moreover, neither prophet is described as hesitant to claim that Yahweh, not Baal, is really the God manifest in nature. Hosea goes so far as to say that Yahweh is, in effect, the real *ba'al*.

From a history of religions perspective it may be true that the ancient world was rife with goddess worship. From the Bible's theological perspective, however, this phenomenon is scarcely noticed at all. Feminine representations of deity are not singled out as any more problematic than masculine ones. It is the idolatrous nature of the representation, whether it is masculine or feminine, that makes it problematic. From a history of religions perspective it may also perhaps seem plausible to claim that any recognition of the divine in nature tends inevitably toward pantheism. From the Bible's theological perspective, however, this inevitability is not recognized. The immanence of God in the natural cycles of fertility is generally taken for granted. Such immanence is not regarded as problematic in itself, but only an idolatrous representation of it.

Because Achtemeier's stereotype misrepresents the Bible so grotesquely, it cannot have come from even the most tendentious reading of the text itself. It must have been derived from some other source and superimposed upon the text. It appears to be largely based on the concept of nature religion, an anthropological category developed in the late eighteenth and nineteenth centuries during the heyday of European colonialism. With this label, the religions of many colonized peoples were identified in terms of the characteristics that made them seem primitive and inferior to the European colonizers, namely, the natives' celebration of fertility and their recognition that women as well as men are important in this regard. The concept of nature religion was also eventually applied to ancient pagan religions so as to differentiate them from biblical religion in these same terms. Achtemeier follows this practice, characterizing the difference between biblical religion and its ancient pagan counterparts in terms of the same superiority complex with which European colonizers characterized the difference between their religion and the so-called primitive religions of their subjects. Her stereotype may thus perhaps be seen as a speculative construct reflecting the modern Western colonialist ideology that Edward Said has called "orientalism."[15]

In any case, the textual evidence does not support the kind of argument advanced by Achtemeier, that those who recognize the Bible's canonicity are precluded in principle from using feminine terminology for God because it inevitably leads to pantheism. On the contrary, the Old Testament generally insists on the nonpantheistic immanence of God in nature and acknowledges the capacity of both masculine and feminine terminology to connote this kind of divine immanence as well as divine transcendence. These claims concerning the Old Testament generally extend to the New Testament. It is widely recognized that the New Testament associates God's nonpantheistic immanence with both feminine and masculine imagery in connection with the incarnation. The Son of God is, after all, "born of a woman" (Gal. 4:4), hence the orthodox recognition of Mary as Mother of God. But the New Testament also readily associates God's nonpantheistic immanence with both feminine and masculine imagery in connection with creation itself, as when Paul uses the metaphor of childbirth to describe the graceful but painful cosmic process through which the world and its inhabitants become related to "the Father" as "sons of God" and are thereby saved (Rom. 8:14–25).

Does the Bible's openness in principle to feminine as well as masculine terminology mean that the Trinitarian nomenclature can be changed? Can the divine name therefore be altered, for example, in the way that Johnson proposes, from God the Father, Son, and Holy Spirit to She-Who-Is Spirit-Sophia, Jesus-Sophia, and Mother-Sophia? There is another crucial issue that needs to be considered before this question can be addressed, namely, the distinction between how God is described and how God is addressed.

In the New Testament the terms "Father," "Son," and "Holy Spirit" are primarily used for relating to God personally, not for describing God impersonally. The New Testament knows virtually nothing of the

---

15. E. W. Said, *Orientalism* (New York: Pantheon, 1978).

later Trinitarian doctrine that God is to be described as three-in-one, but it is permeated everywhere with the Trinitarian assumption that human beings relate to God as they are moved by the power of the Holy Spirit and enabled through the mediation of the Son to call upon the Father.[16] From a biblical perspective, to call God Father, Son, and Holy Spirit is to address God directly and thereby acknowledge a relationship with God, not to make an assertion about the nature of God. The main function of the threefold designation is comparable to one of the main functions served by proper names, which is to address others directly and thereby acknowledge some kind of personal relationship with them. The threefold designation of God as Father, Son, and Holy Spirit thus serves primarily as the proper name by which God is to be addressed, not the doctrinal formula with which God is to be described.

It may be objected that "father" and "son" cannot be proper names, because they denote generic categories to which some persons may belong rather than particular persons. Within the context of personal relationships, however, terms of this sort can be used like proper names, as when a child addresses a parent as "Father," and a parent addresses a child as "Son." It may also be objected that the traditional practice of translating the Trinitarian nomenclature into various languages precludes its being a proper name. Although proper names are generally not translated in many contexts — a Mexican named Pablo, for example, does not become Paul whenever he crosses the border into the United States — it does not necessarily follow that proper names are by definition untranslatable. The possibility of translation is evident from the very fact that the names Pablo and Paul are commonly recognized as being more or less equivalent, and the realization of this possibility would depend upon the function that translation might serve in a particular relational context. Just as Hapsburg kings could be simultaneously known to their Spanish-speaking subjects as Carlos and to their German-speaking subjects as Karl in order to substantiate a political relationship, the God once known to Latin-speaking devotees as *Pater, Filius, et Spiritus Sanctus* could subsequently be known to English-speaking devotees as Father, Son, and Holy Spirit in order to substantiate the divine-human relationship.

Although Trinitarian language obviously has an important role to play in theological discourse about God, in which case it serves to describe the nature of God, it also has a more fundamental role to play in theological discourse addressed to God, in which case it serves to acknowledge a relationship with God. This distinction is neither abso-

---

16. See, for example, O. Cullmann, *Prayer in the New Testament* (trans. J. Bowden; OBT; Minneapolis: Fortress, 1995).

lute nor self-evident, and it can be made only by attending carefully to the function of Trinitarian language in relation to its context. From the standpoint of New Testament theology, however, this distinction is necessary. It is one thing to ask whether we can change the language with which we describe and characterize God, and it is quite another thing to ask whether we can change the proper name by which we call upon and relate to God.

The distinction between describing and addressing God is sometimes confused with the distinction between metaphorical and non-metaphorical language. For example, Alvin Kimel grants that theological language describing God is generally metaphorical and thus subject to change, as Sallie McFague would maintain. He also argues, however, that because the threefold designation of Father, Son, and Holy Spirit is the biblically revealed proper name by which God is to be addressed, it is nonmetaphorical and hence not subject to change.[17] Kimel seems to assume that if the Trinitarian nomenclature were acknowledged to be metaphorical, there would be no basis for any distinction between God's proper name and other descriptions of God — but this is a non sequitur. Philosophers disagree about the ways in which proper names and common nouns exercise their respective referential functions,[18] and with respect to language in general it may be debatable whether proper names can be metaphorical, but with respect to theological language there is no need to exempt God's proper name from the generalization that all terms for God are metaphorical. The very notion of God having a proper name is in itself metaphorical, but this fact does not preclude a meaningful distinction between the names with which God may be properly addressed and the terms in which God may otherwise be aptly described.

On the basis of such a distinction, the general question of whether feminine terminology may be used to describe God can be separated from the more specific question of whether the terms of the Trinitarian proper name may be changed from masculine to feminine. As I concluded in the foregoing critique of Achtemeier's position, the Bible generally acknowledges the capacity of both feminine and masculine terminology to connote God's immanence as well as God's transcendence. When talking about God, theological discourse may therefore evolve by freely following the biblical and other traditional precedents for using feminine terminology for God. When addressing God directly,

---

17. A. Kimel Jr., "The God Who Likes His Name: Holy Trinity, Feminism, and the Language of Faith," in Kimel, *Speaking the Christian God*, 193–94.

18. J. R. Searle, "Proper Names and Descriptions," in P. Edwards, ed., *The Encyclopedia of Philosophy* (8 vols.; New York: Macmillan and Free Press; London: Collier-Macmillan, 1967) 6:487–91.

however, there is more to the matter. We also need to consider whether we are free to change God's proper name.

The difficulty may be explored by asking the analogous question of whether we are free to change anyone's proper name, particularly when our relationship with a person has been based on the long-standing and well-established custom of addressing him or her by that name. If a friend were to tell me that she had decided to call me David instead of Michael but that she expected our relationship to continue just the same, I'm not sure that I could meet her expectations. Although she might affirm that she still appreciated my wonderfully idiosyncratic personality as much as ever, it might be difficult for me to believe this affirmation as long as she insisted on relating to me as someone with a different name.

In such a situation God might well be more easygoing than I, but the nature of the difficulty remains the same. The character of interpersonal relationships depends upon the persistence of the names by which the interrelated persons have customarily addressed one another, and it is hard to imagine how any such relationship could continue if one person thinks that he or she is free to change the other's name. In much the same way, it is hard to imagine how the relationship between God and the community of faith could continue if we think that we are free to change God's name. Can the church reasonably expect to maintain its relationship with God, affirming its appreciation of God's distinctive triune character, while also insisting that God be addressed by some name other than Father, Son, and Holy Spirit?

At this point the analogy between human and divine renaming fails. I certainly know how I would feel about being renamed, but this hardly provides any basis on which to speculate about how God would feel. Kimel seems to think that he can project onto God the affection that a human being might typically have for his or her own name. Kimel smugly asserts that "the triune God has named himself, and he likes his name."[19] But how does Kimel know what God likes? He pretends to know the mind of God in a direct way that seems dangerously close to idolatrous self-deification. We cannot speculate about how God feels about being renamed, but the issue can hardly be avoided by those who want to reaffirm the classical notion of God's radically interpersonal triune character while also changing the Trinitarian names from masculine to feminine. Can the issue be approached in another way?

If we cannot presume to know how God feels about our changing the traditional threefold name, we can at least ask from our human perspective whether the alternative names seem capable of maintaining continuity in our relationship with God. Do the proposed feminine,

---

19. Kimel, "The God Who Likes His Name," 188.

gender-neutral, or gender-transposing names serve as well as Father, Son, and Holy Spirit to describe God's radically interpersonal love toward all creation and God's radically egalitarian shared responsibility for the world? Or do the proposed names have potentially confusing implications with regard to these definitive traits of the triune character? In other words, do the proposed names avoid such classical theological traps as modalism and subordinationism?

Unfortunately, the alternatives thus far proposed generally fail this test. For example, one of the formulas that has recently gained some currency, namely, Creator, Redeemer, and Sanctifier, is blatantly modalistic because it functionally identifies each of the three divine persons in terms of a characteristic that is rightly and radically shared by all three. Such nomenclature might well suggest that God is a monad with three alternate modes of operation, or even that there are in effect three gods. Other examples are not so obviously deficient, but problems of a similar sort are not entirely avoided, even by such a carefully considered proposal as Ruth Duck's alternative Trinitarian name: "God, the Source, the fountain of life; Christ, the offspring of God embodied in Jesus of Nazareth and in the church; and the liberating Spirit of God, the wellspring of new life." In subordinationist fashion this nomenclature seems to arrogate all originative creativity to the first of the three divine persons, that is, "God, the Source."[20] A rose by any other name may smell just as sweet, but it remains to be seen whether God by any name other than Father, Son, and Holy Spirit is just as triune.

This uncertainty leads to an impasse for those who view the reaffirmation of classical Trinitarian theology as the most promising way of extricating Christianity from patriarchy. On the one hand, if the

---

20. R. C. Duck, *Gender and the Name of God: The Trinitarian Baptismal Formula* (New York: Pilgrim, 1991) 185–86. Duck's intention to preserve the insights of classical orthodoxy is explicitly stated (139–58) and is evident in her critique of Creator-Redeemer-Sanctifier and other alternatives (159–84), but J. F. Kay points out that she is not altogether successful in this regard ("In Whose Name? Feminism and the Trinitarian Baptismal Formula," *ThTo* 49 [1993] 531–32). In approaching the Trinitarian name with respect to the baptismal formula, Duck clearly distinguishes the question of changing God's proper name from the question of developing alternative language about God. In contrast, Elizabeth Johnson seems ambiguous on this point. She speaks consistently in terms of finding new alternative ways to speak *about* God, and yet she describes the effect of such language in terms of relating *to* God. In any case, her critics are divided as to whether she avoids classical problems with the terminology of She-Who-Is Spirit-Sophia, Jesus-Sophia, and Mother-Sophia. In two companion reviews of *She Who Is,* for example, one author says, "I would imagine some of the familiar charges of Sabellianism by those dissatisfied with feminist liturgical proposals could be met by this book" (M. M. Fulkerson, *RelSRev* 21 [1995] 23), while the other says that in using *ḥokmāh/sophia* to describe God's relation to the world, Johnson effaces some of the fundamental attributes of the divine persons and thus "runs the risk of conjuring up ... not the female personification of the God known from Christian belief, but another God" (M. A. O'Neill, *RelSRev* 21 [1995] 21).

threefold name of Father, Son, and Holy Spirit is retained along the lines of Gunton's proposal,[21] it is unlikely that the church could break its deep-seated, age-old habit of misusing this masculine terminology to legitimate the subordination of women to men. The fact that such misuse continues virtually unabated, despite the emphatic clarification of voices like Gunton's, shows that there is little hope of significant progress if God's name remains unchanged. On the other hand, if the threefold name is changed along the lines of Duck's proposal, the Trinitarian nomenclature may well lose its capacity to connote clearly the triune character of God. If the new name does not adequately continue to convey the radically interpersonal nature of God's love toward all creation and the radically egalitarian nature of God's shared responsibility for the world, patriarchy will not really be challenged, even if the new name happens to be feminine or gender neutral.

This impasse, which results from a critique of prominent biblical theological claims about the way God is to be described and named, cannot be broken without a reconsideration of the exegetical basis on which any such claims must be grounded. Within the scope of this essay it is impossible to cover all or even some of the texts relevant to the issue at hand, but we can at least deal with an indisputably crucial text so as to suggest the direction that a breakthrough might take.

THE EXEGETICAL BASIS FOR BIBLICAL THEOLOGICAL CLAIMS ABOUT THE DIVINE NAME

The vast majority of Old Testament texts assume that the proper name of God is Yahweh.[22] The status of Yahweh as God's proper name is not diminished by the fact that God can be readily described and even directly addressed in other terms. Titles like King and Shepherd, along with epithets like Rock and Shield, function in relation to Yahweh as complementary nicknames. Nor is the status of Yahweh as God's proper name diminished by the fact that there are substitutes for it. In the Second Temple period the pronunciation of this name became taboo, and the term 'ădōnāy ("Lord") was substituted when reading sacred Scripture aloud. Some "late" texts (e.g., Esther and Ecclesiastes) appear to reflect this custom by similarly avoiding Yahweh in favor of less specific terms. There are also parallel texts in which the generic term for God, 'ĕlōhîm, is in some instances substituted for Yahweh (e.g., Ps. 14:1b–7 par.

---

21. See note 9.

22. This is the best guess of modern philology regarding the vocalization of the consonants in the Tetragrammaton, YHWH. Other vocalizations are possible, but the inevitable ambiguity regarding the pronunciation of the name is irrelevant to the present discussion.

Ps. 53:2–7; Ps. 40:14–18 par. Ps. 70:2–6 [MT]). These facts are often in-terpreted in light of an evolutionary scheme, according to which the attribution of a proper name to any god was an aspect of primitive polytheistic paganism abandoned by biblical religion as it progressed to universal monotheism. This view is reflected, for example, in one of the reasons given by the translators of the New Revised Standard Version for their decision to continue the traditional practice of translat-ing the Tetragrammaton with "the LORD" rather than some vocalization of YHWH.

> The use of any proper name for the one and only God, as though there were other gods from whom the true God had to be distinguished, began to be discontinued in Judaism before the Christian era and is inappropriate for the universal faith of the Christian Church.[23]

Regardless of how the Tetragrammaton may best be rendered in a modern English translation, the phenomenon of the divine name in Scripture is too complex for such a simplistic scheme. This kind of developmental theory is problematic in three major respects. First, the textual data do not conclusively show a trend toward univer-sal monotheism. The substitution of *ʾĕlōhîm* for Yahweh, for example, might well signify a particularization of the generic concept of deity rather than the denaturization of Yahweh by a generic concept of deity. Second, the reluctance to pronounce the divine name was just as charac-teristic of the particularistic forms of Second Temple Judaism as it was of the universalistic forms.[24] And third, in view of the neopaganism and neopolytheism that increasingly characterize postmodernity the very notion of a necessary or unilinear progression from particularistic poly-theism to universalistic monotheism seems suspect. For such reasons it cannot be assumed a priori that the Old Testament shows any pro-nounced tendency to forgo or marginalize the concept of Yahweh as God's proper name.

With this proviso in mind, we now turn to consider the scriptural *locus classicus* concerning the divine name, the call of Moses in Exo-dus 3. This passage has figured prominently in the God and gender debate, but it has often been taken out of context by those who cite it, regardless of which side they are on. More specifically, claims are often made about the meaning of Exod. 3:14–15 without relating its treatment of the theme of God's name to the reappearance of the same theme in Exod. 6:2–4. The failure to connect these two passages is no doubt

---

23. B. M. Metzger, "To the Reader," in B. M. Metzger and R. E. Murphy, eds., *The New Oxford Annotated Bible* (New York: Oxford University Press, 1991) xiii.

24. See M. Rose, "Names of God in the OT," *ABD*, 4:1001–11, and the bibliography cited there.

reinforced by modern source criticism, which explains this phenomenon as the editorial combination of two originally separate versions of the same story, the Elohistic and/or Yahwistic version of the call of Moses in Exod. 3:1–15 and the Priestly version in Exod. 6:2–13. Modern historical criticism has typically been more concerned with assigning such "redundant" episodes to their original documentary sources than with analyzing how they are presently connected.[25] The tendency to read these two episodes apart from each other is, however, not peculiar to modern historical criticism. Although premodern and postmodern commentators are supposed to be more attentive to the canonical form of the text, they have also tended to read Exod. 3:1–15 without relating it to Exod. 6:2–13.[26] One might well ponder why premodern, modern, and postmodern interpretation have all tended to avoid such an obvious intertextual connection,[27] but in any case let us now analyze the narrative that runs from Exod. 3:1–15 to Exod. 6:1–13 so as to show how these two episodes are related. The following outline represents the structure of this narrative:

I. Moses encounters Yahweh at Horeb   3:1–4:17

  A. Yahweh appears to Moses in a burning bush as the ancestral God   3:1–6

  B. Yahweh commissions Moses to be his agent in bringing the Israelites out of bondage in Egypt and into a land of milk and honey   3:7–10

  C. Yahweh and Moses deal with related issues   3:11–4:17

    1. The issue of Moses' qualifications   3:11–12

      a. Moses asks how he could be the one to do such a thing   3:11

      b. Yahweh replies that he can do it because Yahweh will be with him and announces a confirming sign   3:12

    2. The issue of the name of the ancestral God   3:13–4:9

      a. Moses asks what he should say when the people ask him the name of the ancestral God   3:13

25. See B. S. Childs, *The Book of Exodus: A Critical, Theological Commentary* (OTL; Philadelphia: Fortress, 1974) 51–70, 111–14.

26. See Childs, *Book of Exodus*, 84–87. See also the various interpretations of Exodus 3 by Gregory of Nyssa, Nicholas of Lyra, Peter Ochs, Terence E. Fretheim, and Walter Brueggemann in S. E. Fowl, ed., *The Theological Interpretation of Scripture: Classic and Contemporary Readings* (Cambridge, Mass.: Blackwell, 1997) 103–71.

27. As R. W. L. Moberly points out, perhaps it is because critics of all sorts have been much more fascinated with the problem of the apparent contradiction between the frequent use of the name Yahweh throughout the preceding narrative and the notion that this was first revealed to Israel through Moses (*The Old Testament of the Old Testament: Patriarchal Narratives and Mosaic Yahwism* [OBT; Minneapolis: Fortress, 1992] 52–55).

B. Yahweh reaffirms Moses' commission   6:2–12
   1. Yahweh again identifies himself as the ancestral God   6:2–5
   2. Yahweh again sends Moses to announce his plans
      to the people   6:6–9
      a. Yahweh commands Moses to tell them that he will
         free them and bring them into the land   6:6–8
      b. Moses complies but the people remain unconvinced   6:9
   3. Yahweh again sends Moses to confront Pharaoh   6:10–12
      a. Yahweh commands Moses to tell Pharaoh to
         release the people   6:10–11
      b. Moses objects that his failure to convince the people
         portends a similar failure to convince Pharaoh   6:12
C. Yahweh reaffirms the responsibility of Aaron and Moses
   to keep the pressure on both the people and Pharaoh   6:13

From among the many interesting features of this text, for our purposes it must suffice to single out only four of the most important.[28]

First, Yahweh's self-identification as the God of Abraham, Isaac, and Jacob harks back to the ancestral history in Genesis 12–50. More specifically, Yahweh's stated intention to bring the Israelites from their Egyptian bondage into the land of Canaan harks back to the twofold divine promise repeatedly made to these ancestors, the promise of numerous descendants and land.[29] The action in this entire episode is predicated on the fact that this twofold promise is partly fulfilled and partly unfulfilled. The descendants of Israel have indeed become numerous, but they remain farther than ever from Canaan. Moreover, the fulfillment of this part of the promise has proved to be a mixed blessing, as it has been the cause of the initial enslavement of the Israelites (Exod. 1:8–10) and the subsequent worsening of their oppression (Exod. 5:5–9). As the action gets underway, the issue is thus whether the divine promise of land will be fulfilled in a way that makes the life of the Israelites better rather than worse.

Second, the theme of the ancestral God's name is reiterated so as to involve it more deeply in the resolution of this issue. In the first instance, the identification of the ancestral God as Yahweh is not explicitly connected with the promise. Yahweh's motivation for bringing the Israelites into the land is described simply in terms of his compassionate desire to relieve their oppression in Egypt. He has heard their cry and wants to make their life better (Exod. 3:7–8, 16–17). In the second instance, the naming becomes explicitly connected with the promise.

---

28. For a close reading in dialogue with many recent commentators see Moberly, *The Old Testament of the Old Testament*, 7–31.

29. Gen. 12:7; 13:15–16; 15:5, 18; 17:6–8; 22:17; 26:3–4; 28:13–14; 35:11–12; 48:4.

Yahweh's motivation is described in terms of making good on his oath.
He has remembered his covenant with the ancestors and is now determined to bring the Israelites into the land he swore to give them (Exod.
6:4–8). In the second instance, moreover, the identification of the ancestral God as Yahweh is more specifically described in terms of a name
change. The ancestors knew their God by the name of El Shaddai, not
Yahweh, but the same God is now fulfilling under the name of Yahweh
what was once promised under the name of El Shaddai (Exod. 6:2–3).

Third, the theme of God's name change is introduced, not in connection with the recognition of what God's intentions are, but in
connection with the discovery of how difficult it will be for them to
be realized. The people readily believe Moses' announcement that God
has sent him to lead them to freedom (Exod. 4:31), but they lose confidence when Moses fails in his initial attempts to carry out this mission
(Exod. 6:9). This loss of confidence is not prevented by the realization
that God's initiative entails being faithful to an old promise under a
new name. This realization does, however, provide a reason for Moses
and Aaron to keep trying (Exod. 6:10–13). And when God's intentions
to free the people soon do begin to be realized, they see and respond.

Fourth, in this context the famous phrase in Exod. 3:14, "I am who
I am" ('ehyeh 'ăšer 'ehyeh), is comparable to similarly loaded phrases in
other narratives about being named or renamed. These phrases do not
function primarily as etymological explanations for names, however accurate they may or may not be in this regard. Rather, they are puns that
characterize the newly named person and often play upon intertextual
connections with other episodes in the surrounding narrative. For example, the name of Isaac (yiṣḥāq) is "explained" by Sarah's statement
(Gen. 21:6) that "God has brought me laughter (ṣĕḥōq)." Regardless of
whether the name is actually derived from the similar sounding root
meaning "to laugh" (ṣḥq), this pun characterizes Isaac as a child whose
birth was laughable to Sarah and plays upon other episodes in which
she and Abraham laugh at the ridiculous prospect of God giving them
a child in their old age (Gen. 17:17; 18:12–15).[30] Similarly, the name
of Yahweh is "explained" by the statement "I am who I am." Regardless of whether the name Yahweh is actually derived from the similar
sounding root meaning "to be" (hyh), this pun characterizes Yahweh
as one whose identity is self-defined and plays upon the other episode
in which the God of the ancestors is also identified as Yahweh, Exod.
6:2–13.

30. Puns are similarly made on names so as to characterize Jacob (Gen. 25:26; cf. 27:1–
40); Esau, nicknamed Edom and Seir (Gen. 25:25; cf. 25:30 and 27:16, 23–24); Moses (Exod.
2:10); and Peter (Matt. 16:18), and so forth. Cf. also the naming of Jacob's children (Gen.
29:31–30:24).

The intertextual connection between Exod. 3:1–15 and Exod. 6:2–13 is thus to be seen in light of the connotations created by the pun in the former episode. As an integral part of the narrative, the phrase "I am who I am," whatever else it might signify, serves primarily to explain how God can undergo the name change explicitly described in Exod. 6:2–3, from El Shaddai to Yahweh, while maintaining a fundamental continuity in God's personal and historical identity. The God now revealed to the Israelites as Yahweh is none other than the God once revealed to their ancestors as El Shaddai. The fundamental continuity in God's personal and historical identity is evident in the fact that Yahweh is now fulfilling what El Shaddai promised. This is possible because God is who God is.

From a history of religions perspective there is nothing very new in these observations. It has long been supposed that Exod. 3:1–15 and Exod. 6:2–13 both reflect Yahweh's assumption of the role previously played by "the God of the ancestors," who was none other than El in various manifestations. Because these two texts have conventionally been regarded as variant witnesses to one and the same traditio-historical development, the implications of their interconnection in the present form of the narrative have generally been overlooked.[31] The change of divine names is not presented in Exod. 3:1–6:13 as an interesting phenomenon paralleled in other ancient religions, occurring at some point in the tradition that lies behind the text. Rather, it is a historical memory that has been made the subject of theological reflection in the present form of the text. God is characterized here as one who can change names and still be God.

BIBLICAL THEOLOGICAL AND HERMENEUTICAL IMPLICATIONS

There are other Old Testament texts with significant bearing on the theme of the divine name, but none appears to conflict with Exod. 3:1–6:13 regarding its changeability.[32] For the sake of this case study in biblical theological method, we may therefore take it as a general tenet of Old Testament theology that God's name can change. In conclusion we turn to consider whether the New Testament agrees with this claim and what it means for the contemporary debate about the Trinitarian nomenclature.

---

31. See Moberly, *The Old Testament of the Old Testament*, 105–25.

32. For example, the commandment not to take the name of Yahweh in vain (Exod. 20:7 par. Deut. 5:11), the Deuteronomic concept of Yahweh's temple as the place chosen by Yahweh where "he causes his name to dwell" (Deut. 12:5, 11, 21, etc.), and the references in Psalms to the power and efficacy of Yahweh's name (e.g., Ps. 20:1; 44:5; 54:1; 91:14; etc.).

The New Testament does not explicitly consider the issue of the divine name's changeability, but it tacitly agrees with the Old Testament on this score. The New Testament's concept of the divine name is in effect predicated on the assumption that the pattern of divine activity described in Exod. 3:1–6:13 has been replicated in Jesus Christ. If God's name could change from El Shaddai to Yahweh, it could also change from Yahweh to something else. From the New Testament perspective, God has again exercised this option. This time the name has changed from Yahweh to Father, Son, and Holy Spirit without creating any fundamental discontinuity in God's personal and historical identity. If this were not the case, the relationship between the Old and New Testaments would have no theological integrity.[33]

What are the contemporary implications of the biblical theological recognition that God's name can change? These can be discovered by drawing a hermeneutical analogy between the present situation of the church and the situation of the Israelites in Exod. 3:1–6:13. They were at an impasse with respect to God's promise of numerous descendants and land. The Israelites had grown numerous, but the prospect of land seemed as dubious as ever. God changed names as part of the initiative to fulfill in the name of Yahweh what had not been fulfilled in the name of El Shaddai. The church now finds itself in a similar situation. Part of what was promised to our ancestors in the name of Father, Son, and Holy Spirit has indeed been fulfilled, but part of what was promised in this name seems as dubious as ever. The part that has been fulfilled might be summed up in the catchphrase "God with us" (Matt. 1:23), and the part that still seems dubious might be summed up in the catchphrase "in Christ there is no longer male or female" (Gal. 3:28). Might we not expect that the God who changes names precisely in order to break through such impasses will again change names in order to break through this one, and thus fulfill under some still undisclosed new name all of what was promised in the name of Father, Son, and Holy Spirit? If so, the old Trinitarian name would be complemented rather than displaced by the new name, just as the names of El and Yahweh were complemented rather than displaced by their successors. Every true name of God is valid forever (cf. Exod. 3:15), and the revelation given under new names does not diminish the truth of the revelation given under previous names.

In sum, Scripture speaks in a particular way to the struggle to extricate Christianity from patriarchy. We are encouraged to develop fresh language about God and nicknames for God, using both feminine and masculine imagery to connote God's immanence as well as God's tran-

---

33. Cf. Moberly, *The Old Testament of the Old Testament*, 125–46.

scendence. We are cautioned, however, against attempts to change the proper name by which God is directly addressed. God is free to change God's name, and we are not. But God can and does change names. This is not to say that human beings have no part to play in the process. Any revelation of a new name must be mediated through some human act of naming, and the authenticity of any new name can only be discerned through the cumulative experience of the community of faith. There is nevertheless a difference between waiting for a new divine name to be revealed and seeking to devise one.

We must wait on God, but Scripture describes God's name change in a way that encourages us to wait in hope. Precisely when the divine promise is evidently on the way to fulfillment but its complete realization seems blocked, God changes names in the liberating process of breaking through this impasse. With respect to the promise of freedom from patriarchy, the church now seems to be at just such a moment in history. In any case, we have good reason to trust that God will someday assume a name that is conducive to a right relationship between women and men, because God is who God is.

BIBLIOGRAPHY

Childs, Brevard S. *The Book of Exodus: A Critical, Theological Commentary.* Philadelphia: Fortress, 1974.

Duck, Ruth C. *Gender and the Name of God: The Trinitarian Baptismal Formula.* New York: Pilgrim Press, 1991.

Fowl, Stephen E., ed. *The Theological Interpretation of Scripture: Classic and Contemporary Readings.* Cambridge, Mass. and Oxford: Blackwell, 1997.

Gerhart, Mary, and Allan M. Russell. *Metaphoric Process: The Creation of Scientific and Religious Understanding.* Fort Worth: Texas Christian University Press, 1984.

Gunton, Colin. *The Promise of Trinitarian Theology.* Edinburgh: T. & T. Clark, 1991.

———. "Proteus and Procrustes: A Study in the Dialectic of Language in Disagreement with Sallie McFague." In *Speaking the Christian God: The Holy Trinity and the Challenge of Feminism.* Ed. A. F. Kimel Jr. Grand Rapids: Eerdmans, 1992.

Johnson, Elizabeth A. *She Who Is: The Mystery of God in Feminist Theological Discourse.* New York: Crossroad, 1992.

Kay, J. F. "In Whose Name? Feminism and the Trinitarian Baptismal Formula." *Theology Today* 49 (1993).

Knierim, Rolf. *The Task of Old Testament Theology: Substance, Method, and Cases.* Grand Rapids: Eerdmans, 1995.

LaCugna, Catherine Mowry. "God in Communion with Us: The Trinity." *Freeing Theology: The Essentials of Theology in Feminist Perspective.* Ed. C. M. LaCugna. San Francisco: HarperSanFrancisco, 1993.

————. *God for Us: The Trinity and Christian Life*. San Francisco: HarperSan-
Francisco, 1991.

McFague, Sallie. *Metaphorical Theology: Models of God in Religious Language*. 2d ed.
Philadelphia: Fortress, 1985.

————. *Models of God: Theology for an Ecological, Nuclear Age*. Philadelphia:
Fortress, 1987.

Moberly, R. W. L. *The Old Testament of the Old Testament: Patriarchal Narratives and
Mosaic Yahwism*. OBT; Minneapolis: Fortress, 1992.

Searle, J. R. "Proper Names and Descriptions." In *The Encyclopedia of Philosophy*, ed. P. Edwards. 8 vols. New York: Macmillan and Free Press; London:
Collier-Macmillan, 1967) 6:487–91.

Soskice, J. M. *Metaphor and Religious Language*. Oxford: Clarendon, 1985.

Walker Bynum, Caroline. *Jesus as Mother: Studies in the Spirituality of the High
Middle Ages*. Berkeley and Los Angeles: University of California Press, 1982.

Wilson-Kastner, Patricia. *Faith, Feminism and the Christ*. Philadelphia: Fortress,
1983.

11

Justice and Salvation
for Israel and Canaan
John Goldingay

INTRODUCTION

One of the several delights of Rolf Knierim's work is the way he articulates decisive insights in trenchant fashion. Often I find myself responding with a delighted, air-punching "Yes!" to his forthright, swashbuckling advocacy of the Old Testament's insights and his rebuttal of the simpleminded assumption that the New Testament is all that people need. An example of his strongminded asseverations is the declaration that on the one hand, the theme of Yahweh's dominion in justice and righteousness is of key significance in the Old Testament, and on the other hand, that it is incompatible with the kind of belief in Yahweh's special relationship with Israel that makes it possible to think of Yahweh eliminating the Canaanites in order to give Israel a home in their land. On the one hand, "the ultimate vantage point from which to coordinate [the Old Testament's] theologies" is "the universal dominion of Yahweh in justice and righteousness";[1] on the other hand, "the exclusionary election theology represents an insurmountable crisis for the Old Testament's claim to Yahweh's universal justice."[2] Indeed, exclusionary election "represents the most serious theological perversion of the notion of God," a sinful ideology.[3] The centrality of justice and righteousness means that Israel and its election cannot have the significance that many parts of the Old Testament attach to them. This is not to deny Israel's election; it is to affirm that election is particular but not particularistic. The election of Israel does not imply the nonelection of any other people. As a "universalistic paradigm" Israel's election is "a sign of the equal election of all."[4]

Knierim often emphasizes that the task of Old Testament theology revolves around evaluation and criteria. I doubt this. As his paper on Old

---

1. Rolf P. Knierim, *The Task of Old Testament Theology: Substance, Method, and Cases* (Grand Rapids: Eerdmans, 1995) 15.
2. Knierim, *Task of Old Testament Theology*, 451.
3. Knierim, *Task of Old Testament Theology*, 452.
4. Knierim, *Task of Old Testament Theology*, 549.

Testament spirituality splendidly illustrates, it is first of all an exercise in construction. But in his comments on election that emphasis comes home. If the task of theology is to decide who is right, and if it does that in the light of what is central and fundamental, and if righteousness and justice are central, then the kind of election that links with the elimination of the Canaanites can disappear from Old Testament theology.

Yet these key convictions of Knierim's have been subjected to equally trenchant critique.[5] On the one hand, despite (or because of) his passionate concern for the dominion of justice and righteousness, Knierim does not tell us what these words actually mean or provide evidence for their centrality. Neither the meaning nor the centrality is self-evident. For instance, one could read through the whole of Genesis through Kings, and then through Chronicles, Ezra, and Nehemiah (more than half the Old Testament), without realizing that Yahweh was so concerned about dominion, justice, or righteousness. Indeed, it is often argued that dominion is a male preoccupation, and the usual understanding of justice and righteousness may also be affected by gender questions. It is manifestly clear, however, that Genesis through Kings and Ezra, Nehemiah, and Chronicles (to put the point in terms of the narrative framework of the Hebrew Bible) believe that Israel is the special people of Yahweh in a way that Canaan, for instance, is not.

In discussions of the Old Testament's theological value and values the annihilation of the Canaanites will come up sooner rather than later. Knierim has a distinctive take on this matter. Yahweh's liberation of Israel to freedom in Canaan is also Yahweh's oppression of the Canaanites. For all the rationale of Leviticus 18 and Deut. 9:4, they did not deserve this experience more than other peoples. Their annihilation was an act that sits in tension with the commitment to justice that Yahweh claims and that Yahweh expects of Israel. I presume it makes little difference if we believe that their annihilation was a piece of Israelite fiction rather than a factual occurrence. We have to choose between the theology of exclusionary election and the theology of inclusive justice, and we must choose the latter as the more comprehensive framework for our Old Testament theology.[6]

As I have hinted, there is more than one problem with the conclusion to this argument, so we must go back over it. My conviction is that a

---

5. See, for instance, the review of Knierim's book by J. Levenson in *RelSRev* 24 (1998) 39–42.

6. See the comments of D. Jobling and C. Rose on "Canaanite readings" of the Old Testament in "Reading as a Philistine," in M. Brett, ed., *Ethnicity and the Bible* (Biblical Interpretation Series 18; Leiden: Brill, 1996) 381.

substance-critical approach[7] to Knierim's own formulations about election may produce a statement of the significance of election, justice, and righteousness in the Old Testament that are less open to his discomforts. In a moment, I need to make his problem worse in the course of seeking to define justice and righteousness, but eventually I hope to reduce it by seeking to narrow the gap between particular election and exclusive election (between Genesis 12 and Genesis 15).

ELECTION IN A THEOLOGICAL CONTEXT

The problems just referred to are a more formal one and a more substantial one. The more formal problem is that the rejection of Israel's distinctive election appears in a statement about Old Testament theology, yet it involves jettisoning a central and pervasive theme of Old Testament theology. Indeed, H. D. Preuss recently made the theme of election the organizing principle for his Old Testament theology.[8]

Suppose we grant that a substance-critical approach to Old Testament theology might involve disagreeing at a particular point with something that an Old Testament writer says, in the conviction that we could express more accurately what the Old Testament writer was truly after, that we knew Old Testament truth better than it knew itself. Even if this is so, the pervasiveness and centrality of the theme of election makes that a difficult candidate for this treatment. There is a basic implausibility about the claim that this is possible within a treatment of Old Testament theology that seeks to work with the Old Testament's own priorities.[9] The difficulty of jettisoning the theme is heightened if Preuss is right that the idea of a people's election by a deity is also unique in Middle Eastern thinking,[10] though such statements are notoriously hazardous.

As Levenson implies, Knierim might be right that Israel's distinctive election is a mistaken concept, but not that it is an unbiblical concept. "God did not specially elect Israel from among other peoples" is no more a statement that can appear in an Old Testament theology than is "God does not exist" or "Yahweh is not God." Knierim urges an Old Testament theology that draws its criteria and agenda (I would prefer to reverse the words) from the Old Testament itself and thereby dis-

---

7. See Knierim, *Task of Old Testament Theology*, 452. My approach to *Sachkritik* has been shaped by R. Morgan, *The Nature of New Testament Theology* (London: SCM, 1973) 38–52.

8. See H. D. Preuss, *Theologie des Alten Testaments* (2 vols.; Stuttgart: Kohlhammer, 1991–92); ET, *Old Testament Theology* (2 vols.; Edinburgh: T. & T. Clark, and Louisville: Westminster John Knox, 1995–96).

9. For example, Knierim, *Task of Old Testament Theology*, 8–20.

10. Preuss, *Old Testament Theology*, 1:38.

tinguishes itself from systematic theology and biblical hermeneutic.[11] I, too, long for such a thing, but people who affirm its importance often give evidence against the point by their deeds.

There is also the more substantial problem, which heightens the stakes on the question whether the idea of Israel's distinctive election is a mistaken one. Abandoning the idea of Israel's distinctive election significantly affects (I would say skews) the content of Old Testament theology, and not only that, but also of New Testament theology, of Christian theology, and of Jewish theology. Thus, whereas Levenson attributes Knierim's slant to his Christian commitment, R. K. Soulen's study *The God of Israel and Christian Theology* points to a forceful critique of that slant from a Christian angle.[12] If the existence of the Jewish people is a matter of indifference to the God of Israel, this "introduces a note of incoherence into the heart of Christian reflection about God."[13] One might say the same for indifference to the people of Canaan or any other people, but Soulen implies that distinctive questions are raised by the question of the Jewish people.

Soulen notes that there have been two periods when the status of Israel has forced itself on Christian theological reflection: the original separating of the church from Israel, and the recent events of the Holocaust and the establishment of the state of Israel. The period in between was the period of Christendom, which Soulen sees as characterized not only by triumphalism in relation to the Jewish people but also by "a latently gnostic assessment of God's engagement in the realm of public history."[14] There is a topic of concern here for Knierim, for the last thing he wants is a failure of "engagement with human history in its public and corporate dimensions."[15] The question is whether his concern for the Old Testament to influence public life can be advanced if we give up the idea that a distinctive status attaches to that people in Scripture which was especially called to embody God's *mišpāṭ ûṣĕdāqāh* in its public life.

Knierim does not take the classic Christian position of supersessionism, the view that the church replaced Israel in God's purpose. He deprecates anti-Semitism[16] and knows that we must do theology in the light of the Holocaust.[17] But it is worrying that his position resembles the more radical one that Soulen associates with Immanuel Kant

---

11. Knierim, *Task of Old Testament Theology*, 18.
12. R. K. Soulen, *The God of Israel and Christian Theology* (Minneapolis: Fortress, 1996).
13. Soulen, *God of Israel*, 4.
14. Soulen, *God of Israel*, x.
15. Soulen, *God of Israel*, xi.
16. Knierim, *Task of Old Testament Theology*, 452.
17. Knierim, *Task of Old Testament Theology*, 311.

and Friedrich Schleiermacher, that God never had entered into a special relationship with the Jewish people, so that its continuing existence became a matter of theological indifference. Among other things, that certainly facilitated "a further loss of contact . . . with the rough edges of the Hebrew Scriptures and public history."[18] Kant, too, believed that the Jewish people's conviction of its own exclusive election was one of the features of its faith that made it unable to function as a universal moral religion.[19] There is thus a Jewish affirmation of Knierim's position; in due course I will note another, Judith Plaskow's.

There is also, of course, more Jewish critique of it. Soulen does his work in dialogue with that of Jewish theologian Michael Wyschogrod, in particular his book *The Body of Faith: God in the People Israel.*[20] The foundation of Wyschogrod's theology is not (for instance) the Torah but "his affirmation of God's free, irrevocable election of Israel as the people of God."[21] Despite its exclusiveness, for Wyschogrod, that election is an expression of God's affirmation of humanity in its fullness. "God confirms the human creature as it was created to live in the material cosmos."[22] In the words with which Wyschogrod closes his book, Israel is "the carnal anchor that God has sunk into the soil of creation."[23]

"But why," Soulen asks, "should God be God of election at all? Does not God love all persons equally?"[24] It is a variant of Knierim's question about justice. Wyschogrod's answer is that "undifferentiated love" cannot be love that meets individuals in their individuality; that kind of love requires exclusivity.[25] By electing Abraham and his seed, God has chosen in favor of genuine encounter with human creatures in their concreteness. "The distinction between Jew and Gentile — far from indicating a limit or imperfection of God's love — testifies to God's willingness to engage all creation on the basis of divine passion."[26] A friend recently wrote to my wife and me, ending, "With all my love." This might seem hard on her husband and sons. Yet there can be something about love that makes it not necessarily exhaust itself when given

---

18. Soulen, *God of Israel*, 59.

19. See, e.g., I. Kant, *Religion within the Limits of Reason Alone* (trans. T. Greene and H. Hudson; New York: Harper, 1960) 117 = *Religion and Rational Theology* (Cambridge: Cambridge University Press, 1996) 155 (quoted by Soulen, *God of Israel*, 64). Cf. J. Levenson's comments on "Enlightenment rationalism," in *RelSRev* 24 (1998) 41; F. Crüsemann, "Human Solidarity and Ethnic Identity," in Brett, ed., *Ethnicity and the Bible*, 57–58.

20. Michael Wyschogrod, *The Body of Faith: God in the People Israel* (San Francisco: Harper, 1983; repr. 1989).

21. Soulen, *God of Israel*, 5.

22. Soulen, *God of Israel*, 6.

23. Wyschogrod, *Body of Faith*, 256.

24. Soulen, *God of Israel*, 7.

25. Wyschogrod, *Body of Faith*, 61; Soulen, *God of Israel*, 7–8.

26. Soulen, *God of Israel*, 8, summarizing Wyschogrod, *Body of Faith*, 63–65.

wholly to one person; it can mysteriously self-regenerate and multiply in the giving so that it pours out over others than the original object.

Perhaps something like this is presupposed by a comment in *Sifre* on Deuteronomy, chapter 40. God cares for the land of Israel (Deut. 11:12). Does this mean that God does not care for other lands? Job 38:26–27 excludes this. So Deuteronomy implies that God cares not only for this land, "but because of His care for it He cares for all the other lands along with it." Similarly God "keeps" Israel; and Job 12:10 sets all nations in God's keeping. So God keeps not only Israel, "but because He keeps them He keeps every other nation along with them."[27] Wyschogrod sees this as implicit in Gen. 12:1–3, and he sees God's plan to have worked to some degree. Nations have come to experience humanity and history (and justice and righteousness, to revert to Knierim's concerns) with Jewish categories as an outworking of God's distinctive love for Israel and God's love for other peoples.

In principle, then, the particularistic election of Israel and a concern for universal justice and righteousness can work together. There is no inherent tension between them. Old Testament theology does not have to choose between them.

MIŠPĀṬ ÛṢĔDĀQĀH

The same point emerges from a consideration of the use of *mišpāṭ ûṣĕdāqāh* in the Old Testament, which indeed becomes an alternative way of making the same statement.

The RSV phrase "justice and righteousness" has become the standard English equivalent to the hendiadys *mišpāṭ ûṣĕdāqāh*, but it is an unsatisfactory phrase. Both "justice" and "righteousness" are abstract nouns; *mišpāṭ* and *ṣĕdāqāh* are not. Set over against each other, "justice" suggests something about relationships in society, while "righteousness" suggests personal right living. This bears inadequate relationship to the Hebrew expression. Set alongside each other and understood as a hendiadys denoting "social justice," the words suggest the combination of fairness that treats everyone alike and conformity to some norm of rightness. This bears little more relationship to the Hebrew expression. Whatever *mišpāṭ ûṣĕdāqāh* means, it is not "justice and righteousness."

Knierim uses the rendering "just judgment,"[28] and that seems to me a better equivalent, though the "judgment" is not confined to judicial decisions. Whereas "social justice" is an abstract expression, *mišpāṭ*

---

27. R. Hammer's translation in *Sifre: A Tannaitic Commentary on the Book of Deuteronomy* (New Haven: Yale University Press, 1986) 79; cf. Soulen, *God of Israel*, 129.

28. Knierim, *Task of Old Testament Theology*, 121.

and ṣĕdāqāh are both commonly used as concrete nouns. One cannot "do [a] social justice" as one can "do a mišpāṭ" or "do a ṣĕdāqāh." Characteristically, mišpāṭ suggests the declaring and implementing of a decisive judgment, while ṣĕdāqāh denotes the quality of some act, the way it fits into a worldview and a set of relationships that possess, among other things, some moral and social order. Together, mišpāṭ and ṣĕdāqāh thus form a powerful combination. They point to an exercise of authority that has a certain relational and social commitment and to a certain relational and social vision that expresses itself in decisive action. They operate in the court, but also in government and in community relationships. Neither refers directly either to "justice" or to "righteousness."

Whereas "righteousness" suggests conformity to a norm or standard, then, ṣĕdāqāh is a relationship word. That is implicit in its first appearance in Scripture. Abraham manifests a strange willingness to trust Yahweh's word against the odds, though with a little evidence from the events of which we have read in the previous three chapters. And Yahweh counts this as ṣĕdāqāh (Gen. 15:6). This is not a legal fiction whereby he is treated as if he had lived by the norms of right living when he had not. Rather, it is Yahweh's declaration that such trust counts as ṣĕdāqāh. This fits Klaus Koch's contention that ṣĕdāqāh is closely related to faithfulness and loyalty, especially faithfulness and loyalty that go beyond the call of duty.[29] Believing Yahweh's outrageous word is the expression of such faithfulness and loyalty that Yahweh approves. In Yahweh's own case, terms parallel to ṣaddîq are ḥannûn and ḥāsîd.[30] Conversely, in Rom. 9:14 Paul bases his denial that God manifests adikia on the fact that God has carried on showing mercy and compassion to Israel. The consideration that this involved (to our eyes) unfairness to Esau or to the Pharaoh is irrelevant to the question whether God is dikaios.[31] Likewise, Tamar's status as relatively ṣādēq (Gen. 38:26) is intelligible on the basis of an understanding of ṣĕdāqāh that links it with relationships in the community rather than directly with moral norms.

In contrast to ṣĕdāqāh, mišpāṭ is more inherently a matter of the exercise of power or authority. It presupposes, of course, concern for harmony and order in the community; our use of the word "judgment" in English to denote wisdom and insight parallels the way in which a word for giving authority can presuppose that authority is exercised properly. Thus mišpāṭ used on its own can imply "just judgment" (see Isa. 1:17; 32:7; 59:8; 61:8; Jer. 7:5; 10:24; 17:11; Mic. 3:9; Prov. 12:5; 13:23;

---

29. See K. Koch, "ṣedeq," THAT, 2:507–30; ET, TLOT, 3:1046–62.
30. Koch, "ṣedeq," THAT, 2:523; ET, TLOT, 3:1057.
31. See J. D. G. Dunn, Romans 9–16 (WBC 38B; Dallas: Word, 1988) 551.

16:8, 11). The Old Testament can similarly use the verb *šāpaṭ* to speak of judging the needy and the oppressed in the sense of taking fair action on their behalf (e.g., Isa. 1:17, 23; Ps. 10:18; 72:4; 82:3). Yet, in itself *šāpaṭ* simply means "govern" or "rule" or "exercise authority," as *mišpāṭ* signifies authority in action — it often appears alongside words such as *ḥôq* and *miṣwāh*. Thus, the connotation "just judgment" is usually made explicit through the pairing of *mišpāṭ* with some other word, such as *ṣĕdāqāh*. This specifies that the exercise of such authoritative judgment recognizes that the problem in the community was not merely an individual wrong but a breakdown in the harmonious order of the community, and that it is designed to restore this. The word *dîn*, similarly, can require the adjective *yātôm* (Jer. 5:28) or can in itself suggest not merely legal judgment but fair legal judgment (Isa. 10:2).

In keeping with the fact that *mišpāṭ* refers inherently to decisive action more than to just action, Leviticus can quite easily imagine *mišpāṭ* being exercised in a way that reflects *ʿawlāh*, wrong not right. That comes about when those who are involved in *mišpāṭ* favor either poor people or important people (Lev. 19:15; cf. Prov. 24:23; the verb in Mic. 3:11; Ps. 58:2 [1]) or when they cheat in business (Lev. 19:35). The striking prohibition on favoring the poor suggests that the stress elsewhere on judgment *for* the poor implies a concern for them to get their rights, not an arbitrariness about law. Elsewhere, the positive comment regarding the king is that he does not trespass in *mišpāṭ* (Prov. 16:10), but this is a statement of hope; he may exercise *mišpāṭ*, but in a way that involves trespass. Judges will certainly exercise *mišpāṭ*, but it is an open question whether this will be *mišpāṭ-ṣedeq*, to use the interesting construct phrase in Deut. 16:18 (cf. Ps. 119:160; also 119:7, 62, 106, 164 in the plural).[32] There are related verbal expressions in Deut. 1:16, Isa. 11:4, and Prov. 31:9, while the similar phrase *mišpāṭ ʾĕmet*, true judgment, appears in Ezek. 18:8 and Zech. 7:9. Instead of exercising such just *mišpāṭ*, judges rather may bend or twist *mišpāṭ* (Deut. 16:19; cf. Hab. 1:4; Prov. 17:23; 18:5). It is a sign of degeneration when *mišpāṭ* springs up like poisonous weed (Hos. 10:4).[33] It is *ṣedeq* alone that the community is to pursue when it exercises *mišpāṭ* (Deut. 16:20). No tautology is involved in declaring that Yahweh's *mišpāṭîm* have the quality of being *ṣādēq* (Ps.

---

32. Cf. Knierim, *Task of Old Testament Theology*, 118–19. M. Weinfeld says that *mišpāṭ ṣedeq* ("a righteous judgment") is to be distinguished from *mišpāṭ ûṣĕdāqāh*, which signifies "social justice" (*Social Justice in Ancient Israel and in the Ancient Near East* [Jerusalem: Magnes; Minneapolis: Fortress, 1995] 33–34).

33. G. Fohrer's brisk emendation to *mispāḥ* (cf. Isa. 5:7) is a sign that there is a problem here if *mišpāṭ* can easily mean "justice"; see "Der Vertrag zwischen König und Volk in Israel," *ZAW* 71 (1959) 17 = *Studien zur alttestamentlichen Theologie und Geschichte (1949–1966)* (BZAW 115; Berlin: de Gruyter, 1969) 346.

19:10 [9]; 119:75); one could not speak of *ṣĕdāqāh* being exercised in a way that reflects *'awlāh*.

So *mišpāṭ* refers not to "justice" but to the exercise of the authority or power or capacity or willingness to take decisions or to take decisive action. The point is further illustrated by the fact that four times the Torah speaks of Yahweh's *šĕpāṭîm* in Egypt. Twice, the focus is on *šĕpāṭîm* on behalf of Israel (Exod. 6:6; 7:4). Twice, the focus is on *šĕpāṭîm* upon Egypt's gods (Exod. 12:12; Num. 33:4). In none of these passages is the notion of justice present. The idea is that Yahweh will act decisively for or against bringing freedom or exposure.

Apart from this, neither the Torah nor Joshua ever uses *mišpāṭ* or *ṣĕdāqāh* or related words in connection with the Israelites' deliverance from Egypt or their occupation of Canaan, even though a passage such as Exodus 3 does see Israel's deliverance as a response to its *ṣĕ'āqāh* (cry). The language of *mišpāṭ* and *ṣĕdāqāh* is applied to Israel first in connection with the deliverance of Israelite tribes from their oppressors in the book called *Šôpĕṭîm*. Deborah's expression for such acts of deliverance is *ṣĕdāqôt*, though these can be described as Yahweh's or as Israel's (Judg. 5:11). Samuel picks up the word (1 Sam. 12:7) and in his elaboration does include reference to the exodus, though intriguingly, here it is not Yahweh at all who delivers Israel; Yahweh sends Moses and Aaron, and they bring Israel out of Egypt and into Canaan, despite being dead for the latter event.

It is in Deut. 9:4–6 that the Torah comes closest to declaring that Israel's occupation of Canaan is an act of *ṣĕdāqāh*, though even there it does not actually say this. On the one hand, Israel's possession of the land does not issue from its *ṣĕdāqāh*; on the other hand, it does issue from the other nations' *rešaʿ*, the antonym of *ṣĕdāqāh*, and it reflects Yahweh's faithfulness to the promise given to Abraham (which would make it an expression of *ṣĕdāqāh*). In what way it relates to the nations' *rešaʿ* is unstated. Elsewhere, the Canaanites' wickedness was in itself the cause of their loss of their land (see, e.g., Lev. 18:24–30), but the context in Deuteronomy 9 more likely implies that the wickedness of the Canaanites leads to their being removed lest they mislead Israel.[34]

I assume that these statements in Deuteronomy were formulated some centuries after Moses' and Joshua's day, though it is hazardous to base arguments on any view regarding their actual origin. Nevertheless, we can be sure enough that they come from a period when their audience had no prospects of actually annihilating the Canaanites (if Canaanites existed) in the way Deuteronomy enjoins. While the mere question whether Joshua is fact or fiction may make little difference to

---

34. See Knierim, *Task of Old Testament Theology*, 98.

the theological significance or status of its stories about annihilation, the vision that the factual or fictional narrative sets before its audience will vary according to their circumstances. In the late sixth century, for instance, Israel as represented by the people led by King Josiah is a tiny community with little prospect of playing a significant part in Middle Eastern history, while in the late sixth or fifth century the community that appears in Isaiah 56–66, Haggai, Zechariah, Malachi, Ezra, and Nehemiah is even more embattled over against its context. This community's much despised ethnocentricity looks very different to one who belongs to a marginal ethnic group struggling for survival than it looks to secure, mainstream members of a liberal society, and it is to be evaluated differently on the part of minority groups trying to maintain identity than it is on the part of groups with power.[35] Conversely, "When Jews have known relative freedom...they have found it easy to express broadly and comprehensively the worldwide dream of their people. The literature of ancient Alexandria and the Moslem-Jewish symbiosis gives ample evidence of that," as does modern Judaism.[36]

IS YAHWEH FAIR?

If my emphasis regarding the meaning of *mišpāṭ* is correct, that sharpens the question Knierim raises in this connection. The Canaanites may have been *rĕšāʿîm*, but hardly more so than other peoples, and it is therefore difficult to maintain that Yahweh's *mišpāṭ* is *ṣādēq* in treating all peoples alike in the way that Yahweh's own commands require of Israel. "An interpretation of the conquest that ignores the cry of the Canaanites for help, a cry not represented in the Old Testament because it pleads only Israel's case, is in fundamental conflict with the Old Testament understanding of God as the just and merciful judge."[37]

Oddly enough, the Torah does raise the question whether Yahweh's treatment of other peoples is always fair. While it does not refer to Yahweh's acts of *mišpāṭ* or *ṣĕdāqāh* in relation to Israel, it includes an intriguing reference to Yahweh's *ṣĕdāqāh ûmišpāṭ* in relation to Sodom. Genesis 18 is as suggestive for theological reflection as for prayer, and Walter Brueggemann has posited that it was intended thus.[38] It might aid theological reflection on Yahweh's dealings with Israel, but it more overtly does that in relation to Yahweh's dealings with other peoples,

---

35. See M. Brett, "Interpreting Ethnicity," in Brett, ed., *Ethnicity and the Bible*, 16–20, with his references. Cf. the comments of D. L. Smith-Christopher, "Between Ezra and Isaiah," in Brett, ed., *Ethnicity and the Bible*, 122–23.

36. See E. B. Borowitz, "The Dialectic of Jewish Particularity," *JES* 8 (1971) 564.

37. Knierim, *Task of Old Testament Theology*, 318.

38. See W. Brueggemann, *Genesis* (Philadelphia: Westminster, 1982) 162–77.

and specifically with the earlier inhabitants of Abraham's promised land — precisely Knierim's concern. Here, in its first appearance in the Old Testament, ṣĕdāqāh ûmišpāṭ is related to Yahweh's promise to Abraham and also to the intention that Abraham's blessing be significant for all nations. Abraham is responsible for ṣĕdāqāh ûmišpāṭ. This is not a surprising suggestion, for we have already heard of Abraham's ṣĕdāqāh (Gen. 15:6), the word's first occurrence in Scripture. The passage was also the first time we were taken inside Abraham's mind and told something other than what he did. Confronted by Yahweh's promise of progeny, Abraham trusted Yahweh and Yahweh counted this as ṣĕdāqāh. In Genesis 18 Abraham and his family will put ṣĕdāqāh ûmišpāṭ into effect and thus keep Yahweh's way, which implies Yahweh's claim that ṣĕdāqāh ûmišpāṭ are Yahweh's way. The nouns come in the reverse of the usual order, suggesting "rightness that is expressed in decisive action" rather than "decisive action that expresses rightness," but I have not been able to see any significance in this (cf. Ps. 33:5; Prov. 21:3; Hos. 2:21 [19] — Ps. 89:15 [14]; 97:2 have ṣedeq ûmišpāṭ; Ps. 103:6 has ṣĕdāqôt ûmišpāṭîm).

Doing ṣĕdāqāh ûmišpāṭ is here associated with the promise that Abraham's family will become a great and powerful nation and that all the nations of the earth will "bless themselves by him" (Gen. 18:18). The verb bārak is niphal, as in Gen. 12:3 and 28:14, not hithpael, as in 22:18 and 26:4. This might imply that the meaning is passive rather than reflexive, which would strengthen the argument that follows, but I am content to suppose that the two verb forms are rhetorical variants and that the meaning is reflexive. The nations are to "bless themselves by him" (RSV) or to "pray to be blessed as he is blessed" (NEB) rather than explicitly "to be blessed" (NIV). Further, let us acknowledge that in the narrower context the promise that Abraham will become a standard for blessing puts the emphasis on the magnitude of blessing for Abraham rather than directly on hope for other peoples. Nevertheless, the promise implies that a prayer for Abraham-like blessing would be a reasonable prayer for a nation to pray, a prayer to which Yahweh might be expected to respond positively. If Yahweh were instead to respond by questioning whether the dogs can have the children's food, a Canaanite woman will be able to suggest an answer (see Mark 7:24–30).

The assumption that Yahweh might be expected to respond positively to such a prayer is supported by the context on both sides of Gen. 18:18–19. On the one hand, Genesis 1–11 has been concerned with God's blessing of all peoples and with the question whether that blessing will ever find realization, and the first statement of Yahweh's promise to Abraham in 12:1–3 follows directly on those chapters. Knierim himself rightly notes how a motif such as Yahweh's promise to Abraham presupposes Yahweh's concern for the whole world. Then on the other hand, the very prayer for Sodom that follows Gen. 18:1–21 presupposes an interest in all peoples, as Knierim again notes.[39] Even if Sodom becomes a figure for Jerusalem (Isa. 1:9–10), perhaps like Jonah's Nineveh,[40] it is hardly merely that.

The story speaks of a particularly loud outcry against Sodom (Gen. 18:21; 19:13). Such an outcry (*ṣě'āqāh*) is opposite to what is right (*ṣědāqāh*) (cf. Isa. 5:7). So Yahweh will take action against Sodom and thus deliver those it oppressed. Abraham's question is then whether this is actually a way Yahweh can go about being a *šōpēṭ*, a person in authority. "Shall not the *šōpēṭ* of all the earth do *mišpāṭ?*" he asks (18:25). It is a strikingly formulated question, though commentators seem not to have noticed, and translators let the reader off the hook by having Abraham ask whether the judge of all the earth must not do justice; we then read it as if Abraham had asked whether the judge must not do *ṣědāqāh*.

From Abraham's angle, it might seem that the last thing Yahweh needs is a challenge to do *mišpāṭ* if that indeed means merely "decisive action"; God is already on the way to being decisive, and this is what worries Abraham. More likely "do *mišpāṭ*" has its common implication, "execute judgment [on behalf of the righteous or needy]" (see, e.g., 1 Kings 3:28; Ps. 9:17 [16]). In a sense, *mišpāṭ* thus indeed implies judgment that reflects *ṣědāqāh*. Elsewhere, the point is often explicit through the addition of the word *ṣědāqāh* to *mišpāṭ*, but on other occasions it is made through mention of the object or beneficiary of the judgment, and here they have just been mentioned. Abraham's point is, then, "You have to execute judgment [for the righteous in Sodom as well as for the oppressed elsewhere]." We should in any case preserve the concreteness of the question: "Shall not the judge of all the earth execute judgment?"

I have hinted that Yahweh's conversations with Israel's ancestors point to one or two possible responses to any suggestion that Yahweh's giving the land of Canaan to Israel is an act of *'awlāh*. This giving is part of a purpose designed to benefit other nations as well as Israel, and Yahweh has agreed to maintain a concern for the righteous within a wicked nation. Genesis 15:16 also contained a more overt response. Yahweh intends to keep the other promise regarding giving the land of Canaan to Abraham's descendants, but not until the *'āwōn* of the Amorites is full. The questions raised by this rationale, however, are the same as the ones that Knierim raises regarding passages such as Leviticus 18 and

---

39. See Knierim, *Task of Old Testament Theology*, 319–20.
40. See R. E. Clements, "The Purpose of the Book of Jonah," in G. Anderson, ed., *Congress Volume: Edinburgh, 1974* (VTSup 28; Leiden: Brill, 1975) 16–28.

Deuteronomy 9. It does not answer the question, "Why the Canaanites in particular?"

The texts probably imply the conviction that the Canaanites' wickedness was greater than that of other peoples. This raises two difficulties. First, such knowledge as we have from other sources does not paint a picture of the Canaanites as more depraved than other contemporary peoples or, say, the present inhabitants of southern California. Second, we are familiar with the way in which peoples do demonize each other, especially if they need to justify their own attacks on them. Given the trenchant tone of Levenson's critique of Knierim, it is intriguing to note that Levenson has made this point especially in asking, "Is there a counterpart in the Hebrew Bible to New Testament antisemitism?"[41] He sees such a counterpart in the way the Hebrew Bible "caricatures" the Canaanites in order to justify Israel's displacement of them.

Judith Plaskow has offered a parallel Jewish feminist critique of Wyschogrod and of election theology in general.[42] The feminist vision for diversity without hierarchy parallels Knierim's vision for the particular without particularism. Plaskow associates Jewish election theology with patriarchalism; election is a "fundamentally hierarchical" notion.[43] Yet she also notes that election and exclusiveness need not necessarily belong together. Judaism has not spoken or behaved as if its election made it feel superior to the rest of the world. It has been the victim of such views rather than the subject of them. If Judaism lacks a sense of superiority, the explicit emphases of the Torah itself may make this not so surprising, for the context of Deuteronomy's statement of Canaanite wickedness is a denial of Israelite superiority. There was something indefinable that attracted Yahweh to Israel, but whatever this was, it was neither Israel's numerousness nor its righteousness (Deut. 7:7–8; 9:4–6), but rather, the opposite (see 9:7–8 and the passage that follows). Furthermore, the idea that the notion of superiority and domination is key to Israel's understanding of its relationship with Canaan is difficult to fit with its explicit understanding of the annihilation of the Canaanites as a dedication of them to Yahweh (ḥērem). If the latter is some kind of veil for the former, it is one that subverts it.

Additional significance attaches to those statements in Deuteronomy 7–9, given that a handful of passages in that context (4:37; 7:6, 7; 10:15; 14:2) are actually the only ones in Genesis through Joshua that refer to

---

41. JES 22 (1985) 242–60, esp. 248–52. See also Levenson, The Universal Horizon of Biblical Particularism (New York: American Jewish Committee, 1985); revised ed. in Brett, ed., Ethnicity and the Bible, 143–69.

42. See J. Plaskow, Standing Again at Sinai: Judaism from a Feminist Perspective (San Francisco: Harper & Row, 1990), esp. 75–120.

43. Plaskow, Standing Again at Sinai, 99.

Yahweh's choice of Israel (cf. 1 Kings 3:8; Neh. 9:7). We speak as if this is a major theme of the books, but the language is exceptional; it does not even come in Deuteronomy 9.

The theme of election can indeed be present when the word is not. RSV presupposes this in rendering the verb *yāda'* with "choose" at Gen. 18:19. It might have done the same in rendering Jeremiah's account of his "call" (another modern construct that we import into the Bible) where he speaks of Yahweh acknowledging him, distinguishing him, and then appointing him to a task. In Isaiah 40–55 it is the verb *qārā'* ("call, summon") that more often denotes what theology refers to as election. This language underlines that Yahweh's choosing Israel as much resembles a man's summoning a slave or a cook's choosing which pan to use as it does a woman's choosing a man on whom to bestow her love. It is doubtful whether in Isaiah 40–55 or anywhere else (except Isa. 66:19?) it is wise to speak of Israel's being called to a "mission" to the nations (yet another construct from outside the Bible). The suggestion that Israel is elected for service is also an oversimplification, for Israel remains God's chosen even when it fails to serve, while conversely, serving Yahweh does not make one a member of Israel.[44] Yet if Israel is indeed called or summoned or chosen by Yahweh (e.g., Isa. 41:9), then it is as a servant.

We thus need to be wary of reading into the books all that we might mean by the notion of election when their own language works in a different way and points to a notion with different dynamics. This is the more so when we take account of the theological point that is made by explicit talk in terms of choice here and elsewhere. In Deut. 7:6–7, for instance, the point is not at all to encourage Israelite superiority, but to underline a demand for a distinctive Israelite commitment to Yahweh (cf. 10:15; 14:2). In 1 Kings 3:8 it is to underline the demand that leadership lays on the king. In Isaiah 40–55 it is to encourage a people oppressed by a much more powerful overlord. Of a piece with this is the conviction that an awareness of being especially loved by its God (knowing itself chosen) has played a key role in keeping the Jewish people going over subsequent millennia; even Israel's sin will not cancel out its election, because Israel's righteousness was not the basis of its election in the first place.[45]

Perhaps Plaskow is right that election is an inherently particularist notion, and that is one significance of the Old Testament's restraint in explicit use of this language even though it talks more broadly about Israel's special relationship with Yahweh. But we also need to note that

---

44. Cf. Levenson, *Ethnicity and the Bible*, 155–57.
45. See Wyschogrod, *Body of Faith*, 12, 24–25, 213.

election talk's openness to ideological misuse along lines that Plaskow suggests does not in itself establish that there is a question mark about the actual notion of election. Practically everything is open to ideological misuse.[46] Plaskow herself instances the call to obey the Torah, which can encourage "empty legalism,"[47] even as a stress on God's grace can encourage antinomianism (see Romans 6; cf. James 2). Regina Schwartz emphasizes monotheism's potential to encourage the same violent exclusivism as election, though it is not clear why polytheism would be less open to this temptation.[48] The counter to bad election theology need not be no election theology, but rather, the good election theology that Knierim approves, election theology that links election with responsive commitment and a desire to share.

Another instance of election thinking that does not utilize the actual word is the use of the notion of Yahweh's unexplained favor (ḥēn, e.g., Gen. 6:8). J. M. G. Barclay has suggested that "Paul partially deconstructs his own Christological exclusivism by his pervasive appeal to the grace of God."[49] If "finding favor with Yahweh" is another way of speaking of election, then it is striking that the Torah never refers to Yahweh's favor to Israel but does refer to Yahweh's favor to Noah. Along with its assertion that Yahweh's favor is exercised at Yahweh's discretion (Exod. 33:19), the Torah similarly deconstructs its own exclusivism.

THE HARNESSING OF UNFAIRNESS

That peoples do demonize and caricature each other is, of course, not in itself evidence that Israel did so and that the Israelite account of the Canaanites is wrong, and it may be that the Canaanites' religion and life incorporated a distinctively appalling combination of such features as the sacrifice of children and the ritualization of sexual activity.

But let us suppose that the Canaanites were only averagely wicked. What happens to them is not fair compared with what happens to other people, and the Old Testament does not seem to notice the fact. Yet what happens to them is only a spectacular example of a phenomenon that recurs in the Old Testament and in life. There is a randomness about whether people get their comeuppance. If you are in the wrong place

---

46. Cf. the remarks of D. Boyarin, *A Radical Jew* (Berkeley: University of California Press, 1994) 247–48.

47. Plaskow, *Standing Again at Sinai*, 217.

48. See Regina Schwartz, *The Curse of Cain* (Chicago: University of Chicago Press, 1997); see also Miroslav Volf's review of Schwartz's book in *Christianity Today* 27 (April 1998) 32–35.

49. J. M. G. Barclay, " 'Neither Jew nor Greek,' " in Brett, ed., *Ethnicity and the Bible*, 213.

at the wrong time, you experience the disaster you deserve (or do not deserve); if you are lucky, you do not. Most generations of Canaanites, indeed, were not annihilated by the Israelites, in fact or fiction. Most generations of Judean leadership did not get transported to Babylon, even though they may have deserved it as much as did the generation of Jehoiachin and Zedekiah.

This coheres with the fact that the experience of nations in general often seems unfair, as the experience of individual human beings seems unfair. This was as much so for Israel as for any other people: it "has endured its history much more than it has shaped it."[50] This had been the case with Israel before the exodus, and it would in due course seem to be almost systematically so, in such a way as to raise the question whether Israel's election was actually an election to suffering. But in general, different peoples and different individuals have different degrees of giftedness and resources and different degrees of oppression and hurt. While much of that unfairness can be traced to human agencies, much of it cannot, and the implication seems to be that God either is not very interested in fairness or is not in a position to ensure it. What happens in the story in Joshua, then, is that Yahweh utilizes history in its unfairness, getting hands dirty rather than staying unsullied in a heavenly environment in which there would be no accusation of unfairness but nothing achieved either. Admittedly such theological comments are modern observations regarding an issue that does not seem to have been much of a problem for Old or New Testament writers. There is very little evidence that any of them were embarrassed by the story in Joshua.[51] The point is related to the distinctively modern and Western nature of our preoccupation with theodicy. Other cultures have assumed that life should be fair (Israel indeed did), but the nature and the extent of our preoccupation with the questions raised by its unfairness is a modern and Western one.

To put it another way, acceptance of (at least a story of) the annihilation of the Canaanites is actually one of the Old Testament's instances of living with the penultimate that Knierim affirms.[52] But the notion of living with the penultimate presupposes that we believe in the ultimate. The Old Testament lives with a tension between what was designed from creation and what is possible given the obduracy of the human will, and with the same tension understood as holding between what will be at the End and what, given that obduracy, is possible now. Such

---

50. Preuss, *Old Testament Theology*, 1:294.

51. See M. Walzer, "The Idea of Holy War in Ancient Israel," *JRE* 20 (1992–93) 215; against D. Jacobson, *The Story of the Stories: The Chosen People and Its God* (New York: Harper & Row, 1982) 37 (cf. Wyschogrod, *Body of Faith*, 218).

52. Knierim, *Task of Old Testament Theology*, 107, 129–30.

a perspective enables us to articulate an Old Testament theology that does justice to the complexity of the Old Testament's own emphases rather than having to rationalize these.

Perhaps a better way to put it would be to say that Yahweh makes history's "unfairness" the means of putting *mišpāṭ ûṣĕdāqāh* into effect. This is so in two ways.

First, the phrase *mišpāṭ ûṣĕdāqāh* implies that Yahweh behaves in a decisive and committed way to Israel. Joshua could have described Israel's entering into possession of the land of Canaan as an act of *mišpāṭ ûṣĕdāqāh*, even though it does not do so. As Knierim puts it, the concept of justice presupposed by Exodus through Joshua "states that Israel's oppression of the Canaanite nations and Israel's liberation from Egyptian oppression are equally just. It justifies... both liberation of and oppression by the same people.... Justice is what serves Israel's election by and covenant with Yahweh rather than and regardless of a principle of justice that is the same for all nations."[53] Exodus 3:7–8 makes the point vividly.

In themselves, *mišpāṭ ûṣĕdāqāh* are thus not universalizable principles. But Knierim notes that Yahweh is also said to exercise *mišpāṭ ûṣĕdāqāh* elsewhere than in the story of Israel. All Yahweh's work is done in faithfulness, Yahweh loves *ṣĕdāqāh ûmišpāṭ*, and the world is full of Yahweh's *ḥesed*. Psalm 33 follows up these observations with a look back to creation, but even without this its statements have universalized Yahweh's *mišpāṭ ûṣĕdāqāh*. Yahweh is committed to decisive action in the context of a relationship that means doing right by the other party, and is committed in this respect to the whole world. Yahweh decides for the world with *ṣedeq* (Ps. 9:9 [8]; cf. 98:9 — the verb is *šāpaṭ*). The foundation of Yahweh's throne, the throne from which Yahweh rules all the world, is *ṣedeq ûmišpāṭ*, and the heavens proclaim Yahweh's *ṣedeq* (Ps. 97:2).

Following H. H. Schmid, M. Weinfeld saw this exercise of *mišpāṭ ûṣĕdāqāh* as the imposition of order on the cosmos,[54] but this formulation understates the relational implications of *mišpāṭ ûṣĕdāqāh*. But Weinfeld usefully emphasizes three moments of Yahweh's imposition of *mišpāṭ ûṣĕdāqāh* in the Old Testament: creation, the origins of Israel, and the final judgment.[55] One would expect there to be some coherence about these acts of *mišpāṭ ûṣĕdāqāh*. If they must be moments when Yahweh acts decisively to do right by those to whom Yahweh is committed, that has to apply to the world and not just to Israel.

---

53. Knierim, *Task of Old Testament Theology*, 97.

54. Weinfeld, *Social Justice*, 20, referring to H. H. Schmid, *Gerechtigkeit als Weltordnung* (Tübingen: Mohr, 1968). Cf., for example, Knierim, *Task of Old Testament Theology*, 15.

55. For example, Weinfeld, *Social Justice*, 5, 21.

A second way in which the unfairness of history is harnessed to *mišpāṭ ûṣĕdāqāh* is, then, that Israel's occupation of Canaan forms part of a story about the blessing of the world and about Yahweh's bringing *tôrāh* and *mišpāṭ* to the world (Isa. 2:2–4). Paul hints at this point in that midrash on the Old Testament in Romans 9–11, where he includes some discussion of God's fairness. He, too, assumes that God has always been concerned for the blessing of the whole world and that Israel is the means of intention becoming realization. The Pharaoh of the exodus acts, then, as a kind of necessary foil to Israel in the story of how that realization comes about. Paradoxically, Gentile salvation is thus achieved only through Gentile loss.

Perhaps the Canaanites may be looked at the same way. Genesis assumes that for the world to regain blessing it is necessary for Israel to flourish. Deuteronomy assumes that for Israel to flourish it is necessary for the Canaanites to be removed. Knierim suggests that Deuteronomy should have trusted in the inherent power of Israel's theological convictions. If they cannot withstand such pressures, are they worth annihilating for? In the long run they showed themselves able to do this, but perhaps Deuteronomy was only being realistic in recognizing the power of Canaanite temptation when Israelite faith in Yahweh was a newly budded flower.

The fate of Canaan is subordinate to the promise to Israel. But the promise to Israel is in turn subordinate to the fate of the whole world. A temporary unfairness that discriminates for Israel and against Canaan is designed to give way to a broader fairness. Election is exclusive in the short term, but it is designed in due course to benefit others than its short-term beneficiaries. This does not imply that Israel ever ceases to be God's first love, but it could imply that other peoples can be equally loved in their own way.

BIBLIOGRAPHY

Borowitz, Eugene B. "The Dialectic of Jewish Particularity." *JES* 8 (1971).

Boyarin, Daniel. *A Radical Jew*. Berkley: University of California, 1994.

Brett, Mark, ed. *Ethnicity and the Bible*. Biblical Interpretation Series, no. 18. Leiden: Brill, 1996.

Brueggmann, Walter. *Genesis*. Philadelphia: Westminster, 1982.

Clements, Ronald E. "The Purpose of the Book of Jonah." In *Congress Volume: Edinburgh, 1974*. Ed. G. Anderson. Leiden: Brill, 1975.

Dunn, James D. G. *Romans 9–16*. Word Biblical Commentary. Dallas: Word, 1988.

Kant, Immanuel. *Religion within the Limits of Reason Alone*. Trans. T. Greene and H. Hudson. New York: Harper, 1960.

Knierim, Rolf P. *The Task of Old Testament Theology: Substance, Method, and Cases*. Grand Rapids: Eerdmans, 1995.

Levenson, Jon D. "Is There a Counterpart in the Hebrew Bible to New Testament Antisemitism?" *JES* 22 (1985): 242–60.

———. Review of Knierim, *The Task of Old Testament Theology*. *RelSRev* 24 (1998): 39–42.

Morgan, Robert. *The Nature of New Testament Theology*. London: SCM, 1973.

Plaskow, Judith. *Standing Again at Sinai*. San Francisco: Harper & Row, 1990.

Preuss, Horst Dietrich. *Theologie des Alten Testaments*. 2 vols. Stuttgart: Kohlhammer, 1991–92. ET *Old Testament Theology*. 2 vols. Louisville: Westminster John Knox, 1995-96.

Schwartz, Regina. *The Curse of Cain*. Chicago: University of Chicago Press, 1997.

Soulen, R. Kendall. *The God of Israel and Christian Theology*. Minneapolis: Fortress, 1996.

Volf, Miroslav. Review of Schwartz, *The Curse of Cain*. *Christianity Today* 27 (April 1998): 32–35.

Walzer, Michael. "The Idea of Holy War in Ancient Israel." *JRE* 20 (1992–93): 215–28.

Weinfeld, Moshe. *Social Justice in Ancient Israel and the Ancient Near East*. ET Minneapolis: Fortress, 1995.

Wyschogrod, Michael. *The Body of Faith: God in the People of Israel*. San Francisco: Harper, 1989.

12

The Divine Redeemer:
Toward a Biblical Theology of Redemption

Robert L. Hubbard Jr.

Biblical theology is alive and well despite Brevard Childs' well-known obituary on the subject nearly three decades ago.[1] At least, one recognizes that publications on the subject abound.[2] On the other hand, as Rolf Knierim has observed, biblical theology has been and always will be in crisis because of the theological differences between the two Testaments.[3] Indeed, for him, how the two Testaments interrelate theologically remains the crucial issue facing biblical theology today.

The present essay explores the theological theme of redemption in the two Testaments.[4] It represents a longitudinal study that probes the understandings of redemption in the Old and New Testaments.[5] To limit its scope, it draws on a pool of texts that specifically invoke the vocabulary of redemption but that involve God, either as lawgiver or as redeemer. For the Old Testament, the linguistic roots are *pdh* ("to redeem, rescue"), *g'l* ("to redeem, serve as redeemer"), and their deriva-

---

1. B. S. Childs, *Biblical Theology in Crisis* (Philadelphia: Westminster, 1970).

2. Most are collections of essays or *Festschriften*. Some examples are H. T. C. Sun and K. L. Eades, eds., *Problems in Biblical Theology* (Grand Rapids: Eerdmans, 1997); B. D. Ingraffia, *Postmodern Theory and Biblical Theology: Vanquishing God's Shadow* (Cambridge: Cambridge University Press, 1995); S. J. Kraftchick et al., eds., *Biblical Theology: Problems and Perspectives* (Nashville: Abingdon, 1995); S. Pedersen, ed., *New Directions in Biblical Theology* (Leiden: Brill, 1994); F. Watson, *Text, Church and World: Biblical Interpretation in Theological Perspective* (Grand Rapids: Eerdmans, 1994); B. S. Childs, *Biblical Theology of the Old and New Testaments* (Minneapolis: Fortress, 1993). See also C. Stuhlmueller, ed., *The Collegeville Pastoral Dictionary of Biblical Theology* (Collegeville, Minn.: Liturgical Press, 1996); the two thematic series Overtures to Biblical Theology (Fortress) and New Studies in Biblical Theology (Eerdmans); and the two journals *Biblical Theology Bulletin* and *Horizons in Biblical Theology*.

3. R. P. Knierim, "On Biblical Theology," in C. A. Evans and S. Talmon, eds., *The Quest for Context and Meaning* (Leiden: Brill, 1997) 122.

4. An earlier version of this essay was presented at the biblical theology study group of the Tyndale Fellowship in Cambridge, England, on July 3, 1998. I gratefully acknowledge the stimulating conversation that followed and the kindness shown to me by group members on that occasion.

5. Its thematic focus takes its methodological cue in part from the multiplex approach of G. Hasel, *Old Testament Theology: Basic Issues in the Current Debate* (4th ed.; Grand Rapids: Eerdmans, 1991) 204–5. For an overview of redemption in general see J. Unterman, "Redemption (OT)," *ABD*, 5:650–54; G. S. Shogren, "Redemption (NT)," *ABD*, 5:654–57.

tives, terms that flow from the rich conceptual reservoir of Israelite law.[6] The preposition *min* ("from") often occurs with both the above terms, thereby signaling that redemption affords the redeemed a change of location, status, or condition (e.g., Deut. 7:8 [*pdh*]; Gen. 48:16 [*g'l*]). The Old Testament's two linguistic streams flow into two New Testament word groups, *lytroō* ("to redeem") and *agorazō* ("to buy"), and their derivatives.[7] Our task is, first, to explore the theme in each Testament exegetically; and, second, to discuss what Knierim calls their "mutual critical complementarity," that is, the insights that each contributes and the view of the other as seen from the vantage point of its opposite.

REDEMPTION'S ROOTS: OLD TESTAMENT LAW

The Covenant Book (Exodus 21–23) offers probably the Bible's two earliest cases of redemption.[8] These, in turn, launch its long, rich life as a key theological metaphor. The first case concerns the redemption of an Israelite woman sold into a slave-marriage by her father (Exod. 21:7–11; cf. vv. 1–6).[9] Interestingly, the preceding verses (vv. 1–6) make no

---

6. For both roots the foundational study remains J. J. Stamm, *Erlösen und Vergeben im Alten Testament* (Bern: Francke, 1940) 7–44. See also R. L. Hubbard Jr., *"pādâ,"* *NIDOTTE*, 3:578–82; idem, *"gā'al,"* *NIDOTTE*, 1:789–94; H. Cazelles, *"pādâ,"* *ThWAT*, 6:514–22; H. Ringgren, *"gā'al,"* *TDOT*, 2:350–55; J. J. Stamm, *"pādâ,"* *THAT*, 2:389–406; idem, *"gā'al,"* *THAT*, 1:144–45. For the unrelated root *g'l* (II), "to defile," see D. J. A. Clines, *The Dictionary of Classical Hebrew* (4 vols.; Sheffield: Sheffield Academic Press, 1993–98), 2:295–96. The usage of *g'l* is concentrated in Leviticus 25 (vv. 24, 25, 26, 29, 31, 32, 48, 51, 52), Jeremiah 32 (vv. 7, 8), and Ruth 4 (vv. 6, 7); cf. Ezek. 11:15; the qal passive participle *gə'ûlîm* ("redeemed," only Isa. 63:4).

7. See D. H. Field, *"agorazō,"* *TDNT*, 1:267–68; F. Büchsel, *"agorazō,"* *TDNT*, 1:124–28; idem, *"lytron,"* *TDNT*, 4:340–56; K. Kertelge, *"lytron,"* *EDNT*, 2:364–66; J. Schneider and C. Brown, *"lytron,"* *NIDNTT*, 3:189–200; D. Hill, *Greek Words and Hebrew Meanings: Studies in the Semantics of Soteriological Terms* (SNTSMS 5; Cambridge: Cambridge University Press, 1967). As one would expect, the associated Greek prepositions are *apo* ("from"), *ek* ("out of"), and *anti* ("instead of"), whether prefixed to verbs or separate from them.

8. This concurs with the scholarly consensus that the Covenant Book is the Bible's oldest legal code. See, for example, S. Paul, *Studies in the Book of the Covenant in the Light of Cuneiform and Biblical Law* (VTSup 18; Leiden: Brill, 1970) 43–45 (preconquest); D. Patrick, *Old Testament Law* (London: SCM, 1985) 63–66 (the Judges period), F. Crüsemann, *The Torah: Theology and Social History of Israelite Law* (Minneapolis: Fortress, 1996) 166–67 (ninth to eighth centuries); W. Schwendemann, "Recht-Grundrecht-Menschenwürde: Eine Untersuchung von Ex 21,2–11 im Rahmen theologischer Anthropologie," *BN* 77 (1995) 36–40 (era of Amos); contra J. Van Seters, "The Law of the Hebrew Slave," *ZAW* 108 (1996) 534–46 (exilic or postexilic). The most recent literary-critical studies are L. Schwienhorst-Schönberger, *Das Bundesbuch (Ex 20,22–23,33): Studien zu seiner Entstehung und Theologie* (BZAW 188; Berlin: de Gruyter, 1990); Y. Osumi, *Die Kompositionsgeschichte des Bundesbuches Exodus 20:22b–23:33* (OBO 105; Göttingen: Vandenhoeck & Ruprecht, 1991).

9. See G. C. Chirichigno, *Debt-Slavery in Israel and the Ancient Near East* (JSOTSup 141; Sheffield: JSOT Press, 1993) 186–254; V. H. Matthews, "The Anthropology of Slavery in the Covenant Code," in B. M. Levinson, ed., *Theory and Method in Biblical and*

provision for the redemption of male slaves; each simply leaves "a free person" after six years of service (v. 2). But apparently no such time limitation applies to a slave-wife ("she shall not go out as the male slaves do," v. 7).[10] Verse 8 requires the husband-master to permit her redemption, presumably by accepting repayment of the original purchase price, on only one condition: "if she does not please her master."[11] Her master's displeasure with her means that he must "cause her to be redeemed" (*pdh*, hiphil).[12] This is not the place to review all the law's provisions, but two things are striking.[13] First, it affords the slave-wife remarkable protection against oppression. It outlaws her sale to a foreigner (v. 8b) and protects her spousal rights to food, clothing, and conjugal relations (vv. 10–11).[14] Second, it roots the redemption not in the woman's failure to please her husband but in his breach of faith against her (v. 8b, "since he has dealt unfairly with [*bgd b*] her").[15] In other words, the loss of favor is his responsibility — a violation of the understanding, if not trust, between them that, as a consequence, opens for the woman the right of redemption. That redemption benefits her in two ways. It ends her humiliation as a wife out of favor; and it restores

Cuneiform Law: Revision, Interpolation and Development (JSOTSup 181; Sheffield: Sheffield Academic Press, 1994) 119–35; I. Cardellini, *Die biblischen "Sklaven"-Gesetze im Licht des keilschriftlichen Sklavenrechts: Ein Beitrag zur Tradition, Überlieferung und Redaktion der alttestamentlichen Rechtstexte* (BBB 55; Königstein: Hanstein, 1981). Concerning slavery in general see I. Mendelsohn, *Slavery in the Ancient Near East* (New York: Oxford University Press, 1949); M. A. Dandamaev, *Slavery in Babylonia: from Nabopolassar to Alexander the Great (626–331 B.C.)* (trans. V. Powell; rev. ed.; DeKalb: Northern Illinois University Press, 1984).

10. As many have observed, the verb *yṣ'* ("to go out," vv. 2, 7), is a key word that literarily helps to tie vv. 2–6 and vv. 7–11 together.

11. Reading the Qere *lô*, "for himself" (with the LXX, Vulgate, and Syriac; so also NRSV, NIV), for the MT *lō'* in v. 8a. This verse marks the only occurrence of *pdh* hiphil, and its only hophal form also occurs with the redemption of slave-wives (Lev. 19:20). Other cases of redemption (see Leviticus 25) prorated the repayment to the amount of the service or ownership originally paid for. Perhaps the present case also assumes the application of that same principle. See R. L. Hubbard Jr., "The *Go'el* in Ancient Israel: Theological Reflections on an Israelite Institution," *BBR* 1 (1991) 7–8.

12. Its presumed subject, the one who pays for the redemption, is either the woman's father or another member of her family. See C. Houtman, *Das Bundesbuch: Ein Kommentar* (DMOA 24; Leiden: Brill, 1997) 83.

13. For a full discussion see Chirichigno, *Debt-Slavery in Israel*, 244–54; Crüsemann, *The Torah*, 151–59; Houtman, *Das Bundesbuch*, 81–101. Paul (*Book of the Covenant*, 52–53) discusses a similar (but not comparable) case from Mari.

14. If, as seems likely, *'ibrî* (v. 2) means "Hebrew" (vice "Hapiru"), the term "foreign people" (*'am nokrî*) refers to a non-Israelite (cf. Deut. 15:3; 17:15; 23:20), although it could simply designate an Israelite from another city, region, or tribe. See Houtman, *Das Bundesbuch*, 83; Schwienhorst-Schönberger, *Das Bundesbuch*, 315 (fremdes Volk); "another, foreign family," R. Martin-Achard, "*Nēkār*," *THAT*, 2:69; H. Ringgren, "*Nkr*," *ThWAT*, 5:456.

15. For the phrase *bgd b* see Judg. 9:23; Prov. 23:28; Isa. 33:1; Jer. 5:11; 12:6; Lam. 1:2; Hos. 5:7; 6:7; Mal. 2:10, 14, 15.

her to her family, the circle from which she may hope to gain another marriage.[16]

The second case concerns the redemption not of a victim but of a villain. According to Exod. 21:28, when an ox gores someone to death, it loses its own life, but v. 30 adds that, if that death occurs because the owner failed to restrain his ox despite a prior history of goring, the owner also loses his life.[17] Though not intending the death, the owner is legally responsible for it. Notable here is the opening conditional sentence that stipulates when redemption may occur: "If a ransom is imposed on the owner" (*'im kōper yûšat 'ālāyw*, v. 30). In this case redemption is neither automatic nor available on demand but "imposed." But by whom? Although some civil authority might be meant (e.g., local judges or elders), it seems more likely that the ransom provision derives from the recipient of the payment, namely, the victim's family. As J. M. Sprinkle observes, "A victim's family would have little to gain by having the negligent owner put to death, whereas if they accepted a ransom, they would both punish the culprit and compensate themselves."[18] If so, the law permits all parties to make the best of a tragic situation. The condemned man pays a ransom to save his life, the community retains him as a social asset, and the family receives some compensation for its loss.[19]

This brings us to consider next the redemption of the firstborn.[20] Various legal texts lay down two main principles: first, Yahweh owns all firstborn (both human and animal); but, second, Yahweh permits the release of some in exchange for a suitable substitute or stipulated payment.[21] Thus, a sheep will spare a donkey's life for its owner's use (Exod. 13:13a; 34:20a), while the sheep itself (along with the other firstborn not subject to redemption) supplies an animal for sacrifice or meat for priestly meals (Num. 18:17–18). Yahweh even retains rights to un-

---

16. Houtman (*Das Bundesbuch*, 83) suggests that the woman returns to her family circle or becomes the possession of a man of her clan.

17. Cf. the similar law in *ANET*, 163 (§54). For further background see J. J. Finkelstein, *The Ox That Gored* (Philadelphia: American Philosophical Society, 1981); M. A. Katz, "Ox-slaughter and Goring Oxen: Homicide, Animal Sacrifice, and Judicial Process," *Yale Journal of Law* 4, no. 2 (1992) 249–78.

18. J. M. Sprinkle, *"The Book of the Covenant": A Literary Approach* (JSOTSup 174; Sheffield: JSOT Press, 1994) 118.

19. Sprinkle (*Book of the Covenant*, 118–19) even argues that this is the situation's expected outcome, not an exception.

20. See F. E. Greenspahn, *When Brothers Dwell Together: The Preeminence of Younger Siblings in the Hebrew Bible* (New York: Oxford University Press, 1994); R. Syrén, *The Forsaken First-born: A Study of a Recurrent Motif in the Patriarchal Narratives* (JSOTSup 133; Sheffield: JSOT Press, 1993).

21. Exod. 13:2, 12–13; 34:19; Lev. 27:26; Num. 3:12–13; 8:17; Deut. 15:19–20. For legislation concerning agricultural first fruits see Exod. 22:28.

clean firstborn animals, but permits owners to redeem them for a fee or
to sell them outright, in both cases the proceeds going to the sanctuary
treasury (Lev. 27:26–27). Monetary redemption also applies to animal
offerings (Lev. 27:13), houses (v. 15), land (vv. 19–20), and tithes (v. 31).
As for humans, Yahweh originally required the redemption of firstborn
sons at five shekels each (Exod. 13:13b; 34:20b; cf. Num. 8:15–17) but
later took the tribe of Levi in their place (Num. 3:49, 51). One common
element binds the preceding cases of redemption: Yahweh waives his
ownership rights in exchange for stipulated payments, thereby in effect
ceding ownership to Israel.[22]

Finally, this treatment of redemption in Old Testament law ends with
a brief glance at one provision in Old Testament family law.[23] Redemption by a kinsman-redeemer (gōʾēl) is in fact the Old Testament's most
prominent type. The practice centers on the duties of the gōʾēl, a near relative (e.g., a brother, father, uncle, cousin, etc.) legally obliged to assist
kinfolk in distress. According to Leviticus 25, he would buy back their
mortgaged property or houses (vv. 25–34; cf. Jer. 32:7–8) or buy them out
of the slavery into which they had sold themselves (vv. 48–52). These
repurchases had one aim: to restore the unity of family and property,
a metaphysical unity that Israel highly valued. Unlike the two "secular" laws discussed above, this practice articulates its theological roots.
It implements on Israelite soil the redemption won by Yahweh in Egypt
(vv. 42, 55; cf. comments below). In reality Yahweh, not Israel, owns the
land, and he requires the redemption of property and people (vv. 23–
24), lest Israel birth its own cruel Pharaohs and bear a new generation
of impoverished slaves. To deny Israelites redemption is to infringe on
Yahweh's rights by enslaving people who belong to him and, in effect,
to annul the gains of the exodus. Finally, two other duties of the gōʾēl
merit mention. First, the law forbids a ransom payment (kōper) to spare
the life of a premeditated murderer (Num. 35:31), but as "avenger of
blood" (gōʾēl haddām) the kinsman-redeemer could redeem the life of a
relative by killing the killer (Num. 35:19; cf. 2 Sam. 14:11).[24] Mystically,
to restore the relative's lost blood was thought to restore the clan's lost
wholeness, equilibrium, and strength. Second, to die without an heir
similarly weakens the whole clan, so the gōʾēl would also restore clan
strength by marrying the deceased's widow to produce an heir (Ruth
2:20; 3:9, 13; 4:1–14).[25]

---

22. The same principle may underlie the half shekel per person tax after a census,
although the practice is not called "redemption" (Exod. 30:11–16).

23. Hubbard, "The Goʾel in Ancient Israel," 3–19.

24. The killer could, however, seek the protection and formal legal process offered by
a city of refuge (Numbers 35; Joshua 20; 21:13, 21, 27, 32, 38).

25. For the legal issues concerning the marriage of Ruth and Boaz see R. L. Hub-

Now, what do these laws tell us theologically about God, the divine redeemer? At first glance, the two Covenant Book cases seem merely "secular" in nature, treating relationships between humans in the course of daily life rather than relationship with God or his cult. They both lack explicit theological motive clauses from which an inquiring theologian might mine truths. On the other hand, it strikes me as theologically significant that in both cases the speaker is Yahweh himself, not a human lawgiver. That very divine articulation implies divine concern for such mundane matters; indeed, they are of such concern that he requires redemption in the case of the slave-wife and permits it in the case of the ox owner.[26] And what is the character of this redemption? It works for restoration (the return of the slave woman to her family) and against alienation (her sale to a foreigner). It also enforces the ethics inherent in human relationships by holding people accountable for their breaches of faith. But, in the case of the poor ox owner, it also mediates mercy to the irresponsible but not malevolent so that someone may live. As for the law of the firstborn, here Yahweh's personal rights make him a party to redemption, not just its policy maker. Theologically, his policy bespeaks divine generosity, a way in which Yahweh shares his property with Israel. Indeed, in my view, that the once-for-all substitution of the Levites satisfies Yahweh forever reflects extraordinary divine generosity. Over time eleven tribes would likely produce more firstborn than one tribe, yet Yahweh, content with his Levites, requires no further accounting to ensure that he has not been cheated.

Finally, in the *gō'ēl* divine grace works legal redemption to safeguard Israel's freedom and to foster social equality among its people. It also enables the collective family to recover wholeness from weakness after debilitating losses. More importantly, the kinsman-redeemer practice highlights the family connection between redeemer and redeemed, a theme to which I will return below. Through redemption law — its protection of the vulnerable, its restoration of wholeness out of loss — God graciously preserves and fosters among his people the blessing long ago promised to Abram (Gen. 12:1-3).

---

bard Jr., *The Book of Ruth* (NICOT; Grand Rapids, 1988) 48–62. Several Old Testament poetical texts about Yahweh suggest that the redeemer also advocated the cause of a needy relative involved in a lawsuit (Job 19:25; Prov. 23:11) or illegally incarcerated (Jer. 50:34; cf. Ps. 72:14).

26. As is well known, although originating with the gods, the Laws of Lipit-Ishtar and the Code of Hammurabi are articulated by a human king in the first person. For translation and commentary see *ANET*, 159–60, 163–80.

THE DIVINE REDEEMER: THE EXODUS PARADIGM

In the law God as its divine "patron" mandates redemption by humans. But God himself also is redeemer, and the Old Testament paradigm of divine redemption is Yahweh's liberation of Israel from Egyptian slavery. Deuteronomy's speeches recall that episode repeatedly (15:15; 21:8; 24:18), as do other biblical writers (Neh. 1:10; Ps. 78:42; 106:10; 111:9; Isa. 51:10; Mic. 6:4). In my view, the exodus sounds three new, theologically significant themes. First, the exodus redemption frees slaves, not from the relatively humane self-indenture of Leviticus 25 or slave-marriage of Exodus 21, but from a long, brutal, oppressive captivity (Exod. 6:6; Deut. 7:8; 13:5; Mic. 6:4; cf. Exod. 21:8). Pharaoh holds Israel against its will by force, cruelly seeks to control its population, and commands impossible productivity goals under horrible conditions (Exod. 1:8–22). Israel's only hope of redemption is that Yahweh will respond to her bitter, groaning cries (Exod. 2:23–25; 3:7–9). Second, this redemption happens not through repayment of money owed or outright mercy but because Yahweh overpowers Pharaoh in a titanic struggle that finally breaks the oppressor's grip (Deut. 9:26; Neh. 1:10; Ps. 77:15). Third, Yahweh redeems Israel because of his prior covenant relationship with their ancestors. Yahweh identifies himself as the "God of your ancestors" (Exod. 3:15–16; 4:5) and acts to implement his covenant promise to give them land (Exod. 3:8, 17; 6:4, 8; cf. 2:24; 32:13; 33:1; Deut. 7:8; 9:26). Yahweh demands that Pharaoh release "my people" (Exod. 5:1; 7:16; 8:1, 20; 9:1, 13; 10:3; cf. 7:4; 8:21–23; 10:4). In short, Yahweh redeems because of his preexistent personal covenant with this family of clans.

Strikingly, Exod. 6:6 and 15:13 describe this redemptive act with the root of family law, *gō'ēl*, not the more common root, *pdh*. *Gō'ēl* here may simply mean "to rescue (from danger)" as elsewhere, but *gō'ēl* also describes the redemption of Jacob (Gen. 48:16), one of the two ancestors cited in Exod. 6:3–4 (cf. Isa. 29:22). If, as some scholars believe,[27] *gō'ēl* has its family law sense here, Exod. 6:6 and 15:13 would portray Yahweh the redeemer in family terms. In the exodus, Yahweh the kinsman-redeemer releases his "kinfolk" from slavery and restores the "family" wholeness that slavery disrupted. Whatever the case, the exodus forever defined Israel's theology of salvation as rescue from the cruel, resistant grip of an oppressive power. David later revels in how unprecedented and stunning the exodus is: "Is there another nation on earth whose God went to redeem (*pdh*) it as a people, . . . doing great and awesome things for them?" (2 Sam. 7:23; cf. 1 Chron. 17:21). Furthermore, the exodus

---

27. Notably, J. Durham, *Exodus* (WBC 3; Waco: Word, 1987) 72, 78; T. E. Fretheim, *Exodus* (Louisville: John Knox, 1991) 93. The fact that Isaiah 40–66 speaks of the redemption brought by the new exodus with forms of *g'l* may support their view.

created Israel's central ethical ideal. In Deuteronomy it backs up Yahweh's demand that Israel generously supply departing Hebrew slaves (15:13–15), leave food for the poor to glean (24:19–22), and not abuse widows, orphans, and aliens (24:17–18). On the other hand, the exodus reassures Israel that Yahweh will remove, not punish, guilt for an unexplained death (Deut. 21:8) and deliver them from their (and Yahweh's) foes (Ps. 74:2). Finally, the exodus story explains to children why leaven is banished during Passover and why the firstborn receive the special treatment discussed above (Exod. 13:5–8, 11–15).

In the exodus Israel experienced Yahweh as redeemer. Thus, it is no surprise that "redeemer" (*gōʾēl*) becomes a title accorded Yahweh. Paired with "rock" (*ṣûr*) it recalls his powerful protection (Ps. 19:14) or mercy (78:35); paired with "savior" (*môšîaʿ*) it bespeaks rescue from Pharaoh-like oppressors (Isa. 49:26); paired with "father" (*ʾāb*), it remembers Yahweh's intimate kinship with Israel (Isa. 63:16).[28] More theologically significant, Isaiah 40–66 musters allusions to the first exodus, even invoking the root *gʾl* ("to redeem"), to portray Israel's imminent release from captivity in Babylon as a new exodus.[29] Thus, the paradigm of salvation in the past shapes the portrait of salvation in the future. For example, Isa. 52:3–6 (cf. 63:9) offers a clever thumbnail sketch of Exodus 1–6 to explain Yahweh's next move, to liberate his people, held captive illegally, from oppression:

> Long ago, my people went down into Egypt to reside there as aliens;
>   the Assyrian, too, has oppressed them without cause.
> Now therefore what am I doing here, says the Lord,
>   seeing that my people are taken away without cause?
> Their rulers howl, says the Lord,
>   and continually, all day long, my name is despised.
> Therefore my people shall know my name;
>   therefore in that day they shall know that it is I who speak; here am I.[30]

---

28. Ringgren, "*gāʾal*," *TDOT*, 2:355. The title "your redeemer" (often in the messenger formula) dominates Isaiah 40–66 (e.g., 41:14; 43:14; 44:24; 48:17; 54:5, 8; cf. 47:4; 63:16 ("our redeemer"); 44:6; 49:7 ("Israel's redeemer"). The title apparently aims to give reassurance, since it twice occurs with "Fear not!" (41:14; 54:4–5; cf. 44:8).

29. Isa. 43:14–15 NRSV [but cf. NIV]; 51:10–11; 52:3–6, 9; 60:16–17; 62:12; cf. 63:9.

30. Other examples of allusions to the first exodus abound. In the storming of Babylon's gates one hears echoes of Yahweh's overpowering of Pharaoh (Isa. 43:14–15 NRSV [but cf. NIV]; cf. 49:26; 52:9). The picture of the redeemed's return alludes to Yahweh's guidance in the wilderness and provision of water from the rock (Isa. 48:20–21; cf. Numbers 20). The same mighty Yahweh who dried up the Red Sea for the "redeemed" (*gĕʾûlîm*) in Exodus 14–15 will guarantee the joyous return of the "ransomed" (*pĕdûyîm*) to Zion (Isa. 51:10–11; 62:12). In a very creative move, occasionally the oracles in Isaiah 40–66 juxtapose the language of redemption and creation. The result is a clever, almost paradoxical, metaphorical pairing of cosmic sovereignty and familial intimacy (e.g., Isa. 44:21–28). As redeemer, it is Yahweh's duty to redeem his sons and daughters; as creator, he spends

In sum, the exodus reports Yahweh's title as "redeemer," and prophetic reuse of the exodus paradigm achieve two things: the introduction of the theological motif of redemption as release from tyrannical
slavery, and the establishment of God as the redeemer par excellence.

REDEMPTION: SEVERAL OTHER IMPORTANT SENSES

Two other less attested senses of redemption merit brief attention. First,
in some contexts, redemption means simply "to rescue (from danger)"
without implying the legal or social background discussed previously.
Rescuers may be friends (1 Sam. 14:45; Job 6:23), but primarily it is
Yahweh who rescues people from death (Ps. 103:4; Job 5:20; 33:28) or
deathly dangers both national (Ps. 25:22; 1 Macc. 4:11) and personal
(Ps. 26:11; 31:5; 44:22; 55:18; 69:18; 119:134).[31] The "redeemed" credit
God for their rescue (Lam. 3:58; Ps. 71:23; 107:2), and David twice
swears oaths by Yahweh as rescuer (2 Sam. 4:9; 1 Kings 1:29). Theologically, such cases presuppose overpowering, life-threatening danger
whose only counter is Yahweh's superior firepower. But the Old Testament warns that ultimately death is humanly inescapable. According to
Psalm 49, no one, however rich, can buy escape from death — the price
is simply out of reach (vv. 7–8) but God will redeem the faithful from
death by taking them (v. 15). Although we cannot be sure, the psalmist
may allude to some form of afterlife, since the heavenly exits of Enoch
(Gen. 5:24) and Elijah (2 Kings 2:10) both use the same verb "take," *lqḥ*
(cf. Ps. 73:24–26).[32]

Second, several texts associate redemption with the forgiveness of

---

whole countries as mere coins (Egypt, Ethiopia, Seba) to pay for their release (Isa. 43:1–
7). As redeemer, Yahweh will marry widowed Zion and bless her with many children;
as creator he has the power to do so (Isa. 54:1–8). See S. Lee, *Creation and Redemption in
Isaiah 40–55* (Jian Dao Dissertation Series 2; Hong Kong: Alliance Bible Seminary, 1995);
C. Stuhlmueller, *Creative Redemption in Deutero-Isaiah* (AnBib 43; Rome: Biblical Institute
Press, 1970).

31. Some prayers pair "redeem" (*g'l*) with "plead my cause" (*rîb*), metaphorically seeking Yahweh's advocacy as kinsman-redeemer (e.g., Ps. 119:154; cf. Prov. 23:11; Jer. 50:34;
cf. Isa. 35:9–10).

32. In addition, the Old Testament has a concept of eschatological redemption. If redemption frees Israel from captivity, Yahweh's refusal to enact it signals the arrival of
divine judgment against the northern kingdom. Unlike David, Ephraim will not be delivered from national death (Hos. 7:13; 13:14). On the other hand, the return from exile is
divine redemption, Yahweh overpowering Israel's captors (Jer. 31:11; 50:33–34). Even the
assembly of nations to conquer Jerusalem is a setup to later redemption, their later plun-
dering by Zion (Micah 4:10). Isaiah 1:27 seems to imply that justice and righteousness are
Zion's purchase price, but clearly the return gladdens the "redeemed" (Isa. 35:9–10; 51:11)
and includes Ephraim (Zech. 10:7–8). In the end, restored Zion's new name will be "the
Redeemed of the Lord" (Isa. 62:12).

sin, although precisely how redemption relates to forgiveness is not always clear.[33] Of these, Ps. 130:7–8 is probably the most important:

> O Israel, hope in the Lord! For with the Lord there is steadfast love,
>   and with him is great power to redeem.
> It is he who will redeem Israel from all its iniquities.

Though cryptic, the affirmation of Yahweh as "he who will redeem Israel from all its iniquities" (v. 8) presumes that iniquities are an overpowering force, a cruel spiritual Pharaoh, tightly gripping Israel. That is the implication of the preceding line, "with [Yahweh] is great power to redeem" (v. 7). For the first time a redemption text acknowledges sin — both its guilt and its terrible consequences — as a power to be overcome, and only by Yahweh, not by powerless Israel itself.[34] This new insight will wield great influence on New Testament writers.

In summary, speaking broadly, the Old Testament understands redemption as the release by intervention of another of people, animals, or property from the authority, possession, control, or harm exercised by others.[35] These sovereign others may be present or potential, and their subjects enter their control simply by birth in subordinate status, by a sale transacted by another sovereign, by their own errors, by the deserved or undeserved attacks of others, or by capture by force. Thus, the occasion for redemption is their social, physical, or spiritual weakness, if not outright powerlessness. In other words, behind redemption lies a power differential between the two parties, the powerful sovereign and the powerless subject. Thus, redemption requires the intervention of someone strong, socially superior, or rich to effect it, someone at least as strong, prominent, or rich as the current controlling other. That is why God plays such a leading role in biblical redemption: he has overwhelmingly superior power, cosmic stature, and infinite wealth. That also explains why biblical writers so readily adopted the rich, colorful vocabulary of redemption to articulate their theology.

---

33. For example, Isa. 44:22 says, "I have swept away your transgressions like a cloud, and your sins like mist; return to me, for I have redeemed you" (cf. v. 23). The statement makes Yahweh's sweeping away of Israel's sin a prelude to its return to full fellowship, as if that divinely decreed forgiveness removed the only stumbling block to reunion. Presumably, the statement "I have redeemed you" also precedes the return, since it gives the grammatical reason (*kî,* "for") for it. Whether the prophet actually equates forgiveness and redemption is difficult to determine. Perhaps the most one can say is that he at least associates them. On the other hand, in the statement "[Yahweh] will come to Zion as redeemer, to those in Jacob who turn from transgression" (Isa. 59:20), human repentance definitely precedes redemption, the latter perhaps also bringing forgiveness with it.

34. The combination of objective guilt and terrible consequences is inherent in *ʿāwôn.* See R. Knierim, "*ʿāwôn,*" THAT, 2:244–45.

35. Cf. the similar definition in Schneider and Brown, "*lytron,*" NIDNTT, 3:177.

Further, the redeemer — the other whose intervention effects redemption — does so because of a preexisting relationship with the object to be ransomed. Redeemers are no Simon of Cyrene, a total stranger unexpectedly grabbed off the street corner and compelled against their will to effect the ransom. On the contrary, redeemers always have some personal connection with the objects of redemption, whether as owner, husband, close relative, compassionate friend, or covenant God. Finally, redemption imposes ethical demands on the redeemed. The phrase "for you were slaves in Egypt" motivates the redeemed to mirror the compassion and generosity of their redeemer rather than ape the harshness and cruelty of past oppressors.

REDEMPTION IN THE NEW TESTAMENT NARRATIVES

Except for Mark 10:45, Luke-Acts is the only New Testament narrative tradition to mention redemption. In Lukan birth narratives redemption means the realization of Old Testament messianic hopes of political liberation from Israel's enemies and an era of marvelous prosperity. According to Zechariah, his son John's birth signaled that God had "raised up a mighty savior for us in the house of his servant David" (Luke 1:69), the very "redemption" of Jerusalem that Anna saw realized in the newborn Jesus (2:38). Messianic hopes also echo on the Emmaus road after Jesus' crucifixion: "we had hoped that he was the one to redeem Israel" (24:21). Luke clearly regards Jesus' coming as the fulfillment of Israel's expected of deliverance.[36] On the other hand, scholarly controversy surrounds what probably marks the earliest New Testament reference to redemption, Mark 10:45 (par. Matt. 20:28). Dissension crackles among the disciples because James and John have asked for seats of honor in Jesus' kingdom (vv. 35–41). Jesus teaches that, unlike the Gentiles, his kingdom features slaves not masters (vv. 42–45), and he cites himself as the classic example: "For the Son of Man came not to be served but to serve, and to give his life a ransom (*lytron*) for many."

Obviously this is a crucial declaration for many reasons. It may offer a glimpse into Jesus' own understanding of his earthly ministry, that is, to render "service" by giving his life as "a ransom for many." Scholarly opinion, however, remains divided as to whether the saying derives from Jesus himself or from early church teaching retroactively accredited to him.[37] There is no need to engage this discussion at length here.

---

36. Cf. Acts 7, where Stephen lists both Moses (v. 35), Israel's "liberator" (*lytrōtēs*), and Jesus (implicitly, v. 52) among leaders whom rebellious Israel had rejected.

37. For the latter view scholars appeal to the prominence of redemption in Paul, claim that the statement's Greek sounds more Hellenistic than Semitic, and cite its close verbal similarity to 1 Tim. 2:6. They also regard the absence of the ransom idea in Luke's parallel

In my view, there is good reason to assume that Mark 10:45 comes from Jesus and thus to regard it as the root from which the New Testament view of redemption springs.[38]

But what does Jesus' statement mean? I understand it in light of two earlier teachings: his prediction of his imminent betrayal and death (Mark 8:31; 9:31) and his question about what one can give in exchange for saving one's life (8:37).[39] The latter question surely echoes Ps. 49:7–9, a text that underscored that the price was impossibly high for even the richest person to purchase exemption from death. But now Jesus promises to provide such an exemption by giving "his life as a ransom." His death amounts to a "price" paid presumably to God and apparently of sufficient value to satisfy the requirement of Psalm 49. In Mark 10:45 the preposition *anti* ("in place of") means that Jesus' death substitutes for all human deaths, implying that they need not take place. As for the identity of the "many," it seems best to understand the term as referring to an indefinite multitude rather than specifically to believers (cf. Mark 14:24 par. Matt. 26:28).[40] But another important implication follows from this understanding. Since death results from human sin, Jesus' ransom somehow is presumed to remove the effects of sin, thereby making the forgiveness of sin a possibility.

Some scholars believe that the statement alludes to the Suffering Servant (Isaiah 53) and thus believe that Jesus views his death specifically in a sacrificial sense as a sin offering.[41] But the alleged allusions to Isaiah 53 strike me as too illusive to be persuasive. A better cross-reference comes in Jesus' words at the Last Supper concerning "my blood of the covenant... poured out for many" (Mark 14:24). In other words, Jesus understands his death to be a more general covenant sacrifice rather than as specifically a sin offering. By linking his death to betrayal, Jesus

passage on servanthood (Luke 22:24–27) as other evidence. For a detailed discussion with bibliography see R. H. Gundry, *Mark* (Grand Rapids: Eerdmans, 1993) 587–93.

38. The uniqueness of the Markan statement certainly is striking, but its language is Semitic, not Hellenistic, especially when read against 1 Tim. 2:6 (see Gundry, *Mark*, 587–91). Also, only Mark 10:45b uses simple *lytron* ("ransom"), while all later writers use the compound forms *antilytron* ("ransom," 1 Tim. 2:6) and *apolytrōsis* ("release, deliverance," Luke 21:28). This makes development of the latter from Mark 10:45 more likely than the reverse. Finally, the difference in setting — the Last Supper (Luke 22) versus instruction en route to Jerusalem (Mark 10) — may also account for the texts' divergence. See I. H. Marshall, "The Development of the Concept of Redemption in the New Testament," in R. Banks, ed., *Reconciliation and Hope* (Grand Rapids: Eerdmans, 1974) 168–69.

39. Marshall, "Concept of Redemption," 167; cf. L. Williamson Jr., *Mark* (Atlanta: John Knox, 1983) 192.

40. Marshall, "Concept of Redemption," 167. For a discussion of alternatives and alleged links to Isaiah 53 and Qumran see Gundry, *Mark*, 590–91; M. Hooker, *The Gospel According to Mark* (Peabody, Mass.: Hendrickson, 1991) 249–51.

41. For example, W. L. Lane, *Mark* (NICNT; Grand Rapids: Eerdmans, 1974) 383–85. But see the critique by Gundry (*Mark*, 590).

also seems to understand it as that of a martyr. If so, he may here draw on Jewish thought attested in 4 Maccabees that reckoned the death of martyrs as a ransom given for the sins of others (4 Macc. 6:29; 17:21).[42] These, then, are the roots of redemption in the teaching of Jesus. Theologically, while drawing on familiar Old Testament ideas, it focuses redemption in a decisively new way. Redemption relieves humans not from economic hardship, obligations as firstborn, or personal danger but from the death penalty for sin. It involves a personal, human redeemer, but one who pays for it at the cost of his own life. Finally, its beneficiaries are not just the redeemer's family or the nation of Israel but "many," an open-ended term that, for the first time, potentially extends redemption to the whole world.

REDEMPTION AND CHRIST'S WORK: THE EPISTLES

It is the epistles, especially the Pauline ones, that bring redemption theology into full flower. Paul's exposition emerges in his well-known, blunt rebuke of the gullible Galatians (Galatians 3–4). His pastoral concern is that, misled by the Judaizers, the Christians will suffer a spiritual relapse, a retreat from life guided by the Spirit to life ruled by the law (3:1–5). Drawing on Old Testament background, Paul declares that "Christ redeemed us from the curse of the law by becoming a curse for us" (3:13). Citing Deut. 27:26, Paul explains that the "curse of the law" is the death sentence for everyone's failure to keep the law (3:10). But how do we know that Christ was cursed by God? As evidence, Paul cites Deut. 21:23 ("anyone hung on a tree is under God's curse") as proof that Jesus became a "curse" (i.e., "accursed" by God) — his public execution on a Roman "tree" proves it (3:13).[43] So, Christ's death substituted for the death of guilty humans under the curse. His curse-absorbing crucifixion "redeemed us" (*exagorazō*, "to buy out of"), that is, paid a purchase "cost" in exchange for release from slavery. But theologically, Paul must have wondered, how can one man's crucifixion redeem more than himself? Paul's thinking here apparently interweaves two familiar Old Testament precedents: the redemption of the firstborn (i.e., the substitution of one for many) and the redemption of one condemned to death (Exod. 21:29–30; but cf. 30:11–16).[44]

---

42. See Hooker, *Mark*, 249–50; Marshall, "Concept of Redemption," 167.

43. For various views on how Christ relates to the curse see H.-J. Eckstein, *Verheißung und Gesetz* (WUNT 86; Tübingen: J. C. B. Mohr [Paul Siebeck], 1996) 150–70; H. D. Betz, *Galatians* (Hermeneia; Philadelphia: Fortress, 1979) 149–52.

44. The context implies that the newly redeemed also stand justified (i.e., legally innocent) before God (Gal. 3:8, 11, 24). If so, Galatians 3 aligns itself well with Paul's view

But Christ redeemed humans not only from the law's death penalty but also from slavery "under the law" (Gal. 4:5). In this "slavery" the slave masters are "the elemental spirits of the world" (or, "basic principles of the world," τὰ στοιχεῖα τοῦ κόσμου, 4:3, 9; cf. Col. 2:8), a term Paul apparently borrows from Stoic popular philosophy but stamps with his own meaning. For Paul, the term incorporates both trust in the Jewish Torah as a path to salvation (cf. the reference to special calendrical days, 4:10) and the Gentile idolatry of the Galatians' pre-Christian life (i.e., "beings that by nature are not gods," 4:8).[45] From that repressive slavery, Paul argues, Christ has set the Galatians free, and for a purpose: God can adopt them as his very own children.[46] Why, he asks, would his audience choose slavery over being God's children and heirs (4:7, 9)? On the contrary, he urges them, don't abandon your freedom in Christ for the burdensome yoke of slavery (5:1). In sum, in both Gal. 3:13 and 4:5 redemption denotes a past event of manumission.[47]

In Hebrews 9 a very different metaphorical and theological atmosphere greets us. In vv. 11–14 two Old Testament items — the tabernacle and the high priest's work on the Day of Atonement (Leviticus 16) — lie in the background.[48] In my view, this marks an especially bold and creative theological departure, since no texts thus far covered in either Testament directly associate redemption with either the tabernacle or Yom Kippur. The writer contrasts the temporary, external, and ineffective sacrifices of the old sanctuary (vv. 8–10) with the final, comprehensive high priestly work of Christ. Its uniqueness derives from two things — in the words of William Lane, "the uniqueness of the sanctuary that he entered and . . . the uniqueness of the sacrifice that he

of redemption as atonement through a sacrifice (i.e., Christ's death on the cross) as the means of justification (Rom. 3:24–25; cf. 1 Cor. 1:30).

45. E. Plümacher, "stoicheion," EDNT, 3:277–78; cf. H. Paulsen, "physis," EDNT, 3:444. For the view that the term may designate a Hellenistic syncretism that worshipped celestial bodies, see G. Delling, "stoicheion," TDNT, 7:670–87; E. Schweitzer, "Slaves of the Elements and Worshipers of Angels: Gal 4:3, 9 and Col 2:8," JBL 107 (1988) 455–68. Cf. Wisd. 13:1–11.

46. For the intersection of redemption and adoption in Paul's thinking see Rom. 8:23; Eph. 1:5 8.

47. In my view, however, the metaphor derives from contemporary Greco-Roman practices, not from the book of Exodus. For example, in Gal. 4:9 Paul describes the "elemental spirits" as "weak" (asthenē) and "beggarly" (ptōcha), not oppressive or overpowering.

48. Verse 13 also recalls the purificatory ritual of the red heifer (Numbers 19). At first glance this seems an odd allusion, but the author may here draw on a Jewish exegetical tradition (e.g., Josephus, the Mishnah) that understood this sacrifice also to be work of the high priest. See the evidence and discussion in H. W. Attridge, The Epistle to the Hebrews (Hermeneia; Philadelphia: Fortress, 1989) 249–50. The allusion to Numbers 19 aims to highlight the superior purity that Christians enjoy before God because of Christ's shed blood. For the Old Testament text see J. Milgrom, "The Paradox of the Red Cow (Num. XIX)," VT 31 (1981) 62–72.

presented."[49] Christ entered the permanent, God-made, heavenly Holy Place, not the temporary, man-made, earthly one (vv. 11–12, 24). He gained entrance not by offering animal blood but his own blood (v. 12), and the upshot is that he wins "eternal redemption" (αἰωνίαν λύτρωσιν), a freedom from sin that presumably cannot be lost and thus never need be won again (vv. 25–28).[50] Verse 15 interprets his self-sacrifice as a "ransom" (ἀπολύτρωσιν) from sins under the old covenant, probably (as in Galatians 3) from the covenant curse or death penalty that blood shed in covenant-making symbolized.[51]

Theologically, Hebrews 9 assumes a high Christology (who else is sinless [v. 14; cf. 4:15] and thus able to enter the heavenly Holy Place?), and the substitution of Christ's life for the lives of sinful humans (vv. 12, 25–26). Although the writer leaves it unstated, he probably would attribute the efficacy of Christ death, as does 1 Pet. 1:18–19, to the precious value of Christ's blood, value based on his eternal existence (see 1 Pet. 1:20–21), perhaps his perfection as God. In any case, his death easily pays the full "price" for redemption from slavery to what Peter regards as futile religions.

CONCLUSION

This longitudinal study of divine redemption has carried us through much complex exegetical terrain. We have seen that as redeemer, God lovingly requires redemption of humans by humans in the law, demonstrates it in the exodus, and consummates it in Christ. Its subthemes are rescue from danger and death, freedom from tyranny, restoration to wholeness, and unbelievable joy. Paradoxically, it frees and enslaves at the same time, freeing the redeemed from cruel tyrants only to become slaves of the living, loving God.

As for the two Testaments' mutual critical complementarity, a few brief remarks must suffice. One is struck by the dominance of a central, divine redeemer in each Testament, Yahweh in the Old and Christ in the New. One observes also the benevolence of both redeemers in that each liberates the enslaved or rescues the endangered from threatening

---

49. W. L. Lane, *Hebrews 9–13* (WBC 47B; Dallas: Word, 1991) 237.

50. Contextually, in v. 12 the aorist participle εὑράμενος suggests an action coincident with or subsequent to (i.e., "obtaining") that of εἰσῆλθεν ("he entered") rather than one antecedent to it (so NRSV; Lane, *Hebrews,* 230; Attridge, *Hebrews,* 249–50 ["another case of 'coincident' aorist"]; E. Grässer, *An die Hebräer* (3 vols. in 1; EKKNT 17; Zürich: Benziger, 1990) 2:154 ["one and the same action"]; contra NIV ["having obtained"]). The term "eternal redemption" also occurs in *Palestinian Targum* to Gen. 48:18; 1QM 1:12; 15:1; 18:11.

51. The context (vv. 16–22), especially its emphasis on blood, seems to point in this direction. See Lane, *Hebrews,* 241–42; contrast Attridge, *Hebrews,* 254. For the blood of the covenant see Exod. 24:6–8.

circumstances. Granted, both also make the redeemed their own slaves, but the redeemed apparently raise no complaints against that servitude. On the other hand, significant differences distinguish the treatment of the theme of divine redemption in each Testament. In the Old Testament the arena of redemption is the here-and-now, whether release from slavery to another Israelite, Pharaoh, or the Babylonians, or divine rescue from horrible dangers and death. Several texts, however, show awareness of divine redemption from sin, thereby paving the way for New Testament writers, but they are comparatively few. In the Old Testament divine redemption applies almost exclusively to Israelites. By contrast, the New Testament's view of redemption is preoccupied with the problem of sin and the death of Christ to solve it. Redemption centers on Jesus' crucifixion, and in Pauline thought the arena of redemption's impact becomes cosmic and universal in scope. Occasionally, New Testament writers discuss redemption by drawing on Old Testament motifs that Hebrew writers themselves did not associate with redemption, for example, when Hebrews 9 draws on the Old Testament motifs of the tabernacle and the Day of Atonement.

The Old Testament complements the New Testament by keeping alive God's universal concern for the whole world, especially those oppressed and abused by the powerful. It challenges the New Testament tendency to otherworldliness, forcing readers to reckon with issues of social ethics, international politics, and justice. It also reminds readers of the divine protection and rescue from danger available to God's people. It portrays the life of faith as one living with its feet on the ground, amid the rough-and-tumble, dust-and-grime of daily threats to life and blessing, laboring to bring liberation of the weak from the powerful. On the other hand, the New Testament complements the Old Testament by treating redemption's cosmic and eternal nuances. The New Testament reminds readers that sin and eternal death are as cruel and catastrophic as any human Pharaoh. It challenges the Old Testament to sharpen its own cosmic understanding of reality, that is, to consider sin and death as cosmic realities with eternal implications. It poses its central figure, Jesus Christ, as a new vantage point from which to view the Old Testament.

Broadly speaking, the Bible understands redemption as an experience, a status, a mandate, and a destiny. It is an experience: humans actually leave the brutal Pharaohs of political and spiritual tyranny, actually feel free of the death penalty for sin, and in fact enjoy the forgiveness of their many and grievous sins. It is a status: people are "the Lord's redeemed,"[52] God's own adopted children, his own family pride and joy. It is a mandate: past acts of redemption — "you were slaves in

---

52. Cf. Ps. 107:2; Isa. 35:9; 51:10; 62:12.

Egypt" and "you were bought with a price" — obligate the redeemed to model their treatment of others after the treatment received from their redeemer, thereby adding new members to the circle of the redeemed. It is a destiny: it awaits the final "day of redemption," the full experience of being God's own children, the ultimate release of creation from physical decay, and entrance into eternal life.

BIBLIOGRAPHY

Büchsel, F. "agorazō," TDNT 1 (1964).
———. "lytron," TDNT 4 (1967).
Chirichigno, G. C. Debt-Slavery in Israel and the Ancient Near East. JSOTSup 141. Sheffield: JSOT Press, 1993.
Delling, G. "stoicheion," TDNT 7 (1971).
Field, D. H. "agorazō," TDNT 1 (1964).
Hill, D. Greek Words and Hebrew Meanings: Studies in the Semantics of Soteriological Terms. SNTSMS 5. Cambridge: Cambridge University Press, 1967.
Houtman, C. Das Bundesbuch: Ein Kommentar. DMOA 24. Leiden: Brill, 1997.
Hubbard, Jr., Robert L. "The Go'el in Ancient Israel: Theological Reflections on an Israelite Institution." BBR 1 (1991).
Katz, M. A. "Ox-slaughter and Goring Oxen: Homicide, Animal Sacrifice, and Judicial Process." Yale Journal of Law 4/2 (1992).
Kertelge, K. "lutron," EDNT 2 (1991).
Knierim, Rolf P. "On Biblical Theology," In The Quest for Context and Meaning. Ed. C. A. Evans and S. Talmon. Festschrift for J. A. Sanders. Leiden: Brill, 1997.
Marshall, I. Howard. "The Development of the Concept of Redemption in the New Testament." In Reconciliation and Hope. Ed. R. Banks. Festschrift for Leon Morris. Grand Rapids: Eerdmans, 1974.
Paulsen, Henning. "physis," EDNT 3 (1991).
Plümacher, E. "stoicheion," EDNT 3 (1991).
Ringgren, Helmer. "ga'al," TDOT 2 (1975).
Schneider, J., and C. Brown. "lytron." Ed. C. Brown. NIDNTT 3 (1978).
Schweitzer, Eduard. "Slaves of the Elements and Worshipers of Angels: Gal 4:3, 9 and Col 2:8." JBL 107 (1988).
Shogren, G. S. "Redemption (NT)," ABD 5 (1992).
Sprinkle, J. M. "The Book of the Covenant": A Literary Approach. JSOTSup 174. Sheffield: JSOT Press, 1994.
Stamm, J. J. Erlösen und Vergeben im Alten Testament. Bern: A. Francke, 1940.
Stuhlmueller, Carroll. Creative Redemption in Deutero-Isaiah. AnBib 43, Rome: Biblical Institute Press, 1970.
Unterman, J. "Redemption (OT)," ABD 5 (1992).

13

Toward an Old Testament Theology of Concern for the Underprivileged

Mignon R. Jacobs

INTRODUCTION

The concern for the underprivileged is represented throughout the Old Testament by semantic indicators, conceptual formulations, and aspects shared with other theologies, for example, the theology of justice and the theology of hope. Through its interrelationship with these theologies, the concern for the underprivileged contributes to the theological pluralism within the Old Testament. This pluralism characterizes Old Testament theology and precipitates its fundamental challenge.[1] Even so, the challenge is not simply the existence of plurality[2] nor the complex of discernibly heterogeneous theologies that is here termed theological pluralism.[3] Rather, the challenge is the coexistence and the

---

1. Knierim, *The Task*, 1–20, esp. 1, 5.
2. Plurality itself does not necessarily signify difference among elements. Rather, it signifies the multiplicity of the elements. Pluralism exists inasmuch as differences are present among the elements. The particular nature of the plurality is what determines whether or not it is pluralism. Thus, while plurality is essential and necessary for the existence of pluralism, pluralism is neither essential nor necessary for the plurality.
3. Knierim, *Task of Old Testament Theology*, esp. 1, 5.
This pluralism has long been recognized and has generated many articulations of the task of both biblical theology and Old Testament theology. See G. von Rad, *Old Testament Theology* (2 vols.; San Francisco: Harper & Row, 1962–65); W. Pannenberg, *Basic Questions in Theology* (trans. G. H. Kehm; 2 vols.; Philadelphia: Fortress, 1970–71) volume 1. A brief survey of literature from the last two decades further illustrates the attempts to address this theological pluralism: B. S. Childs, *Old Testament Theology in a Canonical Context* (Philadelphia: Fortress, 1985); H. G. Reventlow, *Problems of Biblical Theology in the Twentieth Century* (Philadelphia: Fortress, 1986); G. F. Hasel, *Old Testament Theology: Basic Issues in the Current Debate* (4th ed.; Grand Rapids: Eerdmans, 1991); idem, "The Future of Old Testament Theology: Prospect and Trends," in B. C. Ollenburger, E. A. Martens, and G. F. Hasel, eds., *The Flowering of Old Testament Theology: A Reader in Twentieth-Century Old Testament Theology, 1930–1990* (Winona Lake, Ind.: Eisenbrauns, 1992) 373–83, proposes a "multiplex canonical Old Testament theology" that is historical in nature; he therefore insists that this theology interprets the final form, allows for the uncovering of the rich diversity of the Old Testament, and in that uncovering illustrates the development of the various constitutive concepts, themes, and motifs; P. D. Hanson, *The Diversity of Scripture: A Theological Interpretation* (OBT 11; Philadelphia: Fortress, 1982); C. Westermann, *Elements of Old Testament Theology* (Atlanta: John Knox, 1982); J. J. Collins, "Is a Critical Biblical Theology Possible?" in W. H. Propp et al., eds., *The Hebrew Bible and Its Interpreters* (Winona

interrelationship of these discernibly heterogeneous theologies within
one corpus, the Old Testament. Thus, Knierim contends,

> The theological problem of the Old Testament does not arise from the sep-
> arate existence of its particular theologies. It arises from their coexistence.
> The coexistence of these theologies in the Old Testament demands the in-
> terpretation of their relationship or correspondence, a task that is more
> than and different from the interpretation of each of them in its own
> right. . . . [4]

As significant as it is to the task of Old Testament theology, theological pluralism itself does not define that task. Rather, pluralism
is essential to defining the theological task to the extent that Old
Testament theology (1) critically assesses its constitutive theologies,[5]
and (2) seeks to understand pluralism's nature and anatomy[6] in light
of its particulars. Insofar as the existence, nature, and validity of
the constitutive theologies define their interrelationship within the
whole, the magnitude of the task of Old Testament theology is further demonstrated by their inherent pluralism.[7] The reconstruction of
Old Testament theology must be preceded by the reconstruction of
its constitutive theologies and by an understanding of their inherent
pluralism, namely, the pluralism signaled by semantic indicators and
conceptual formulations.

Lake, Ind.: Eisenbrauns, 1990) 1–17, esp. 9, 14, postulates the possibility of a critical biblical theology and defines its task as that of "clarify[ing] the meaning of truth-claims of
what was thought and believed from a modern critical perspective"; he recognizes that
this task involves critical assessment of the theologies themselves if, as he asserts, the
theologian is to clarify "the basis for the claims, and the various functions they serve";
W. Brueggemann, *Theology of the Old Testament: Testimony, Dispute, Advocacy* (Minneapolis: Fortress, 1997), proposes that Old Testament theology is a testimony (mode), dispute
(content), and advocacy (role); fundamental to his work is his assertion that pluralism
pervades the text as well as the interpretive methods and communities; W. Schweiker and
M. Welker, "A New Paradigm of Theological and Biblical Inquiry," in C. L. Rigby, ed.,
Power, Powerlessness, and the Divine: New Inquiries in Bible and Theology (Atlanta: Scholars
Press, 1997) 1–20.

4. Knierim, *Task of Old Testament Theology*, 1–2.

5. Collins, "Critical Biblical Theology," 14.

6. Anatomy is defined here as the structure of the theology, including its parameters
and the system of relationships that exists among its elements. By this definition anatomy
also suggests the limitations of the theology. Cf. Knierim, *Task of Old Testament Theology*, 5.

7. Schweiker and Welker, "New Paradigm," 8–11. In light of their assessment of the
tendencies in theological construction, these authors propose a theology that is both systematic and pluralistic. This proposal addresses two fundamental challenges: "to achieve
a balance between coherence and complexity and thereby to avoid reductionist modes of
thought or *ad hoc* accounts of traditions, texts, and communities" (12). They further propose that these are achieved by developing a "coherent, . . . systematic mode of thought
equal to the complexity of [the] subject matter" (11–12). Cf. Hanson, *Diversity of Scripture*,
10f.

There are at least two compelling ways of approaching the Old Testament theology of concern for the underprivileged. The first is to engage in a critical reconstruction of the theology through analysis of its occurrences in the Old Testament. To this approach belongs the delineation of the essential aspects of the theology. The second approach is to examine the place of the theology within Old Testament theology. This necessitates analysis of the relationship of the theology with other theologies. Using concept-critical analysis, the present essay focuses on the first approach and indicates a few aspects of the second.

The most salient and typical semantic indicators of concern have been the focus of many etymological studies — for example, ענו/עני "afflicted";[8] אביון "needy";[9] דל "poor, lowly";[10] רש "poor, famished."[11] Others have taken a more thematic approach in considering the אלמנה "widow"; יתום "orphan"; גר "sojourner."[12] Even these tend to focus exclusively on the typical semantic field. While the investigation of the semantic field is necessary, this tends to result in the exclusion of other significant articulations which lack the typical semantic field.[13] To address this limitation of previous studies, the present essay includes groups of underprivileged usually excluded from the analysis (e.g., "servants and slaves," "oppressed"). These groups of underprivileged do not employ the semantic field typically associated with the concern for the underprivileged; they do, however, exhibit the characteristics of those underprivileged identified by the typical semantic indicators.[14]

---

8. E. Gerstenberger, "ענה II," ThWAT, 6.247–70; L. J. Coppes, "ענה III," TWOT, 2.682–84; F. Hauck and S. Schulz, "πτωχός," TDNT, 6.888–94, esp. 888.

9. G. J. Botterweck, "אבה," ThWAT, 1.23–43; idem, "אביון" TDOT, 1.25–41; L. J. Coppes, "אבה," TWOT, 1.4–5; C. F. Fensham, "Widow, Orphan, and the Poor in Ancient Near Eastern Legal and Wisdom Literature," JNES 21 (1962) 129–39.

10. H.-J. Fabry, "דל," ThWAT, 2.221–44; L. J. Coppes, "דלל," TWOT, 1.190.

11. P. D. Miscall, The Concept of the Poor in the Old Testament (Ph.D. diss.: Harvard University, 1972).

12. Fensham, "Widow, Orphan, and the Poor"; D. H. Engelhard, "The Lord's Motivated Concern for the Underprivileged," CTJ 15 (April 1980) 5–26; R. J. Coggins, "The Old Testament and the Poor," ExpTim 99, no. 1 (1987) 11–14; R. D. Patterson, "The Widow, the Orphan and the Poor in the Old Testament and Extra-Biblical Literature," Bibliotheca Sacra 130 (1973) 223–34.

13. Miscall (Concept of the Poor) recognizes the limitation of etymological studies and attempts to identify the Israelite concept of the poor. While he does so, and expands the consideration to include אלמנה, and גר, יתום, along with the typical semantic indicators, דל, and עני, אביון, the limitation of his work is that his analysis excludes others whose circumstances are the same as those he categorizes as poor. W. D. Tucker Jr. (The Reign of Yahweh and the Theology of the Poor in the Final Shape of the Psalter [Ph.D. diss., Southern Baptist Theological Seminary, 1997]) also recognizes the tendency to limit analysis of the theology the poor to typical semantic fields, and therefore proposes to expand the analysis to include others, such as דל, רש, אביון, יתום, עשוקים.

14. See M. R. Jacobs, Conceptual Coherence of the Book of Micah (Ph.D. diss., Claremont Graduate School, 1998) chapter 2. This includes a discussion of the types of semantic and

Through its examination of the persons concerned and the aspects of concern (e.g., its aims and extent), this essay demonstrates that the concern for the underprivileged in the Old Testament (1) encompasses a wide range of persons, but is limited in some ways to the underprivileged of the covenant community; and (2) presupposes a system of responsibilities and therefore advocates regulating the practices of the society rather than radically changing the infrastructure of the society in order to actualize care for the underprivileged. This essay therefore concludes by identifying some aspects shared with the theology of justice and some limitations of this theology for hermeneutical reflections.

PERSONS CONCERNED

Basic to the concern for the underprivileged in the Old Testament is the belief that their rights and well-being are safeguarded by God. Within this conceptual framework two sets of persons come into focus, namely, the underprivileged and those responsible to ensure their livelihood and well-being.

The Underprivileged

The term "underprivileged" is used to characterize those who by their relative status and circumstances — regardless of duration or cause — are subservient to others; lack the basic freedom afforded to others in the society; and/or lack the basic resources for self-sustenance, self-determination, and self-protection (i.e., in the ways that self-determination is manifested in that society); and lack of resources to participate in cultic ceremonies. This section explores the characteristics of these persons in order to illuminate their vulnerability and hence the aspects of concern for them.

The Poor

The inherent pluralism in this theological reconstruction is evident in the various semantic indicators for the "poor." While the different terms may be indicative of socio-economic difference, or at least differences in the voiced concern, the characteristics of the persons unite them in this category.

The עני "poor, afflicted" is a person experiencing distress or adversity. The nature of the distress may be economic (Exod. 22:25f.; Deut. 15:11;

---

conceptual indicators that represent a concept and the significance of addressing all these types.

24:14–15) as well as physical (Isa. 51:21; Ps. 88:16 [15])[15] and spiritual (cf. Ps. 22:25 [24]; 25:16; 34:7 [6]). The shared characteristics of the עני and the אביון "needy" are signaled by their occurrence together — for example, the formula עני ואביון (e.g., Deut. 24:4; Jer. 22:16; Ezek. 16:49; Ps. 35:10; 37:14; 40:18 [17]); עני//אביון (e.g., Deut. 15:11; Isa. 29:19; Ps. 72:4; 140:13 [12]; Prov. 30:14; Amos 8:4).[16] These characteristics include the need for food (Lev. 19:10) and other economic resources required for daily sustenance (Deut. 24:14–15), and the need for protection against oppression. It is the latter characteristic that is attributed to the עניים, the poor of God.

עני is also used to describe a social condition;[17] for example, the אח "brother" (Deut. 15:7f.) and the שכיר "hired servant" (Deut. 24:14–15) are described as poor. Their condition includes the need to borrow from others and, in the absence of any other resources, the need to give one's garment as pledge (Exod. 22:25–26).

The term אביון "needy, poor" refers to a person whose economic situation is constituted by landlessness, lack of the basic means of sustenance, and reliance on the provisions made to address poverty.[18] The needy were susceptible to robbery, oppression, and enslavement (cf. Lev. 19:13; Amos 2:6; 4:1; 8:6), and stood on the brink of servitude or slavery as a means of self-preservation (cf. Lev. 25:39). These persons also sustained themselves by borrowing (Deut. 15:7–11; 24:10f.). Their vulnerabilities also made them susceptible to injustice in legal matters. Thus, those responsible for the execution of justice in the court are prohibited from denying justice to the אביון (Exod. 23:6; cf. 23:3 [דל]; Prov. 22:22–23). In some instances, however, the אביון may have been denied a hearing (Amos 5:12; cf. Isa. 10:1–2).

The "needy" (אביון) are usually mentioned with the "poor/afflicted" (עני).[19] Like עני, the term אביון is used as a description of a person's economic status (Deut. 15:2, 7; 24:12, 14, 15; cf. Exod. 22:24 [25]; Prov. 22:22 [דל]). The term is also used to indicate a restrictive aspect of concern for the underprivileged. Such use is seen in the designation "in your land" (בארצך) to further characterize אביון (Deut. 15:7, 11; 24:14; cf. Lev. 19:33,

---

15. Square brackets indicate the NRSV versification where it differs from that of the Hebrew text.

16. G. J. Botterweck, "אביון," ThWAT, 1.31ff.

17. Coppes, "ענה III," TWOT, 2.683. The significance of the עני is a complex matter that has occupied scholarly attention. For a comprehensive review of the discussion see Miscall, Concept of the Poor, chapter 1.

18. See Miscall, Concept of the Poor, 32–33, 76; A. Gélin, Les pauvres de Yahvé (Paris: Cerf, 1956) 19–20.

19. The previous discussion of עני has references. See Botterweck, "אביון," ThWAT 1.31f. Note other parallel uses of אביון and דל (e.g., 1 Sam. 2:8; Isa. 14:30; Amos 4:1; 8:6; Ps. 72:12), and of אביון and צדיק (e.g., Amos 2:6; 5:12).

גר בארצכם "the sojourner in your land"). This restrictive use is further signaled by the use of the second person pronominal suffix (ך) to identify the poor as part of the covenant community (e.g., אבינך, Exod. 23:6; אחיך האביון, Deut. 15:7, 9; cf. עניך, Deut. 15:11).[20]

While the אביון are marginalized by their economic status, the concern for their well-being makes them central to the blessing, punishment, and existence of the community (Ezek. 18:12f.; Amos 4:1–3; 5:12; 8:f.; cf. Jer. 22:13–16 — knowing God is defined as caring for the needy; Ps. 72:1–4, 12–14).

The term דל "weak, lowly, poor" occurs most frequently in the book of Proverbs (14:31; 19:4, 17; 21:13; 22:9, 16, 22; 28:11, 15; 29:7, 14). In its broadest sense דל refers to physical or psychological weaknesses (Judg. 6:6; 2 Sam. 3:1; 13:2).[21] This characterization facilitated its use with terms typically used of the "poor" — for example, אביון (1 Sam. 2:8; Isa. 14:30; Amos 2:7; 5:11; 8:6; Ps. 72:13; 82:4; 113:7; Prov. 14:31) and עני (Isa. 10:2; 26:6; Zeph. 3:12; Ps. 72:13; 82:3; Prov. 22:22).[22] Socioeconomically, the weak (דלים), though poorer than others, were not of the same dependent status as the servants/slaves (שׂכיר, אמה, עבדה), the sojourner (גר), or even the needy (אביון). Instead, the דלים are believed to have been small-scale farmers who had the economic resources to sustain themselves. Thus, like the rich (עשׁיר), they were required to pay one atonement price (Exod. 30:15). No exceptions were made to account for their poverty.[23] They also had the means to fulfill the requirements for guilt, sin, and burnt offerings in accordance with their economic resources (Lev. 14:21f.).[24]

The vulnerabilities of the דל lie in limited power and possessions. Thus, like the other groups of underprivileged, their well-being is a point of concern, that is, justice in court (Exod. 23:3; Lev. 19:15), safeguard against oppression (Amos 2:7; 4:1; 8:6; Mic. 2:1–2; cf. Prov. 14:31; 19:17), and provision for participation in the cult (Lev. 14:21f.).[25]

---

20. In the book of Psalms the term אביון is typically used of the destitute and of the righteous who are ravaged by enemies. Regarding the enemies of the poor and needy see Botterweck, "אביון," *ThWAT*, 1.37f.; Gélin, *Les pauvres de Yahvé*, 46f. See also R. Martin-Achard, "Yahwé et les ʿanawîm," *TZ* 21 (1965) 349–57; Tucker, *Reign of Yahweh*.

21. H.-J. Fabry, "דל," *TDOT*, 3.216; cf. Gélin, *Les pauvres de Yahvé*, 20.

22. Fabry, "דל," *TDOT*, 3.216. Cf. instances where דל is used in association with אלמנה "widow" and/or יתום "orphan, fatherless" (Isa. 10:2; Ps. 82:3).

23. Fabry, "דל," *TDOT*, 3.219.

24. Note that provisions are also made for others with limited economic resources. While these are not designated as דל, the fact that they are of limited resources places them in the same category (women seeking purification after childbirth, Lev. 12:6f.; the person of limited resources bringing a guilt offering, Lev. 5:7f.). See J. Milgrom, *Leviticus 1–16* (AB 3; New York: Doubleday, 1991) 860f.; M. Noth, *Leviticus* (trans. J. S. Anderson; OTL; Philadelphia: Westminster, 1965) 110; cf. Fabry, "דל," TDOT 3.219.

25. Miscall (*Concept of the Poor*) does not share this perspective. He proposes that "the

רָשׁ (רָאֹשׁ) "poor" is found mostly in the book of Proverbs (13:8, 23; 14:20; 17:5; 18:23; 19:1, 7; 22:2, 7; 28:3, 6, 27; 29:13; cf. 30:8; 31:7). It is often contrasted with the rich (עָשִׁיר) (Prov. 13:8; 14:20; 18:23; 22:2; 28:6, 7), the fool (כְּסִיל) (Prov. 19:1), and the liar (אִישׁ כָּזָב) (Prov. 19:22). In contrast to the rich, the רָשִׁים refer to persons of limited economic resources who because of this status may be disfavored by others (Prov. 14:20; 18:23; 19:7). Even so, the רָשִׁים are favored by God, and how they are treated results in either blessing or curse on the community (Prov. 17:5). Further indication of concern for the רָאשׁ is found in 2 Sam. 12:1f. There, the contrast is between rich (עָשִׁיר), one with an abundance of resources, and poor (רָאשׁ), one with limited resources (cf. 1 Sam. 18:23, רָשׁ). In this context the mistreatment of the poor by the rich is considered a capital offense.

Less frequently represented is the concern for the מִסְכֵּן "poor" (Eccl. 4:13; 9:15–16). This person is usually contrasted with the great as a person of wisdom whose wisdom does not keep him from being despised. There are also those whose poverty and distress place them in this category. The book of Proverbs represents these as people whose poverty is a direct result of their own negative behaviors, such as slothfulness (עָצֵל/עַצְלָה) (Prov. 12:11, 14; 13:4; 18:9; 19:15; 20:4; cf. Prov. 21:17; 24:33).[26] This characterization of the lazy/slothful (עָצֵל) presupposes that they had the means of self-sustenance but chose not to take advantage of these means for their own self-preservation. Thus, they become poor and hungry while in possession of resources such as fields. Even so, their protection and well-being are safeguarded (cf. Prov. 14:31).[27]

Sojourner, Widow, and Orphan

Typically, the sojourner, widow, and the orphan are mentioned together (Exod. 22:20–23 [21–24]; 23:6; Deut. 24:17, 19–21; 27:19; Jer. 7:6).[28] Their marginalized status makes them vulnerable to others and thus predisposes them to economic deprivation and oppression.

The גֵּר (גֵּרִים) "stranger(s), sojourner(s)" are persons who live outside their kinship community and depend on the hospitality of a selected resident community.[29] As sojourners (גֵּרִים) their vulnerability includes

---

[dāl] is the lower class in society but is not given any particular consideration or help; 'ani and 'ebyôn indicate the poor who are accorded such privileges" (75).

26. Cf. Fabry, "דל," 220.

27. Contrast Botterweck, "אֶבְיוֹן," TDOT, 1.34. He believes that the slothful are not included in the concern expressed toward the underprivileged. He further argues that their slothfulness excludes them from the concern.

28. Cf. poor, widow, and the orphan (Isa. 10:1–2; Job 29:12–13; 31:16–17); orphan and widow (Isa. 1:23; Ps. 68:1–5); poor and fatherless (Ps. 82:3); sojourners, orphans, and widows with the Levites (Deut. 14:29; 26:12).

29. Contrast the גֵּר "stranger/sojourner" and the נָכְרִי "foreigner." The latter usually

their need for food, shelter, and protection of their life and well-
being. Because of these vulnerabilities, sojourners could at anytime lose
their protection and be mistreated (e.g., Israel's enslavement in Egypt).
Among Israelites, sojourners were allowed some of the same rights as
the citizens of Israel (Lev. 19:33–34; 24:22; Num. 15:14–15; cf. Exod.
22:20–23 [22:21–24]). Among these were the right to receive basic sustenance (Deut. 24:19–21), justice in judicial proceedings (Deut. 1:16; 27:19),
asylum (Num. 35:15), and participation in the cult.[30]

Although sojourners may have been poor, it does not necessarily follow that they were poor prior to their sojourning (cf. Gen. 12:10; 47:4f.;
2 Kings 8:1f.) or during their sojourning. Sojourners who became resident aliens could become rich while natives could become poor (e.g.,
Jacob in Gen. 30:43; 31:17f. cf. Lev. 25:47f.). Their economic status was
not dependent on the status of the natives. Rather, the reason for their
sojourning usually affected their economic resources.

First, because of famine, the גר chooses a community for self-
preservation — for example, Abram (Gen. 12:10); Jacob and his sons in
Egypt (Gen. 47:4f.; cf. 26:3; 1 Kings 17:20; 2 Kings 8:1–6; Ruth 1:1).[31] In
these instances the choice to become a sojourner, though it may address
the basic need of sustenance, may also create further needs — for example, protection against oppression and legal protection. Second, Levites,
who were landless according to law, became sojourners in trying to
find a place where they could be priests and have means of sustenance (Judg. 17:7f.; cf. Deut. 12:18–19; 14:29). Third, while some freely
choose to become sojourners, others reluctantly enter that way of being.
Among them are those seeking refuge because of war (Isa. 16:3–4)[32] or
bloodguilt (cf. Gen. 4:12f.), or to escape adversity (Gen. 27:42f.).

The concern for the אלמנה "widow"[33] and for the יתום "orphan,

---

has a negative connotation, as in the sense of a foreign god, or the adulteress (Prov 2:16;
5:3; 6:24). R. Martin-Achard, "גור," *TLOT*, 1.307–10, esp. 308; M. R. Wilson, "נכרי," *TWOT*,
2.579–80.

30. H. G. Stigers "גור," *TWOT*, 1.331. P. Bovati (*Re-Establishing Justice: Legal Terms, Concepts, and Procedures in the Hebrew Bible* [trans. M. J. Smith; JSOTSup 105; Sheffield: JSOT
Press, 1994] 312) makes reference to the complaint as a form used by the poor to assert
their rights. See also H. E. von Waldow, "Social Responsibility and Social Structure in
Early Israel," *CBQ* 32 (1970) 182–204, esp. 186.

31. D. Kellermann, "גור," *TDOT*, 2.443; Stigers "גור," *TWOT* 1.156–57. Abram is regarded as an alien in Canaan (Gen. 17:8; cf. Abraham, Isaac, and Jacob in Exod. 6:4).
Elisha instructed the Shunammite woman to sojourn to the land of the Philistines in
order to avoid famine (2 Kings 8:1–6).

32. Kellermann, "גור," *TDOT*, 2.443. Cf. 2 Sam. 4:3.

33. H. A. Hoffner, "אלמנה," *TDOT*, 1.287–91; J. Kühlewein, "אלמנה," *TLOT*, 1.127–30.
See H. K. Havice, *The Concern for the Widow and the Fatherless in the Ancient Near East: A
Case Study in Old Testament Ethics* (Ph.D. diss.: Yale University, 1978); Fensham, "Widow,

fatherless"[34] is one of the primary articulations of concern for the under-privileged in the Old Testament (Exod. 22:21–23 [22–24]; Deut. 10:18; 24:17; 27:19; Isa. 1:23; 10:1–2; Jer. 7:6; 22:3; cf. Job 29:12–13; 31:16–18, 21–22; Ps. 68:5; 82). Without a male protector (husband, father), the אלמנה "widow" and יתום "orphan, fatherless" are vulnerable to oppression and poverty and have little or no judicial protection (cf. 2 Kings 8:1–6).[35]

The widow (אלמנה) is a woman whose husband died. Her economic status is reduced by the loss of her primary provider, and further re-duced if she is childless or has lost her adult male children (Ruth 1; 2 Sam. 14:5–7; cf. 1 Kings 17:20). Whether or not the widow could in-herit the property of her deceased husband remains an open question. She may have been permitted to assume the rights of the property if she had no adult male children or a brother-in-law.[36] Her options were to remain with her children, return to her father's house, or remarry.[37] In cases in which the widow has no sons and has a brother-in-law in the same household, the brother-in-law is required to marry the widow in order to provide for her and to preserve his brother's name (Deut. 25:5f.; cf. Genesis 38; contrast Ruth 4). However, there are those whose hus-

---

Orphan, and the Poor"; Coggins, "The Old Testament and the Poor," 11–14; Patterson, "The Widow, the Orphan and the Poor."

34. The term may not mean orphan as defined in modern society, that is, one whose father and mother have died. Most likely, in the Old Testament it refers to one whose fa-ther is dead but whose mother may be still alive. See Hoffner, "אלמנה," *TDOT*, 1.290; W. C. Kaiser Jr., *Toward Old Testament Ethics* (Grand Rapids: Zondervan, 1983) 162. Von Waldow ("Social Responsibility," 187) sees the likelihood of the mother's presence as further in-dicative of social tensions for the child. This option in the interpretation of the term is not considered by many who have written on the subject; cf. J. E. Hartley, "יתום," *TWOT*, 1.419; Fensham, "Widow, Orphan, and the Poor"; Patterson, "The Widow, the Orphan and the Poor."

35. See Engelhard, "The Lord's Motivated Concern," 5; Kaiser, *Toward Old Testament Ethics*, 161–62.

36. Hoffner, "אלמנה," *TDOT*, 1.290; von Waldow, "Social Responsibility," 187. Cf. P. S. Hiebert, "'Whence Shall Help Come to Me?' The Biblical Widow," in P. Day, ed., *Gen-der and Difference in Ancient Israel* (Minneapolis: Fortress, 1989) 124–41; F. Frick, "Widow in the Hebrew Bible: A Transactional Approach," in A. Brenner, ed., *A Feminist Compan-ion to Exodus to Deuteronomy* (FCB 6; Sheffield: Sheffield Academic Press, 1994) 148. Frick critiques Hiebert's analysis as failing to examine the sociological aspects of the widow's existence. He uses the story of Judith (Jdt. 8:4f.) to argue against those who assume the poverty and marginalized status of the widow in Israelite society, and proposes that a childless widow could be a self-sustaining, reputable member of the community without returning to her father's household or entering into a levirate marriage. Contrast E. W. Davies, "Inheritance Rights and the Hebrew Levirate Marriage," *VT* 31 (1981) 138–39.

37. Provisions for levirate marriages attempt to protect the widow. Cf. Frick, "Widow in the Hebrew Bible," 145–48; J. B. Scott, "אלמנה," *TWOT*, 1.47, for discussion of the stip-ulations regarding the widow's choices. For example, a widow of a priest may return to her father's house if she has no children (Lev. 22:13). She may marry a priest if her hus-band was a priest (Ezek. 44:22). See Hoffner, "אלמנה," *TDOT*, 1.290; von Waldow, "Social Responsibility," 187.

bands died to whom the term was not applied, namely, Abigail (1 Sam. 27:3; 30:5; 2 Sam. 2:2; 3:3).

The יתוֹם "fatherless" is not necessarily poor but may have an inheritance that is being safeguarded by his mother until he is of age to assume responsibility.[38] The vulnerability of the fatherless in these cases is that they do not have an adult male to protect that inheritance and may become prey to those who seek to rob them (cf. Prov. 23:10). Likewise, if they leave the household of their father in order to return to the family of their mother, they may suffer as an outsider.

Servants and Slaves

The שָׂכִיר "hired servant" is a free person who hired himself out for wages.[39] This person lacks economic resources and depends on daily work for these resources. A poor Israelite may sell himself in which case he is considered a hired servant (Lev. 25:39f.). The hired servant is vulnerable to those who may attempt to withhold daily wages (Lev. 19:13; Deut. 24:15; cf. Jer. 22:13; Mal. 3:5). He is also vulnerable to enslavement as a means of survival.

The term עֶבֶד "servant, slave"[40] has a range of connotations, including that of the slave to a master. This is the connotation being considered here. The עֶבֶד "servant, slave" is restricted in areas of self-sustenance, self-determination, and protection against oppression. Even so, slavery of Hebrews (insiders) had a limited duration of six years (Lev. 25:39f.; Exod. 21:2). Thereafter they were free, unless they chose to remain slaves. In such cases they would give up their right to freedom in exchange for a lifetime of servitude (Exod. 21:5f.; Deut. 15:12). Nonetheless, slaves were not to be mistreated or killed (Exod. 21:20). If they were mistreated and sustained bodily injury, they were to be freed as compensation (Exod. 21:26–27). Their injury may be regarded as oppression (cf. Lev. 24:18f.; Deut. 19:21); and the penalty to the owner was loss of property.[41]

As in the cases of the עָנִי and אֶבְיוֹן, a distinction is made between the underprivileged of the community and outsiders. In contrast to the Israelite slave, slavery of a "stranger/sojourner" could be perma-

---

38. Hoffner, "אלמנה," TDOT, 1.290.

39. von Waldow, "Social Responsibility," 199; C. Rogers, "שׂכר," TWOT, 2.878 (1 Sam. 2:5). The other servants are to be considered in this category as those whose labor was protected by the Sabbath day rest.

40. C. Westermann, "עבד," TLOT, 2.819–32. The term could apply also to those who while in service to the king were not underprivileged in the sense of lacking food, influence, or the means of self-protection (cf. 1 Sam. 27:5, 12).

41. See B. S. Childs, The Book of Exodus (OTL; Philadelphia: Westminster, 1974) 473; J. I. Durham, Exodus (WBC 3; Waco: Word, 1987) 324.

nent. These people were considered property and as such could be bequeathed to an heir (Lev. 25:45f.).[42]

Oppressed

The עשׁקים "oppressed" are characterized as those whose status and vulnerability predisposed them to mistreatment. This group may include the poor, the stranger, the widow, fatherless, sojourner, slave, and any whose relative power and status exhibit points of vulnerability (Jer. 22:3; Amos 4:1; Ps. 146:7–9; cf. Eccl. 4:1). Thus, this category also includes adult males (self-supporting, landowner) who nonetheless are oppressed due to their limited power. This latter group was vulnerable to those whose greed and power allowed them to forcibly take land from others (Mic. 2:1–2; cf. Isa. 5:8–10). In such instances the oppression may result in the reduction of these persons to a state of poverty.[43]

The Privileged

Considering the privileged in this theological construction is necessitated by the primacy of the presupposition that there are those who are responsible for the well-being of the underprivileged. This responsibility is most clearly evident in the formulations regarding provisions to be made for the underprivileged (food, loans without interest, justice, protection from oppression, participation in the cult). The responsibility is further presupposed by the consequences associated with the choice of providing or not providing for the underprivileged, consequences that presuppose the ability of those addressed to fulfill the stated requirements.

The privileged are characterized as those, in a hierarchical social order, who by their relative status and circumstances have the freedom afforded to others in the society — resources for self-sustenance, self-determination, and self-protection — as well as the power to affect the well-being and existence of others.[44] Typically among these are rulers/leaders, landowners, judges, elders, priests, and the rich. Their status predicates a role and therefore certain responsibilities.

It is the responsibility of rulers (king and princes) to promote and maintain a just society in which the underprivileged are protected and

---

42. Noth (*Leviticus*, 191–92) notes that Lev. 25:40f. stands in tension with Exod. 21:1–11 and Deut. 15:12–18. Here, the story of Hagar (Gen. 16:1f.; 21:16f.) further illustrates the slave's lack of self-determination.

43. See Jacobs, *Conceptual Coherence*, chapter 4.

44. See Havice, *Concern for the Widow*, 23f., 190f., 223. She identifies aspects of the responsibilities to the underprivileged and notes the hierarchical nature of the system of responsibilities. Cf. H.-J. Boecker, *Law and the Administration of Justice in the Old Testament and Ancient East* (Minneapolis: Augsburg, 1980) 29f.

provided for (Isa. 11:1–5, esp. v. 4; Psalm 72; Prov. 31:1–9; cf. Isa. 1:16–
17; 23; Mic. 3:1, 9).[45] The articulation of the characteristics of the ideal
king identifies justice and righteousness (particularly for the underprivileged) as the measure of his reign (Isa. 11:3–5; Psalm 82). Judges
were to execute justice without partiality and without the inducement
of bribes (Deut. 16:18–20; cf. Mic. 3:10f.). Field owners were to provide gleaning privileges to the underprivileged. The rich and those
with excess were to loan to the underprivileged without efforts to increase their own wealth or to further jeopardize the well-being of the
underprivileged.

The underprivileged and privileged statuses are not mutually exclusive; therefore, responsibilities to care for the underprivileged may fall
on persons who themselves at one time or another may be considered
underprivileged. It is this aspect of concern that indicates the relativity
of the status and the hierarchy of responsibilities. In this respect the גר
who sought the protection of the community may become wealthy and
in that status have influence over others, including natives (Lev. 25:39f.).
Furthermore, in that situation the responsibility for the well-being of
the underprivileged also falls on the גר in spite of his status. Likewise,
the people are responsible for the landless Levites (Deut. 18:1f.). The
"poor" (גבר רש) also have a responsibility to the underprivileged "poor"
(דל) not to oppress them.

Finally, the fundamental assertion of concern for the underprivileged
and the basis of their hope is that Yahweh assumes responsibility for
their well-being. This responsibility is then delegated to the leaders,
judges, and those in positions to affect the well-being of the underprivileged. Oppression is therefore considered a sin against God and
is subject to punishment (Lev. 5:20–26 [6:1–7]; Deut. 28:29; Ps. 72:4;
Prov. 14:31; Isa. 10:1–2; Amos 2:6f.; 4:1f.; Mic. 2:1f.; 3:1–12; 6:9f.). Yahweh protects the oppressed (Ps. 9:9) and guards them by responding
to their cry, blessing those who fulfill their responsibilities to them,
and punishing those who neglect those responsibilities. Furthermore,
the well-being of the underprivileged is linked to order in the universe
in such a way that their violation is a violation of the world order. This
universal aspect of concern stands alongside the particularistic nature
of concern, concern for the underprivileged of Israel.

---

45. The ruler's responsibility for the underprivileged is seen in the ancient Near Eastern traditions — for example, the Tale of Aqht, the Legend of King Krt; the prologues to
the Codes of Urukagina and Ur-Nammu; the epilogue to the Code of Hammurabi (see
ANET). See Fensham, "Widow, Orphan, and the Poor," 130f.; Patterson, "The Widow,
the Orphan and the Poor," 226–228; Engelhard, "The Lord's Motivated Concern," 11–14;
K. Whitelam, The Just King: Monarchical Judicial Authority in Ancient Israel (JSOTSup 12;
Sheffield: JSOT Press, 1979) 24f., 34f.

ASPECTS OF CONCERN

The basic concern for the underprivileged is that their life and well-being are preserved within their historical and societal context. The concern neither proposes a change in the structure of the society nor guarantees removal of the underprivileged from their circumstances as a means of addressing their adversities (contrast Exodus 3f.). In spite of this, the concern constitutes a basis of hope inasmuch as it sets out realistic measures for actualizing the care of the underprivileged.

Aims of Concern

Provision of Economic Resources

The physical life of the underprivileged is jeopardized by their lack of means of sustenance. "In the Old Testament, regular daily eating and drinking are considered the actualization, before all else and as the basis of all else, of the sustenance of life vis-à-vis death."[46] Thus, the availability, accessibility, and acquisition of food are imperative to life for all persons, including of the underprivileged. Other resources such as wages, loans, and other monetary aid provided the means to acquire food and clothing.

The accessibility of food constituted one aspect of the realistic hope of the underprivileged in that it is an ongoing provision spanning the seasonal harvests, the third-year tithe, and the sabbatical year. Two of these allow for the underprivileged to gather food directly from the land.

First, as prescribed in Lev. 19:9–10, they were allowed to glean after the fields were harvested (also Lev. 23:22; cf. Deut. 24:19–21; Ruth 2:2f., 15).[47]

Reapers are forbidden to clear the entire field. The borders are to be left unharvested. Furthermore, the portion of the field that is harvested ought not to be cleared of all its yield. Anything that is missed on the first attempt or accidentally falls is to remain for the underprivileged (Deut. 24:19–21), "for the poor and the sojourner" (Lev. 19:10, לֶעָנִי וְלַגֵּר), "for the sojourner, orphan, and widow" (Deut. 24:21, לַגֵּר לַיָּתוֹם וְלָאַלְמָנָה). No conditions regarding the abundance of the harvest are placed on the deliberate effort to provide for the underprivileged in this way. Thus, the provision of the food is not dependent on the owner's satisfaction with the harvest or on the circumstances contributing to that season's yield, that is, rain or drought. The hope for the underprivileged lies in the fact that regardless of the yield or value of the crop (whether wheat

---

46. Knierim, *Task of Old Testament Theology*, 232.
47. See Engelhard, "The Lord's Motivated Concern," 15; Hoffner, "אלמנה," *TDOT*, 1.291; Miscall, *Concept of the Poor*, 58.

or the less expensive barley), the owners of the fields and vineyards must provide for the underprivileged. Their hope also lies in the regularity of this provision and the types of food provided, namely, wheat, barley, olives, grapes, and other fruits. These foods included the staples; therefore, it was possible for the underprivileged to maintain a healthy diet. Nonetheless, the provision does not apply to the totality of the available food supply. Consequently, food resources are limited regardless of the extent of the need among the underprivileged. This aspect of the provision indicates that the concern is not to distribute food resources equally among all, but to make food accessible to all.

Second, during the sabbatical year — in the absence of the seasonal harvest — the underprivileged were allowed to reap the land of any spontaneous yield (Exod. 23:10–11).

While the provision is for the "poor, needy" (אֶבְיוֹן) in Exod. 23:11, in Lev. 25:6 the focus of concern includes "male and female slaves" (עֶבֶד and אָמָה), the hired servant (שָׂכִיר), and sojourners (גֵרִים). The provision is not that the underprivileged use the sabbatical year to sow the fields. They too are to observe the seventh-year rest. The provision is that they have access to the entire yields of the land during the sabbatical year.

Third, at the end of each third year, the tithe of all of the yields of the land, including the grain, wine, and firstborn of the herd and flock, was reserved for the underprivileged — Levites, sojourners, widows, and orphans (Deut. 14:28–29). They could eat to their content of what is provided. They were to partake of the tithe in a designated place and in this way show reverence for God (Deut. 14:23). As with the remains gleaned from the field, this provision addresses only part of the total resources. Likewise, it does not address instances where the provisions are insufficient to meet the need of the underprivileged.

In addition to food, economic assistance was available to the underprivileged by several means including wages and loans.

The underprivileged may earn their wages. When they did so, the wages were to be paid to them on the day that they are earned (Lev. 19:13; Deut. 24:14–15). The rationale is that the hired servant is poor and needs the resources promptly. It is further assumed that the servant has no reserves and will be in further hardship without regular influx of resources.

Since loans (money and other resources)[48] were to help the underprivileged, they were subject to conditions that safeguarded the poor from succumbing to further adversity. The first condition is that loans are released at the end of the seventh year (Deut. 15:2). This condition was to ensure that the underprivileged would not be permanently in-

---

48. Cf. Deut. 23:19f.; Prov. 28:8.

debted. It was feasible that one could receive a loan without means of repayment. In that case the sabbatical year offered a release from the loan. Armed with this knowledge, creditors — those with excess resources — were likely to refuse loans. Therefore, stipulations were also made to assist the underprivileged, namely, that the underprivileged be readily lent money or its equivalent. Consequently, the basic requirement for lending is poverty and the economic misfortune of a once self-sustaining person (Lev. 25:35).

The second loan condition is that loans to fellow Israelites were to be given without interest (נֶשֶׁךְ) (Exod. 22:24 [22:25]). Extending a loan to those without economic means was to be done for the purpose of helping them and not for securing additional economic resources via interest or profit.[49] Furthermore, to take interest on the loan would be to increase the indebtedness of the borrower, thus increasing the probability of further hardship and lifetime servitude for the repayment of the loan.

While the lenders were not to exact interest, they could hold collateral for the loan in the form of pledges (עבט). As with the loan, the pledges were subject to conditions that safeguarded the well-being of the underprivileged. One of the basic conditions is that items that were vital to maintain the life of the underprivileged were not to be taken as pledge. Thus, taking a mill or millstone was prohibited (Deut. 24:6). This prohibition does not extend to clothing (cloaks) in the same way. It is permissible to take a cloak in pledge, but not the cloak of a widow (Deut. 24:17). When taken as a pledge from the poor (עני), the cloak must be returned by nightfall so that the debtor may use it as covering (Exod. 22:25; cf. Deut. 24:12–13). Yet another condition is placed on the lender who accepts collateral for the loan. The lender is prohibited from entering the residence of the debtor to secure a pledge. This disallowed the lender from taking anything other than what was offered in pledge.

The third, and possibly the basic, condition of the loan is the relationship between the lender and the borrower — insider (רע "neighbor" or his אח "brother" in the broader sense of "kin") and outsider (נכרי "foreigner"). While the lender may not exact interest from his רע "neighbor" or his אח "brother" in the broader sense of "kin,"[50] he may exact

---

49. See Noth, *Leviticus*, 191. M. C. Fisher ("נֶשֶׁךְ," *TWOT*, 2.604–5) proposes that the stipulation did not disallow for charging interest but allowed for interest. Thus, Fisher proposes that the stipulation is against a second interest that would result in lifelong enslavement. This proposal is made on the basis of the interpretation of Lev. 25:35–54 as addressing cases of debtor enslavement and his interpretation of the verb חזק, which he takes to mean "seize" — forcibly enslave. But the verb may more likely refer to supporting, restoring, retaining, helping (cf. Judg. 7:8; 2 Sam. 11:25).

50. J. M. Hamilton (*Social Justice and Deuteronomy: The Case of Deuteronomy 15* [SBLDS

it from the נכרי "foreigner" (Deut. 15:3; 23:20). That the poor person is to be treated as a גר "sojourner" in Lev. 25:35 further illustrates that the גר was considered a resident of the community and treated as such in some matters, such as loans. The mention of the נכרי is secondary to identifying a motivation for the release of the loan and prohibition against charging interest, namely, contrasting the treatment of the insider (Deut. 15:2) with the outsider (Deut. 15:3a; 23:20a). Clearly, the concern for the נכרי "foreigner" is not the same as for the underprivileged of Israel. The difference in the concern signals that the nature of concern for the underprivileged is contingent on membership in the covenant community.

That the concern of the text is the insiders is further indicated in Deut. 15:4, 7, 9, 11. The declarative statement in Deut. 15:4a indicates that there will be no אביון in the midst of those who are being addressed. The formulation אחיך האביון in Deut. 15:7 and 9 makes explicit the connection between אח "kin" and אביון "poor/needy," thus identifying the אח "kin" as אביון "poor/needy." In this way, the concern is for the underprivileged of the community (עניך, אחיך, אביונך, Deut. 15:11; cf. Lev. 19:33–34; 25:35; Deut. 23:19) rather than for foreigners. As such, the very motivation underlying the conditions of the loan is the motivation for caring for the underprivileged: they are kin and part of the covenant community.

Safeguarding Justice

The safeguarding of justice extends to legal matters, such as the lawsuit, and more broadly to other matters, including provision of food and other economic resources. With regard to justice in legal matters, two prohibitions apply: perversion of the justice (משפט) due the underprivileged of the community and partiality toward them (Exod. 23:3, 6 ["needy," אבינך]; Lev. 19:15; cf. Deut. 24:17 ["orphan and widow," ואלמנה יתום]; 27:19, 25). The reason cited is that such partiality toward one party in the suit, regardless of his or her status, jeopardizes the possibility for the person in the right to receive justice (Exod. 23:8; cf. Prov. 22:22–23; 24:23; 28:21). There is no presumption that rendering in the favor of the underprivileged is unquestionably an act of justice. Rather, it is presumed that justice in a lawsuit is not determined by the status of the parties involved. Consequently, to rule in favor of the underprivileged simply because they are underprivileged is as much a perversion of justice as ruling in favor of the rich or powerful simply because they are

---

136; Atlanta: Scholars Press, 1992] 34–40) observes that Deuteronomy frequently uses אח with the nuance of "kin" (Deut. 15:2, 3, 7, 9, 11, 12; 17:15; 19:18f.; 22:1–5; 23:20f.; 25:3). See H. Wolff, "אחה," TWOT, 1.31–32.

rich. Even so, the provision of food and other resources builds on a measure of partiality or benevolence toward the underprivileged to ensure their right to life.

The perversion of justice may also take the form of bribes. Bribes would be used to secure a favorable judgment in a case. In that instance the underprivileged would be at a disadvantage to the extent that they lack the means to secure a bribe. The prohibition against the bribe aims at ensuring that the guilty and innocent receive their due regardless of their status. The safeguarding of justice also means that the judicial system is preserved as a fair system for all concerned.

In the broader sense God executes justice for the underprivileged by being impartial, not taking bribes, and providing food and clothing (Deut. 10:17–18). These provisions are considered the right of the underprivileged because of their dependent status. To withhold such provisions, then, is to act unjustly toward the underprivileged by denying them their right to life and well-being. Thus, God responds to the cry of the underprivileged.

> If you do afflict them, and they cry to me, I will surely hear their cry; and my anger will burn, and I will kill you with the sword, and your wives shall become widows and your children orphans. (Exod. 22:22–23 [23–24])

"[T]his 'cry' is not just a personal outburst or a simple instinctive reaction to suffering: it is essentially addressed to someone (*'el...*) and demands to be heard in the name of right.... In this way a complaint reveals another aspect of what constitutes it; it is a request for help addressed to an 'authorized' person, juridically bound by the actual cry."[51] The cry of the underprivileged affects Yahweh's response. Even so, the nature of the response may vary — for example, judgment on the oppressors or removal of the underprivileged from the situation of distress (cf. Exodus 3; 22:22; Deut. 19:9; 24:15).

Safeguarding Freedom

The divergent articulations of concern for the underprivileged are evident in this area. Here, one must ask whether this divergence represents a different conceptual basis or a different contextualization of the same basic concern. An examination of the relevant texts shows that the divergence exhibits a common conceptual basis: to the slave, the fundamental needs include means of subsistence, safeguard of freedom, and protection from oppression (Exod. 21:5f.; Lev. 25:39f.; Deut. 15:12f.). In

---

51. Bovati, *Re-Establishing Justice*, 317. He cites various examples, including Gen. 39:14; 15:18; 2 Sam. 13:19. Cf. Boecker, *Law and the Administration of Justice*, 49f.; Deut. 22:23–27; 1 Kings 8:1–6.

Deut. 15:12–18 the concern is to protect the slaves from involuntary life-time servitude. The slaves are members of the covenant community — אָחִיךָ הָעִבְרִי אוֹ עִבְרִיָּה "your kin, a Hebrew man or a Hebrew woman"[52] — who became slaves through acts of selling themselves (מכר "to sell," niphal).[53] The law stipulates that the owner of such slaves free them (שלח, piel) after six years of service.

Notably, the provision is not for the abolition of slavery but for its regulation as an institution. Thus, the formulation of the law indicates that the responsibility for the freedom of the slave lies in the hand of the owner as well as the slave. The owner is responsible for freeing the slave, thus ending the servitude of that slave (cf. Exod. 21:5; Lev. 25:39). Furthermore, the law requires that the owner generously pro-vide that freed slave with material possessions and livestock, that is, the economic basis on which to establish a measure of independent ex-istence.[54] The slave is also free to choose whether or not to remain a slave. The choice, however, is motivated by love for the owner (Deut. 15:16). In Deut. 15:12f. no specification is given concerning those born into slavery (contrast Exod. 21:5f.).

Safeguard against Abuse and Oppression

The concern to safeguard the underprivileged from oppression is artic-ulated within the conceptual framework that designates oppression as sin (Isa. 59:13) and an insult to God (Prov. 14:31). The vulnerabilities of the underprivileged predisposed them to various forms of disfavor and abuse from any with opportunity and motive to oppress (cf. Prov. 14:20; 28:3). Therefore, the safeguard against oppression[55] extended to the various groups of underprivileged — for example, the widow, or-phan, sojourner, and hired servants (Jer. 7:6; 21:12; Amos 4:1; Zech 7:10; Mal. 3:5). The paradigmatic manifestation of the provision against op-pression is the exodus (Exodus 3f.), the removal of the oppressed from the oppressive situation. As with the exodus account, other formula-tions regard oppression as a violation of the underprivileged (Lev. 19:13; Deut. 24:14) and cause for judgment (Jer. 6:6; Amos 2:6; 4:1f.; Mic. 2:1f.;

---

52. Concerning the inclusion of women in this formulation vis-à-vis the absence of this reference in Exod. 21:5f. see M. A. Fishbane, *Biblical Interpretation in Ancient Israel* (Oxford: Clarendon, 1985).

53. Contrast Exod. 22:3f. Fishbane (*Biblical Interpretation*, 340–41) sees Deut. 15:12f. as a restricted use of the earlier *traditum*.

54. See G. Braulik, *The Theology of Deuteronomy* (trans. U. Lindblad; BIBAL Collected Essays 2; North Richland Hills, Tex.: Bibal Press, 1994) 140f.

55. See R. B. Allen, "עשׁק," *TWOT*, 2.705–6; cf. C. F. Mariottini, *The Problem of Social Op-pression in the Eighth-Century Prophets* (Ph.D. diss.: Southern Baptist Theological Seminary, 1983), esp. 31f.

Mal. 3:5; cf. Prov. 14:20). Regarding the sojourners and servants, oppression included physical abuse, such as overworking, bodily injury,
and denial of rest as prescribed by the Sabbath laws (Exod. 23:12).

Participation in the Cult

Participation in the cult was important as the manifestation of the covenant relationship between Israel and Yahweh. Participation required
gifts and other resources that may have been beyond the means of the
underprivileged. Thus, provisions were made to insure that they were
not excluded because of their lack of resources or marginalization. The
provisions allowed for participation by the sojourner, widow, and orphan in the festivals — the Passover (Exod. 12:48; Num. 9:14), Day of
Atonement (Lev. 16:29), and Festivals of Weeks and Tabernacles (Deut.
16:9f.). In the case of the גר, he was allowed to participate in hearing
the reading of the law (Deut. 31:12). While the underprivileged were to
be provided for as members of the covenant community, they were also
subject to the requirements of the cult. They were to observe the Sabbath (Exod. 20:10), observe the purification laws (Lev. 17:8–16; 18:26),
and bring the required sacrifices for their sins. Since their participation
in the cult could have been restricted by their lack of resources, further provisions were made for fulfilling the requirement for the various
sacrifices according to the resources available to the poor (Lev. 14:22f.).

Motivation for the Concern

The fundamental motivation for articulating the concern for the underprivileged is to ensure their well-being. This motivation, however, is
different from the motivation to adhere to the actions prescribed in
the articulated concern. This section considers the motive clauses ac-
companying the formulations of concern, using them to identify the
motivation or inducements offered to those responsible for actualizing
care for the underprivileged.

Humanitarianism

This motivation is constituted by its appeal to the humanity of the addressees. The conceptual framework for this motivation is the covenant
relationship. Even though the motivation is humanitarian in nature its
framework of validity is the covenant. Through understanding the experience of others one may gain empathy for their circumstances. Such
understanding may be had through shared experiences or knowing
more about the circumstances.

The appeal to shared experiences is made in several instances,
including the release of slaves and generosity toward slaves when released (Deut. 15:13–15). In this context the shared experience is the end

of the enslavement and the provisions made to the Israelites for their well-being.[56]

In other contexts the appeal to shared experience is made to de-ter oppression against a גֵר "stranger." For example, "You shall not wrong a stranger or oppress him, for you were strangers in the land of Egypt"(Exod. 22:20 [21]).

The experiences being alluded to are the status of Israel in Egypt as sojourners and the oppression suffered there. In this respect the memory of the oppression may deter if not prevent Israelites from op-pressing one another (Exod. 23:9; cf. Deut. 24:18, 22). The appeal was also made to safeguard justice for the sojourner, widow, and orphan (Deut. 24:17–18; cf. 10:19).

Empathy for the underprivileged may also have been secured through knowledge of their circumstances. For example, the motiva-tion cited for paying daily wages is that the poor are dependent on them (Deut. 24:25). The rationale is that the addressee would know the gravity of the circumstances and thus act to alleviate the need of the poor.

The perpetual existence of the poor within the covenant community is cited as a motivation for helping the poor. In this respect the very existence of the poor is the essence of the motivation to protect them (Deut. 15:11). It presumes that the provisions themselves are a part of the reality of the perpetual poverty. It further presumes that the hope of the underprivileged lies in regulating of the societal practices. The provisions, therefore, do not hold out the hope of the termination of all poverty and adversity.

Reward and Punishment

Another aspect of the motivation is the prospect of receiving rewards. These rewards may take the form of blessing and increased economic resources (Deut. 15:10). Thus, the motivations for freeing the slaves in Deut. 15:18 are that the time of service has been profitable and that God will bless the owner for releasing the slaves.

As there are positive motivations for fulfilling one's responsibility to the underprivileged, there are also negative motivations, namely, the avoidance of punishment.

---

56. Cf. the absence of the motivation in Exod 21:3f. Also, the perspective of this text seems to differ from that of Deut 15:12f. In the Exodus passage no provision is made for establishing the livelihood of the freed person. Furthermore, a person must leave behind his family if that family was acquired during slavery. Thus, the freedom of the slave seems to be curtailed by the interest of the owner. Cf. Braulik, *Theology of Deuteronomy,* in light of its contribution to our understanding of human rights.

You shall not wrong or oppress a resident alien.... You shall not abuse any widow or orphan. If you do abuse them, when they cry out to me, I will surely heed their cry; my wrath will burn, and I will kill you with the sword, and your wives shall become widows and your children orphans. (Exod. 22:20–23 [21–24])

This negative motivation is also seen in Deuteronomy (15:9; 24:15, 17; cf. Prov. 22:22–23) and in the judgment speeches of the prophets. In the latter, the reason for punishment is the oppression of the underprivileged and, generally speaking, the failure to fulfill one's responsibility toward them (Isa. 10:1f.; Amos 2:6f.; 4:1f.; 8:6f.; Mic. 2:1–2; 3:1–12).

Reverence for Yahweh

As articulated in Prov. 14:31, "Those who oppress the poor insult their Maker; but those who are kind to the needy honor him." Therefore, out of reverence to God one would treat the underprivileged kindly. This appeal is further evident in the motive clause "I am the Lord your God" (Lev. 19:10; 23:22; 24:22). This clause functions as a reminder of the source of concern for the underprivileged. It also places the imperative to care for them on the recognition of the character and being of God, the Creator and God of the covenant.

Finally, God exemplifies the concern for the underprivileged. Thus, God is portrayed as the God of justice who executes justice for the underprivileged and establishes justice as the foundation of God's reign (cf. Deut. 10:18f.; Psalms 72, 82)

Extent of Concern

The concern for the underprivileged consists of its distinctive and essential components that characterize this concern and distinguish it from other theological formulations. These components are the semantic indicators, typical formulaic expressions and the conceptual frameworks of concern. The theology of the underprivileged is further constituted by theological concepts whose presence is necessary to its character and without which that theology would exhibit significantly different aspects. Such is the relationship of the theology of justice to the theology of concern for the underprivileged. Its relationship with the theology of concern for the underprivileged manifests itself primarily with regard to the nature of the responsibility for its execution and the extent of concern.

With Respect to Persons

Issues of the extent of the Old Testament concern for the underprivileged arise with the observation that the primary concern is articulated about the underprivileged of Israel. As noted in the use of the various qualifiers, the texts are aware of the existence of others whose circumstances mirror those of the underprivileged of Israel. Yet, in the provision of the loans distinctions are made between the treatment of the underprivileged of Israel and foreigners. Nonetheless, the extent of concern is as much a factor of the perspective from which it is articulated as the circumstances that stimulated the articulation of concern. It is this contextualization of concern that accounts in part for its exclusivistic character. Still, the focus on the underprivileged of Israel and the covenant relationship as the framework place concern for others in the background if not entirely out of sight.

With Respect to the Existence of Poverty and Injustice

While the concern for the underprivileged addresses the needs of the underprivileged within their circumstances, it does not address itself to changing these circumstances. Consequently, the concern is not to remove the circumstances that generate poverty or injustice, but to care for the underprivileged within those realities. Thus, while the declaration is made that there will be no poor, this declaration is qualified (Deut. 15:4b) to indicate limited application of the declaration with respect to the addressees and the condition for the nonexistence. The כִּי clause signals that the blessing of Yahweh is the precondition for the nonexistence of the poor.[57] However, as signaled by the conditional clause (רק אם "if only"), there is a condition to the blessing itself: obedience (Deut. 15:5). This condition is followed by a hypothetical statement that further specifies how the poor ought to be treated if they exist in the land (Deut. 15:7–8). Perhaps the ideal of Deut. 15:4 is balanced by the reality of Deut. 15:11, a reality resulting from disobedience.[58]

Thus, as significant as it is to the theology of concern for the underprivileged, the fact of the existence of the underprivileged remains a presupposition to the concerns. The provision concerning food and economic resources allows for the provision of food and loans, but noticeably not for equal access to the totality of those resources by all persons.[59]

---

57. For discussion of the nature of that declaration in v. 4 as compared to v. 11 see Miscall, *Concept of the Poor*, 101f.; Hamilton, *Social Justice and Deuteronomy*, 15ff.; G. von Rad, *Deuteronomy* (trans. D. Barton; OTL; Philadelphia: Westminster, 1966); P. Craigie, *The Book of Deuteronomy* (NICOT; Grand Rapids: Eerdmans, 1976).

58. Craigie (*Book of Deuteronomy*, 237) endorses the possibility that the text reflects the contrast between the ideal and the reality of disobedience resulting in the existence of the poor. He also leaves open the possibility that the text reflects the contrast between the present reality and hope for the future.

59. Knierim (*Task of Old Testament Theology*, 106f.) discusses social justice in a stratified society.

CONCLUSION

There are dangers in all theological reconstruction. The first danger is that the resultant theology is invalidated by the material selected in the construction of that theology. The second danger is that although the theology is validated by its constitutive components, its implications for hermeneutical reflections create daunting challenges.

The first of these challenges is the exclusive nature of concern. Is God the God of all underprivileged or of those of Israel only? This is essentially the question that today's underprivileged must confront in their use of the Old Testament in their hermeneutics of liberation, justice, and hope.[60] This confrontation must consider how the portrayal of God as the God who addresses the needs of some of the peoples of the earth is to be reconciled with the portrayal of an omnipotent, omnipresent, and benevolent God. The present underprivileged must confront the challenge of the persistence of their circumstances and examine the basis of their hope. Perhaps the basis of hope for Israel's underprivileged as suggested by the Old Testament may differ in nature from the basis of hope for today's underprivileged. This is an aspect of the limitation of the theology.

To say that a theology has limitations is nothing more than to define the parameters of that theology. Nonetheless, the limitations of one theology affect the parameters of the whole. Consequently, the theology of justice cannot ignore the aspects of concern of the underprivileged; nor can the concern for the underprivileged ignore the aspects of justice that it both presupposes and articulates. The theology of concern for the underprivileged is therefore essential and necessary to the theology of justice and to Old Testament theology if that theology seeks to be legitimate to its constitutive elements.

BIBLIOGRAPHY

Allen, Ronald B. "עשׁק," TWOT 2 (1980).
Boecker, Hans-Jochen. Law and the Adminstration of Justice in the Old Testament and Ancient East. Minneapolis: Augsburg, 1980.
Botterweck, G. Johannes. "אביון," TDOT 1 (1977).
———. "אבה," ThWAT 1 (1973–77).
Bovati, Pietro. Re-Establishing Justice: Legal Terms, Concepts and Procedures in the Hebrew Bible. Trans. Michael J. Smith. JSOTSup 105. Sheffield: JSOT Press, 1994.

---

60. See C. L. Rigby, "Someone to Blame, Someone to Trust: Divine Power and the Self-Recovery of the Oppressed," in Rigby, ed., Power, Powerlessness, and the Divine, 79–102. D. Williams (Sisters in the Wilderness [Maryknoll, N.Y.: Orbis, 1993]) discusses the limited extent of God's liberating action.

Coggins, Richard J. "The Old Testament and the Poor." *ExpT* 99/1 (1987).

Collins, John J. "Is a Critical Biblical Theology Possible?" In *The Hebrew Bible and Its Interpreters.* Ed. William H. Propp et al., 1–17. Winona Lake, Ind.: Eisenbrauns, 1990.

Coppes, Leonard J. "ענה III," *TWOT* 2 (1980).

———. "דלל," *TWOT* 1 (1980).

———. "אבה," *TWOT* 1 (1980).

Davies, E. W. "Inheritance Rights and the Hebrew Levirate Marriage." *VT* 31 (1981).

Engelhard, David H. "The Lord's Motivated Concern for the Underprivileged." *Calvin Theological Journal* 15 (April 1980).

Fabry, H.-J. "דל," *TDOT* 3 (1977).

Fensham, Charles F. "Widow, Orphan, and the Poor in Ancient Near Eastern Legal and Wisdom Literature." *JNES* 21 (1962).

Fisher, Milton C. "נשך," *TWOT* 2 (1980).

Frick, Frank. "Widow in the Hebrew Bible: A Transactional Approach." In *A Feminist Companion to Exodus to Deuteronomy.* Ed. Athalya Brenner, 139–51. Sheffield: Sheffield Academic Press, 1994.

Gerstenberger, Erhard. "ענה II," *ThWAT* 6 (1973–77).

———. "דל." *TDOT* 3 (1977).

Hamilton, Jeffries M. *Social Justice and Deuteronomy: The Case of Deuteronomy 15.* SBLDS 136. Atlanta: Scholars Press, 1992.

Hanson, Paul D. *The Diversity of Scripture: A Theological Interpretation.* OBT 11. Philadelphia: Fortress Press, 1982.

Hartley, John E. "יתום," *TWOT* 1 (1980).

Havice, Harriet K. *The Concern for the Widow and the Fatherless in the Ancient Near East: A Case Study in Old Testament Ethics.* Ph.D. dissertation, Yale University. Ann Arbor: University Microfilms International, 1978.

Hiebert, P. S. " 'Whence Shall Help Come to Me?' The Biblical Widow." In *Gender and Difference in Ancient Israel.* Ed. P. Day, 124–41. Minneapolis: Fortress Press, 1989.

Hoffner, Harry A. "אלמנה," *TDOT* 1 (1977).

Kellermann, Diether. "גור," *TDOT* 2 (1977).

Knierim, Rolf P. *The Task of Old Testament Theology: Substance, Method, and Cases.* Grand Rapids: Eerdmans, 1995.

Kühlewein, J. "אלמנה," *TLOT* 1 (1997).

Martin-Archard, R. "גור," *TLOT* 1 (1997).

———. "Yahwé et les ᵃⁿnawîm," *TZ* 21 (1965).

Miscall, Peter D. *The Concept of the Poor in the Old Testament.* Ph.D. dissertation: Harvard University, 1972.

Patterson, Richard D. "The Widow, the Orphan and the Poor in the Old Testament and Extra-Biblical Literature." *BSac* 130 (1973).

Rigby, Cynthia L. "Someone to Blame, Someone to Trust: Divine Power and the Self-Recovery of the Oppressed." In *Power, Powerlessness, and the Divine: New Inquiries in Bible and Theology.* Ed. Cynthia L. Rigby, 79–102. Atlanta: Scholars Press, 1997.

Rogers, Cleon. "שכר," *TWOT* 2 (1980).

Rook, J. "Making Widows: The Patriarchal Guardian at Work." *Biblical Theology Bulletin* 27/1 (1997).

———. "When Is a Widow Not a Widow?: Guardianship Provides an Answer." *Biblical Theology Bulletin* 28, no. 1 (1998).

Schweiker, W., and M. Welker. "A New Paradigm of Theological and Biblical Inquiry." In *Power, Powerlessness, and the Divine: New Inquiries in Bible and Theology.* Ed. Cynthia L. Rigby, 1–20. Atlanta: Scholars Press, 1997.

Scott, Jack B. "אלמנה," *TWOT* 1 (1980).

Stigers, Harold G. "גור," *TWOT* 1 (1980).

von Waldow, H. Eberhard. "Social Responsibility and Social Structure in Early Israel." *CBQ* 32 (1970).

Westermann, Claus. "עבד," *TLOT* 2 (1997).

———. *Elements of Old Testament Theology.* Trans. Douglas W. Stott. Atlanta: John Knox, 1982.

Whitelam, Keith. *The Just King: Monarchical Judicial Authority in Ancient Israel.* JSOTSup 12. Sheffield: JSOT Press, 1979.

Wilson, Marvin R. "נכרי," *TWOT* 2 (1980).

Wolff, H. "אחה," *TWOT* 1 (1980).

14

The Task of
Hebrew Bible/Old Testament Theology—
Between Judaism and Christianity

A Response to Rolf Knierim's
*Task of Old Testament Theology**

Isaac Kalimi

Have we not all one father?
Has not one God created us?
Why then are we faithless to one another,
profaning the covenant of our fathers?

—Malachi 2:10

STRUCTURE AND CONTENT

Since Rolf Knierim (b. 1928) is a former student of the renowned Heidelberg theologian Gerhard von Rad (1901–71), we are not surprised to learn that Knierim had pursued biblical thinking from the early stages of his life. In the beginning of his career, forty-five years ago, he published a popular article, "Biblisches Denken," in the monthly newsletter of his German Lutheran congregation (1955).[1]

The book under discussion here, *The Task of Old Testament Theology: Substance, Method, and Cases*, is not simply one more typical (biblical) theology of the Old Testament. It is a collection of articles that were originally published in several languages (English, German, and Portuguese) and in various periodicals and *Festschriften*. They were written over a span of approximately three decades, in different places, and under different circumstances. In *The Task of Old Testament Theology* Knierim combined them into one volume, which represents his com-

---

*Rolf Knierim, *The Task of Old Testament Theology: Substance, Method, and Cases* (Grand Rapids: Eerdmans, 1995). The main part of this essay was originally delivered as a response to the book at the AAR/SBL annual meeting in San Francisco on November 24, 1997.

1. See Knierim, *Task of Old Testament Theology*, xii.

plete and updated opinion on the issue in contemporary lingua franca, that is, English.

The book deals mainly with biblical theology and with the theology of the Hebrew Bible and its fundamental task according to the author. Although it was not originally designed so, it is comprised of two major sections.

The first, and more significant, section is a methodological program for Hebrew Bible theology as a field of study, as indicated by the opening chapter, "The Task of Old Testament Theology." It is followed by three critical responses from other scholars (see below) and concludes with Knierim's answer to them. The extensive chapter "The Interpretation of the Old Testament" concentrates on general topics, such as biblical exegesis; theology and hermeneutics; the method of Old Testament theology; justice in Old Testament theology; and the Old Testament, the New Testament, and Jesus Christ. Here, the author furnishes important knowledge about basic issues in the discipline and guides readers toward a better understanding of his own terminology, methods, and distinctions.

The second section includes several detailed case studies of Old Testament theology. Most of these essays treat a comprehensive biblical subject, such as "Revelation in the Old Testament," "Cosmos and History in Israel's Theology," "Food, Land and Justice" (the first, to the best of my knowledge, to treat extensively the theology of food in the Bible), "Hope in the Old Testament," "The Spirituality of the Old Testament," "The Old Testament — The Letter and the Spirit," "Israel and the Nations in the Land of Palestine in the Old Testament," "The Composition of the Pentateuch," "The Book of Numbers," "Science in the Bible" (which fills in a gap in the study of Old Testament theology), "On the Contours of Old Testament and Biblical Hamartiology" [= sin, I.K.]. Some essays, such as "Conceptual Aspects in Exodus 25,1–9" and "On the Theology of Psalm 19," concentrate on specific biblical texts. The essay "A Posteriori Explorations" completes this section.

The book concludes with an extensive chapter (appendix?), "On Gabler." Right now this chapter represents the most fundamental and detailed research on the famous 1787 inaugural lecture of Johann Philipp Gabler (1753–1826) at the University of Altdorf (Bavaria, Germany), in which Gabler distinguished biblical theology as an independent discipline separate from dogmatic theology.[2] The book also contains a bibliography and several useful indexes.

2. See also M. Sæbø, "Johann Philipp Gabler at the End of the Eighteenth Century: History and Theology," in *On the Way to Canon: Creative Tradition History in the Old Testament* (JSOTSup 191; Sheffield: Sheffield Academic Press, 1998) 310–26; L. T. Stuckenbruck, "Johann Philipp Gabler and the Delineation of Biblical Theology," *SJT* 52 (1999) 139–57.

Despite Knierim's statement that "other essays already published or on file which do not exemplify the task of Old Testament theology, or exemplify it less, were excluded from the collection,"[3] it seems that not all the essays are good cases of Old Testament theology. In fact, some of them have little to do with it, at least directly. For instance, the essay "The Composition of the Pentateuch" (in which the author attempts to identify the Torah as *Vita Mosis* — a biography of Moses — including the book of Genesis!) is stimulating for its own sake (even if one does not agree with the author in every point), but is not a good illustration of Knierim's writings on Old Testament theology.[4] The same can be said of the interesting and meticulous essay "The Book of Numbers," which does not bear much significance for the main subject of the volume.

Although six of the book's essays (and part of a seventh) are published for the first time,[5] nearly two-thirds of them have appeared previously in diverse contexts. Therefore, it is unfortunate that the author did not designate their sources. For example, the first three chapters derive from Knierim's lecture at the annual meeting of the Society of Biblical Literature in 1983, which was followed by responses from other scholars, namely, Walter Harrelson, W. Sibley Towner, and Roland E. Murphy, along with Knierim's reply to them. All these were published in *Horizons in Biblical Theology* 6 (1984) and are republished in the book. The reader who is unaware of this background wonders why responses of these scholars, specifically Americans, were included in Knierim's book, and not those of well-known European theologians. Notes like those on the chapters "The Interpretation of the Old Testament" and "Israel and the Nations in the Land of Palestine in the Old Testament," which clarify why these chapters have the style of oral presentation,[6] contribute to a better understanding of the pieces. In short, it would benefit readers to know the background of all the essays, that is, to whom they were addressed, and how, when, and where.

A previous reviewer, Richard J. Coggins, remarked that "the book

---

3. Knierim, *Task of Old Testament Theology*, xiii.

4. The centrality of the Sinai pericope in the Pentateuch (around 42 percent, almost half of the Pentateuch text) has, of course, important theological consequences. Note the saying of the Sages: "the whole world and the fullness were not created but for the sake of the Torah" (*Gen. Rab.* 1:4). Unfortunately, Knierim's article did not develop in this direction.

5. The unpublished essays include "Food, Land and Justice," "Hope in the Old Testament," "The Spirituality of the Old Testament," "On the Contours of Old Testament and Biblical Hamartiology," "A Posteriori Explorations," "On Gabler," and the first part of "On the Theology of Psalm 19."

6. See Knierim, *Task of Old Testament Theology*, 57 n. 1 (this essay is based on the lectures that Knierim gave at the United Methodist Seminary in São Paulo, Brazil, in 1989); 309 n. 1 (this article is based on the lectures that Knierim gave at the Lutheran Theological Seminary in Gettysburg, Pennsylvania, in 1978).

has much to say about 'Method' and discusses many 'Cases'; there is not the substance of an Old Testament theology here."[7] Accordingly, the absence of the word "substance" from the subtitle of the book's cover is considered to be a Freudian slip. And indeed, if we take the word "substance" to mean "concreteness," "actuality," "worthiness," "usefulness," "significance," and so forth, there is some justification for Coggins's remark. Nevertheless, one cannot ignore the possibility that Knierim uses "substance" as an equivalent for the well-known German terms *Sachkritik* or *Inhaltskritik*, that is, subject, theme, or content criticism of the Hebrew Bible. From this viewpoint there is clearly much of "substance" in Knierim's book.

SOME CRITICAL METHODOLOGICAL AND THEOLOGICAL VIEWPOINTS

In the following pages I present a number of critical perspectives on several methodological and theological aspects of Knierim's book. Some of the perspectives have to do with the nature of biblical scholarship in general and biblical theology as a self-defined discipline in particular, while others specifically concern Jewish-Christian relationships.

First and foremost, I share Knierim's comprehensive methodological outlook, that is, to view a defined subject within a comprehensive issue; to see a limited picture (the micro) within the entire framework (the macro); to understand the bound biblical text, topic, or thought not only within the close context — that is, paragraph, literary unit, book, composition of the school, or literary genre — but also within the whole broad biblical perspective.[8] Moreover, at least concerning the theologies of the biblical authors and editors, I believe that we must greatly broaden our perspective. This means that we should observe them not only from the perspective of the all-inclusive biblical horizon, but also be aware of their own historical time, their ancient Near Eastern and Mediterranean background and cultural context, as much as possible. Obviously, the biblical authors and editors, like any other creative writers, are conditioned by their own time, place, and specific historical circumstances and religio-cultural norms and atmosphere. No one can ignore these. Only from this wide perspective, and not in isolation, will we be able to grasp the uniqueness of biblical thoughts and be able to evaluate properly their special contribution. Only from this wide perspective of the entire biblical horizon within its Oriental context (and not from Western secular philosophical viewpoints or

---

7. See R. Coggins, "Old Testament Theology — How?" *ExpTim* 107 (1996) 309.
8. See, for example, Knierim, *Task of Old Testament Theology*, 469.

any of the religious/confessional points of view and biases, either Jewish or Christian) can we deepen our understanding of the theologies of Hebrew Bible writers and editors.

Knierim did not refrain from placing at least some of his theological discussions in the ancient Oriental spectrum. For instance, in his essay "Revelation in the Old Testament" he states that "what has been said must be viewed within the broader horizon of ancient Near Eastern ontology and epistemology, to which the Old Testament belonged." Accordingly, he dedicates a special detailed subdivision to that issue.[9] And in the article "The Book of Numbers" he discusses the narrative genre of the cultic campaign. He refers to other ancient cultures and notes that this genre is unique neither to the Priestly writers nor to Israel: "Egyptian sources report about both the planning stage in Pharaoh's court and the execution of the plan."[10] In this case, however, Knierim refers neither to a specific example nor to any bibliography, as the subject demands.

Knierim focuses essentially on the final form (*der Endtext*) of the Hebrew Bible, that is, the Scripture as it is in front of us, the form that has been canonized and authorized. Usually, he does not deal with the earlier stages of the biblical beliefs, thoughts, ideas, and so forth, which might be revealed by historical-critical methods. In other words, Knierim researched the Hebrew Bible theologies primarily from the synchronic viewpoint. It appears that in his research and writing he distinguishes between the nature and methods of the scholarly investigation of the history of the Israelite religion in the biblical period on the one hand, and Old Testament theology(ies) on the other. These are two different aspects of the same literary corpus, and they are incompatible.[11] Unlike some biblical scholars, Knierim avoids confusion between the two independent concepts.[12]

---

9. Knierim, *Task of Old Testament Theology*, 145–48.

10. Knierim, *Task of Old Testament Theology*, 387.

11. For detailed discussion on this issue see I. Kalimi, "History of Israelite Religion or Old Testament Theology? Jewish Interest in Biblical Theology," *SJOT* 11 (1997) 100–109.

12. In reaction to the German version of my 1997 *SJOT* article (*Jahrbuch für Biblische Theologie* 10 [1995] 45–68; see n. 11) Professor Knierim wrote to me in his letter of July 25, 1996, "Lassen Sie mich nur sagen, daß Ihre Bestimmung des *Unterschiedes* der beiden und der eigenständigen Berechtigung (ich würde sagen: der eigenständigen *Notwendigkeit* für...) jeder der beiden vollkommen klar und unwiderleglich ist. Daß dies in USA fast kaum diskutiert, in England ([here a British scholar is named] et al.) nicht verstanden, und auch in Deutschland vermasselt ist, ist eigentlich ein bedauerliches Zeichen intellektueller Unfähigkeit der Gilde, die Probleme klar zu analysieren und zu rekonstruieren. Ich selbst bin seit meinem Artikel für die 1971 von Rad *Festschrift* (nun in Englisch in meinem Buch, dessen *Programm, auch* in der Komposition der Artikel, ja kaum von jemand verstanden wird), also: seit 1971 bin ich in einem anderen Lager bezüglich des Programmes für AT Theologie als dem v. Rad'schen."

Over generations many Christian theologians attempted to uncover and define (sometimes even impose) one central unifying theological idea of the whole Hebrew Bible. Concepts such as "covenant," "salvation history," "promise," "God is the Lord who imposes his will," and "kingdom of God" are among the many suggestions offered in biblical theological scholarship for this central theme.[13] Just recently Horst Dietrich Preuss (1927–93) has suggested that the unifying theological center of the Old Testament is "JHWH's historical activity of electing Israel for community with his world and the obedient activity required of this people (and the peoples)."[14] But how does the biblical Wisdom literature (Proverbs, Job, and Ecclesiastes, for example) correlate with this central theology? The reader is offered no reply. Knierim accurately emphasizes[15] that the Hebrew Bible does not contain a single central theology but several different theologies.[16] This plurality of theologies coexists in the Hebrew Bible and demands the interpretation of their relationship, that is, how they are related to one another in the same corpus. Some of them complement each other. There are also, however, some parallels and contradictions between theologies in the Hebrew Bible, the contradictions occasionally occurring even within the very same book.[17] How could this diversity of parallel and contradictory theologies coexist in the same book, literary complex, or corpus?

Indeed, contrary to the New Testament, in which almost everything is centered on Jesus Christ,[18] there is no distinct, prominent center point — *die Mitte* — that the entire Hebrew Bible/Old Testament surrounds.[19] If all parts of the Hebrew Bible share any common issue, it

---

13. For a survey of different suggestions see H. G. Reventlow, *Problems of Old Testament Theology in the Twentieth Century* (Philadelphia: Fortress, 1985) 125–33; Kalimi, "History of Israelite Religion," 105–6.

14. See H. D. Preuss, *Old Testament Theology* (2 vols.; Edinburgh: T. & T. Clark, 1995) 1:25. In the original German version: "So soll 'JHWHs erwählendes Geschichtshandeln an Israel zur Gemeinschaft mit seiner Welt', das zugleich ein dieses Volk (und die Völker) verpflichtendes Handeln ist, als Mitte des AT, damit als Grundstruktur atl. Glaubens,...bestimmt werden" (idem, *JHWHs erwählendes und verpflichtendes Handeln* [vol. 1 of *Theologie des Alten Testaments*; 2 vols.; Stuttgart: Kohlhammer, 1991] 29). Obviously, this idea is reflected already in the subtitle of the book.

15. See, for example, Knierim, *Task of Old Testament Theology*, 1–4.

16. Cf. Kalimi, "History of Israelite Religion," 100–123.

17. Cf., for example, Gen. 6:6–7, "And *the Lord repented* that he had made man," and Exod. 32:14, "*And the Lord repented* of the evil which he thought to do to his people" (see also 2 Sam. 24:16 par. 1 Chron. 21:15; Jer. 26:19; Jon. 3:10), with Num. 23:19 and with 1 Sam. 15:29, "And also *Israel's Everlasting One* [i.e., the Lord] *does not deceive and does not repent;* for he is not a man that he should repent." Similarly, cf. 1 Sam. 15:11, "*I* [the Lord] *repent* that I have made Saul king," with v. 29 of the same chapter.

18. Although the Epistle of James does not specifically mention Jesus.

19. On this issue see Reventlow, *Problems of Old Testament Theology*, and compare Kalimi, "History of Israelite Religion," 100–123.

is monotheism.[20] After all, this corpus is an anthology of a variety of literary genres written and edited over hundreds of years, during different eras (i.e., kingdom era, exilic and Second Temple periods), under many circumstances, in many places (i.e., Israel, Judah, Babylon), by numerous authors, editors, and schools (Deuteronomic, Priestly, Holiness, etc.). This leaves no space for any sort of homogeneity of a single, central thought in the Hebrew Bible. It is natural, therefore, that this heterogeneous literary complex contains a variety of theologies, which together in a single corpus reflect somehow a chaotic, and, from time to time, complicated conglomerate. This heterogeneity of thoughts and theologies is not at all surprising. On the contrary, it would be surprising if the Hebrew Bible did not contain an anthology of diverse lines of thoughts and theologies. Nonetheless, generally, biblical scholars and theologians have not emphasized or described these crucial problems. Knierim, on the other hand, justifiably attempts to put this issue at the top of the Hebrew Bible/Old Testament theological agenda as a fundamental and central problem. He calls for a theological criterion to interpret and understand this problem, and to examine "the relationship or correspondence of the individual theologies within this theological pluralism."[21] "In order to determine the relationship among the Old Testament's theologies," says Knierim, "we must be able to discern theologically legitimate priorities. We must ask which theology or theological aspect or notion governs others, and which is relative to, dependent on, or governed by others. Ultimately, we must ask whether there is one aspect that dominates all others, is therefore fundamental, and must be understood as the criterion for the validity of all others."[22] Knierim emphasizes, however, that he neither envisions nor proposes harmonizing the Old Testament, "at least not in the sense that the plurality of theological notion is replaced by one notion; that one notion is expected to be found everywhere; that it is imposed on others without the recognition of their own place and validity; that all notions

---

20. Note that the book of Esther does not mention the name of God at all. Perhaps only Esth. 4:14, "For if you keep silence at such a time as this, relief and deliverance will rise for the Jews from another quarter," can be read as alluding to God (see LXX and Targumim ad loc.; Josephus, *Ant.* 11.227; *Esth. Rab.* 8:6). Nonetheless, all these could be considered as late theological commentary on the biblical verse. Indeed, Vetus Latina, the Vulgate, and the Syriac version of the verse are not leading to this direction (see also Rabbi Abraham Ibn Ezra's commentary on Esth. 4:14). Similarly, the Song of Songs does not contain the name of God.

21. Knierim, *Task of Old Testament Theology*, 5. For other central problems of biblical theology see, for example, B. S. Childs, *Biblical Theology in Crisis* (Philadelphia: Westminster, 1970); H.-J. Kraus, *Die Biblische Theologie: Ihre Geschichte und Problematik* (Neukirchen-Vluyn: Neukirchener, 1977); Reventlow, *Problems of Old Testament Theology*; G. Hasel, *Old Testament Theology: Basic Issues in the Current Debate* (Grand Rapids: Eerdmans, 1991).

22. Knierim, *Task of Old Testament Theology*, 8–9.

mean the same; and that contradictions are excluded and differences overlooked."[23]

Of course, there is nothing wrong with diverse portraits of God in the Hebrew Bible. It is, however, necessary to be aware of these theological features — all canonized and authorized — to compare them for better understanding of the uniqueness of each individual theology, and to look for the possibility of their potential correlation with other biblical theology(ies).

Generally, Christian biblical theologians consider what they call the Old Testament as a prehistory (*Vorgeschichte*), a preparation to the New Testament, and thus the latter as a fulfillment of the former (*Verheißung-Erfüllung*).[24] They are combining both Testaments, and alternating back and forth between the Old and the New and from the New to the Old. They read the Old Testament in the light of the New Testament, and utilize Christian dogmas stated in the New Testament as the only criteria for evaluation of the Old Testament. "Alle Theologie ist Christologie," says Otto Procksch.[25] Later on he stresses, "Ist Christus der Mittelpunkt der Theologie, so scheint das Alte Testament außerhalb einer geschichtstheologischen Betrachtung zu liegen. Denn in Geschichte und Glauben Israels liegt eine vorchristliche Geisteswelt vor, die höchstens in Jesus Christus ihren Schlußpunkt findet. Der Neue Bund tritt dem Alten gegenüber und hebt ihn auf."[26] So the Christian biblical theologians ignore the distinctive characters and principles of the Hebrew corpus. They select some parts of it that are found appropriate to impose the Christian doctrines on and they neglect the others.

This attitude has been expressed in almost all Christian theological legacy from the earliest times until the present. In the modern era it is reflected not only in the writings of theologians such as Johann Philipp Gabler over two hundred years ago,[27] and Otto Procksch

---

23. Knierim, *Task of Old Testament Theology*, 52.

24. This appears already in Luke 24:27: "And beginning with Moses and all the prophets, he interpreted to them in all the scriptures the things concerning himself." It emerges repeatedly, however, in the works of many Christian theologians — for example, B. S. Childs, *Biblical Theology of the Old and New Testaments: Theological Reflection on the Christian Bible* (Minneapolis: Fortress, 1993) 452 ("The old covenant is a preparation for the new"); G. B. Caird, *New Testament Theology* (completed and edited by L. D. Hurst; Oxford: Oxford University Press, 1994) 57–62.

25. See O. Procksch, *Theologie des Alten Testaments* (Gütersloh: C. Bertelsmann Verlag, 1950) 1.

26. Procksch, *Theologie des Alten Testaments*, 7.

27. Although Gabler distinguished between biblical theology and dogmatics, he maintained that the New Testament must be the exclusive criterion for Christian study of the Old Testament. See Knierim, "On Gabler," *Task of Old Testament Theology*, 554–56.

just fifty years ago,[28] but also in those of some contemporary Christian scholars. Antonius H. J. Gunneweg (1922–90), for instance, was of the opinion that from a Christian theological viewpoint the New Testament is the exclusive measure for the legitimacy and understanding of the Old Testament: "Das Neue Testament war und ist für die Rezeption des Alten Testaments als Buch der christlichen Kirche das Kriterium, und nicht etwa umgekehrt."[29] And in his monograph *Biblische Theologie des Alten Testaments* Gunneweg treated the Old Testament's issues in the light of the New Testament.[30] A similar view is stated by Brevard S. Childs. Childs, too, is of the opinion that Christian scholars and theologians have the "fundamental goal to understand the various voices within the whole Christian Bible, New and Old Testament alike, as a witness to the one Lord Jesus Christ, the self-same divine reality."[31] In another place Childs expresses the view that "Jesus Christ, God's true man, who is testified to in *both testaments,* is *the ultimate criterion of truth for both testaments.*"[32]

This view of biblical theologies obviously represents the needs of at least some Christian communities, if not all. They bind the two corpora in their written theology, just as they profess and believe.[33] Nonetheless, this attitude of Christian theologians toward the Hebrew Bible as a non-self-contained corpus, as an incomplete production without the New Testament, giving central place to the New Testament in Old Testament interpretation and theology, is unacceptable not only from the Jewish viewpoint but also from a scholarly one.

From the Jewish viewpoint this sort of theology contains anti-Jewish features. The παλαιᾶς διαθήκης of Paul in 2 Cor. 3:14, for example, which is usually translated as the "old testament" or the "old covenant," is invalid and replaced by the "new covenant," commonly called the "new testament."[34] This "new testament," to cite J. P. Gabler, is "newer and

---

28. See Procksch, *Theologie des Alten Testaments,* 1, 7.

29. A. H. J. Gunneweg, *Biblische Theologie des Alten Testaments: Eine Religionsgeschichte Israels in biblisch-theologischer Sicht* (Stuttgart: Kohlhammer, 1993) 36; compare Gunneweg's *Vom Verstehen des Alten Testaments: Eine Hermeneutik* (GAT 5; Göttingen: Vandenhoeck & Ruprecht, 1977) 183–87 ("Das Neue Testament als Kriterium der kanonischen Geltung des Alten").

30. See, for instance, his discussion on covenant (*Bund*) on pp. 68–75; cf. R. Rendtorff, "Recent German Old Testament Theologies," *JR* 76 (1996) 334. Gunneweg was also of the opinion that Christians understand the Hebrew Bible better than Jews: "Der christliche Glaube wagt es, die Textworte besser zu verstehen, als sie sich selbst verstehen — besser auch, als die Juden sie verstanden und immer noch verstehen" (*Biblische Theologie,* 52).

31. See Childs, *Biblical Theology of the Old and New Testament,* 85; cf. 452.

32. Childs, *Biblical Theology of the Old and New Testament,* 591 (italics added).

33. Cf. Kalimi, "History of Israelite Religion," 114–15.

34. See also 2 Cor. 3:6; 5:17.

better."[35] Only the "new/true Israel" (that is, the church), carries on the spirit of ancient, original "Biblical Israel," not the so-called "Talmudic Jews."[36] In the same chapter (2 Cor. 3:6) Paul introduces himself as minister of "the new testament, not of the letter, but of the spirit, for the letter kills, but the spirit gives life." It means in Christianity that "the Old Testament has been considered to be the document of a false religion, a religion of laws and the letter, whereas the New Testament represents the true religion — a religion of the gospel and the spirit."[37] This attitude, the negation of Judaism and the Jewish people, has motivated the well-known, terrible persecution of and discrimination against Jews by Christians over generations, and it leaves no room for cooperation between Jewish and Christian biblical scholars and theologians.[38]

From a scholarly viewpoint New Testament supersessionist theology is unacceptable as well, first and foremost because it lacks any scientific objectivity. The methods of such theologians have an a priori, one-sided confessional bias. Moreover, the New Testament is not a continuation of the Hebrew Bible. There is no real organic connection between the two corpora, either literally and historically or linguistically (Hebrew and Aramaic versus Greek)[39] and philosophically (Oriental-Semitic thought versus Greco-Roman). They are somehow connected theologically to each other presumably sometime in the early stage of Christianity, when Jewish-Christians accepted their new religious direction but simultaneously associated with their original religious heritage. Appar-

---

35. On this see Knierim, *Task of Old Testament Theology*, 537.

36. The concept that Christianity is a continuation of "Biblical Israel" is deeply rooted in Christian theology. See, for example, Matt. 8:11–12; Luke 13:24–30; Acts 15:14–17; 28:28; cf. R. R. Ruether, *Faith and Fratricide: The Theological Roots of Anti-Semitism* (New York: Seabury, 1974) 84–86; R. Rendtorff, "Das 'Ende' der Geschichte Israels," in *Gesammelte Studien zum Alten Testament* (TB 57; Munich: Kaiser, 1975) 267–76. It should be mentioned that in the last decades there are also different voices heard among Christians. For example, in 1980 the Synod of the Evangelical Church of the Rhineland (Germany) declared, "We believe the permanent election of the Jewish people as the people of God and realize that through Jesus Christ the church is taken into the covenant of God with his people" (see *The Theology of the Churches and the Jewish People: Statements by the World Council of Churches and Its Member Churches* [with commentary by A. Brockway, P. von Buren, R. Rendtorff, and S. Schoon; Geneva: World Council of Churches, 1988] 93, §4). Some German theologians protested against this declaration, and Gunneweg (*Biblische Theologie*, 73) defined it as "eklatante Häresie" (clear heresy). Cf. Rendtorff, "Recent German Old Testament Theologies," 335, and his sharp criticism of Gunneweg's statement there.

37. Knierim, *Task of Old Testament Theology*, 298.

38. On this issue see Kalimi, "History of Israelite Religion," 106–7.

39. It is possible, however, that Matthew's Gospel was originally written in Aramaic (see W. F. Albright and C. S. Mann, *Matthew* [AB 26; Garden City, N.Y.: Doubleday, 1971] vii). For the presumed Semitic background of several passages in the New Testament see J. A. Fitzmyer, *Essays on the Semitic Background of the New Testament* (London: Geoffrey Chapman, 1971).

ently, they would have liked also to base their new religious ideas on the well-known and widely accepted ancient Hebrew traditions of the Prophets and Psalms, for example.[40]

Nonetheless, only the New Testament reflects the unique Christian religion. As of today, the relationship between the two "Testaments" — the "New" (*novum*) and the "Old" (*vetus*) — is an unsolved question even in Christianity itself. An essay such as "Zur Frage der Notwendigkeit des Alten Testaments" (in the Christian canon, of course),[41] or "Warum gehört die Hebräische Bibel in den christlichen Kanon?" published in *Berliner Theologische Zeitschrift* just a few years ago,[42] verifies this claim. Furthermore, in his 1993 monograph Gunneweg defined the historical and theological relationship between the two "Testaments" as the most difficult problem of Christian theology: "Er sieht sich mit dem wohl schwierigsten Problem der christlichen Theologie konfrontiert, nämlich mit der Frage nach der historisch und theologisch angemessenen Verhältnisbestimmung von Altem und Neuem Testament."[43] One can only agree with Preuss's conclusion in the last section of the second volume of his *Old Testament Theology*. In that section Preuss discusses the "openness of the Old Testament," stressing that such openness "does not necessarily imply or even mean an openness to the New Testament. Only a Christian theologian is able to speak of the Old Testament's openness to the New Testament. Such a theologian comes to the Old Testament by way of the New Testament using it as the basis to approach the Old Testament critically and questioningly."[44]

---

40. Since Jesus and at least some of his adherents (e.g., the apostles) were Jews — raised and educated in Judaism — it is very hard, if not impossible, to understand the New Testament without knowledge of and background from the Hebrew Bible/Old Testament and early Judaism.

41. H. G. Geyer, "Zur Frage der Notwendigkeit des Alten Testaments," *EvT* 25 (1965) 207–37.

42. M. Heymel, "Warum gehört die Hebräische Bibel in den christlichen Kanon?" *BTZ* 7 (1990) 2–20. For further discussion on this issue see H. von Campenhausen, "Das Alte Testament als Bibel der Kirche," in *Aus der Frühzeit des Christentums* (Tübingen: Mohr [Siebeck], 1963) 154ff.; J. Schreiner, "Das Verhältnis des Alten Testaments zum Neuen Testament," in *Segen für die Völker: Gesammelte Schriften zur Entstehung und Theologie des Alten Testaments* (Würzburg: Echter, 1987) 392–407; W. H. Schmidt, "Das Problem des Alten Testaments in der christlichen Theologie," in *Festschrift H. Donner* (Wiesbaden: Harrassowitz, 1995) 243–51; F. Watson, "The Old Testament as Christian Scripture," *SJT* 52 (1999) 227–32.

43. Gunneweg, *Biblische Theologie,* 52; see also idem, *Vom Verstehen des Alten Testaments,* 37–41, where Gunneweg writes (41), "[D]as hermeneutische Problem des Verhältnisses der beiden Kanonteile und der christlichen Geltung des Alten Testaments bleibt eine jetzt erst recht unerledigte."

44. Preuss, *Old Testament Theology,* 2:306. In the original German version: " 'Offenheit des AT' meint damit nicht sofort oder gar nur dessen Offenheit hin zum NT. Von letzterer kann nur ein christlicher Theologe sprechen, der bereits vom NT herkommt und von ihm

Contrary to all those Christian theologians who relate the Old Testament to the New Testament, Knierim focuses on the Old Testament "in its own right."[45] He wants "to give back to the Old Testament the right of its own voice."[46] He clarifies for Christians that an interpretation of their Old Testament "must be mindful of that dissensus [i.e., distinction] and, therefore, rest on the Old Testament itself and not on their New Testament or on an a priori combination of both."[47] He stresses that "Old Testament theology must systematize the theological traditions of the Old Testament."[48] Although according to Knierim "a united biblical theology should not be assumed to be ultimately elusive," he emphasizes that "a separate focus on the theology of each testament is required so that, before any biblical theology is proposed, each testament receives the right to its own case without interference from the other."[49] To be sure, Knierim makes clear the necessity of dealing with the Old Testament by Christians: "Because the Old Testament is part of our canon, one way or another we must come to grips with it."[50] But how do these statements by Knierim coordinate with what he says in other places? Two examples follow.

1. "With regard to the question of the validity of the theology of Exod. 3,7–8 ..., either this theology must be *replaced* by a theology of God's universal justice found elsewhere, partly in the Old Testament and partly in the New Testament, or its own paradigm must be *reconceptualized.* ... A reconceptualization is legitimate precisely because of the claim, found in both the Old and the New Testaments, that all humanity is elected into the blessing of God's universal justice and salvation. ... Inasmuch as Jesus Christ is proclaimed to be the ultimate revelation of the reign of God, *he, too, will have to be understood as representing this criterion.*"[51] In this case, obviously, Knierim is not that far, for instance, from the previously cited statements of Childs.

2. "It seems that the Old and the New Testaments complement each other in that each helps rectify the deficiency of the other and in that

---

her an das AT forschend und fragend herantritt" (idem, *Israels Weg mit JHWH* [vol. 2 of *Theologie des Alten Testaments*; Stuttgart: Kohlhammer, 1992] 326).

45. See Knierim, *Task of Old Testament Theology,* 1 n. 1, 9 n. 6.

46. Knierim, *Task of Old Testament Theology,* 299. Knierim (310) also says, "I prefer to give the Old Testament its own say. ... I prefer this route to the other in which the New Testament speaks for the Old Testament, thereby depriving it of its own voice and authenticity."

47. Knierim, *Task of Old Testament Theology,* 1 n. 1.

48. Knierim, *Task of Old Testament Theology,* 9 n. 6.

49. Knierim, *Task of Old Testament Theology,* 73.

50. Knierim, *Task of Old Testament Theology,* 309.

51. Knierim, *Task of Old Testament Theology,* 135 (italics added in the last sentence).

each is partly in need of reconceptualization in light of the legitimate emphasis of the other."[52]

Like many other Christian theologians and biblical scholars, Knierim employs the common Christian term "Old Testament." In Christian theology this term originally had negative and anti-Jewish connotations. Knierim is aware of this, and therefore emphasizes that "the Christian designation of the Jewish Bible as their Old Testament must not be interpreted negatively." According to him it "can only mean antecedence to the New Testament historically, even as this antecedence is not the basis for determining the relationship of the two testaments."[53] But "Old" and "New" mean, to use the words of Gunneweg, "eine theologisch nicht auflösbare Zuordnung an: das Alte ist alt nur im Verhältnis zum Neuen, das Neue neu nur in seinem Bezug zum Alten."[54] I have no doubt that Knierim does not intend any negative connotation in using this term. But I wonder why he did not use simply a term like "First Testament" (*Erstes Testament*), if not "Hebrew Bible/Scripture," Tanak, or *Mikra,* in order to avoid the problematic term. Moreover, the designation of the Jewish Bible by the term "Old Testament" is inaccurate. These two terms are incompatible. After all, the order and the classification of the historical, prophetical, and so-called hagiographical books, the number of the books included in the Old Testament, and the content of some other books are quite different from those in the Jewish Bible.[55] The sequence of the books in the Jewish Bible and in the Old Testament, for instance, has considerable theological implications, as I have illustrated in another study.[56]

The biblical concept regarding the election of Israel as the people of God from among all nations is well known, especially from Deuteronomistic literature and Deutero-Isaiah.[57] Knierim knows and acknowl-

---

52. Knierim, *Task of Old Testament Theology,* 137. See also below in this essay p. 246.

53. Knierim, *Task of Old Testament Theology,* 2 n. 1.

54. Gunneweg, *Vom Verstehen des Alten Testaments,* 36.

55. For the different order and content of the Christian Old Testament in comparison with the Hebrew Bible/Tanak see E. Zenger et al., *Einleitung in das Alte Testament* (Kohlhammer Studienbücher Theologie 1/1; Stuttgart: Kohlhammer, 1996) 30.

56. See I. Kalimi, "History of Interpretation: The Book of Chronicles in Jewish Tradition — From Daniel to Spinoza," *RB* 105 (1998) 5–41, esp. 24–25.

57. See, for example, Deut. 4:19–20; 7:6–8 par. 14:2; 10:14–15; 26:17–19; 32:8–9 (in verse 8 read בני אל, with LXX and 4QDeut[q] [in 4QDeut[j]: בני אלהים], instead of MT בני ישראל; cf. Deut. 4:19–20); 1 Kings 3:8a; Isa. 41:8–9; 44:1–2, 8–10; see also Exod. 19:5–6; Ezek. 20:5; Ps. 33:12; 105:43; 135:4. The concept is unique to the Israelites and unknown among other ancient Near Eastern religions. For scholarly literature on the issue see Preuss, *Israels Weg mit JHWH,* 305 n. 1, as well as his own discussion on pp. 305–27; F. W. Golka, "Universalism and the Election of the Jews," *Theology* 90 (1987) 273–80 (for the German version of the article, see idem, "Die Geschöpflichkeit des Menschen und die Erwählung Israels," in *Jona* [Calwer Bibelkommentar; Stuttgart: Calwer, 1991] 25–33).

edges this concept: *"Israel's election is valid."* "But," he continues, "the entire Old Testament overwhelmingly testifies to the fact that the elect community was at no time in its history without sin and guilt. *It never was what it was called to be."* Knierim then affirms equitably, "Nor has Christianity ever been what it was called to be. In light of the central claim of Christianity, this is an even *more serious deficiency."*[58]

It is an entirely different attitude than that of traditional church fathers and many Christian theologians over generations. They used Israel's prophets' rebukes and confrontations with guilt and sin (often greatly exaggerated) against Israel, and considered Jews a stubborn people and children of those who killed God's messengers and prophets (e.g., Matt. 5:12; 23:30–37; Luke 11:47–51; 13:34; 16:31). To cite Acts 7:50, "You stiff-necked and uncircumcised in heart and ears, you do always resist the Holy Spirit. As your fathers did, so do you."

As a biblical researcher and exegete, Knierim points out that "the prophetic texts contain the record of Israel's failure to live up to and maintain the conditions of its election history. Israel failed specifically with regard to internal societal justice and exclusive loyalty to its savior God, Yahweh, and the purity of Yahweh's cult."[59] Therefore he sees, correctly, a serious "tension between Israel's election and failure." Is there anything wrong with confronting this problematic theme as it appears in the Hebrew corpus? Should we not at least admit it as it is without any bias and apologetic? If one ignores or attempts to cover it, will it disappear from the Bible? Nonetheless, Knierim views this as a paradigm for humanity: "Israel would thus be the symbol not for a new but for the old, imperfect humanity through the toleration of the tension at the crossroads of election and failure."[60]

Knierim emphasizes that in the Torah and the Deuteronomistic history, Israel's election "is both the purpose and aim of creation and the condition wherein the nations can be blessed or cursed. The status of the nations depends on whether they bless or curse Israel" (Gen. 12:1–3; cf. 27:29b; Num. 24:9b).[61] Accordingly, says Knierim, "it is nowhere said, except for the attempt in Numbers 22–24, that the Canaanites cursed Israel. Hence, in the light of their experience vis-à-vis the conquest, why are they cursed when they do no more than fail to bless Israel and become Yahweh worshippers?"[62] But biblical statements such as "Not because of your [Israelites'] righteousness ... are you going in to possess their [Canaanites'] land; but *because of the wickedness of these nations*

---

58. Knierim, *Task of Old Testament Theology*, 440 (italics added).
59. Knierim, *Task of Old Testament Theology*, 450.
60. Knierim, *Task of Old Testament Theology*, 450.
61. Knierim, *Task of Old Testament Theology*, 451.
62. Knierim, *Task of Old Testament Theology*, 451; cf. 134–35, 317.

the Lord your God is driving them out from before you" (Deut. 9:5; cf. 9:4; 18:12; Lev. 18:24–28, 30; 20:23–24), clarify that the occupation of the Canaanites' land was not because "they do no more than fail to bless Israel and become Yahweh worshippers," but because of their own long-term, accumulative heavy transgression and guilt.[63] Knierim does not mention these verses here, but he discusses them in another place and defines them as "traditio-historically, and especially substantively, a secondary, derivative rationalization."[64] He states, "In the book of Genesis (from Gen 12:1, 7 on), the sins of the Canaanites play no role as a reason for that promise [i.e., Yahweh's promise to give the land to the patriarchs]."[65] But what about Gen. 15:16, "And they [the Israelites] shall come back here [to Canaan] in the fourth generation; for *the iniquity of the Amorites* [i.e., Canaanites][66] *is not yet complete.*" Knierim's statement "If they did, it would not make [any] sense anyway" is unconvincing. Moreover, it seems that in this case, at least, there is no controversy between the election theology and the biblical "claim to Yahweh's universal justice." According to the theology of Gen. 15:16 and Deut. 9:5, etc., the conquest of Canaan absolutely does not negate the affirmation "that Israel's God, Yahweh, does not violate justice."[67] This theology does not confirm the rest of Knierim's conclusion: "[B]y subjecting the theology of creation to the theology of exclusionary election, it discredits the claim that Yahweh is truly and justifiably the universal deity."[68] From the biblical-theological viewpoint the Canaanites were conquered and dispossessed because of their wickedness, just as in the earlier time the whole generation of the flood (except for the Noachic remnant) was destroyed because of its corruption and wickedness (Gen. 6:1–8:19). This viewpoint is reflected later on by the punishment of the Israelites themselves. The kingdoms of Israel

---

63. It is also worth noting that the attempt in Numbers 22–24 to curse the Israelites was made by the Moabites and Midianites with the help of Balaam the son of Beor the Aramean (Num. 22:5; Deut. 23:4–5). The Moabites, Midianites, and Arameans are not included among the six/seven/ten nations that inhabited the promised land/Canaan (Gen. 15:19–21; Exod. 3:8; 23:23; 34:11; Deut. 7:1; Josh. 3:10). Indeed, according to Deut. 2:9 the Lord ordered, "Do not harass Moab or contend with them in battle, for I will not give you any of their land for a possession, because I have given Ar to the sons of Lot for a possession." Moreover, Numbers 22–24 together with Deut. 2:9 are opposed to the idea of Gen. 12:3: the Moabites who cursed Israel not only were not cursed by God, but received His protection.

64. Knierim, *Task of Old Testament Theology*, 96–100, esp. 98.

65. Knierim, *Task of Old Testament Theology*, 98.

66. The name Amorites in the Hebrew Bible is occasionally parallel to the name Canaanites, and thus "the land of Amori" to "the land of Canaan." See, for example, Josh. 10:6, 12; 24:8; Amos 2:9–10.

67. Knierim, *Task of Old Testament Theology*, 452; see also 318.

68. Knierim, *Task of Old Testament Theology*, 452.

and Judah were conquered and destroyed, their inhabitants exiled, and the land inherited by others because of their social sins and disloyalty to God (2 Kings 17:4–23; 24:18–25:21; 2 Chron. 36:11–20).

If, however, one observes the biblical material otherwise, that is, not from the theological viewpoint of Knierim but from that of history, as done, for instance, by Friedemann W. Golka,[69] one comes to a different conclusion. Golka surveys the theology of the election of Israel versus the theology of the creation of the world and humanity in the Hebrew Bible. On the basis of the Israelites' connections with the other nations in the ancient Near East during the biblical period, he concludes that at least "in post-exilic literature the priority of creation [i.e., all humans are God's creatures and hence participate in his blessing] over the election of Israel has been fully recognized."[70]

Knierim points out that the Hebrew Bible is not, throughout, "particularly concerned with Israel's election." The question of "where this concern reflects a particularistic paradigm for the exclusivity of Israel's election at the expense of the election equally of all, and where it reflects a universalistic paradigm of Israel's election as a sign of the equal election of all"[71] is still unanswered. But the clarification of this question affects the Hebrew Bible's claim of the universality of the God of the whole world (monotheism) as a God of universal justice and righteousness.

Knierim uses within one small paragraph the words "the election equally of all" and the words "the equal election of all." Is he of the opinion that each religious group (including Christians, naturally) has its own equal process of election? Is he trying to say that the Christian community, as well as Israel, is elected by God? In another section of the book Knierim expresses what is probably the New Testament's perspective: "Inasmuch as Israel's election is recognized and not replaced by the equally problematic Christian community, it is recognized as a servant in God's plan of universal salvation, *together with and alongside the Christian community.*"[72] Does he here hint at this "equal election"? In any event, at least from a scholarly viewpoint, this "equal election" is not confirmed in the Jewish Scriptures.

Being a Protestant theologian (who was also trained as a pastor in the Evangelisch-theologische Fakultät of Ruprecht-Karls Universität Heidelberg for many years) generally does not affect Knierim's academic objectivity (as much as that is possible). But let us not forget that

---

69. See Golka, "Universalism and the Election of the Jews," 273–80.
70. Golka, "Universalism and the Election of the Jews," 280.
71. Knierim, *Task of Old Testament Theology,* 549.
72. Knierim, *Task of Old Testament Theology,* 135 (italics added).

after all every person is connected, consciously or unconsciously, to his or her own original religious roots, and it is not easy to be released from them completely. Furthermore, contrary to the history of Israelite religion(s), the nature of theology of the Hebrew Bible/Old Testament is generally ahistorical, and occasionally subjective or even confessional.[73] Thus, it is not entirely surprising that Knierim's book, which includes in its title the words "Old Testament Theology," reflects from time to time the individual religious views of its author and/or "the Christian voice."[74] In fact, Knierim declares, "I prefer to give the Old Testament its own say in the hope that it may tell something which is in the spirit of Christ."[75] Later on the same page he inquires, "Where in these events is Jesus Christ whom we confess to be Lord?" On another occasion he discusses Paul's statement in 2 Cor. 3:6[76] and confesses frankly, "I do not want to belittle the importance of this Christology, even as it affects the understanding of the Old Testament."[77]

But should Hebrew Bible theology, as a branch of university study, necessarily be related to the New Testament? Must it always be confessional? As I have stated elsewhere, the learning of Hebrew Bible theology at university level can and must proceed objectively — as much as that is achievable — from academic, intellectual viewpoints. Then the synagogue and the church can apply the results of such research as they see fit.[78]

Unfortunately, Knierim sometimes is imprecise in his accounts of specific biblical or historical data. Three examples follow.

1. In the chapter "Israel and the Nations in the Land of Palestine in the Old Testament" he writes, "What was important for the Jews was their return to their land after more than twenty-five hundred years of exile, and their claim of independence in that land after twenty-five hundred years of dependence on foreign empires."[79] Knierim refers here to the epoch from the destruction of Jerusalem and the Babylonian exile

---

73. See Kalimi, "History of Israelite Religion," 100–102.

74. Knierim, *Task of Old Testament Theology*, 309.

75. Knierim, *Task of Old Testament Theology*, 310; other examples are on 135, 137, 309, 311, 317, 321, 549.

76. See the discussion on this verse, above, p. 239.

77. Knierim, *Task of Old Testament Theology*, 298.

78. Kalimi, "History of Israelite Religion," 106.

79. Knierim, *Task of Old Testament Theology*, 310. Knierim (314) also says, "In 722 BCE and in 586 BCE, respectively, that control [of the land] was lost; it remained so until 1948 and 1967. For 2,500 years, the land was a province under foreign powers (the Babylonians, the Persians, the Greeks, the Romans, Constantinople [Byzantine Empire], the Arabs [what about the 'Kingdom of Jerusalem,' which was established by Crusades?], the Turks, and the British Mandate)."

in 586 B.C.E. to the establishment of the state of Israel in 1948 C.E. But he overlooks some important historical events:

The first event, almost fifty years after the Babylonian exile, when at least a portion of the Jews returned to Zion (Cyrus's decree of 538 B.C.E.; Ezra 1–2; Nehemiah 7; 2 Chron. 36:21–23), was the rebuilding of the temple, resettlement of Judah, and achievement of a religio-cultural autonomy that existed for a long time.

The second event, from the time of the high priest Simon the Hasmonaean (ca. 142 B.C.E.; 1 Macc. 13:41–42) until the invasion of Judea by the Roman commander Pompey (63 B.C.E.) almost eighty years later, was the Jews controlling their own destiny in an independent kingdom in the Land of Israel.

The third event, after the capture of Jerusalem by Pompey, was the Jewish people losing their political and military independence, even though their entity in Judea existed — in one form or another — until the destruction of Jerusalem and its temple by Titus (70 C.E.).

2. Later on Knierim states, "That was the time from 1200 to 900 B.C.E., . . . the time from Joshua through David and Solomon. It was the time of conquest, settlement, and integration of the land."[80] But the particular time span of this period as designed by Knierim is inexact. On the one hand, Israel is mentioned in the stela from the fifth year of Pharaoh Merneptah (ca. 1220 B.C.E.) as a people defeated by him in his campaign to Canaan.[81] That is, Israel as an entity already existed in the land of Canaan at the beginning of the last quarter of the thirteenth century. Obviously, this evidence cannot be ignored by anyone who speaks about the time of conquest. On the other hand, King Solomon died probably circa 928 B.C.E. Thus, the era that Knierim refers to is actually 1225 to 928 B.C.E., not 1200 to 900.

3. At the end of the same chapter Knierim writes, "Lot (Edom!) is offered the choice of land by Abraham (Genesis 13 [1–2, I.K.])."[82] But Lot is considered in the Bible as eponymous of the Ammonites and Moabites (Gen. 19:37–38), not the Edomites, who were related to Esau (Gen. 25:30; 36:1).

Finally, the task of Hebrew Bible/Old Testament theology is to demonstrate the full viewpoint of the Scriptures — not only the "nice sides" of God, the light and the friendly sides, but also God's "dark sides," such as vengefulness, excommunication, wrath, perverseness, which are associated with God in the Bible. One would expect some of Knierim's cases to deal particularly with these issues as well.[83]

---

80. Knierim, *Task of Old Testament Theology,* 314.
81. See *ANET,* 376–78, esp. 378.
82. Knierim, *Task of Old Testament Theology,* 320.
83. On these issues see, for example, J. Ebach, "Der Gott des Alten Testaments — ein

LANGUAGE, STYLE, AND BIBLIOGRAPHY

It would have been better if Knierim had unified the diverse styles
(i.e., oral and written presentations) of the book's essays (most of them
originally prepared for and presented to a varied audience) into one
scientific style.

One of the responders to Knierim's essay "The Task of Old Testament Theology," Walter Harrelson, refers to the "clarity" of that essay,
"to have been written magnificently."[84] Eugene H. Merrill stated in
his review in *Bibliotheca Sacra* that "the volume is good reading."[85]
These statements could be construed as cheap flattery or bitter irony,
although it is unlikely that these scholars meant either. But either of
their remarks could be interpreted as a lack of respect for a first-
rate scholar. Unfortunately, there are numerous unclear sentences and
inaccessible paragraphs in this collection (even if the reader is a leading biblical scholar whose mother tongue is English).[86] Thus, *The Task
of Old Testament Theology* becomes a real task for any reader, biblical
scholar and theologian as well as intellectual layperson. More than
once I have wished that Knierim's arguments would be stated in German, his mother tongue. Moreover, the style of the book generally is
repetitive. Many paragraphs are duplicated — the same idea in other
words without adding anything new. Certainly the style could be im-
proved, and the text could be shortened and made clearer and more
fluent without hurting the content. It would be beneficial if the book
were reread and edited by someone whose mother tongue is English,
and if some linguistic and stylistic emendations were made to clarify
Knierim's views.

In the bibliographical items Knierim brings full reference once in the
footnotes and once again, quite differently, in the comprehensive bibliography that concludes the book.[87] For example, on page 381 note 3
the author lists "Dennis Olson, *The Death of Old and the Birth of the New:
The Framework of the Book of Numbers and the Pentateuch*, Brown Judaical
Studies 71 (Chico, CA: Scholars Press, 1985)." On page 563 the same
item appears as "Olson, D. *The Death of Old and the Birth of the New: The*

Gott der Rache?" *Biblische Erinnerungen: Theologische Reden zur Zeit* (Bochum 1993) 81–
93; N. Lohfink, "Der gewalttätige Gott des Alten Testaments und die Suche nach einer
gewaltfreien Gesellschaft," *Jahrbuch für Biblische Theologie* 2 (1987) 106–36; W. Dietrich
and C. Link, *Die dunklen Seiten Gottes: Willkür und Gewalt* (2nd ed.; Neukirchen-Vluyn:
Neukirchener, 1997).

84. W. Harrelson, "The Limited Task of Old Testament Theology," in Knierim, *Task of
Old Testament Theology*, 21.

85. E. H. Merrill, review of Rolf P. Knierim, *The Task of Old Testament Theology:
Substance, Method, and Cases*, BSac (October–December 1996) 494.

86. See Coggins, "Old Testament Theology — How?" 309.

87. See Knierim, *Task of Old Testament Theology*, 557–67.

Framework of the Book of Numbers and the Pentateuch. Brown Judaical Studies 71. Chico, Calif.: Scholars Press, 1985."[88] In other words, there is a lack of consistent style in citing sources. Moreover, it would have been better if short-form citations had been used in the footnotes for items that Knierim refers to repeatedly, and these items detailed only at the end of the book.

As is true of virtually every book, Knierim's book is not entirely free of typographical errors (for instance, on page 2 note 1: "absolished" instead of "abolished"). Here, I list some misspelled Hebrew words. On page 329: מלינ instead of מלין; on page 601: אדסה instead of אדמה; אני אוה instead of אני הוא; דער instead of דעת; הטא instead of חטא; טבה instead of טובה.

CONCLUSION

It is customary not to agree with an author on every explicit detail or distinct part of a book. In spite of some of my critical viewpoints, however, I can conclude that *The Task of Old Testament Theology: Substance, Method, and Cases* as a whole is an original study, distinguished by its depth and breadth. It makes an essential contribution to biblical scholarship in general and to biblical theology in particular. Knierim handles the problematic issue of the plurality of Hebrew Bible theologies from comprehensive methodological viewpoints. He presents several particularly interesting cases as well, showing respect for the "mother religion."

During the preparation of this essay the words of Rabbi Oshaia from the Babylonian Talmud (*Pesachim* 87b) several times came to mind:

אמר רבי אושעיא מאי דכתיב "צדקת פרזונו בישראל"
צדקה עשה הקדוש ברוך הוא בישראל שפזרן לבין האומות

Rabbi Oshaia said: What is meant by the verse, "even the righteousness of His Ruler in Israel" [Judges 5:11]? The Holy One, blessed be He, showed righteousness/mercy unto Israel by scattering them among the nations.[89]

I seriously question this theodicy of rabbis that attempts to justify the tragic historical circumstances of the Jewish existence among the nations as the righteousness/mercy of the Almighty unto them — circumstances that caused them to pay such a high price for keeping their identity and their unique religio-cultural heritage. Nevertheless, I allow

---

88. Compare also, for example, the reference to G. W. Coats on p. 355 n. 4 with that on p. 559; the references to B. S. Childs and R. Rendtorff on p. 380 nn. 1 and 2 with their forms on pp. 558, 564; the reference to J. Durham on p. 396 n. 8 with that on p. 559.

89. For the English translation compare H. Freedman, *Pesahim* (vol. 5 of *The Hebrew-English Edition of the Babylonian Talmud;* 30 vols.; ed. I. Epstein; London: Soncino, 1967).

myself to paraphrase this rabbinical statement by saying, "Blessed be Professor Rolf P. Knierim, who showed his righteousness/mercy unto biblical scholars and theologians by collecting these scattered essays from among multilingual nations as well and from many periodicals and *Festschriften* to form one comprehensive, impressive, and valuable volume!"

BIBLIOGRAPHY

Caird, G. B., and L. D. Hurst. *New Testament Theology.* Oxford: Oxford University Press, 1994.

Childs, Brevard S. *Biblical Theology in Crisis.* Philadelphia: Westminster, 1970.

———. *Biblical Theology of the Old and New Testaments: Theological Reflection on the Christian Bible.* Minneapolis: Fortress, 1993.

Dietrich, W., and C. Link. *Die dunklen Seiten Gottes — Willkür und Gewalt,* 2. erweiterter Auflage. Neukirchen-Vluyn: Neukirchener Verlag, 1997.

Ebach, J. "Der Gott des Alten Testaments — ein Gott der Rache?" *Biblische Erinnerungen — Theologische Reden zur Zeit.* Bochum: 1993.

Geyer, H. G. "Zur Frage der Notwendigkeit des Alten Testaments." *Evangelische Theologie* 25 (1965): 207–37.

Golka, Friedemann W. "Universalism and the Election of the Jews." *Theology* 90 (1987).

Gunneweg, Antonius H. J. *Biblische Theologie des Alten Testaments: Eine Religionsgeschichte Israels in biblisch-theologischer Sicht.* Stuttgart: W. Kohlhammer, 1993.

———. *Vom Verstehen des Alten Testaments: Eine Hermeneutik.* Grundrisse zum Alten Testament — Das Alte Testament Deutsch Ergänzungsreihe 5. Göttingen: Vandenhoeck & Ruprecht, 1977.

Hasel, Gerhard. *Old Testament Theology: Basic Issues in the Current Debate.* Grand Rapids: Eerdmans, 1991.

Kalimi, Isaac. "History of Interpretation: The Book of Chronicles in Jewish Tradition — From Daniel to Spinoza." *RB* 105 (1998).

———. "History of Israelite Religion or Old Testament Theology? Jewish Interest in Biblical Theology." In *SJOT* 11 (1997).

Knierim, Rolf P. *The Task of Old Testament Theology: Substance, Method, and Cases.* Grand Rapids: Eerdmans, 1995.

Kraus, H.-J. *Die Biblische Theologie: Ihre Geschichte und Problematik.* Neukirchen-Vluyn: Neukirchener Verlag, 1977.

Lohfink, N. "Der gewalttätige Gott des Alten Testaments und die Suche nach einer gewaltfreien Gesellschaft." *Jahrbuch für Biblische Theologie* 2 (1987).

Preuss, Horst Dietrich. *Old Testament Theology.* Vol. I. Edinburgh: T. & T. Clark, 1995.

Rendtorff, R. "Das 'Ende' der Geschichte Israels." In *Gesammelte Studien zum Alten Testament.* Theologische Bücherei 57. Munich: Chr. Kaiser, 1975.

———. "Recent German Old Testament Theologies." *JR* 76 (1996).

Ruether, R. R. *Faith and Fratricide: The Theological Roots of Anti-Semitism.* New York: Seabury, 1974.

Reventlow, Henning G. *Problems of Old Testament Theology in the Twentieth Century*. Philadelphia: Fortress, 1985.

Sæbø, M. "Johann Philipp Gabler at the End of Eighteenth Century: History and Theology." In *On the Way to Canon: Creative Tradition History in the Old Testament*. JSOTSup 191. Sheffield: Sheffield Academic Press, 1998.

15

Wrestling with Israel's Election:
A Jewish Reaction to
Rolf Knierim's Biblical Theology
Joel S. Kaminsky

Professor Knierim's *The Task of Old Testament Theology: Substance, Method, and Cases* contains a wealth of valuable scholarship on a wide variety of issues connected to the study of the Hebrew Bible and its theological interpretation. Whatever criticisms I make over the course of the next few pages should not eclipse the fact that Professor Knierim has written an important book that is a major contribution to, and will have a lasting impact upon, the field of biblical studies. Furthermore, I know only too well that it is much easier to criticize a constructive theology than it is to produce a coherent alternative.

Because each person inevitably brings certain assumptions to his or her own reading of any text (perhaps more so to one's reading of a religious text or a scholarly reflection upon a religious text), I make known that I, for better or worse, cannot avoid reading both the Bible and Knierim's erudite reflections on biblical theology with the eyes of a Jewish biblical scholar. One result of my respect for Jewish tradition is that whenever I quote Knierim's work, I devocalize the Tetragrammaton. Another is that this response focuses on the parts of Knierim's book that touch upon issues of Jewish-Christian dialogue. Thus, most of this discussion centers on Knierim's program for doing biblical theology rather than on the other parts of this book in which Knierim, often brilliantly, works out his vision of biblical theology in relation to various biblical concepts and through close readings of certain texts.

Christian biblical scholarship is becoming ever more sensitive to questions of anti-Semitism and the supersessionist presuppositions that frequently animate such views. Although Knierim clearly is aware of the past transgressions committed by many Christian biblical scholars, one still sees certain problems in his approach. The primary one is that Knierim wishes to devalue all particularistic and/or nationalistic ideas unless they contain some element that can be universalized. The chief victim of such a theological approach is the notion of Israel as the specially elect people of God. I am aware that Knierim would deny that he has rejected the idea of Israel's election, but rather, would contend that he has extended this elect status to all peoples and nations. Such a theological move, however, is tantamount to denying the concept as it has been put forward within the Hebrew Bible, as well as how this notion has been understood by Jewish and even by important streams of Christian tradition. If election means anything, it must mean that some are elected and others are not. This does not mean that these others are left out of God's providential plans, but rather, as I will argue further below, that God's plans for other nations are worked out through his special relationship with the elect people of God. That Knierim has indeed rejected the notion of Israel's special election is confirmed by statements like this one: "It is true that a major reason for the Old Testament's *theological deficit* lies in its understanding of the inseparable connection between Israel the people of God and the historical nation and society of Israel."[1] It should be said that Knierim jettisons the concept of election for the noblest of reasons. It is his contention that the centerpiece of any theology of the Hebrew Bible is *"the universal dominion of YHWH in justice and righteousness."*[2] Furthermore, Knierim must be complimented for not simply replacing Jewish exclusivist claims with Christian supersessionist claims that are equally exclusivist. As he makes clear, he wishes to eliminate all such exclusivist claims. "A reconceptualization is legitimate precisely because of the claim, found in both the Old and the New Testaments, that all humanity is elected into the blessing of God's universal justice and salvation."[3]

Although Knierim's reconceptualization sounds quite enticing, before one assents to it, I wish to test its major assumptions as well as explore what is lost by such a theological maneuver. The obvious place to begin such an inquiry is to examine whether universal justice is the centerpiece of the theology of the Hebrew Bible. I have nothing against the notion that God should deal justly with everyone and always use the same standard when judging individuals or nations. My concern is twofold: Does the Hebrew Bible endorse this view, and if it does, is this notion so central to biblical theology that it can trump particularistic ideas, such as God's election of the Jewish people? After having written a book on cases of divine retribution that are quite troubling from a modern individualist perspective, I reached the conclusion that the authors of the Hebrew Bible certainly noticed that sometimes God's justice appeared to differ from human justice. Biblical writers reacted to

---

1. Rolf P. Knierim, *The Task of Old Testament Theology: Substance, Method, and Cases* (Grand Rapids: Eerdmans, 1995) 107 (italics added).

2. Knierim, *Task of Old Testament Theology*, 15 (italics original).

3. Knierim, *Task of Old Testament Theology*, 135.

this fact in different ways. Some simply acknowledged that there were two scales of justice and that we were in no position to judge God as unjust. "For my thoughts are not your thoughts, nor are your ways my ways, says the Lord. For as the heavens are higher than the earth, so are my ways higher than your ways and my thoughts than your thoughts" (Isa. 55:8–9). Other biblical writers, like the author of Ezekiel 18, argued that in spite of appearances to the contrary, God is just in the way that humans are. But it is not clear that this latter set of theological ideas ever fully displaced all other views that are less sure that humans and God share the same scale of justice.[4]

The Hebrew Bible contains many narratives in which God acts in ways that are morally troubling. Often God is seen as delivering arbitrary or extreme punishments (Genesis 3; 2 Samuel 24; Ezek. 20:25–26). As Jon Levenson notes, "In texts like these, divine sovereignty takes precedence over divine goodness. God's goodness is subordinate to his greatness and not identical with it. Man's task is to accept humbly the lordship of God without subjecting him to moral critique."[5] Although I do not wish to argue that these troubling instances of divine retribution are central to any theology of the Hebrew Bible, their presence in the text should raise some question about Knierim's claim for the ubiquity of the concept of God's justice and righteousness. A more serious challenge to Knierim's theology is posed by another group of texts that contain some of the most important theological ideas concerning God's character. These texts speak of a God who is mysterious, often arbitrary and more than occasionally unjust. The texts that I have in mind include passages in which God forgives certain human beings, even when justice demands that they be punished more severely. One thinks of Cain in Genesis 4, or Israel after the golden calf episode (Exodus 32–34). I would contend that mercy quite often involves a suspension of justice and that in the Hebrew Bible there is a bias toward mercy over and against justice. One of the major claims of Christianity, as I understand it, is that this bias toward mercy is amplified in the New Testament. If this is true, one would be hard pressed to agree with Knierim that God's universal justice is, or even should be, the centerpiece of all biblical theology.[6] Of course, another idea that I would argue may be just as,

4. Joel S. Kaminsky, *Corporate Responsibility in the Hebrew Bible* (JSOTSup 196; Sheffield: Sheffield Academic Press, 1995) 139–89.

5. Jon D. Levenson, "Cataclysm, Survival and Regeneration in the Hebrew Bible," in Daniel Landes, ed., *Confronting Omnicide: Jewish Reflections on Weapons of Mass Destruction* (Northvale, N.J.: Aronson, 1991) 52.

6. For an expanded treatment of this issue see Joel S. Kaminsky, "The Sins of the Fathers: A Theological Investigation of the Biblical Tension between Corporate and Individualized Retribution," *Judaism* 46 (summer 1997) 319–32.

if not more, important to the theology of the Hebrew Bible than the idea of God's universal justice, is the idea of his mysterious election of Israel.

As I noted, Knierim claims that one must abandon the notion of election because it is ultimately at odds with God's universal justice. A careful reading of Knierim's book suggests that what led him to the notion "that a nationalist covenant justice is incompatible with equal justice universally"[7] was primarily the destruction of the Canaanites by the Israelites. Knierim rightly notes that in the Hebrew Bible Israel's war against the Canaanites is made out to be as just as Israel's liberation from Egypt. He sees this as engendering a problem of two mutually exclusive views of justice that are ultimately resolved only "by reference to the concept of Israel's election as YHWH's people. On this basis, justice is what serves Israel's election by and covenant with YHWH, rather than and regardless of a principle of justice that is the same for all nations."[8] Although there are many troubling aspects of God's apparent command to annihilate the Canaanites, it is by no means clear that the way out of these murky waters is by surrendering what many Jews and Christians deem as one of the most treasured biblical concepts: God's free and sometimes mysterious choice to show grace to a particular person or a specific nation (Rom. 9:6–18).

Knierim's analysis of this complex issue is at times a bit confusing. He is outraged that Israel believed it had the divine right to annihilate the Canaanites, but he is aware that this may never have happened. This is not to say that if the anti-Canaanite polemic were only religio-political rhetoric it would be unproblematic. A rhetoric that endorses the total annihilation of a group of people is problematic, but it is a less serious problem than the actual annihilation of a group of people. In fact, there is evidence to suggest that much of the anti-Canaanite polemic, rather than precipitating the destruction of the Canaanites, may be a late reaction that grew out of the failure to destroy the Canaanites. According to a theory like Mendenhall's, only a few tyrannical Canaanites would have been killed, and they may have been done in by fellow Canaanites.[9]

Aside from the historical question of how many Canaanites were killed by the Israelites, Knierim dismisses all those texts that speak of the sinfulness of the Canaanites as irrelevant to the question of God's justice. He does so on the basis that "the reference to the sins of the Canaanites as the reason for their destruction is not a rationale for

---

7. Knierim, *Task of Old Testament Theology*, 121.

8. Knierim, *Task of Old Testament Theology*, 97.

9. For a summary of the basic theories surrounding the conquest traditions see J. Maxwell Miller, "The Israelite Occupation of Canaan," in John H. Hayes and J. Maxwell Miller, eds., *Israelite and Judean History* (Philadelphia: Westminster, 1977) 213–84.

justice independent of the theology of Israel's exclusive election. It depends on and serves that theology."[10] In Knierim's opinion, the sinful Canaanites must be destroyed because they will tempt the disobedient Israelites. This is one possible reading of the Bible's view of the Canaanites and why they must be totally uprooted, but another view is that they were uprooted because they had committed so many evil deeds (Gen. 15:16; Lev. 20:22–23). I grant that a later Deuteronomic editor blamed the fall of the northern and southern kingdoms on the evil Canaanites who tempted the Israelites and the Judeans. I also agree that God's promise of land to a wandering tribal group means that someone is bound to be driven off a currently occupied piece of land. But I would not presume, as Knierim does, that the Canaanites were in no sense evil. Knierim believes that because certain highly developed elements of the anti-Canaanite polemic are late, the whole polemic must be false. In fact, he portrays the Cannanites in quite positive terms and speaks of "the Canaanites' own ethos of loyalty to their religious traditions."[11] Although his construction is possible, it is equally possible that the Canaanites did, in fact, engage in practices abhorrent to God. If this latter contention proved to be true, although one might object to a call for their total destruction, one could at least understand why certain biblical authors advocated such a position and believed that it was within the universe of divinely prescribed moral behavior. Knierim argues that the liberation of Israel from Egypt and the annihilation of the Canaanites are based on two mutually exclusive views of divine justice, but he is only able to make this argument because he has ignored the text's rationale that the Canaanites were evil by claiming that this rationale is secondary. If one leaves the text intact, however, one sees that it is the same God using a single standard of justice who punishes an evil Pharaoh and also calls for the destruction of the evil Canaanites.

Part of what drives Knierim to read the destruction of the Canaanites in such a negative light is his strong feeling that the Hebrew Bible views war as incompatible with the true flowering of justice. Thus his assertion that "even YHWH's wars, represent, if not injustice altogether, at best a degree of subordinate justice. They are never legitimate in themselves either as means or as ends, especially when compared with their opposite, the justice of peace or the peace of justice."[12] Once again, one can sympathize with Knierim's strong opinions against war. But the question is, Does the Bible generally support Knierim's views on war, or does it hold a completely different view? The evidence sug-

---

10. Knierim, *Task of Old Testament Theology*, 98.
11. Knierim, *Task of Old Testament Theology*, 99.
12. Knierim, *Task of Old Testament Theology*, 104.

gests the writers of the Hebrew Bible believed that certain wars were endorsed by God and that such wars were in no way less just than a just peace. In fact, Knierim seems to be aware of the actual biblical view of war when he asserts "that the Old Testament is only very infrequently critical of warfare. It legitimizes war. Indeed, YHWH's own warfare is a manifestation of justice in history."[13] What leads Knierim to reject this view is his antielection position. He believes that a God who favors Israel in warfare is inherently an unjust God. Since God's justice is paramount, all other texts in tension with this are relativized. What is interesting about this turn in Knierim's argument is that he is no longer simply arguing for the theological centrality of God's justice but is using a modern set of preferences to redefine what the biblical text should mean by God's justice. And he does this even when the text itself seems quite clear that something Knierim considers unjust, it considers a manifestation of God's justice in history.

The result of Knierim's reading of the Hebrew Bible is that not only does he develop the theological centrality of God's justice and righteousness at the expense of many equally important biblical ideas, but he also distorts some of the Hebrew Bible's most explicit statements on God's justice and righteousness. His basis for doing so seems to be a series of ideas having little to do with the Hebrew Bible or ancient Israel. Knierim favors pacifism and socialism, and is opposed to particularism and, most especially, nationalism. These biases are all tied up with each other in a complex fashion. His pacifism inevitably forces him to view as unjust even those wars that the Hebrew Bible considers just. In order to do this, he must remove the rationale provided for these wars, which he does by calling it propaganda. Now the Canaanites become just another nation and Israel becomes their oppressor. Israel commits a wrong against the Canaanites because it believes it has been elected by God, and according to Knierim this is a misunderstanding of God's relationship to Israel. "When it comes to YHWH's struggle for justice through his presence in this world, his presence in Israel's society is nothing but a paradigm for his presence in humanity. In this sense, Israel's own struggle for justice is a symbol and a paradigm for the same struggle everywhere in humanity, and not a symbol of a claimed justice in the service of Israel's exclusive election."[14] Of course, replacing Israel with the church is no solution. *Mutatis mutandis* the same goes for the believing Christian community. There must be no election, and any action that God performs on behalf of any person or nation is only of interest because it is paradigmatic and can be universalized. To elimi-

---

13. Knierim, *Task of Old Testament Theology*, 99.
14. Knierim, *Task of Old Testament Theology*, 136.

nate the problem, Knierim must eliminate any concept of election and all notions of group identity too.

I concur with Professor Towner when he says that one "senses that the categories of universal rulership and justice and righteousness are selected as central partly for subjective reasons, because Knierim wants to select them as central."[15] I would go further and argue that Knierim has a whole series of subjective preferences that have influenced not only his decision to place such importance on the concept of God's universal justice and righteousness at the expense of other ideas, but also his understanding of this idea itself. That Knierim begins his theologizing from certain subjective preferences does not, in and of itself, mean that his theology is fatally flawed; it may just mean that he prefers to work inductively from contemporary human experience back to the God of the Hebrew Bible, rather than deductively from the God of the Hebrew Bible to contemporary human experience.[16] Knierim is correct in his insight that inevitably some parts of the Bible will become more central to our understanding of God and some more peripheral, and that the plurality of views within the Bible insures that this will always be the case. Furthermore, he is not wrong in assuming that doing biblical theology involves making a series of correlations between the contemporary situation of the reader and the biblical text. But one becomes troubled about Knierim's specific theological enterprise when one notices that ideas of lesser theological import are elevated to a central status and now come to overshadow, or even to displace totally, many truly profound theological ideas. The result is that a series of subjective modern preferences become the controlling feature of Knierim's reading of the biblical text rather than part of a process of mutual dialogue. Instead of having a conversation between the contemporary reader and the biblical text in which each truly challenges the assumptions of the other, one ends up with a Bible stripped of any idea that might pose a challenge to the contemporary outlook.

Before concluding, I turn to one other aspect of Knierim's rejection of the concept of election that deserves attention. Knierim believes that there is an irresolvable tension between God's universal justice and Israel's election, and thus he tells readers that they must choose one or the other. But Knierim has done some injustice to the notion of Israel's elect status by reducing it to a simple form of divine favoritism, and not fully reckoning with the complexity of the Hebrew Bible's view of election. It is true that some Jews in the ancient, medieval, and modern

---

15. Knierim, *Task of Old Testament Theology*, 27.

16. Such an approach is advocated by Peter Berger, *A Rumor of Angels* (rev. ed.; New York: Doubleday, 1990) 55–85.

periods have misused the notion of election by proclaiming that election means that God loves them at the expense of the Gentiles. In turn, certain Gentiles, misunderstanding the concept of election and becoming indignant at the notion that the Jews claim to be the specially chosen people of God, have either rejected this notion totally or, more usually, claimed this elect status for themselves.[17]

The Bible itself outlines the ways that election can be misused and misunderstood by both the elect and those not elected and actually provides a corrective to this situation. The clearest example can be found within the Joseph story. Although this story is not specifically about Jews and non-Jews but about one chosen brother (probably representing one chosen tribal group) among others, it clearly evokes how election can be misused by its recipient and misunderstood by those others closely related to the elect one. Both Joseph and his brothers initially assume that his dreams in which his brothers symbolically bow down to him are prophecies about how he will attain fame and fortune at his brothers' expense. But in the end, although his dreams came true and his brothers did indeed bow down to him, he (along with the reader) realizes that the whole purpose of God bringing this about was so that Joseph could keep his extended family alive (Gen. 45:5–7; 50:20). Thus, by the end of the narrative Joseph and his brothers, along with the reader, come to see that the chosen one is favored not to lord it over the nonchosen ones, but to protect them and even to save their lives through active intervention. Thus, election is for everyone's benefit. The lesson to be learned from the Joseph story is not that Jacob was wrong in his favoring of Joseph, but that both Joseph and his brothers acted poorly in relation to each other.[18]

One can apply this same insight to God's election of Israel and the response of the nations to Israel's election. Although Israel often falls into the error of viewing election as equivalent to a form of special divine protection (Jeremiah 7), God's chosen people are constantly reminded that the notion of election is more one of responsibilities than of special privileges: "You only have I known of all the families of the earth; therefore I will punish you for all your iniquities" (Amos 3:2). And even though the nonelect have sometimes resisted the notion that God is specially connected to the people of Israel (Exodus 1–15), there are other

---

17. See Jeffrey S. Siker, *Disinheriting the Jews: Abraham in Early Christian Controversy* (Louisville: Westminster John Knox, 1991).

18. For an accessible and thoughtful literary analysis of the Joseph story see Robert Alter, *The Art of Biblical Narrative* (New York: Basic Books, 1981) 155–77. For a deeper theological analysis see Jon D. Levenson, *The Death and Resurrection of the Beloved Son* (New Haven: Yale University Press, 1993) 143–69.

times that they have come to see that this special relationship is for
their benefit too (Rom. 9:4–5; 11:28–32).

If one understands the concept of election simply as a type of divine
favoritism, as Knierim does, it is easy to see why he has rejected this
idea as a misinterpretation of God's general relationship to all humanity. According to his interpretation God should look upon all human
communities with the same favoritism, and thus all humanity would be
God's elect. But the question is, Is this an accurate portrayal of ancient
Israel's understanding of election? I would contend that the evidence
I have cited indicates that the notion of election espoused by the Hebrew Bible is more complex and profound than Knierim's portrayal of
it, and therefore that the people of Israel are not an incidental part of a
universal story that the Hebrew Bible tells. Rather, the Hebrew Bible is
a story about God's mysterious and unique relationship with the Jewish people. This story does indeed involve the other, nonelect nations of
the world (Gen. 12:3; Exod. 19:5–6; Isa. 2:2–4; 66:18–21; Zech. 8:20–23),
but it does so through God's special relationship to the Jewish people.
To ignore this fact by universalizing the notion of election is to risk
distorting substantial portions of the biblical text and miss one of its
central theological ideas. Furthermore, to do so is also another form of
supersessionism, even though it does not replace Israel with the church.
It still replaces Israel, inasmuch as Israel becomes a stand-in for anyone
or everyone.

Knierim's particular program is certainly a step in a correct direction. He has in some sense reckoned with what are, from the Jewish
perspective, the two most problematic aspects of most Christian writing on the theology of the Hebrew Bible: Christian supersessionism,
and a tendency to homogenize the text rather than to take account of
the plurality of theologies one finds in the Hebrew Bible.[19] But his particular solutions remain unsatisfactory, and I find that in spite of his
deep commitment to avoiding these two pitfalls, he has in some sense
not succeeded. Although he is constantly reminding the reader of the
plurality of theologies within the Hebrew Bible, ultimately his modern socio-political biases lead him to flatten its theological landscape.
And even though he ingeniously seeks to avoid the problem of supersessionism by arguing that the centrality of God's justice means that all
people are elected by God, not just Israel, his position amounts to a new
type of supersessionism. In terms of the plurality of theologies in the
text, I think that Knierim has taken the first giant step by arguing that

---

19. For the most comprehensive statement of why Jews are troubled by Christian bib-
lical theology see Jon Levenson, "Why Jews Are Not Interested in Biblical Theology," in
The Hebrew Bible, The Old Testament, and Historical Criticism (Louisville: Westminster John
Knox, 1993) 33–61.

this plurality constitutes a problem inasmuch as it frequently requires readers of the Bible to make hard choices. But I wonder whether a Christian thinker could write a theology of the Hebrew Bible that preserves more nuances and permits various theological insights to stand on their own, even when they are in sharp tension with other equally valid insights. In terms of supersessionism, I find it difficult to choose between a traditional Christian reading of the Hebrew Bible that takes the concept of election seriously, but believes Israel has been displaced, and one, like Professor Knierim's, that eliminates such supersessionism but does so by denying Israel's election. I personally prefer the exegetical integrity of the more traditional Christian reading, even while I admire both Knierim's attempt to rein in Christian anti-Semitism and his attempt to make the theology of the Hebrew Bible useful to those who are seeking to create a more just world. Of course, I still hope that eventually a Christian biblical scholar will produce a theology of the Hebrew Bible that is not supersessionistic but still affirms the basic biblical principle that the Jewish people have a continuing special relationship with God and that the unfolding of this relationship has implications for all of humanity.[20]

BIBLIOGRAPHY

Alter, Robert. *The Art of Biblical Narrative*. New York: Basic Books, 1981.

Berger, Peter. *A Rumor of Angels*, rev. ed. New York: Doubleday, 1990.

Kaminsky, Joel S. *Corporate Responsibility in the Hebrew Bible*, JSOTSup 196. Sheffield: Sheffield Academic Press, 1995.

———. "The Sins of the Fathers: A Theological Investigation of the Biblical Tension Between Corporate and Individualized Retribution," *Judaism* 46 (summer 1997) 319–32.

Knierim, Rolf P. *The Task of Old Testament Theology: Substance, Method, and Cases*. Grand Rapids: Eerdmans, 1995.

Levenson, Jon D. "Cataclysm, Survival and Regeneration in the Hebrew Bible." In *Confronting Omnicide: Jewish Reflections on Weapons of Mass Destruction*. Ed. Daniel Landes. Northvale, N.J.: Jason Aronson, 1991.

———. *The Death and Resurrection of the Beloved Son*. New Haven: Yale, 1993.

---

20. Although I have not seen a book produced by a biblical scholar that manages to accomplish this difficult and challenging task, I have seen a few Christian theologians do so. See R. Kendall Soulen, *The God of Israel and Christian Theology* (Minneapolis: Fortress, 1996); Paul M. van Buren, *Discerning the Way: A Theology of Jewish Christian Reality* (New York: Seabury, 1980). This is not to say that Christian biblical theologians have ignored the concept of election. One recent two-volume theology of the Old Testament has used the notion of election as its organizing principle: Horst D. Preuss, *Old Testament Theology* (2 vols.; OTL; Louisville: Westminster John Knox, 1995–96).

————. "Why Jews Are Not Interested in Biblical Theology." In *The Hebrew Bible, The Old Testament, and Historical Criticism*. Louisville: Westminster John Knox, 1993.

Miller, J. Maxwell. "The Israelite Occupation of Canaan." In *Israelite and Judean History*. Ed. John H. Hayes and J. Maxwell Miller. Philadelphia: Westminster, 1977.

Preuss, Horst D. *Old Testament Theology*. OTL, 2 volumes. Louisville: Westminster John Knox, 1995, 1996.

Siker, Jeffrey S. *Disinheriting the Jews: Abraham in Early Christian Controversy*. Louisville: Westminster John Knox Press, 1991.

Soulen, R. Kendall. *The God of Israel and Christian Theology*. Minneapolis: Fortress, 1996.

van Buren, Paul M. *Discerning the Way: A Theology of Jewish Christian Reality*. New York: Seabury, 1980.

16

Gender Complementarity
in the Hebrew Bible
Hyun Chul Paul Kim

INTRODUCTION

One of the unique features of the Hebrew Bible is the plurality of texts, traditions, concepts, worldviews, and theologies that lie within its pages. It contains not only a coherent thread of messages but also a contending divergence of stories, recountings, and expressions of faith by various authors and communities. We must also bear in mind, however, that there is a dynamic meeting between the diverse perspectives of the text and the diverse perspectives of the reader. For example, suppose I had been a male, Asian, Christian scholar living in Medieval times, residing in a society where upholding any view favorable toward women was anathema. In that world would I have been able to write honestly and openly about female perspectives in the Hebrew Bible? Could I have articulated the concept of gender equality and mutuality? Or, could I have had the courage to say or write what I believed to be a right or honest interpretation, regardless of societal response?

The fact of the matter is that our reading is deeply controlled by where we are coming from, how we are reading, and why we are reading.[1] This essay argues that competent biblical interpretation requires a

---

This essay is an expanded version of a paper presented to the Feminist Theological Hermeneutics of the Bible group at the annual meeting of the Society of Biblical Literature in Orlando, Florida, in November 1998. I express special thanks to the chairpersons of that group, Nancy R. Bowen and Richard D. Weis. It is an honor to dedicate this essay to Professor Rolf P. Knierim in celebration of his seventieth birthday, with deep gratitude for his mentorship and with sincere wishes for many blessings in the years to come.

1. David J. A. Clines (*Interested Parties: The Ideology of Writers and Readers of the Hebrew Bible* [JSOTSup 205; Sheffield: Sheffield Academic Press, 1995] 24–25) writes, "We all do this kind of concealment of our motivations, and perhaps there is nothing wrong in it. Perhaps you do not even want to know what unexpressed reasons I have for writing this book, and perhaps I could not tell you the most of them even if I wanted to. Perhaps you do not know for what hidden reasons you are reading it.... There is, I should hope, a good deal of scholarly rigour within it, but I would be deceiving myself if I thought that I (or any of us) were capable of disinterested scholarship." Alice Bach ("Reading Allowed: Feminist Biblical Criticism Approaching the Millennium," *Currents in Research: Biblical Studies* 1 [1993] 192–93) writes, "Male critics who have analyzed texts from a feminist perspective

more dynamic awareness of plurality not only within the biblical texts, but also within ourselves. Thus, the biblical text inherently invites the reader to be aware of the vitality of diverse concepts that convey the living testimonies of peoples of faith and invites the reader to join in her or his religious dialogue with comparison, disagreement, and reinterpretation. Subsequently, this calls for a dynamic correlation of the theologies and ideologies among the texts as well as between the texts and the readers. For this, Rolf P. Knierim's contributions deserve special attention.

This essay thus starts with a recap (by no means exhaustive) of Knierim's theory, methods, and theology in the biblical interpretation. Then it presents a case study for the biblical portrayals of gender relationship in selected biblical texts that display implicit concepts and ideologies of gender mutuality. I attempt to utilize some of Knierim's interpretative tools to exegete, interpret, reinterpret, and theologize coherent and contending concepts, unified and plural ideologies, of gender issues in dialogue with the horizon of the biblical canon and today's ever changing worldviews.

EXCERPTS OF KNIERIM'S METHODOLOGY

This essay selects and corresponds to those elements and aspects of Knierim's scholarship that are pertinent to my goals and methods. They are briefly summed up as follows.

Revitalization of Form Criticism through a New Orientation

Form criticism, despite its immeasurable usefulness for biblical studies, has been a key factor in the atomization of the texts. This has often resulted in the neglect of the text as a whole. Along with James Muilenburg, Knierim reoriented the primary attention of form criticism to start its study from the extant form of the text.[2] Only then can one backtrack to the traditio-historical and redactional prestages. Paying attention to the extant form, the reader can appreciate the intention of the final redactor(s) who put the whole of a text together.

---

have ignored the ideology of masculinity, that is the social construction of the male and masculine sexual stereotypes. While women's roles are being reexamined, masculinity, although equally problematic, remains neglected as a subject for analysis."

2. See James Muilenburg, "Form Criticism and Beyond," *JBL* 88 (1969) 1–18; Rolf Knierim, "Old Testament Form Criticism Reconsidered," *Int* 27 (1971) 436–68; idem, "Criticism of Literary Features, Form, Tradition, and Redaction," in D. Knight and G. Tucker, eds., *The Hebrew Bible and Its Modern Interpreters* (Chico, Calif.: Scholars Press, 1985) 123–65.

Biblical Theology for Each Testament in Its Own Right and for the Mutual Contributions of the Hebrew Bible/Old Testament and the New Testament

In between the fences of reading the biblical texts descriptively and prescriptively biblical interpreters have been wrestling with the texts' claims of truth vis-à-vis the complexities of changing worlds. Often these claims of truth have been adumbrated or filtered by dogmatic doctrines or readers' prerogatives. The Hebrew Bible has been read from — and only from — the eyes of the New Testament not infrequently with Christian supersessionism. Knierim's ongoing effort as a biblical theologian has been to read the Hebrew Bible in its own text, context, and theology before proofreading or checking it with the New Testament.[3] Only then would it be appropriate for Christians to read and compare the two Testaments with a view toward how one contributes to the other for any constructive, critical, and corrective biblical theology and hermeneutics.

The Concepts of Creation and the Universal Dominion of Yahweh-God with Justice and Righteousness

Biblical texts, inasmuch as they are rooted in history, sociology, and politics, are inherently embedded in theological queries, issues, and answers. Accordingly, biblical theologians have attempted to construct and interpret the essential concepts that have spanned the bulk and history of the Hebrew Bible (e.g., *Heilsgeschichte,* covenant, law and promise, and so on). Amid these concepts Knierim's theological insights highlight the dynamic interrelationship between the concept of God as the Creator of all humanity and that of justice and righteousness.[4] The vantage points in biblical theology can be seen neither as "the canon within the canon" nor as the "monolithic" or "normative" truth, but in the dynamic mutuality, fusion, and critique between the concepts of the universality of God and the particularity of justice and righteousness. On the one hand, among many other concepts from the texts of the Hebrew Bible it is the concept of God as the Creator of all that en-

---

3. R. Knierim ("On Biblical Theology," in C. Evans and S. Talmon, eds., *The Quest for Context and Meaning: Studies in Biblical Intertextuality in Honor of James A. Sanders* [Leiden: Brill, 1997] 120) writes, "From this Christian theology of religion, the theology of the Jewish Bible has from the earliest Christian writings on appeared to be at best preliminary, preparatory, penultimate, relative, an example for how not, or no longer, to believe, and at worst irrelevant, negligible, or to be rejected. The relationship between these writings and the Old Testament was not one of mutually equal openness, an openness in which the Old Testament and these writings could jointly determine the scope of the religious understanding of reality. This relationship was unilaterally predetermined by Christians and their Christian agenda." See also Rolf Knierim, *The Task of Old Testament Theology: Substance, Method, and Cases* (Grand Rapids: Eerdmans, 1995) 72–74, 123–30.

4. See Knierim, *Task of Old Testament Theology,* 1–20, 33–56.

compasses, and functions as one of, the most fundamental concepts for other concepts and perspectives. Without God the integrity of the Hebrew Bible would collapse. Even the concept of salvation history resides within the boundary of the concept of creation.[5] In that system creation also includes the universal reign of Yahweh-God over all humanity without any barriers of race, gender, class, ideology, or religion. On the other hand, this theological presupposition marks a dynamic correlation with the concepts of justice and righteousness. In other words, creation with the universal dominion of the Creator must account for the diverse aspects of justice and righteousness, and vice versa. For this reason Knierim defines manifold meanings of justice and righteousness.[6] There is not one form, case, or definition of justice, but many of them, which need to be reconstructed and compared in light of the worldviews of the texts vis-à-vis our worldviews and existential cases.

Exegesis, Theology, and Hermeneutic as the Interpretive Modes of the Texts of the Hebrew Bible

Biblical exegetes implement numerous ways, methods, and steps in the exegetical process. Knierim's way of exegeting a biblical text involves three interpretive steps or dimensions: exegesis, theology, and hermeneutic.[7] Exegesis indicates the selecting and reading of a delimited text in light of its composition, context, and conceptuality. Theology denotes the holistic comparison of the implications of the studied text with those of other texts in the Hebrew Bible and/or the New Testament. Hermeneutic implies not hermeneutics (i.e., interpretation) per se, but rather, a specific case, event, or issue in today's world that may be significantly relevant and comparable to the cases, ideologies, and theologies of the text in the biblical world. Each of the three steps is interdependent upon the other two. The interactive relationship of these steps requires a dialogical mode of interpretation.

Structural Analysis of a Text for the Tasks of Examining the Text's Contextuality, Intratextuality, and Intertextuality and Reconstructing Its Infratextuality (Underlying Concepts)

Just as the composition of a biblical chapter or book is more than a mere anthology, so is a text more than an assembled unit. Both con-

---

5. See, for instance, Knierim's essay "Cosmos and History in Israel's Theology" in *Task of Old Testament Theology*, 171–224.

6. For the various aspects (at least sixteen different ones) of justice in the Hebrew Bible see Knierim, *Task of Old Testament Theology*, 89–122.

7. See Knierim, *Task of Old Testament Theology*, 58–71. For Knierim's concise definitions of the three tasks see "On the Task of Old Testament Theology," in E. Carpenter, ed., *A Biblical Itinerary: In Search of Method, Form, and Content* (JSOTSup 240; Sheffield: Sheffield Academic Press, 1997) 153.

tain carefully programmed structures. Hence, to study the structure of a text involves more than dividing or outlining a text. The structure is not merely a sum total of subunits but also a result of the author's intended order, design, and purpose. A text's structure is intricately connected to the text's contextuality, intratextuality, intertextuality, and infratextuality, all of which deserve careful examination. Contextuality suggests the intended purpose of the text's relationship to its preceding and following texts. Intratextuality displays the hidden conceptual movement, sequence, and emphasis within the relationship of the verses of the text. Intertextuality can help in understanding the authorial meaning and intention of the usage of specific words, phrases, or metaphors that echo other texts in the Hebrew Bible and beyond. Infratextuality denotes the subsurface concepts that govern the whole formation of the text's contextuality, intratextuality, and intertextuality in its extant form.

Reconceptualization of the Concepts of a Text with Heuristic Comparison as a Mode of Rereading

No preacher preaches a text without the filtering of her or his own interpretation and reinterpretation in light of various contexts of the text, biblical theologies, and corresponding occasions vis-à-vis the congregation.[8] Recent efforts in semiotics and hermeneutics have helped incorporate the legitimacy of rereading, such as reader-response criticism, into the modes of biblical interpretation. Knierim brings up the task of reconceptualization as a mode of the ongoing reinterpretation of the biblical texts for today's application. How do the motifs, themes, and concepts of the biblical texts become relevant to our concerns in the coming twenty-first century? When the concept of a text directly conflicts with another text in the Bible, what shall we do with their confrontation vis-à-vis issues of today's reality? For these ongoing questions Knierim suggests that the reader conscientiously account for the dynamic relationship between a concept and its conflicting concept within the Bible, as well as the relationship between a concept and today's worldview. Central to this hermeneutical task is the reader's integral effort to compare differing or conflicting ideologies for the changing society vis-à-vis justice and righteousness. Such comparing implies that there may be no absolute norm or answer.[9] Rather, it is

---

8. Knierim (*Task of Old Testament Theology,* 471) writes, "No preacher can speak of the wrath or anger of God in the Old Testament without an interpretative filter."

9. Knierim ("Comments on the Task of Old Testament Theology" [paper presented at the annual meeting of the Society of Biblical Literature, San Francisco, November 1997] 5–6) writes, "And last but not least, I do believe that the amount of aspects to be studied is endless, and that in this regard no volume will ever be able to say it all. I also believe, that

constantly subject to correction, criticism, and revision for the sake of that which is "better" in the encounter between the biblical world and our world on the basis of our ongoing study of God, justice, and righteousness.

BIBLICAL CASES

Bible readers, ancient and modern, have wrestled with the biblical portrayals and implications concerning various relationships: between God and humanity, between God and the gods, between heavens and earth, between a king and the people, between nature and humankind, between men and women, and so forth. Among these relationships are the gender roles in the Hebrew Bible (social settings and ideologies) that display perspectives that are greatly imbalanced. Modern feminist scholarship has not only pointed out such imbalance, but has also projected hermeneutical modes in addressing various concepts of gender relationship. Within those various concepts this essay focuses on some evidences of hidden effort by the biblical authors to balance out the complementarity between male and female heroes.[10] Particular attention is given to Exodus 15 and Judges 4–5, dealing with questions of how gender relationship is depicted within its unique sociocultural contexts, how the authorial intentions compare and differ between the two texts and in the horizons of the Hebrew Bible and New Testament, and what it means for us to reinterpret the limitations and potentials of the texts' underlying concepts for today's contexts with regard to the dynamics of mutual respect, competition, challenge, and solidarity in gender relationship.

Genesis 1 and 2

These two chapters, so-called P and J narratives, contain the creation stories that share many common elements. At the same time, however, they also exhibit different depictions. Even concerning the portrayals

---

the process of systematization by comparison will always be heuristic, one of finding, and continue to finding ever clearer, what we do not yet know, rather than one that becomes fixed let alone one that would be externally predetermined by fixed doctrines. Whether or not this method for the search of the truth in the historical sources of the Old Testament lends itself to making a contribution to our discussions in our modern or so-called postmodern world — who am I, or who is anyone, to decide that in advance?"

10. The term "complementarity" in this essay implies an idea of the relationship of two distinct parties who share mutual needs, interdependence, and respect. This term is to be distinguished from the connotation of a hierarchical relationship of two parties where one is subordinate to the other. Rather, it is used to include the ideas of mutuality, balance, and equality, while maintaining the uniqueness and distinctiveness of each party rather than homogeneity.

of gender relationship both accounts narrate many different contents. In Genesis 1 the creation accounts are described in a theological expression with the "word" of Elohim and in an orderly manner with the symmetrical six-day events, culminating in the creation of humankind (1:26–31; note "it was *very* good" in v. 31) and in the Sabbath on the seventh day (2:1–3). According to this narrative human beings, who are created in the image of God and have dominion over the world, are described as male and female. From the evidence of the text there is no preference for or discrimination against one gender or the other. Rather, in a collective sense both male and female comprise the whole of humankind.[11] Thus, the famous verse depicts that "in the image of God he created *them*" (1:27) — in the third person plural form. This passage suggests the concept of equality of the gender relationship under the same creation, guidance, and protection of their God.

In Genesis 2 Yahweh Elohim, who is described in a more anthropomorphic way, creates man first. Moreover, the motif of making the animals, birds, and living creatures is to give them as a "companion" (עֵזֶר) for the man (2:18–20a). Eventually the creation story culminates in the creation of the woman who is brought to the man as a companion (2:22). The creation of woman out of man's rib has been the topic of endless scholarly discussions. It has been highlighted, abused, and paraphrased, oftentimes for the purpose of denigrating the status of women (3:16). Regardless of the subsequent debates on this story, it is certain that there is a conceptual difference, if not contrast, between Genesis 1 and 2 concerning gender relationship. Although the translation of the Hebrew word as "companion" instead of "helper" may connote an equal status of the woman with the man in Genesis 2,[12] the text implies pri-

---

11. Susan Niditch ("Genesis," in C. Newsom and S. Ringe, eds., *The Women's Bible Commentary* [Louisville: Westminster John Knox, 1992] 12–13) writes, "Without establishing relative rank or worth of the genders, the spinner of this creation tale indicates that humankind is found in two varieties, the male and the female, and this humanity in its complementarity is a reflection of the deity." Helen Schüngel-Straumann ("On the Creation of Man and Woman in Genesis 1–3: The History and Reception of the Texts Reconsidered," in A. Brenner, ed., *A Feminist Companion to Genesis* [FCB 2; Sheffield: Sheffield Academic Press, 1993] 75) writes, "So this statement *explicitly* excludes men's rule over women! Oddly enough, this has not been noticed before. An analysis of the wording in Gen. 1.26–28 results in precisely this, however: man and woman rule over the rest of creation, and this implies only too clearly that one gender may not claim power over the other."

12. See, for example, Phyllis Trible, *God and the Rhetoric of Sexuality* (Philadelphia: Fortress, 1978) 72–94; Carol Meyers, *Discovering Eve: Ancient Israelite Women in Context* (New York: Oxford University Press, 1988) 84–85. An example of a contrasting view is expressed by Pamela J. Milne ("The Patriarchal Stamp of Scripture: The Implications of Structuralist Analyses for Feminist Hermeneutics," in Brenner, ed., *Feminist Companion to Genesis*, 167–68): "It was my view then, and it remains my view now, that the 'reformist' feminist goal of reclaiming the Bible from its own patriarchal biases, and from those of its interpreters through the centuries, is simply not a viable one. I used Genesis 2–3 as an example text to

mary attention to the man, who by naming his mate assumes a hidden authority. Whether one reads the accounts of Genesis 1 and 2 independently or holistically, the concept of equality and complementarity between man and woman is more vividly implied in Genesis 1. Therefore, in comparison with the portrayal of a woman in Genesis 2, Genesis 1 potentially signifies the mutual gender status between male and female in God's creation of humankind. Before God, male and female are the same creature, components of what is called humankind.

Thus, what we see in the extant form of the two chapters is not only the conceptual continuity but also the conceptual tension and diversity in the creaturehood of male and female — without hierarchy in Genesis 1, and with androcentric patriarchy in Genesis 2. Therefore, in terms of gender relationship the subtle tension, continuity, and reiteration in the first two chapters of the Tanak can be seen as a microcosm of the diverse, discrete, and often imbalanced perspectives within the entire corpus of biblical texts, among which Exodus 15 and Judges 4–5 display unique exceptions.

Exodus 15

The two songs in Exodus 15 (the Song of Moses in vv. 1–19 and the Song of Miriam in vv. 20–21) are considered by many scholars as ancient poetry, due particularly to their old Hebrew language and syntax. These songs, as climactic hymns, play a significant role within the surrounding literary contexts: they culminate the victory of Yahweh and Israel in the preceding texts and anticipate unfolding events of wonder in the wilderness in the following texts. In other words, although these songs could have been independent of the surrounding contexts, they heighten the intentionality of the whole literary development and together stand as a central part of the entire book of Exodus with various significant conceptual ramifications.

Within those contexts the Song of Moses is followed by the Song of Miriam. In the former, Moses is joined by the "sons of Israel" in praise to Yahweh for their victorious liberation and the defeat of the oppressing Egyptians by the might of Yahweh. In the latter, Miriam is joined by "all the women" in praise to Yahweh in a song that summarizes with artistic succinctness the lengthy and redundant song of their brothers. Here we may find some significant implications from the conceptual relationship between the two songs by comparing their placement, similarity, and differences.

---

illustrate my position. . . . David Clines, for example, has re-examined Trible's claim that 'ēzer connotes a relationship of 'equality' rather than that of an inferior 'helper.' He argued that in this context being a 'helper' is simply not a Hebrew way of being 'equal' and that the only way in which Eve 'helps' Adam is in producing offspring."

First, it is peculiar that Miriam is depicted not as Moses' sister but as Aaron's sister. The reader is reminded of the anonymous description of her in Exodus 2 as "his [Moses'] sister." The reader may speculate in various ways. For example, in Exod. 2:1–10 every character is unnamed except for the son, who is named at its climax as Moses (v. 10). The other characters remain as backdrops for Moses, but their anonymity implicitly underscores their titles — for example, a *Levite* woman, and the daughter of *Pharaoh*. Thus, the text intends to highlight the Levitical lineage of Moses and his fateful connection to the house of Pharaoh. Regardless of these speculations we find one evident fact: from the extant form of the text the reader is invited to identify that unnamed sister of Exodus 2 with Miriam. There is a conceptual development from an unknown sister to the identified Miriam. There is also a linkage from a Levitical family to a female leader, Miriam. For this reason Miriam could have been perceived as a priest.[13] It is perhaps due to this intention that she is called Aaron's sister, as the name Aaron implies a closer tie to the house of Levitical priests than does Moses. Alternatively, it may be due to the fact that Aaron was the firstborn son of the family. All these important evidences lead to another significant fact: Miriam is described as a "prophetess" (נביאה). Although she is called Moses' sister in Exodus 2, now she is called a prophet in the line of Levites. This deliberately elevates her status as an important counterpart for Moses the prophet.[14] Therefore, the present text — which offers the names of two prophets — implicitly emphasizes the female leadership in that Miriam is no longer merely a sister of Moses or Aaron but a prophet in her own right.

Second, the placement of Miriam's song directly after that of Moses may indicate the primary significance of Moses and his song, as it precedes that of Miriam. The present text implies that the women were respondents to the men (v. 21, "Miriam sang to them [third person masculine plural]"), as the women's significance remains a peripheral

---

13. Drorah Setel ("Exodus," in Newsom and Ringe, eds., *Women's Bible Commentary*, 29) writes, "Exodus contains several indications that Israelite women originally may have had a religious status from which they were later barred. The lineage, actions, and title ('prophet') attributed to Miriam, as well as Zipporah's connections to a priestly household (2:16) and an apparently sacrificial act (4:25), point to a cultic status that was forgotten or repressed in the compilation of the text as it has been handed down."

14. Setel ("Exodus," 31) writes, "Miriam's designation as a prophet and her unquestioned leadership of the victory celebration in Exodus 15 indicate that ancient Israelites were also familiar with forms of female authority that did not survive into later periods." Similarly, Phyllis Trible reconstructs the hidden tradition of Miriam's leadership in light of Mic. 6:4 and Jer. 31:4: "In early Israel Miriam belonged to a trinity of leadership. She was the equal of Moses and Aaron" ("Bringing Miriam out of the Shadows," in A. Brenner, ed., *A Feminist Companion to Exodus to Deuteronomy* [FCB 6; Sheffield: JSOT Press, 1994] 181).

backdrop.[15] Scholars debate which song was composed first, the shorter one or the longer one. Here, it is helpful to pay attention to the compositional relationship between Exod. 15:19 and 15:20–21. Verse 19 starts as prose in distinction with the poetry in vv. 1b–18. What, then, is the function of v. 19 and its intratextual relation to vv. 20–21? Here it should be noted that the content of 15:19 corresponds to that of 14:26–31. There is a substantive parallel between the two. Just as the narrative of 14:26–31 sets the stage and reason for the subsequent song of victory in 15:1–18, so does 15:19 provide a background summary for the subsequent song in 15:20–21. Just as the Song of Moses is very much dependent upon the narrative of 14:26–31 with regard to form and content, so is the Song of Miriam closely tied to the narrative of 15:19. In this sense, although 15:19 is a recapitulation of 14:26–31, it also functions as a narrative background for the following passage, 15:20–21. It thereby makes a substantive division with the Song of the Sea as a whole.[16]

For what purpose, then, are the two similar but distinct accounts put together? Two conceptual implications can be reconstructed from the authorial intention: the two songs are put together to reduce or replace the significance of the female role and, at the same time, to convey the implicit concept of togetherness in the chorus of the whole community. Let us start with the first implication. One should note that this kind of redundancy and duplication is a common compositional feature in the Pentateuchal literature (e.g., a J account and a P account adjacent to each other). Accordingly, one can posit that there once existed two independent traditions, that is, the Song of Moses and the Song of Miriam. In other words, in the relationship between the two text traditions, the Song of Miriam may have represented a different or dissenting voice for another tradition, if not another community.[17]

---

15. Fokkelien van Dijk-Hemmes ("Some Recent Views on the Presentation of the Song of Miriam," in Brenner, ed., *Feminist Companion to Exodus to Deuteronomy*, 205–6) writes, "However, this positive conclusion regarding the presentation of Miriam does not alter the fact that, in the interpretations discussed so far, her performance in Exodus 15 has been placed in the shadow of Moses' performance."

16. This means that the placement of 15:19 is not merely a postscript of 15:1–18 but rather a bridge for a new unit, that is, 15:19–21. Jorge Pixley (*On Exodus: A Liberation Perspective* [trans. R. Barr; Maryknoll, N.Y.: Orbis, 1987] 97) notes, "This short passage [15:19–21] serves to relate the hymn to the exodus account generally. Its version of how the Israelites 'had marched on dry ground right through the sea' is based on the prose account, and here serves to clarify ambiguous expressions in the hymn."

17. Ellen Frankel (*The Five Books of Miriam: A Woman's Commentary on the Torah* [New York: G. P. Putnam's Sons, 1996] 110) writes, "Even though Moses' triumphant Song at the Sea is eighteen verses long, while Miriam's is only one verse (and even that single verse is a direct quote from her brother's song), this imbalance reflects later editing, not Miriam's second-class status in her own time. In fact, some of us believe that Miriam's song was censored or lost, due to a later generation's uneasiness with female leadership."

By having the preliminary narrative in v. 19, the Song of Miriam thus portrays a tradition that could have been as independent and valid as the Song of Moses. Furthermore, in 15:1 Moses and the "sons of Israel" start their song with the (collective) first person jussive form of the verb, "I will sing to Yahweh." In 15:22 Miriam and the women start their song with the imperative verb, "Sing to Yahweh" (note that the imperative verb is in the second person masculine plural form in the MT), rather than the cohortative or jussive form.[18] From the interaction of the imperative and cohortative verbs we can deduce that the Song of Moses was meant to be a response to the invocation by the Song of Miriam. For this reason scholars view the Song of Miriam possibly to have generated the Song of Moses, while in the present text the formation is reversed.[19] Therefore, in the extant form the placement of the song by Miriam and the women (15:20–21), initiated by Moses and the men (15:1–18) and marginalized by the unusual brevity (15:21), stands quite naturally with the common intentionality of the narrative contexts that portray Moses as the predominant figure over Miriam or any other female heroes. Nevertheless, the extant text hints at another conceptual element: if it were the authorial intention to diminish the significance of the female protagonists, it could have been done much better. Instead, the prophet Miriam is included along with her fellow musicians, implying the concept of togetherness in the setting of the chorus of both genders and all statuses. To this concept we now direct our discussion.

Third, the extant text displays a subtle intention to maintain a literary balance in that the reader is invited to read and listen to both songs, not one. Admittedly, throughout the book of Exodus, and indeed the entire Pentateuch, Miriam stays in the background of the main plots, or Miriam's significance as a coleader and prophet is deliberately minimized or ignored. In this pivotal chapter, however, the two songs purposefully correspond to each other as they build a nice chorus — the songs by men and women, respectively, of the same community. How do they echo each other and build a chorus? It is helpful to compare the contents of the two songs:

---

18. The LXX, *Targum Pseudo-Jonathan*, and Vulgate have this verb in the first person plural form, following the same line as 15:1, but not that of 15:22 of the MT.

19. Frank M. Cross and David N. Freedman have argued for the antiquity and originality of the Song of Miriam, as this song concludes the entire Song of the Sea in Exodus 15 ("The Song of Miriam," *JNES* 14 [1955] 237–50). Van Dijk-Hemmes ("Presentation of the Song of Miriam," 202) states, "It would be more plausible to assume that the Song of Miriam belongs to an older tradition and that the Song of the Sea is a later amplification thereof."

Exod. 15:1 (Song of Moses)	*Exod. 15:21 (Song of Miriam)*
I will sing to Yahweh,	Sing to Yahweh,
for he has triumphed gloriously;	for he has triumphed gloriously;
horse and rider	horse and rider
he has thrown into the sea.	he has thrown into the sea.

The Song of Miriam echoes the very first line of the Song of Moses. Except for the first line, the verses are the same. That the Song of Miriam is a recap of the initial line of the Song of Moses may indicate that, as already discussed, the Song of Miriam was much longer than what the received text contains. Additionally, it can allow the reader to hear the same song sung by both male and female in unison, harmony, and consonance. Again, in the typically patriarchal text and culture, women normally did not gain main attention, and this text follows that familiar tradition. Nonetheless, the presence of the imagery of the female leadership and participation in this text displays subtle but important significance. Just as the song by Moses and the "sons of Israel" marks the climax of the whole exodus movement, so does the seemingly subsidiary song by Miriam and her fellow women give another stamp to the significance of the entire plot. The unexpected or marginalized roles of the women in the sense of "unauthorized leadership," as Drorah Setel refers to it, now reach their own invaluable climactic juncture at the Song of Miriam.[20] To put it another way, the subtle emphasis on the importance of the roles of women in the fate of Moses (Exod. 1:15–22; 2:1–22; cf. 4:24–26), and thereby the whole people of Israel, culminates in the duet of Moses and Miriam, where the reader is invited to remember and acknowledge the audacious roles of women, particularly Miriam.[21] Likewise, in the correlation between cohortative and imperative verb forms the reader finds an authorial sketch of the interaction between the two parts of the choir, as if sopranos and altos sing the invitational hymn while tenors and basses echo with the responsive arias, and vice versa. In the corresponding interaction there is a concept of unity and mutuality between Moses and Miriam, between the men and the women of Israel.

---

20. Setel ("Exodus," 29) notes, "One way in which the women of Exodus provide unauthorized leadership is through acts of intervention."

21. J. Cheryl Exum delineates the significant role Miriam plays in the story of Moses as she describes Miriam whose "resourcefulness at a strategic moment determines Moses' future and who later becomes a leader of the exodus in her own right.... Without Moses there would be no exodus, but without these women there would be no Moses!" (" 'Mother in Israel': A Familiar Figure Reconsidered," in L. Russell, ed., *Feminist Interpretation of the Bible* [Philadelphia: Westminster, 1985] 80–81).

Carol Meyers argues that one of women's primary religious roles during this period was to participate in and lead public festivities after military victories. One of the signifiers of this is the word *tōp* (plural: *tuppîm*), which is usually translated "tambourine," but Meyers argues convincingly to render it "hand-drum." The occurrences of this word in the biblical references reveal, she concludes, a unique musical tradition in which the female musicians played a central role and even possessed public power during the performance.[22] Here, one question still remains to be addressed: if women are the primary victory singers, dancers, and drummers, then why does the extant text add the song by Moses and the sons of Israel? When music is to be performed by the female choir, why are Moses and his male folks shown to join the choir (note also Barak joining with Deborah for the song in Judg. 5:1)?[23] One possibility is that the androcentric author or redactor stole this unique female tradition. But it is unclear how making the male leader a singer can elevate men's (i.e., Moses') status over women's (Miriam's) status in that cultural context. In 1 Sam. 18:6–7 only women sing for David and Saul, and though David himself must have been a gifted musician, the fact that the text does not include him or any other men in that choir neither degrades nor elevates men's status. Hence, it is more plausible to reason that the author/redactor of the Exodus text intended to imply that the chorus was to be performed by all of the community members, both female and male. Admittedly, the patriarchal bias does exist in the background of the contextual depiction of Moses' predominant role over Miriam (Miriam's song follows his and has a much shorter form). By having two songs in one chapter and one context, however, the extant form conveys the concept of community togetherness in the joy of victory through Yahweh's might, celebrated by all the people of Israel.

Last, but not least, concerning the setting and conceptuality of the correlation of the two songs and two leader-prophets over against many other typically male-oriented texts, what is unique and peculiar about these songs? Is there an implication for the source of power, strength, and solidarity in music? In the setting of these songs, the reader can easily imagine the communal event where Moses and Miriam are surrounded by the fellow chorus members and the audience. In other words, these songs depict the affairs of the community in that both women and men take essential parts. When the community joins together for the common songs and celebration, there is a strong sense of solidarity. Gender divisions can function for the sake of making the

22. Carol L. Meyers, "Of Drums and Damsels: Women's Performance in Ancient Israel," *BA* 54 (1991) 16–27.
23. I owe this insight to Nancy R. Bowen.

music harmonious and the dances more adoring. Toward the more fundamental common goals they can join their voices, hands, and hearts together — warriors and singers, leaders and congregation, mothers and fathers. Likewise, in every group there is a figure who leads and influences the group. In this text Moses and Miriam (as prophets!) share the leadership: Moses leads the brothers and Miriam leads the sisters. In the leadership of these two (with that of an implicit third leader, Aaron), mutual complementarity functions as a key model for the unity and efficiency of the entire community.[24]

To summarize, Miriam's status as prophet implies its significant concept of balance as a counterpart to Moses, also a prophet. Although the Song of Miriam comes after the much longer Song of Moses, the two songs build a nice duet in that these songs represent two different groups of people joining together for the same goal and purpose. Even the textual formation indicates the compositional significance of the Song of Miriam, adjoined by its narrative (15:19 for 15:20–21) in parallel with the Song of Moses (14:26–31 for 15:1–18). Together, they depict the sounds of harmony among different leaders, groups, and genders united by shared faith, experience, and solidarity. In that unity, though Moses assumes a more prominent role, the two songs imply the concept of complementarity of Moses and Miriam, not only brother and sister, but also coleaders and copartners.

Judges 4–5

The song of Deborah and Barak can be connected to the Songs of Moses and Miriam with this fact (among others): both are considered to be ancient, if not archaized. In addition to their antiquity these songs share motifs of Yahweh's victory and deliverance of the Israelites with the instrumentality of heroic leaders. In the book of Judges the leaders are commonly called "judges" (שׁפט), and their role was similar to that of Moses in rescuing, delivering, and leading the people of Israel. In Judges 4–5 Deborah is depicted as the leader of Israel (4:4, "At that time Deborah...was *judging* Israel"). Peculiarly, however, Deborah is also called a "prophetess" (cf. Miriam in Exod. 15:20), and her direct leadership of Israel was not so much that of a military liberator as it was that of a visionary seer and spokesperson for Yahweh. The role of a military commander is given to Barak. Hence, it is not certain whether it is Deborah or Barak who should be given the title of "judge" as the main

---

24. Setel ("Exodus," 32) notes, "In biblical references outside of Exodus (Num. 12:2; Micah 6:4), Miriam is grouped with Moses and Aaron in such a way as to suggest that the three of them formed a leadership triad."

protagonist. It is precisely this question that I want to reexamine with regard to the relationship and dual leadership of Deborah and Barak.

First, the plot of Judges 4 signals the conceptuality of Deborah's predominant status and superior role in comparison with Barak. If Moses receives the primary spotlight in comparison with Miriam in Exodus 15, in Judges 4 it is Deborah who marginalizes Barak. The most explicit evidence is the sharp contrast between Deborah's courage and Barak's cowardice. Throughout the narrative Deborah's courage in boldly delivering Yahweh's command to Barak sharply contrasts Barak's wimpy hesitance in carrying out the command. Deborah is the initiator and Barak the reluctant follower. Deborah is the strategist and Barak the executor.[25] Against this background the story develops with the subtle implication that the real heroic honor goes to the women, Deborah and Jael, as opposed to the men, Barak and Sisera. Moreover, even as Deborah is the initiator of the entire military strategy, at the beginning stage Barak is endowed with the promise and honor of victory, into whose hand Yahweh will give Sisera (4:7). In the immediate response to Barak's conditional attitude, however, Deborah delivers the message of an altered plan: "Yahweh will give Sisera into the hand of a woman," not that of Barak (4:9). The story concludes, ironically, with the valiant acts of Jael, a woman with wit and a brave heart, who encounters Barak and shows him the already slain Sisera (4:22). Accordingly, the reader can sense from the movement of the plot that Deborah, along with other women of courageous deeds, deserves special and more significant attention than Barak. It is no wonder that this passage is considered an exception to the typically patriarchal culture of the Hebrew Bible. In the narrative (Judges 4) that offers a setting for the subsequent song (Judges 5) the reader finds an unusual and unexpected concept of the status of women, one that ironically surpasses that of men.

Second, despite the evident hierarchical interrelationship between Deborah and Barak, there is another hidden signifier that depicts the concept of teamwork and mutuality. Throughout the two chapters the texts almost unequivocally convey the message that the readers/

---

25. It should be noted that Arie van der Kooij illustrates a parallel between the hierarchical relationship of Deborah and Barak and that of Samuel and the "failing" Saul. According to this view the place where Deborah is said to dwell ("between Ramah and Bethel in the hill country of Ephraim," Judg. 4:5) is strikingly similar to the home of Samuel in Ramah (1 Sam. 7:17). Also, the depiction of Deborah as prophet and judge (Judg. 4:4) is remarkably similar to that of Samuel ("prophet," 1 Sam. 3:20; "judge," 1 Sam. 7:15f.). By the same principle, just as the depiction of Deborah parallels Samuel, so is the description of Barak as the military leader comparable to that of Saul, the "failing" leader. See Arie van der Kooij, "On Male and Female Views in Judges 4 and 5," in B. Becking and M. Dijkstra, eds., *On Reading Prophetic Texts: Gender-Specific and Related Studies in Memory of Fokkelien van Dijk-Hemmes* (Leiden: Brill, 1996) 141.

audience should pay attention to both Deborah and Barak. It is as though the author consistently intended to balance the two protagonists. Or alternatively, we may argue that to the community and audience their heroes were not one, but two, if not three (Deborah, Barak, and Jael). In other words, within the dynamic interaction between Deborah and Barak there are implicit signifiers that suggest the concepts of mutual respect, negotiation, and tolerance based on each other's merits and concerns. There are open talks between the two. Deborah instructs and Barak reacts. Deborah responds and Barak follows through. From the communications of the two characters in the narrative the reader may imagine the scene of a whining son talking with his mother. The mother constantly listens to the son and embraces him. It is no surprise that we find in the song the naming of Deborah as "a mother in Israel" (5:7). Presumably, the motherhood of Deborah would anticipate the fatherhood of Barak as a coleader. In a deliberate shift of the plot, however, Barak, overshadowed by more courageous and more mature women, is portrayed as a yet-to-grow up child, an image that intensifies the sovereign Godhood of Yahweh.[26]

In the flows, ironies, and changes of the narrative motifs the concept of teamwork remains in that both leaders reveal their willingness to be open to and cooperate with each other. Together they build a team with mutual respect, communication, and correction. The only peculiarity is that in spite of the reciprocal relationship, Barak remains a follower. These hidden implications of mutually interactive dialogue between the two can be found in the subsurface level of the texts. Athalya Brenner, in her study reconstructing the "infrastructure" of the plot in Judges 4–5, delineates the carefully designed "conceptual parallel":

> The structural complementarity is the message. Such is the world, such are historical events, such is society, that synchronous cooperation of the divine and the human — with a distinction or division but without an exclusion or bias of sex and gender — is a prerequisite for the successful fruition of the shared effort. This is demonstrated by the two strata of the single narrative presented to us by Judges 4 and 5.[27]

---

26. In a similar way Athalya Brenner explicates the ironic downfall of Sisera before Jael, whose relation to Sisera in that dramatic scene depicts aspects of a mother in a complex way: "Sisera sinks down (thrice), falls (thrice), and lies (once) between — so the Hebrew — Jael's legs. The unmistakable sexual connotations have an additional echo: they are reminiscent of a natural birth scene, when the woman sits on her haunches and the baby has to be caught by somebody, so that it does not fall to the ground (cf. Gen. 30.3). Thus Jael embodies aspects of both Deborah and Sisera's mother: she is a 'good' mother for us Israelites, a 'bad' one for Sisera; sexually attractive, like the would-be Israelite spoils of Sisera, but active rather than passive" ("A Triangle and a Rhombus in Narrative Structure: A Proposed Integrative Reading of Judges 4 and 5," in A. Brenner, ed., A Feminist Companion to Judges [FCB 4; Sheffield: JSOT Press, 1993] 103).

27. Brenner, "A Triangle and a Rhombus," 108.

According to her study the structure of these texts does not exhibit the concept of imbalance or exclusion of one plot (character), gender (male versus female), or chapter (Judges 4 versus Judges 5) over against the other. Rather, the whole structure is shaped around the underlying conceptuality that points to the complementarity of various parts, all in congeniality.

In addition, in the two chapters, whenever the names Deborah and Barak occur, both are frequently mentioned together in a pair (4:6, 9, 14; 5:1, 12, 15; cf. also 5:7, "mother in Israel," and 5:9, "commanders of Israel"). In 4:6, 9, and 14 there are exchanges of words, ideas, and plans between the two. In 5:1 the evidence of the extant text shows that the song is sung by both Deborah and Barak. In Exodus 15 there are two songs, one by Moses (and the "sons of Israel") and the other by Miriam (and the women). In Judges 5 there is only one song, but it is sung by both Deborah and Barak — at least that is what the heading of the received text conveys to the reader.[28] Likewise, in 5:12 there is a moving convocation that invokes both Deborah and Barak. It is the same with 5:15. Evidently, in all these cases the name Deborah precedes Barak. Again, these verses hint at the intention of the significance of both Deborah and Barak in their interactive leadership and celebration with teamwork and mutual openness.

Finally, the union of two distinct genders and roles is made possible also for a common goal and a greater cause. Within the very struggles for survival of the same people Deborah and Barak exemplify the concept of unity within diversity. Athalya Brenner succinctly describes this concept:

> The two worlds are different and distinct. Yet they reflect each other — hence the parallel structure. One cannot operate without the other.... The

---

28. Van der Kooij ("Male and Female Views," 143) argues for Deborah's authorship of this song. This argument is based on the several relevant evidences. Whereas Deut. 32:44 indicates that the Song of Moses in Deuteronomy 32 was said by Moses and Joshua, the credit should go to Moses. In the Song of Moses in Exodus 15, though the singers are described as both Moses and the people of Israel, the implied author is Moses. Accordingly, Deborah, whose name occurs first in the pairing with Barak, must be the supposed author of the song in Judges 5. Although this interpretation is convincing, its argument is mainly concerned about the authorship of the famous songs. The question still remains as to why the headings and other contexts express that both Deborah and Barak, just like both Moses and the "men" of Israel, sang the song together. Here, attention can be distinguished between authorship and singers. Whereas the author(s) of these songs may have been a single hero and leader, the texts clearly read that the songs were sung by more than one. Who was to sing the song in Judges 5? At least from the final redactor's point of view, therefore, this song was sung by both Deborah and Barak in the hearing of the community of both of them. The underlying concept indicates not only that Deborah assumes a more important status than Barak, but that the reader should picture the copartnership of a duet, not a solo.

combination of the usually distinct gender-and-role worlds is essential
for the victory. By dividing the cast into two formally equivalent groups,
groups that have to penetrate each other in order to be effective, the need
for male and female cooperation is emphasized in chap. 5 far beyond its
"factual," slightly pejorative counterpart version in chap. 4.[29]

For the greater goal of survival and victory the distinctions of gender
and class are reinterpreted as potentials for the various functional components of the whole of community. The text suggests the concept of
complementarity by acknowledging and respecting different functions
of the two genders. A good example is 5:12, which points out the unity
of two leaders in their distinctive functions or talents:

Deborah	*Barak*
Awake (עוּרִי עוּרִי)	Arise (קוּם)
utter a song (דַּבְּרִי־שִׁיר)	lead away your captives (שְׁבֵה שֶׁבְיְךָ)

The comparison shows a conceptual indication to distinguish different roles that Deborah and Barak should play. Deborah's role is to speak
a song as a prophet, judge, and music leader. Barak's role is to engage
in a military battle as a warrior — these quite different roles the text
puts together.[30] The text acknowledges and differentiates the functions
of the two. Yet their different functions build a conceptual harmony
and mutuality. The two leaders, who are quite distinct and different
in character, office, personality, ability, and gender, now join together in
common praise of Yahweh's deliverance of their community and people.
It is not his community or her community, but their community.

To summarize, Judges 4–5 displays unusual (in its patriarchal milieu)
concepts of the wisdom and might of female characters, which sharply
contrasts with their male counterparts. The texts also imply, however,
the concept of balance toward equality by means of the radical paradigm shift and role reversal between Deborah and Barak on the one
hand, and through compositional effort to mention the two names together on the other. Furthermore, in light of the song tradition (apart
from the Song of Hannah, a different kind of battle song) the Song of
Deborah and Barak forms a nice pairing with the Song of the Sea in Exodus 15. Both songs are sung after victory in battle. Both are considered
archaic. Both songs are preceded by historical narratives. In Exodus 15
there are two songs, one of Moses and one of Miriam, but they share

---

29. Brenner, "A Triangle and a Rhombus," 105.

30. From the perspective of comparative studies it is intriguing to note that in the
ancient history of Korea there is a similar epic of the heroic, camaraderie, and loyalty between Sun Duk, the female king, and Yu Shin Kim, the male commander-in-chief, during
the era of Shilla dynasty.

common contents and motifs. In Judges 5 there is one song, but by two heroes and leaders. Read (or sung) together, these two ancient hymnic traditions suggest a chiasm in that the leadership of Moses (male) led or joined by Miriam (female) is nicely matched with the leadership of Deborah (female) led or joined by Barak (male).[31] Though canonically set apart from each other, these unique and famous songs remotely echo each other for the concept of balance and mutuality.

New Testament

In the broader horizon of the Hebrew Bible the preceding depictions of gender relationship are quite distinct from those in other parts of the book. This is true also in the New Testament, where there are texts that depict gender mutuality and texts that depict a clear hierarchy of man over woman.

There is an example of copartnership and coleadership in Aquila and Priscilla (Acts 18; cf. Rom. 16:3; 1 Cor. 16:19; 2 Tim. 4:19). In Romans 16 ten female "coworkers" and "apostles" are mentioned. In 1 Tim. 3:11, along with the male deacons, "women deacons" or "wives" are admonished with appropriate guidances as leaders of the church. But 1 Tim. 2:8–15 (esp. v. 12) demonstrates the idea that a woman's place is under the authority of men in the church. First Corinthians 11:2–16 provides a similar portrayal of women in their hierarchical relationship to men. Admittedly, these texts must be read in their own unique contexts and ideologies. It has been argued that in the process of the textual formation the Roman ideology of gender relations was influential toward "pressing Christian women into submission to male authority and obscur[ing] the record of their earlier involvement."[32] Thus, from the outset there are apparent differences in the concepts of gender relationship in the New Testament pertaining to the role and status of women within church and society.

How, then, is Gal. 3:27–28 to be read in light of those diverse concepts? How shall we read and reconceptualize this passage for today's hermeneutic?

> For all of you who have been baptized in Christ have clothed yourselves with Christ. There is neither Jew nor Greek, there is neither slave nor free, there is no longer male and female; for all of you are one in Christ Jesus. (Gal. 3:27–28)

---

31. This observation of the correlation and balance between Exodus 15 and Judges 5 is borrowed from David N. Freedman, "Early Israel in Poetry and History" (lecture delivered at the University of California, Riverside, November 6, 1996).

32. Bart D. Ehrman, *The New Testament: A Historical Introduction to the Early Christian Writings* (New York: Oxford University Press, 1997) 341.

In this text there is a conceptual relationship between v. 27 and v. 28. The denial of ethnic, class, or gender barriers (v. 28) is grounded in people being baptized "in Christ" (v. 27).[33] Those barriers and differences are subordinated to the greater purpose of their faith and commitment to Christ. Here is the concept of equality and mutuality. In this verse today's reader may easily be reminded of the ideals of the Civil War and the emancipation of slaves. But does this passage simply negate all differences? Would we no longer find, for example, Jew or Greek, male or female? Rather, the passage implies that the dismissal of race, class, or gender barriers is confined within the primary context of the faith confession and baptism in Christ and of unity among the converts. Thus, it also means that the implicit ideology of this passage does not call for the abolition of the slavery system, just as it does not signify giving up Jewishness, Greekness, maleness, or femaleness.[34]

How, then, shall we reconceptualize this passage? What limits and potentials of the implied concepts of this passage can be relevant to our interpretation of gender relationship? In light of the concept of mutuality and balance of other texts in the Hebrew Bible and New Testament this passage can be reread to imply that in our struggle toward justice and righteousness it is important to respect one's own identity and distinctiveness.[35] In any effort to pursue equality we need to be reminded of the uniqueness of each party: togetherness cannot be

---

33. Richard N. Longenecker (*Galatians* [WBC 41; Dallas: Word, 1990] 159) writes, "Gal 3:26–29 focuses on being 'in Christ' and the new relationships that result from that status — new relationships spiritually ('sons of God,' 'clothed with Christ') and new relationships societally and culturally ('neither Jew nor Greek, slave nor free, male nor female')....Being 'in Christ' is the essence of Christian proclamation and experience."

34. For the views that differentiate the religious-soteriological dimension and the social dimension of Gal. 3:28 see, for instance, D. Boyarin, "Galatians and Gender Trouble: Primal Androgyny and the First-Century Origins of a Feminist Dilemma," *Center for Hermeneutical Studies Protocol Series* 1 (1995) 1–38; G. Röhser, "Mann und Frau in Christus: Eine Verhältnisbestimmung von Gal 3,28 und 1 Kor 11,2–16," *Studien zum Neuen Testament und seiner Umwelt* 22 (1997) 57–78; J. Moncho Pascual, "La asimetria como principio rector de la sociedad antigua," *Ciudad de Dios* 210, no. 2 (1997) 473–93.

35. Not only concerning gender relationship but also concerning Jewish-Christian dialogue one should note Marvin A. Sweeney's remark on the two traditions — two distinctive readings of the Hebrew Bible: "Although some might argue that these differences point to fundamental and irreconcilable differences between the two traditions, it is important to keep in mind that it is essential for each tradition to recognize and accept the reality of different points of view as a basis for establishing any meaningful dialogue. Although well intentioned, attempts to find a common Jewish-Christian reading of the Hebrew Bible run the risk of assimilating the distinctive identities of either or both traditions. True dialogue can take place only when both traditions can speak on the basis of their unique understanding of scripture, and acknowledge the legitimacy of their differences" ("Tanak versus Old Testament: Concerning the Foundation for a Jewish Theology of the Bible," in H. Sun and K. Eades, eds., *Problems in Biblical Theology: Essays in Honor of Rolf Knierim* [Grand Rapids: Eerdmans, 1997] 372–73).

achieved merely by mingling or collapsing together two distinct groups, but rather by mutual respect and reconciliation, and oftentimes by one yielding to the "disenfranchised" other. At the same time, it is important to find, identify, and reinterpret those sometimes explicit and sometimes hidden ideals of equality in Christ in a broader sense. This is where the dynamic interaction between the text and the reader (e.g., reader-response hermeneutics of rereading) can be a significant factor of Bible reading in that the conceptual ideals of repudiating barriers become essential parts of the meanings of Gal. 3:27–28. Admittedly, Paul, like Jesus, would not have urged a social revolution on this basis. Nevertheless, later tradents were and will be wrestling with that concept — the ideals of the equality of slave and free, male and female — in that someone could say, "They are to be equal," not only in the spiritual realm but also in the social and political reality.

CASES OF THE HERMENEUTIC

Reconceptualization of Biblical Cases

This study of the portrayals of women and men and the conceptuality of their significance both in ancient society and in the theology of the Hebrew Bible shows various implications of the roles and functions of men and women. On the one hand, these implications indicate conceptual differences or conflicts concerning the gender relationship within the ideological plurality of the Hebrew Bible. On the other hand, they also offer the hermeneutical quest for application of the encounter between the biblical concepts and the relevant events or issues of today's world. In light of the multiple concepts within the Hebrew Bible and the hermeneutical encounters, what can we draw from the preceding examinations for the interpretation of both critical limits and positive potentials on the issue of gender complementarity?

First, we have observed that biblical texts display not monolinear but plural, and at times contending, concepts and ideologies of gender relations. As is well known, many biblical stories and narratives are deeply embedded in the cultural milieu of patriarchal androcentrism. There are, however, other texts and hidden implications that signify understanding toward balance, mutuality, and equality. We have dealt with a good example in two ancient songs (Exodus 15 and Judges 5), which depict a biblical worldview of dual leadership by male and female heroes. The two songs independently denote the idea of gender complementarity, along with the idea of mutual interrelatedness in a harmonious chorus of solidarity. The two songs, read together canonically, connote the idea of gender balance and mutuality. There are phrases, texts, and ideologies that depict patriarchal androcentrism in a hierarchical division of male and female. Yet there are also phrases, texts, and ideologies that signify mutuality in balance. What shall we, the readers, do with this collection of plural theologies and ideologies in the Hebrew Bible and the New Testament? It is the reader's task to read and analyze the texts, and then to reread, reinterpret, and find their relevance for the issues, hopes, and struggles of today's society.

Second, even though the conceptual aspects of the role and status of women in the studied texts differ from typically patriarchal concepts in the Hebrew Bible, these women represent exceptional cases. Both Miriam and Deborah are leaders of the people. Together with their partners they are truly a few good men and women. Nonetheless, these rare heroic persons demonstrate positive implications in such a way that they are not simply exceptions but models for the readers and audiences to carry into their own life settings. Amidst, or in contrast with, the divergent concepts of gender relationship, these stories provide exemplary ideals that challenge the status quo of the patriarchal culture and thereby carry their own ideological influences to later generations, today and tomorrow.

Third, the texts examined suggest ideologies and concepts more in theory than in praxis. We need to be reminded of the limitations of theory in the face of reality. Has there been any time in human history in which equality was actually and fully achieved? If so, equality by whose measure? What is said in the texts remains a good case, but how will it meet our problems? As a response, the conceptual aspects of the present texts can offer some constructive principles, however theoretical or utopian these may be. Admittedly, the depiction of gender balance from the two ancient songs in the Hebrew Bible does show its own limitations in terms of its cultural setting and its location among androcentric biblical texts. Likewise, the immediate meaning of Galatians 3 is limited to its baptismal metaphor, and is not literally inclusive of the ideology of social reform. Nonetheless, the concept of balance and mutuality in line with multiple concepts is significant for the readers in their engagement with the text. As a text can have more than one meaning, so the readers need to weigh, compare, and correct the plural meanings of a text vis-à-vis other texts in the Bible. For instance, the concept of God's love toward all humanity and living creatures may not be an immediate or explicit concept in many biblical stories. Nevertheless, the ideals of God's *agapē* love, not only in the New Testament but already in the Hebrew Bible, have been a source of human freedom and justice in our history (as in the post–Civil War emancipation of slaves). The concept is there, but it often takes a long time to be acted out. By the same token, the ideals of gender equality can be found in those examined biblical texts. Though the road may be steep and long, it has been and will be rewarding to continue to pursue those ideals. That endeavor requires a mutual awareness of the need to improve and change, and a willingness to strive toward balance. As in Taoism, neither *yin* nor *yang* is bad, but when their balance is broken, as in patriarchal androcentrism, a problem arises.

As a result we can add several ways to implement praxis, which then can be explored, evaluated, and corrected. One is the need to change the perspectives of both parties through education. The awareness of problems should arise in both parties — at least for some members of each party — both the dominant and the dispossessed. It starts with an awareness of problems and the audacious, conscientious, and authentic change of perspectives. Jay McDaniel argues for the significance of such awareness in theology and education:

> When theologians speak, few academicians listen. But some forms of Christian theology do have considerable influence outside secular colleges and universities. They influence faculties in seminaries, who in turn influence church leaders, who in turn influence practicing religious communities.... In this way one of the least prestigious of intellectual endeavors in the academy is one of the most influential in the world. And for this reason it is immensely important that theology seek to become postpatriarchal.[36]

This change of perspectives then intricately leads to a paradigm shift, role reversal, or other similar actions. As perspectives and worldviews are changed and transformed, alternative practices need to be exercised in the forms of yielding, role reversal, and teamwork. Afterwards, and all along, there needs to be a pursuit of dialogue and openness toward improvement, because change toward equality, or rather, balance, cannot and should not be rigid, but should be as fluid and multidimensional as the complexity of our society. Hence, a brief discussion of this last element is in order.

Finally, in those cases in which the biblical texts demonstrate the concepts of solidarity of the people within a community, there still remains the issue of multicommunal hermeneutic. This is particularly true in our ever shrinking global environment. In talking about the solidarity of the community, questions may arise. Whose community are we talking about? Which community and for whom? The biblical examples call for the concepts of communal solidarity both within and beyond one's own existence. For example, while reflecting on the concept of the exodus from Egypt, what shall we say about the conquest of

---

36. Jay B. McDaniel, *Of God and Pelicans: A Theology of Reverence for Life* (Louisville: Westminster John Knox, 1989) 117.

Canaan? While pondering ethnic solidarity, what shall we say about the
fate of other nations? While reading and retelling the heroics of Moses,
Miriam, Deborah, and Barak, how shall we regard the Egyptians and
Canaanites? Will the concerns for race and class be extended to the
concerns for kindred creatures and environment? It is of no minor importance that feelings of solidarity must involve concern and sensitivity
for the outside groups as well. We need to be reminded of the complexities of reality in that a member of one party may be easily regarded as
a member of a second party by virtue of another factor (race, gender,
class, etc.), then also of a third party, and so on. Pui-lan Kwok takes
full account of this multidimensional awareness in her exemplification
of "postcolonial reading" of "multiple identities" of a woman:

> A postcolonial reading insists that a woman should not be treated solely
> as a sexualized subject, because her identity is also shaped by her class,
> language, ethnicity and so on. Thus, a feminist reading should not simply
> emphasize the sex-gender system that is at work in the story, but also pay
> attention to the intersection of class, race, ethnicity and other factors.[37]

This multidimensional awareness and sensitivity should encompass all
aspects of community — gender, ethnicity, class, religion, geography,
and many more. When a form of solidarity within a specific group or
community is built, the people must be alert to the new need and new
ideology that may arise from its accomplishment and consequence. In
this dynamically fluid awareness there can be an ever changing and
ever improving struggle toward solidarity, teamwork, and equality.

Encounter with Today's World

For the encounters between the biblical cases and relevant issues or
events in today's society, let me deal with two worlds familiar to me,
Korean and American. First, the concept of mutual respect in gender
relationship from these well-known biblical texts can speak to current
situations in Korean society. Despite socioeconomic growth there still
remain many women who receive no attention, let alone respect, from
society. Also, some women do get attention, but only in a superficial

---

37. Pui-lan Kwok, "Overlapping Communities and Multicultural Hermeneutics," in
A. Brenner and C. Fontaine, eds., *A Feminist Companion to Reading the Bible: Approaches,
Methods and Strategies* (FCB 11; Sheffield: Sheffield Academic Press, 1997) 215. See also
the examples of the womanists' effort to include other groups within their solidarity —
for example, Karen Baker-Fletcher's definition of "womanist": "It is important not to ignore [Alice] Walker's inclusion of all women of color, and not only Black women, in her
definition of 'womanist.' Such inclusion indicates to me that Black womanists must be
open to and in solidarity with cultural perspectives of other women of color." (Karen
Baker-Fletcher and Garth Kasimu Baker-Fletcher, *My Sister, My Brother: Womanist and Xodus God-Talk* [Bishop Henry McNeal Turner/Sojourner Truth Series in Black Religion 12;
Maryknoll, N.Y.: Orbis, 1997] 5).

way as peripheral citizens. Quite often they are pressured to be subordinate to men by custom, culture, or law. The exemplifications and ideals of mutual openness and complementarity can continue to convey important messages concerning these perennial problems. Moreover, they require more urgent attention in the church, politics, and academia on the one hand, and in society, culture, and families on the other. Within the church, for instance, we can model the coleadership of Moses and Miriam, Deborah and Barak. As a step toward this, the issue of women's ordination needs to be addressed in the wide range of the ecclesiastical setting, especially in the context of Korean and Korean American churches. Even if, theoretically, in rules and regulations, Korean church leadership adopts the ordination of women, it is another matter for male parishioners to accept and respect the leadership of a female minister and for male leaders to consider female leaders as colleagues.[38] Hence, there need to be still more calls for a paradigm shift to mutual openness and respect. This requires efforts to find and establish role models in copartnership and coleadership among church leaders in pursuit of gender complementarity and mutuality. This also requires an open dialogue between the two gender groups in pursuit of the greater goals of teamwork in the ministry beyond self-serving purposes of a single group.[39] This dialogue must include conversation between believing communities and their nonbelieving neighbors. Again, the concepts of yielding, role reversal, and change of perspectives will be necessary, starting with the church leadership. Otherwise, when a rapidly chang-

---

38. For an example of the ongoing patriarchal biases of many churches in Korea note the comment of Hyun Kyung Chung (*Struggle to Be the Sun Again: Introducing Asian Women's Theology* [Maryknoll, N.Y.: Orbis, 1990] 12): "Citing the Bible, many male clergy said that women should be quiet in the church; therefore women's ordination and public leadership were denied. If women wanted to be of any good, they should suffer as Christ suffered on the cross." Sang Nim Ahn ("Feminist Theology in the Korean Church," in V. Fabella and S. Park, eds., *We Dare to Dream: Doing Theology as Asian Women* [Maryknoll, N.Y.: Orbis, 1990) 131, 133] states, "One of the reasons most Korean Churches do not ordain women is that Jesus and his disciples were all men.... The church is the body of Christ, so men and women should participate equally in all its activities, committees and gatherings. We have to change our attitudes, customs and systems to enable men and women to work together in decision-making and in activities of services. As a result, many women elders and ministers should be ordained and they should be able to find places to serve without difficulty, and they should receive equal treatment with men in similar conditions."

39. Here, one should note Karen Baker-Fletcher's remark for the importance of dialogue both within and outside the same gender group: "For me, this suggests that there will be times when women will need to meet separately to discuss particular issues relating to women. The same is true for men. But it is also important for women and men to come together and engage in conversation with each other about their particular understandings of spiritual development in order (1) to understand differences and (2) to discover and share some common themes" (Baker-Fletcher and Kasimu Baker-Fletcher, *My Sister, My Brother,* 166).

ing society and culture invade the church, more confusion may result in those communities of faith that are not ready for such change.

In addition, concerning current situations in the United States, the beauty of multiethnic groups living together inevitably entails a multi-dimensional awareness and dialogue.[40] And indeed there needs to be constant awareness of and alertness to the multidimensional and complex interrelationship of peoples and communities. So often it is easy to pursue the solidarity of a single group. This is especially the case when there is an urgent need for that group to survive and acquire rights of which it has been deprived. At the same time, however, just as each context is different for its unique situation, acquiring the rights of one group has to account for other groups. In a complex society, commonly called "a melting pot" or "a salad bowl," being open to and aware of the needs of other groups can be essential steps toward the ideals of balance and equality. The pursuit of justice and righteousness may be achieved more easily through solidarity within the same gender, race, and class. Biblical concepts, however, at least in view of what we have retrieved and reconceptualized from the studied texts, also imply that a genuine sense of solidarity as fellow human beings must meet its fulfillment beyond the boundaries of gender, race, class, and so on. However difficult or utopian this task may be, the hidden norms of balance, complementarity, equality, mutual respect, and teamwork can all point to the wider range of openness through dialogue and the willingness to take courage for a greater cause, learn from and share with each other's needs, and correct oneself for the sake of the other.

CONCLUSION

Biblical portrayals of gender relationships vary, just as their depictions of other relationships are manifold. Amidst those diverse perspectives, however, is a common struggle that moves toward the manifestation of God's presence with justice and righteousness. Concerning the struggle regarding gender relationship, biblical texts warn us to be cautious in our interpretation but also encourage us to go forward on our journey. Those positive ideals of the studied texts give us faith and hope that the Bible can and should continue to be relevant to us. What, then, can we learn from the limits and potentials of those texts that display gender

---

40. Delores S. Williams (*Sisters in Wilderness: The Challenge of Womanist God-Talk* [Mary-knoll, N.Y.: Orbis, 1993] 203) writes, "Since feminists and womanists come from many cultures and countries, womanist-feminist dialogue and action may well provide some of the necessary resources. Recognizing and honoring our differences and commonalities can lead in directions we can perhaps both own."

mutuality in terms of today's world, religious communities, and ministries? Finding the limitations can offer sound warnings for us to be constantly aware of the inevitable gap between theory and praxis and sensitive toward others within the complex relations of ethnic diversity, privileged versus underprivileged, male and female, and peoples with diverse religious backgrounds. Finding the potentials can present tangible goals and procedures that we may engage for the tasks of ongoing adaptation, change, and improvement, however idealistic or utopian they may be.[41] In the dynamic hermeneutical relationship between those limits and potentials the task for us is to build a chorus of various voices, as diverse elements complement one another to produce an exceptional harmony that a single element cannot make.[42] In that chorus another important task is to listen to other members as much as to sing one's own part fully and correctly. Such tasks, undertaken in pursuit of the goal of togetherness through dynamic interaction among the diverse members of the chorus, are indeed part of a journey worthwhile to take and share.

BIBLIOGRAPHY

Ahn, Sang Nim. "Feminist Theology in the Korean Church." In *We Dare to Dream: Doing Theology as Asian Women*. Ed. Virginia Fabella and Sun Ai Lee Park. Maryknoll, N.Y.: Orbis Books, 1990.

Bach, Alice. "Reading Allowed: Feminist Biblical Criticism Approaching the Millennium." *Currents in Research: Biblical Studies* 1 (1993).

Baker-Fletcher, Karen, and Garth Kasimu Baker-Fletcher. *My Sister, My Brother: Womanist and Xodus God-Talk*. Maryknoll, N.Y.: Orbis Books, 1997.

Brenner, Athalya. "A Triangle and a Rhombus in Narrative Structure: A Proposed Integrative Reading of Judges 4 and 5." In *A Feminist Companion to Judges*. Ed. A. Brenner. Sheffield: JSOT Press, 1993.

Chung, Hyun Kyung. *Struggle to Be the Sun Again: Introducing Asian Women's Theology*. Maryknoll, N.Y.: Orbis Books, 1990.

---

41. For an exemplary goal for the ideals note Elisabeth Schüssler Fiorenza's call for the pursuit of "the practice and vision of the discipleship of *equals* which inspires those women *and* men in biblical religion who struggle for liberation from patriarchal oppression" (*But She Said: Feminist Practices of Biblical Interpretation* [Boston: Beacon, 1992] 5 [italics added]).

42. Sharon H. Ringe's proclamation deserves our (i.e., both female and male) attention: "Interpretation is therefore best done as a community project, where the voices of poor women and rich women, white women and women of color, single women and married women, women from one's own country and from other parts of the world, lesbians and heterosexual women can all be heard, if not in person, at least in their writings. With the involvement of many voices, the chorus of interpretation can begin to convey the rich texture of the biblical traditions themselves" ("When Women Interpret the Bible," in Newsom and Ringe, eds., *Women's Bible Commentary*, 7).

Clines, David J. A. *Interested Parties: The Ideology of Writers and Readers of the Hebrew Bible.* JSOTSup 205. Sheffield: Sheffield Academic Press, 1995.

Cross, Frank M., and David N. Freedman. "The Song of Miriam." *JNES* 14 (1955).

Dijk-Hemmes, Fokkelien van. "Some Recent Views on the Presentation of the Song of Miriam." In *A Feminist Companion to Exodus to Deuteronomy.* Ed. A. Brenner. Sheffield: Sheffield Academic Press, 1994.

Exum, J. Cheryl. " 'Mother in Israel': A Familiar Figure Reconsidered." In *Feminist Interpretation of the Bible.* Ed. L. M. Russell. Philadelphia: Westminster Press, 1985.

Fewell, Danna N. "Reading the Bible Ideologically: Feminist Criticism." In *To Each Its Own Meaning: An Introduction to Biblical Criticisms and Their Applications.* Ed. S. L. McKenzie and S. R. Haynes. Louisville: Westminster John Knox, 1999.

Frankel, Ellen. *The Five Books of Miriam: A Woman's Commentary on the Torah.* New York: G. P. Putnam's Sons, 1996.

Knierim, Rolf P. "On Biblical Theology." In *The Quest for Context and Meaning: Studies in Biblical Intertextuality in Honor of James A. Sanders.* Ed. Craig A. Evans and Shemaryahu Talmon. Leiden: Brill, 1997.

———. *The Task of Old Testament Theology: Substance, Method, and Cases.* Grand Rapids: Eerdmans, 1995.

———. "On the Task of Old Testament Theology." In *A Biblical Itinerary: In Search of Method, Form, and Content — Essays in Honor of George W. Coats.* Ed. Eugene E. Carpenter. JSOTSup 240. Sheffield: Sheffield Academic Press, 1997.

Kwok, Pui-lan. "Overlapping Communities and Multicultural Hermeneutics." In *A Feminist Companion to Reading the Bible: Approaches, Methods and Strategies.* Ed. A. Brenner and C. Fontaine. Sheffield: Sheffield Academic Press, 1997.

McDaniel, Jay B. *Of God and Pelicans: A Theology of Reverence for Life.* Louisville: Westminster John Knox, 1989.

Meyers, Carol. *Discovering Eve: Ancient Israelite Women in Context.* New York: Oxford University Press, 1988.

———. "Of Drums and Damsels: Women's Performance in Ancient Israel." *BA* 54 (1991).

Newsom, Carol A., and Sharon H. Ringe, eds. *The Women's Bible Commentary.* Louisville: Westminster John Knox Press, 1992.

Pixley, Jorge V. *On Exodus: A Liberation Perspective.* Trans. R. R. Barr. Maryknoll, N.Y.: Orbis Books, 1987.

Schüngel-Straumann, Helen. "On the Creation of Man and Woman in Genesis 1–3: The History and Reception of the Texts Reconsidered." In *A Feminist Companion to Genesis.* Ed. A. Brenner. Sheffield: Sheffield Academic Press, 1993.

Schüssler Fiorenza, Elisabeth. *But She Said: Feminist Practices of Biblical Interpretation.* Boston: Beacon, 1992.

Sweeney, Marvin A. "Tanak versus Old Testament: Concerning the Foundation for a Jewish Theology of the Bible." In *Problems in Biblical Theology: Essays in Honor of Rolf Knierim.* Ed. Henry T. C. Sun and Keith L. Eades. Grand Rapids: Eerdmans, 1997.

Trible, Phyllis. *God and the Rhetoric of Sexuality.* Philadelphia: Fortress, 1978.

van der Kooij, Arie. "On Male and Female Views in Judges 4 and 5." In *On Reading Prophetic Texts: Gender-Specific and Related Studies in Memory of Fokke-lien van Dijk-Hemmes.* Ed. Bob Becking and Meindert Dijkstra. Leiden: Brill, 1996.

Williams, Delores S. *Sisters in Wilderness: The Challenge of Womanist God-Talk.* Maryknoll, N.Y.: Orbis Books, 1993.

17

Liberation Theology and the Bible:
A Methodological Consideration
A Response to J. Severino Croatto
Wonil Kim

Arthur McGovern has noted four distinct themes that recur most frequently in liberation theology's use of the Bible: "God as liberator, with the Exodus as a special prototype; God's command to 'do justice,' reflected in the denunciations of the prophets; Jesus, liberation, and the kingdom of God; and Jesus and the confrontations in his life which gave a 'political dimension' to his actions."[1] As a methodological test case, I will examine J. Severino Croatto, a liberationist and an Old Testament scholar in Buenos Aires, as he builds his methodological case on the first of these categories: "God as liberator, with the Exodus as a special prototype." I must make it clear, however, that Croatto is only one of many liberationist biblical scholars. His method, therefore, does not represent liberation theology's diverse approaches to the Bible in their entirety. I have chosen Croatto because his methodology represents a particular perspective that is pertinent to the discussion of methodology of Jewish Bible/Old Testament theology. Thus, my critique of Croatto is not tantamount to a critique of liberation theology's appropriation of the Bible in general.

Long before liberation theology emerged, Ernest Wright's phrase had become a truism: "history is the chief medium of revelation."[2] This axiom, of course, reflects the long-established tradition of *Heilsgeschichte*, to which Wright belongs. As Albrektson[3] and Childs[4] point out, "revelation in history" is stressed in contrast with an alternative view of how revelation takes place, namely, through the word, or through a static, propositional doctrine of eternal truth. The classic Protestant view of

---

1. A. McGovern, "The Bible in Latin American Liberation Theology," in N. Gottwald, ed., *The Bible and Liberation: Political and Social Hermeneutics* (Maryknoll, N.Y.: Orbis, 1984) 462.

2. G. E. Wright and Reginald H. Fuller, *The Book of the Acts of God: Christian Scholarship Interprets the Bible* (Garden City, N.Y.: Doubleday, 1960) 13.

3. B. Albrektson, *History and the Gods* (Lund: Gleerup, 1967) 11–13.

4. B. S. Childs, *Biblical Theology in Crisis* (Philadelphia: Westminster, 1970) 39–40.

the divine word in the Bible has given way to this other concept of revelation that emphasizes "the action of God in history, his revelation in events."

Gerhard von Rad, the chief proponent of *Heilsgeschichte,* therefore does not hesitate to call the Old Testament "a history book,"[5] and an adherent of the von Rad school, Bernhard Anderson, finds the most distinctive feature of the Jewish people in their "sense of history."[6] He asserts that "if historical memory were destroyed, the Jewish community would soon dissolve."[7] This historical memory, simply put, is the memory of what God has done for and in the community. The Old Testament, according to Anderson, "is the narration of God's action."[8] Among many of God's actions, the event of the exodus stands out as by far the most important occurrence in Israel's history. Thus, Ernest Wright notes,

> At the center of Israel's faith was this Supreme act of divine love and grace. The very existence of the nation was due solely to this act; the beginning of Israel's history as a nation was traced to this miraculous happening. In confessions of faith it is the central affirmation.... Who is God? For Israel it was unnecessary to elaborate abstract terms and phrases.... It was only necessary to say that he is the "God who brought thee out of the land of Egypt, out of the house of bondage" (Ex. 20:2).[9]

Thus, by the time of the Medellín conference,[10] and by the time Cone[11] and Gutiérrez[12] first published their works, "history" as the main category of biblical theology had been well established. In this milieu students of the Old Testament had already recognized the exodus as one of the most important events, if not the central event, that shaped Old Testament traditions. And liberation theology's affinity to the legacy of the *Heilsgeschichte* school has been recognized.[13] Liberation

---

5. Gerhard von Rad, "Typological Interpretation of the Old Testament," in *Essays on Old Testament Hermeneutics,* ed. Claus Westermann, Eng. trans. ed. James Luther Mays (Atlanta: John Knox Press, 1979) 25ff.

6. B. Anderson, *Understanding the Old Testament* (Englewood Cliffs, N.J.: Prentice-Hall, 1966) 2. In the 1986 edition he changes "history" to "tradition."

7. Anderson, *Understanding the Old Testament,* 2. In the 1986 edition he changes "destroyed" to "erased."

8. Anderson, *Understanding the Old Testament,* 2.

9. Wright and Fuller, *Book of the Acts of God,* 77.

10. The Second General Conference of the Latin American Bishops, held in Medellín, Colombia, in 1968, is considered not only the official beginning of liberation theology but also one of the most important events in the history of Latin American Christianity. See E. Dussel, *History and the Theology of Liberation* (Maryknoll, N.Y.: Orbis, 1976) 113.

11. J. Cone, *A Black Theology of Liberation* (Philadelphia: Lippincott, 1970).

12. G. Gutiérrez, *A Theology of Liberation* (Maryknoll, N.Y.: Orbis, 1973).

13. See, for example, Cone, *Black Theology,* 92–106. See also J. Severino Croatto, *Exodus: A Hermeneutics of Freedom* (trans. S. Attanasio; Maryknoll, N.Y.: Orbis, 1981) v. For

theology thus entered into dialogue with biblical theology dominated by the vocabulary of "history" as the main theological category, and predicated its theology on that nomenclature. Croatto's method under investigation here represents one example of this dialogue. A critique of Croatto, therefore, entails a critique of the more fundamental theological framework operating under the rubric of "history" and "narrative."

As would be expected, the "God of history" provides the "hermeneutic key" for Croatto. In the language strongly reminiscent of G. E. Wright, Croatto declares that

> the biblical God is not the God of the Sources (an object of study and of reason) but the God-of-history of which the Sources speak to us as a kerygmatic "memory" that sheds light on the God in action now. The biblical message wells up from the salvific happening — *this is the hermeneutic key* I shall hark back to again and again.[14]

Croatto thus takes "salvific happening" as the point of departure for theology, and insists that theology born of praxis is the starting point for biblical theology itself.

Croatto wrote his first systematic treatment of the biblical theme of liberation, however, in order to "contribute a few epistemological elements to the theology of liberation."[15] Salvific events are, of course, important to Croatto. But he concentrates on the question of *"how* the kerygma of liberation is treated as a theme in the Bible," because he wants to find a paradigm for our own hermeneutic process.[16] He knows that the Bible has ample data of liberation motifs, but it is an epistemology that he goes after. He wants to know how the Bible produces and develops a kerygma of liberation. Or, put another way, he wants to know how the Bible knows what it knows about the kerygma of liberation. And ultimately, he wants to know what the Bible's own epistemology tells us about how we, in turn, know the kerygma of liberation for our own time. This is the crux of his book *Exodus: A Hermeneutics of Freedom.*

The object of Croatto's study, then, is not so much the historical, salvific events as their kerygma, "the word 'signifying' the salvific events lived by Israel."[17] The chief methodology is midrashic, combined with a "Ricoeurian approach to philosophical and religious hermeneu-

---

a defense of this affinity, see C. E. Gudorf, "Liberation Theology's Use of Scripture: A Response to First World Critics," *Int* 41, no. 1 (January 1987) 10.

14. Croatto, *Exodus*, v (italics added).

15. Croatto, *Exodus*, iv.

16. Croatto, *Exodus*, iv.

17. Croatto, *Exodus*, 4.

tics."[18] In the absence of the author and the original audience, the "distanciated" text now attains a new world of its own with a possibility for different interpretations. Employing a Ricoeurian terminology to describe this textual-interpretive phenomenon — polysemy[19] — Croatto now sees the text as a reservoir of a "surplus of meaning." And as such the text renders a new world that stands "in front of it." In contrast and in addition to what traditional exegesis finds "behind" the text — such as author, original setting, traditions, and so forth — it now offers a new kerygmatic meaning standing "in front of it." To this foreground meaning of the text hermeneutics adds another meaning in the new situation of the new reader.[20]

This process operates with a "hermeneutic circularity," the key interpretive configuration for Croatto. A hermeneutic circle exists between an event and its kerygma on the one hand, and between the kerygma and a new situation on the other. An event generates a kerygma as a response to it, and the kerygma in turn spawns a hermeneutical response in a new generation of readers, and so on. In this continuing process the second circle models itself after the first one, but also goes beyond it. Thus Croatto insists that

> a hermeneutic reading of the biblical message occurs only when the reading *supersedes the first contextual meaning* (not only that of the author but also that of his first readers). This happens *through the unfolding of a surplus-of-meaning disclosed by a new question addressed to the text.*[21]

In these hermeneutic circles, then, lie the Bible's own epistemology and Croatto's method of determining "precisely what the biblical kerygma ... makes explicit and precisely what it permits us to 'explore' from our *own* perspective."[22]

Croatto senses a certain *kairos,* a "favorable moment" in today's struggle for liberation throughout the world in general, and in Latin America in particular. This, he believes, provides us with a new hermeneutical moment to address "a new question to the text."[23] Reread from this perspective the biblical text renders a new theme: liberation. And it begins with the exodus account as the "founding text" because that account is "a characteristic, provocative, creative, inexhaustible kerygmatic 'locus....' [It] models the faith of Israel.... [Without it] neither

---

18. Croatto, *Exodus,* 1. See P. Ricoeur, *Interpretation Theory: Discourse and the Surplus of Meaning* (Fort Worth: Texas Christian University Press, 1976); idem, *The Conflict of Interpretation: Essays in Hermeneutics* (Evanston, Ill.: Northwestern University Press, 1974).

19. Croatto, *Exodus,* 2.

20. Croatto, *Exodus,* 2.

21. Croatto, *Exodus,* 3.

22. Croatto, *Exodus,* 4.

23. Croatto, *Exodus,* 6–10.

Israel's faith nor the formation of its religious traditions and sacred books are understandable."[24] Hermeneutically, it provides "a *radical* da-tum...*in which* both Israel and we...must interpret God and ourselves. ...[As such,] it becomes an inexhaustible 'reservoir-of-meaning'...[and its] 'donation-of-meaning' is unlimited."[25] The exodus was "the most decisive event in [Israel's] history,"[26] and the exodus account furnishes the pivotal point around which both intrabiblical kerygma of liberation and our own hermeneutics of liberation revolve.

I reiterate that Croatto's main interest lies not so much in the event of the exodus as in the kerygmatic function of the exodus account in its midrashic, canonical development. For him, the decisive meaning of an event emerges not when it occurs but "only *after* the mediation that time effects, after it has 'donated' its recreative energy."[27] The exodus, there-fore, takes on its historical significance only when it is hermeneutically understood and expressed — "reflected upon, pondered, and explored by faith" after the fact, from the perspective of the community's present reality. And such reflection, pondering, and exploration take shape as an account of the event, in other words, in and as language. This means that the exodus finds its real import as a linguistic phenomenon of word — spoken, written, read, rewritten, and reread, always functioning as a "memory" and an "announcement."[28] It is a word-event.

In his second book, *Biblical Hermeneutics,*[29] Croatto gives a theoret-ical analysis of this linguistic aspect of liberation kerygma. Here, he places and identifies the function of the exodus account within the more comprehensive and familiar field of hermeneutics. He asserts that

> there is no such thing as a *biblical* hermeneutics distinct from a philosoph-ical, a sociological, a literary hermeneutics....There is but one general hermeneutics, with many "regional expressions." The method and phe-nomenon coincide in all cases.[30]

Croatto takes us through this route of general hermeneutics because he wants to establish a legitimate scientific basis for the biblical epistemol-ogy of liberation kerygma. He wants to ground it as a phenomenon of what is true of hermeneutics in general by showing how it works according to a science of language.[31]

---

24. Croatto, *Exodus,* 12.
25. Croatto, *Exodus,* 13.
26. Croatto, *Exodus,* 28.
27. Croatto, *Exodus,* 13.
28. Croatto, *Exodus,* 14–15.
29. J. Severino Croatto, *Biblical Hermeneutics: Toward a Theory of Reading as the Production of Meaning* (Maryknoll, NY: Orbis, 1987).
30. Croatto, *Biblical Hermeneutics,* 2.
31. Croatto, *Biblical Hermeneutics,* 9–11.

To accomplish this goal, Croatto turns to the field of signs, that is, semiotics, and more specifically, narrative semiotics.[32] He fully subscribes to one of this field's first Ricoeurian tenets: the "death" of the author. He refuses to believe that "the" meaning of a text coincides with the author's intention, and rejects any such notion as "the snare of exegetical 'historicism.' "[33] This "death" in fact extends beyond the author to the first addressees and to the "horizon of the original discourse." They all die along with the author. The "text," not the author or the author's setting, then, becomes the locus of "meaning."[34] Croatto believes "this concentration in the text [allows us] to explore the possible meanings of the text *as text*."[35] This shift then sets the text free from the constraints of the original setting to a new realm of meanings. "The author's finite horizon is replaced by a textual infinitude. The account opens up ... to a polysemy,"[36] to "a production of meaning,"[37] not because of its inherent ambiguity but because of "its capacity to say many things at once."[38]

According to the rules of semiotics, however, a text opens up only to be closed once again. Just as the grammar of language in a speech-act brings the polysemic signs into a closure of a "single direction" so that they can "say something about something,"[39] the same principle applies to a text:

> The laws of the linguistics of the sentence are repeated and broadened on the level of the account. There is actually a grammar and a syntax of the account. A text is something structured and finished ... as an organized totality [requiring its own grammar].[40]

Despite the plurality of the potential meanings of a text, therefore, an actual reading, in order to be a reading, cannot let the text say everything about everything, but only something about something — hence the need for a closure of many meanings into one. "Reading as production of meaning" calls not only for an openness to a polysemy but also for a closure to a monosemy.[41] "Every reading, therefore, involves a closure of meaning.... [There is a paradoxical] alternating play of polysemy in the text and monosemy in the reading."[42]

32. Croatto, *Biblical Hermeneutics*, 13–35.
33. Croatto, *Biblical Hermeneutics*, 21.
34. Croatto, *Biblical Hermeneutics*, 15–20.
35. Croatto, *Biblical Hermeneutics*, 17.
36. Croatto, *Biblical Hermeneutics*, 18.
37. Croatto, *Biblical Hermeneutics*, 20–35.
38. Croatto, *Biblical Hermeneutics*, 21.
39. Croatto, *Biblical Hermeneutics*, 15–20.
40. Croatto, *Biblical Hermeneutics*, 16.
41. Croatto, *Biblical Hermeneutics*, 30–35.
42. Croatto, *Biblical Hermeneutics*, 32.

Furthermore, such a closure entails "an appropriation of meaning,"[43] because a reading, at the moment of closure, "[leaves] nothing to another reading." It appropriates all other meanings of the text, generating a conflict of interpretations.[44] To be sure, a reading will itself once again become a text, and as such will "regain its polysemous value." But at the moment of reading it is nevertheless "totalizing, exclusive, seeking to appropriate *all* meanings."[45] Yet, this is a basic phenomenon of the text described by semiotics.[46] This phenomenon provides a critical support for Croatto's reading of the liberation kerygma in the Bible. He knows that the reading of the Bible by liberation theology is a totalizing, exclusive appropriation of a text. But he sees no need to apologize for it, because a liberationist does only what the rules of semiotics allow, in fact, require.[47]

Croatto thus establishes a theoretical legitimacy for liberation theology's reading of the liberation kerygma in the Bible. He appeals to semiotics to open up the text to a polysemy and to set it free not only from the traditional historical exegesis but also from any monopolizing interpretation with a finality. The text is now made available to liberation theology. Then Croatto resorts to semiotics once more, this time to its closuring character, so that liberation theology can have its fair share of an appropriation in a venture of hermeneutics.

The text that liberation theology appropriates, however, extends beyond the exodus account to the whole Bible. The closuring character of narrative semiotics applies to the entire canon. Croatto takes this canonical approach because he sees the canon as a "single text"[48] constituted by "the hermeneutic effort of the primitive church."[49] He is aware, however, of the difficulties that this single text presents, not the least of which is the problem of diversity within the canon, as well as the middle-class perspectives prevalent throughout its structure.[50] But narrative semiotics demands that "the message of a text [be] not in a fragment of the account, but in its totality, as a structure codifying a meaning."[51] A text, therefore, is "not the cumulative sum of plurality . . . [but] the unification of a linguistically coded central kerygma."[52]

---

43. Croatto, *Biblical Hermeneutics*, 30–35.
44. Croatto, *Biblical Hermeneutics*, 31.
45. Croatto, *Biblical Hermeneutics*, 40.
46. Croatto, *Biblical Hermeneutics*, 33.
47. Croatto, *Biblical Hermeneutics*, 33.
48. Croatto, *Biblical Hermeneutics*, 56–60.
49. Croatto, *Biblical Hermeneutics*, 57.
50. Croatto, *Biblical Hermeneutics*, 51.
51. Croatto, *Biblical Hermeneutics*, 54.
52. Croatto, *Biblical Hermeneutics*, 57.

At this juncture Croatto introduces probably his most important methodological stipulation. He knows that many different "semantic axes" exist in the Bible along which any number of totalizings into a single text can occur.[53] And he seems aware that the Bible on its own neither privileges any of these axes nor suggests if or how such privileging should be done. Croatto, therefore, considers it the reader's burden to decide which "semantic axes" to privilege, and how. For Croatto, this act of privileging certain semantic axes into a codified structure of meaning throughout the Bible constitutes the task of biblical hermeneutics. And this hermeneutical task requires organizing, not juxtaposing, the axes: "The hermeneutic enterprise does not consist in *listing* relevant *themes*. It consists in the *structuration* of these themes in the total work that is the Bible."[54]

As Croatto locates liberation theology's privileged axes in the kerygma of liberation, he justifies this choice on two grounds. First, to state the obvious, the kerygma of liberation constitutes a semantic axis in the Bible. The biblical text "was marked by profound experiences of suffering...oppression [and] liberation," not only in its origin but throughout its history. The kerygma of liberation, therefore, characterizes the biblical literature from its inception through its end. This is a semiotic phenomenon of the biblical text requiring a semiotic treatment: "This understanding of the Bible...falls under the rubric of a totalizing reading...through [its] 'axes of meaning,' which it offers in its condition as *single text,* or extended account."[55]

Second, privileging the liberation kerygma is justified on the ground that the oppressed themselves choose to do it in their struggle for liberation. For Croatto, this choice is more than a simple selection according to taste from a smorgasbord of theologies. For him, it has to do with the totalizing question of "to whom the Bible pertains and belongs,"[56] a matter of who "owns" the Bible:

> Inasmuch as the generality of human experience is that of suffering, wretchedness, sin, and oppression, it is not difficult to recognize that the most adequate "ownership" of the Bible, the most adequate "pertinency" for rereading the kerygma of the Bible, is with the poor. That kerygma belongs to them "preferentially" — first and foremost.[57]

Here, we see Croatto make a methodological jump from the orbit of semiotics into that of praxis. We might well have anticipated

---

53. Croatto, *Biblical Hermeneutics,* 58.
54. Croatto, *Biblical Hermeneutics,* 58 (italics added).
55. Croatto, *Biblical Hermeneutics,* 64.
56. Croatto, *Biblical Hermeneutics,* 60–65.
57. Croatto, *Biblical Hermeneutics,* 63.

this transition, because his point of departure was not semiotics but praxis. Semiotics serves only to legitimate liberation theology's reading of the Bible as a scientific phenomenon. Having accomplished this goal, Croatto now returns to a home port of liberation theology: praxis. Semiotics and praxis, of course, mutually condition, even constitute, each other. But in Croatto's scheme the former serves the latter, not vice versa.

This primacy of praxis entails a significant methodological ramification. For all he said in a book length discourse on the indispensable role of semiotics, Croatto knows its crucial limitation: semiotics describes how a hermeneutic reading of the Bible happens according to the scientific rules of language, but it does not offer any normative material that evokes a particular hermeneutic reading. That material comes from a source outside semiotics, namely, the praxis of liberation. Croatto apparently has no misgivings about this, for he reserves "the decisive point" of the hermeneutics of liberation not for semiotics but for praxis.[58] For him, "*what* really generates the rereading of the Bible, and gives it its orientation, are [not semiotics but] successive practices [of the reader]."[59]

I have noted that Croatto focuses his attention more on the biblical epistemology of liberation kerygma than on the exodus event itself. We can readily understand why he does this when we consider his chief aim: establishing a hermeneutical legitimacy for liberationists' reading of the Bible. But this should not deter us from appreciating Croatto's paramount theological concern: God who acts in history. Semiotics, at best, serves as a methodological detour for a better understanding of the God who works for and in liberation. God did liberate Israel in the exodus. God still does liberate the oppressed in today's world. Without this *theologoumenon* as the most important presupposition, Croatto has no use for hermeneutics.

For this reason the word-event of the exodus account for Croatto is no ordinary anthropological phenomenon. To the extent that the faith community perceives God's involvement in the original event, its signifying word emerges as the Word of God. It is a God-talk, a theology with a truth claim. Although Croatto does not elaborate the point at length, it is this God-factor in both the exodus and today's struggle for liberation, and not just the Bible's own epistemology with its hermeneutic circles and other semiotic phenomena, that makes our hermeneutics possible. We might even say that it mandates a herme-

---

58. Croatto, *Biblical Hermeneutics*, 65.
59. Croatto, *Biblical Hermeneutics*, 65.

neutics from us. Because of this God-factor the exodus account "is still *unconcluded:*"[60]

> [It enjoins us] to prolong the Exodus event because it was not an event solely for the Hebrews but rather the manifestation of a liberative plan of God for all peoples. According to a hermeneutical line of thinking it is perfectly possible that we might understand ourselves *from* the perspective of the biblical Exodus and, above all, that we might understand the Exodus *from* the vantage point of our situation as peoples in economic, political, social, or cultural "bondage."[61]

Croatto's hermeneutic effort "by way of semiotics," with his deft adaptation of Ricoeurian theory, has generally received favorable responses.[62] But the critics of liberation theology, of course, have disapproved the use of "the Exodus as a special prototype" before and after Croatto published his works. I will selectively examine some of these criticisms before returning to Croatto.

John Yoder's 1976 *Sojourners* article[63] seems to have laid a foundation for criticisms of this kind. In it we can anticipate elements of subsequent criticisms. One of the most frequent objections to liberation theology's appropriation of the exodus has to do with what J. Andrew Kirk labels a "horizontalizing" of the exodus account.[64] Yoder correctly perceives the exodus as Yahweh's holy war filled with miracles. As such, it was "not a matter of human strategizing," and "winning it was not an effect of preponderant human power."[65] The Israelites trusted Yahweh only with "a leap of faith," and "the Red Sea event is for the whole Old Testament the symbol of the confession that the Israelites do not lift a hand to save themselves."[66] To this we can add Kirk's observation that "any hypothetical history of a group of slaves struggling for and gaining their own freedom has been entirely eliminated from the sources (hypothetical or real) which make up the present narrative."[67] Kirk asks if a praxis-oriented interpretation can change the text's *sensus litteralis.*[68]

---

60. Croatto, *Exodus,* 14.

61. Croatto, *Exodus,* 15.

62. Even some of the favorable reviews, however, criticized his effort as being overly pedantic and theoretical, and therefore, counterproductive to the spirit of the theology that purports to have grassroots appeal. See, for example, Robert Polzin, review of J. Severino Croatto, *Biblical Hermeneutics, HBT* 10, no. 2 (December 1988) 83–85.

63. J. H. Yoder, "Exodus: Probing the Meaning of Liberation," *Sojourners* 5 (September 1976) 27–29.

64. J. A. Kirk, *Liberation Theology: An Evangelical View from the Third World* (Atlanta: John Knox, 1979) 152.

65. Yoder, "Exodus," 27.

66. Yoder, "Exodus," 27–28.

67. Kirk, *Liberation Theology,* 152.

68. Kirk, *Liberation Theology,* 150.

Norbert Lohfink, while examining the exodus tradition through the so-called credo of Deuteronomy 26, also confirms these arguments. He does so not only on textual grounds but also on the basis of his own theological and sociological presupposition: "A deed like this is impossible for human beings."[69] Curiously, however, Lohfink betrays a methodological ambivalence as he recognizes, regarding the plagues story, that every happening in history has both mundane and providential sides, and admonishes us not to let the portrayal of God's direct involvement distract us.[70]

Another criticism dealing with the language of miracles and divine intervention is raised by David Tracy, but from an opposite direction. Reflecting the sentiments of certain Marxist critics, he questions the intelligibility of liberation theology's commitment to supernaturalist language. He wants to know how Christian liberationists can continue to claim "an exclusive understanding of revelation and christology" and still make sense to the modern and postmodern secular liberationists who feel "threatened" by such a claim.[71] With this argument Tracy charges liberation theology with "neoorthodoxy." Christine Gudorf, however, poignantly responds by reminding us that the majority of the world does not fit Tracy's description of the modern experience of "Enlightenment," much less "post-modernity."[72] She sees in this kind of contention an insistence that Euro–North American concerns and methods set the definitive parameters for theological dialogues. Calling such an assertion an intellectual "imperialism,"[73] Gudorf turns Tracy's challenge around and calls for a "remythologization" of the modern world.[74]

Gudorf also includes in her countercriticism Schubert Ogden, who reproaches liberation theology for focusing on the God of ethics "without dealing at all adequately with the metaphysical being of God in himself," because religion should be about both.[75] She replies to Ogden by asking, "How many of the religions of the world would meet this

---

69. N. F. Lohfink, *Option for the Poor: The Basic Principle of Liberation Theology in the Light of the Bible* (trans. L. M. Maloney; Berkeley: BIBAL Press, 1987) 42–43.

70. Lohfink, *Option for the Poor*, 41.

71. D. Tracy, *Blessed Rage for Order: The New Pluralism in Theology* (New York: Seabury, 1975) 245.

72. Gudorf, "Liberation Theology's Use of Scripture," 13.

73. Gudorf, "Liberation Theology's Use of Scripture," 17.

74. Gudorf, "Liberation Theology's Use of Scripture," 14.

75. S. Ogden, *Faith and Freedom: Toward a Theology of Liberation* (Nashville: Abingdon, 1979) 33–34. For a systematic critique of Ogden's criticism of liberation theology see A. K. Min, *Dialectic of Salvation: Issues in Theology of Liberation* (Albany: State University of New York Press, 1989).

test?"[76] She then suggests that metaphysics is already implicit in ethics and spirituality, and a "developed" metaphysics is a step that liberation theology's new ethics and spirituality can cultivate later, as was the case with the history of Christian metaphysics.[77] Then, in her compelling appeal to the "northern" theologians, Gudorf asks them to "recognize [and respect] alternative ways of testing truth claims" in Latin America, that is, against the lived reality of liberation, within a system of mythological language and symbols.[78]

In addition to the accusation of "horizontal" (or "non-horizontal") reading, we also typically encounter the charge of liberationists' "selective" use of the Bible.[79] José Míguez Bonino, a liberationist himself, already challenged his colleagues from early on to go beyond the exodus account to find liberation motifs. Yoder picks this up to build his own case against the "exclusive" use of the exodus. Gudorf correctly points out, however, that liberation theologians generally do not devote their attention disproportionately to the exodus in comparison with other themes, such as kingdom, crucifixion, and resurrection.[80] This is true even of Croatto's book with the explicit title *Exodus*. Use of the exodus as a "prototype" does not necessarily mean an exclusive use. Perhaps the more serious charge of "selective" reading is the one made against the use of liberation kerygma itself. Kirk, for instance, argues that the *"too narrow* praxiological vantage point" of liberation theology deprives the text of its riches instead of releasing its reserve of meaning.[81]

The phenomenon of selective reading, of course, is as old as the Bible itself, and the problem of "a canon within the canon" as archaic as that of biblical interpretation. Thus, Gudorf observes that

> all use of Scripture is selective. The Bible is a collection of accounts of the actions of God toward human beings spread out over many centuries, in many historical contexts, interpreted by authors from very different perspectives. If one is to make any attempt to relate the texts to the lives of people today, one must interpret the various narratives into a coherent whole with major and minor themes. This requires selection.... In all ... approaches to Scripture one has been selective.[82]

---

76. Gudorf, "Liberation Theology's Use of Scripture," 15.
77. Gudorf, "Liberation Theology's Use of Scripture," 15.
78. Gudorf, "Liberation Theology's Use of Scripture," 15–16.
79. See, for example, Kirk, *Liberation Theology*, 151.
80. Gudorf, "Liberation Theology's Use of Scripture," 16–17.
81. Kirk, *Liberation Theology*, 151.
82. Gudorf, "Liberation Theology's Use of Scripture," 17. See also M. B. G. Motlhabi, "Liberation Theology: An Introduction," in P. G. R. de Villiers, ed., *Liberation Theology and the Bible* (Pretoria: University of South Africa, 1987) 8ff.

Gudorf is certainly not the first to notice selectivity as an inherent element of biblical hermeneutics, nor will she be the last. Croatto carries out his project, as we have seen, acutely aware of this unavoidably selective nature of reading the Bible hermeneutically. In a way, we can see his *Biblical Hermeneutics* as a response to the criticism of "selective" reading. Instead of criticizing liberationists for their "selective reading," then, we should ask the more pertinent question of the validity of any given selected axes.

Yoder presents what he calls "the way of Diaspora" as a counterparadigm to the exodus model.[83] He finds this model operating in Joseph in Egypt, Jeremiah's counsel to seek the welfare of the city in the exile, Daniel under Nebuchadnezzar, Mordecai in Persia, the New Testament church, and rabbinic Judaism. Yoder equates the individuals in this model with a "moral minority," and describes their function as that of improving the quality of the "pagan oppressor" without destroying him. They do so by forcing the evil power "to renounce its self-mythologizing religious claims and to recognize the higher sovereignty...proclaimed by the Hebrew monotheists."[84] Hermeneutically, this Diaspora model provides a paradigm for the countercommunities in today's world, a paradigm that will follow that of their predecessors.

Few will question that Yoder's hermeneutics represent a selective reading as much as that of any liberationist's. Notice a striking formal similarity between Yoder's and Croatto's methods. Like Croatto, Yoder finds certain "semantic axes" in the Bible, structures them into an appropriating "closure," and draws certain hermeneutical conclusions from the closure. Croatto chooses the "liberation axes" because he stands in solidarity with the oppressed of Latin America and accepts a revolutionary method as a moral necessity. Yoder selects his axes because he believes improving the oppressive government without destroying it is morally superior to "the paradigm of leaving Egypt and destroying Pharaoh on the way."[85] When Kirk argues that the liberationist's reading of the exodus kerygma springs from an already committed political stance,[86] he somehow neglects that his observation applies to Yoder as well. As we have seen, Croatto methodologically includes his political stance as the point of departure in his hermeneutical process. Yoder apparently does the same, albeit without giving a comparable methodological stipulation in his article.

Whose axes, then, give a better argument? We may find it tempting

---

83. Yoder, "Exodus," 29.
84. Yoder, "Exodus," 29.
85. Yoder, "Exodus," 29.
86. Kirk, *Liberation Theology,* 152.

to suppress this evaluative question in this time and age of "reader-response criticism,"[87] "reception theory,"[88] and "deconstruction." But we need to ask if we can afford to say simply that Croatto is right in his Latin American situation and Yoder is right in his North American situation, that we can keep both readings in a "dialectical tension," and go on to celebrate the rich diversity of the canon. We would participate in such a celebration only if we are ignorant of, or choose to ignore, the conflictive nature of this plurality. Each of these two scholars "appropriates" the text with his own axes diametrically opposed to those of the other. We have already heard from Croatto on this. Now Yoder:

> This Joseph/Daniel/Mordecai model is so characteristic in the Hebrew Bible that *we have to claim* that this kind of elite contribution to the reforming of the existing order is more often the fitting contribution to the pagan community than any theocratic take over.[89]

Can a responsible reader of the Bible avoid taking a side in this "conflict of interpretations"? It is one thing to admit the difficulty of the question or to suggest an alternative hermeneutics. But it is another thing to say both Croatto and Yoder can be valid, if for no other reason than that Yoder is not talking about the North American situation. Both hermeneuts are addressing the Latin American situation. A "conflict of interpretations" is not a game played on the computer keyboards of careerists. A "conflict of interpretations" is a conflict of worldviews, anthropological self-perceptions, theologies, political ideologies, and for many, a conflict of life and death. In the face of this conflict, to say that the Bible contains diverse theologies is not only saying nothing new but amounts to saying nothing at all. The diversity includes conflicts of truth claims in the name of God, demanding our response. These conflicts are already built into the definition of the hermeneutical task. To say that there is "diversity in the canon" solves nothing. It only marks the beginning of the problem.

In looking at Yoder's argument for the moral superiority of the reformist model over the revolutionist, we must express our doubt that any sane liberationist would disagree with Yoder's moral argument in abstract principle. Revolutionaries do not take up arms because they enjoy war games. Pedro Casaldáliga, a Spanish bishop living in Brazil,

---

87. See J. P. Tompkins, ed. *Reader Response Criticism: From Formalism to Post-Structuralism* (Baltimore: Johns Hopkins University Press, 1980); E. V. McKnight, *Postmodern Use of the Bible: The Emergence of Reader-Oriented Criticism* (Nashville: Abingdon, 1988); idem, *The Bible and the Reader: An Introduction to Literary Criticism* (Philadelphia: Fortress, 1985).

88. See R. C. Holub, *Reception Theory* (London: Methuen, 1984).

89. Yoder, "Exodus," 29 (italics added).

proclaims "You ask me about my faith. . . . I answer with my life"[90] not because he believes there is some mysterious virtue in shedding blood. The liberationists who turn to military means do so as the last resort in what they perceive to be an impossible situation. They think of it as a legitimate self-defense.[91] Yoder at least acknowledges that such an impossible situation does require a forceful measure when he attributes the "plagues and death" in Egypt to "the hardness of Pharaoh's heart [that] would not permit the Exodus to be peaceful."[92] He tries to justify it by saying that Yahweh, not the people, did it. This line of argument is questionable, to say the least. We need to ask since when a moral argument has depended on whether God or a human carries out a certain action, and if we can really make a moral judgment on the basis of the agent and not of the substance of the action.

Yoder also tries to discredit the liberation fronts by charging that neither their records nor "the inherent quality of their vision" gives "substance to their [postrevolution] existence" after the model of the covenant people at Mount Sinai. And he blames "the liberating elite" for imposing its revolutionary values on the unwilling population while turning itself into an oppressor.[93] The horrors of the Stalinist legacies in the former Soviet Union and elsewhere should not obscure from our view, however, the socialist vision for communal democracy.[94] Socialist struggles, including the ones in Latin America, have had their share of aberrations and corruptions, but corruption in the name of a theory is no proof of the theory's fallacy. When Yoder derogatively labels liberation theology a "guerrilla theology,"[95] then, he oversimplifies and undersells liberationists, giving the impression that he does not fully understand their visions and agenda, not to mention their existential angst.

The textual examples that Yoder cites for his "Diaspora model" also present serious exegetical problems. We need to know to what extent the individuals in the model constitute a "moral" minority, and in what sense such a minority intends to "reform" or "improve" the oppressive governments under which it suffers. Should we not wonder about Nebuchadnezzar's sweeping decree that "any people, nation, or language which speaks anything against the God of Shadrach, Meshach,

---

90. M. Randall, *Christians in the Nicaraguan Revolution* (trans. M. Velverde; Vancouver: New Star, 1983) 11.

91. For one of the best testimonies of this argument see J. P. Cannon, *Socialism on Trial* (New York: Pathfinder, 1986).

92. Yoder, "Exodus," 28.

93. Yoder, "Exodus," 29.

94. For a definitive work on Marxist vision of democracy see S. Farber, *Before Stalinism: The Rise and Fall of Soviet Democracy* (London: Verso, 1990).

95. Yoder, "Exodus," 29.

and Abednego shall be torn limb from limb, and their houses laid in ruins (נְוָלִי = garbage heap, outhouse)" (Dan. 3:29)? What "reform" or "improvement" does such a decree envision? Do we not need to question the intention of the text, conscious or unconscious, for reporting the content of such a decree? Are we to find the decree morally justifiable because it now protects the "Hebrew monotheists"? And what about "the children and the wives" of Daniel's accusers whose bones the lions crushed to pieces (Dan. 6:24)? Should we not wonder why the "believing community" has preserved such a report?

And what should we make of the book of Esther? How are we to read the last chapters (8–10) of the book? The Jewish minority goes out with a royal decree to smite "all their enemies with the sword, slaughtering and destroying them," and to do "as they [please] to those who hated them," and not before but after they were liberated, at that (Esth. 9:5). (I will leave out the question of whether the last chapters depict a simple self-defense or vengeance, although I find it difficult to argue only for the former.[96]) How do they prove their moral superiority with such behavior, much less reform or improve the Persian government or society in the fashion envisaged by Yoder? Furthermore, having no Yahweh to do the bloody work for the Jews in Persia seems to present no problem for Mordecai in this book that has not a single reference to God.[97] Nor does it seem to present problems for Yoder. Far from "not lifting a hand to save themselves," Mordecai and his company lift a legion of hands, supposedly killing more than seventy-five thousand. In view of this depiction we cannot deny "the intensity and bitterness of the Jewish-Gentile conflicts in the book . . . pictured as 'fights to the finish.' "[98] Contrary to Yoder's wish, some scholars have therefore more fittingly placed Esther in the tradition of the exodus.[99]

We cannot even call these flawed readings exegetical fallacy. It is a simple matter of reading the stories with a flagrant selectivity and carelessness, on the level of Sunday school or Bible story moralizing, at that.

---

96. See D. J. A. Clines, *Ezra, Nehemiah, Esther* (NCB; Grand Rapids: Eerdmans, 1984) 321–22.

97. I do not necessarily disagree with Clines, who sees God's role in the story becoming "more conspicuous the more he is absent" (*Ezra, Nehemiah, Esther*, 269). But this picture of God's involvement in Israel's history already marks a radical departure from the picture we have in the exodus. It more readily fits what von Rad describes as a "secularized historiography" (*Old Testament Theology* [trans. D. M. G. Stalker; 2 vols.; New York: Harper, 1962–65] 1:306–24).

98. N. Gottwald, *The Hebrew Bible: A Socio-Literary Introduction* (Philadelphia: Fortress, 1985) 562.

99. See G. I. Emmerson, "Esther," in R. J. Coggins and J. L. Houlden, eds., *A Dictionary of Biblical Interpretation* (London: SCM, 1990) 205. This does not, of course, deny one aspect of Yoder's point, namely, that the book of Esther does not promote an exodus.

Only with an incredible irony, therefore, can Yoder charge liberationists with "selective" reading. The question of the merits of Yoder's moral argument aside, his use of these texts for the "Diaspora model" proves untenable — not because he reads them "selectively," but because his selective reading distorts the texts. In order to appropriate these texts for his argument, Yoder would first have to read them accurately, and also give a theoretically sound reason for selecting the given texts. He does neither.

Although it is not directly included in his "Diaspora model," Yoder wants to embrace the exodus story to serve his paradigm as well. Here, he correctly observes that the exodus means "literally going out," and overturning the oppressive regime in the land "is very strikingly *not* what the Exodus did."[100] Then he goes on to claim the story for his paradigm: "[If]...the model of Exodus were to be taken seriously,...it would point far more clearly to the creative construction of relatively independent counter-communities, and less to a seizure of power in the existing society."[101]

Seizure of power it is not. But why do the Israelites "very strikingly" not do it? And does the exodus really "point far more clearly to the creative construction of independent counter-community"? If so, what kind of "counter-community"? With these questions we now return to Croatto.

Croatto calls our attention to "the language of the Promise" in his reading of the exodus. As we have seen, in Croatto's hermeneutical circle of event and kerygma, not only does the event produce the kerygma but also the kerygma produces the meaning of the event. In this "retrospective signifying" the kerygma understands the exodus as part of a plan. The event of the exodus "retrospectively becomes 'promise,'" forming the patriarchs-Moses-deliverance-land axis.[102] Seen in this light, "the Exodus is [a part of the] *programmatic event*" that culminates in the land.[103] I will not discuss here the tradition history of the promise of the land. For the purpose of this discussion I note only that Croatto reads the exodus kerygma programmatically. His reading gives a picture of a deliberative *post factum* reflection by the community ("reflected upon, pondered, and explored by faith"). And the community reflects "from the vantage point of the fulfillment of the promised land": "the two moments of the 'departure' (from Egypt) and of the 'entry' (into the promised land) are correlates. The former points to the

---

100. Yoder, "Exodus," 27.
101. Yoder, "Exodus," 28. See also McGovern, "Bible in Latin American Liberation Theology," 468.
102. Croatto, *Exodus*, 15–16, 25.
103. Croatto, *Exodus*, 15–16, 25 (italics added).

latter; the entry not only completes the departure but it also *deepens its meaning*."[104]

Although Croatto reads the text accurately as he places the exodus in the promise-settlement axis, we must ask Croatto how he perceives the precise "meaning of the departure" that "the entry deepens." He knows that the departure is for a land. But certainly he knows too that the land is not empty. Surely he has read what immediately follows "a land flowing with milk and honey." After all, the sentence does not end there but continues: "to the place of the Canaanites, the Hittites, the Amorites, the Perizzites, the Hivites, and the Jebusites" (Exod. 3:8). We have to wonder what Yahweh intends to do with them as he brings his people into their land. We cannot simply truncate a sentence after the first half and ignore the other half, semiotics (or "midrash," "reader-response criticism," "reception theory," "deconstruction," "death of the author and her/his initial addressees," "the new world of kerygma standing 'in front of' the text") or not. No self-respecting proponent of any of these literary theories would approve it anyway.[105]

To the extent that the exodus constitutes a part of the programmatic events of the promise-settlement axis, as Croatto sees it correctly, its stated destiny — not only the land of agricultural abundance, but also the land identified as belonging to specific peoples with names — is part of that program. We do not have to look "behind" or "in front of" the text to see this. We only have to look at it. So, then, what is "the meaning of the departure" that "the entry deepens"? Liberation? The beginning of a conquest? A strange hybrid of both?

Croatto does not answer these questions, because he does not raise them to begin with. Neither does the majority of critics. Strangely, many "faulty" aspects of the exodus model preoccupy them, but not this. We encounter some exceptions, such as Klaus Nürnberger, who criticize liberation theology for its silence on this question.[106] Rolf Knierim, who counts himself solidly among the liberationists, has also noted this problem, and gives it a systematic treatment. He scrutinizes the text (Exod. 3:7–8) exegetically in the context of the Pentateuch, then also "in light of biblical theology."[107]

---

104. Croatto, *Exodus*, 25 (italics added).

105. See, for example, J. Derrida, *Acts of Literature* (New York: Routledge, 1992) 33–75; *Limited Inc* (Evanston, Ill.: Northwestern University Press, 1988) 146.

106. K. Nürnberger, *Power and Beliefs in South Africa* (Pretoria: University of South Africa Press, 1988) 218. See also Motlhabi, "Liberation Theology," 8.

107. In 1978 Knierim gave a lecture on this problem that was subsequently published as "Israel and the Nations in the Land of Palestine in the Old Testament," *Lutheran Theological Seminary Bulletin* 58, no. 4 (November 1978) 11–21, and now in *The Task of Old Testament Theology: Substance, Method, and Cases* (Grand Rapids: Eerdmans, 1995) 309–21. For a fuller

Knierim identifies the exodus event in the concentric circles of a literary environment — a Yahweh speech that, in turn, is located in a "story," namely, the Pentateuch narrative: "The text refers to a real impending event. It is a story. The text does not communicate an abstract idea."[108] He does not stop, however, with the story. He strives to find the "concept" of the story, and seems to engage the story and its "concept" in a dialectical relation. While he uses the story as a window to its concept, he also uses its concept to understand the story better. He thus says, "[W]ithout a concept, the story would be without clarity. What is the theological concept of the story?"[109]

Knierim first distinguishes between the "cause" and the "reason" for the exodus. On the most immediate level the oppression is the cause for the liberation. But Knierim sees the reason for the liberation elsewhere: the need for the exodus. With the entire Pentateuch narrative in mind, he even goes so far as to say, "It could be that the need for Israel's exodus is in the first place the reason for their oppression."[110] He substantiates this notion by observing that Yahweh considers no alternatives for solving the problem of the oppression. Not all the Pharaohs were oppressive. Taking care of this one Pharaoh, therefore, could have solved the problem. Nor does Yahweh introduce any of "the viable alternatives also [found] in the Old Testament," such as the book of Esther.[111] (We should not conclude, however, that Knierim condones Yoder's "Diaspora model" with his reference to the book of Esther). Thus, concludes Knierim, "[I]t seems that the intention to lead Israel away from Egypt is at the outset the conceptual reason for the liberation of Israel for which the oppression is the actual cause."[112]

Knierim now needs to answer the most obvious question: Why does Yahweh, then, have his mind set on the exodus? Why the need for it? Answer: the promised land. He notes "how directly our text connects Israel's departure from Egypt with the goal of its subsequent immigration.... No alternatives are considered, not even Sinai."[113] The entry into the land is, then, the main concept of our text. Both oppression and liberation serve this concept.

And what does our text say about this goal, the land? Knierim notes the two aspects that comprise the text's depiction of it: perma-

---

understanding of Knierim's treatment of this question we also need to see his arguments in his Brazil lecture, found in *Task of Old Testament Theology*, 130–34.

108. Knierim, *Task of Old Testament Theology*, 131.
109. Knierim, *Task of Old Testament Theology*, 131.
110. Knierim, *Task of Old Testament Theology*, 131.
111. Knierim, *Task of Old Testament Theology*, 131.
112. Knierim, *Task of Old Testament Theology*, 132.
113. Knierim, *Task of Old Testament Theology*, 132.

nent settlement (land with milk and honey) and the conquest (the six peoples occupying the land). To confirm the second of these, he refers to the text's place in the tradition history of the conquest, and to its Deuteronomic/Deuteronomistic language.[114] In other words, he sees the conquest theology already embedded in the language of the departure from Egypt. Furthermore, this conquest theology is based on the theology of the land. And the ultimate rationale for the theology of the land comes from another theology on which it stands: the theology of election.[115] These exegetical observations yield an unavoidable conclusion for Knierim:

> The theology of Exodus 3:7–8 is the theology of the land of Israel as Yahweh's own people. All other notions, including the notion of liberation from oppression, stand in the service of this theology.... [The] story of liberation is not self-evidently based on a concept or theology of liberation. ... [I]t is [therefore] not automatically clear in a given case whether liberation aims at nothing but the removal of injustice, or whether it serves an alien purpose which itself involves oppression of others by the liberated, and which discredits the credibility of liberation itself.[116]

The election theology[117] then legitimates the conquest theology. Conquest presupposes election. Whatever we may think of an election theology per se, no theology of justice can tolerate an election theology that legitimates and fosters a conquest theology.

We now ask Croatto once more, What is "the meaning of the departure" that "the entry deepens"? The departure alone may mean liberation. But the meaning of the departure "deepened by the entry into the land" certainly signifies something more than liberation, as Knierim's analysis has shown us. It spells conquest. Denying this as an embedded element of the text would make as much sense as saying that Hitler's *Mein Kampf* contains no anti-Semite or anti-Bolshevik elements. Croatto would have to do more than "select" a certain part of this text to negate the conquest theology in it. He would have to destroy it. While I do not criticize his "selecting," "appropriating," and "closuring" the liberation axes, I do have a problem with his destruction of a text in order to accomplish his feat. Before we can talk about the "codified structure of meaning" of an axis of texts, we need to learn to respect the "codified structure" of a sentence. After all, "the laws of the linguistics" he applies to "the level of account" are, by his own ad-

---

114. Knierim, *Task of Old Testament Theology,* 132.
115. Knierim, *Task of Old Testament Theology,* 132.
116. Knierim, *Task of Old Testament Theology,* 133; see also 309–21.
117. For a recent systematic treatment of election as the fundamental aspect of the Old Testament see Seock-Tae Sohn, *The Divine Election of Israel* (Grand Rapids: Eerdmans, 1991).

mission, "the laws of the linguistics of the *sentence*."[118] The author may or may not have "died," but the sentence has not. And we certainly do not have the right to kill it, if only in the name of justice.

(This also prompts me to note an important hermeneutical concern. The programmatic nature of the conquest theology in the text — to the extent that the text mirrors the deliberative *post factum* reflection by the faith community, as Croatto sees it — carries a grievous hermeneutical ramification: it fits all too well the description of that notorious genre of history-writing from the perspective of the "winners" who justify their actions in the name of God.[119])

If we wish to address the exodus from a biblical-theological perspective, which Yoder and Croatto, as well as others in this discussion, attempt to do, it appears that we must begin to ask a different set of questions with a different set of criteria. We need to move beyond the questions and the issues raised in the debate that surrounds the exodus model we have examined. The most crucial question is not whether Yahweh or humans destroyed the Pharaoh (Yoder, Kirk, Lohfink). If Yahweh did it, he did it not so much to liberate an oppressed people as to set the prelude for the conquest of other peoples' land.[120] In fact, the more we believe that Yahweh did it, the more of a problem we have with this God. The "intelligibility" or "non-intelligibility" of supernaturalist language (Tracy) does not test the validity of the truth claim inherent in the story. (Incidentally, not all Marxists feel threatened by the "mythological" language of liberation theology.[121]) The real question of intelligibility has to do with whether Yahweh and his people act justly in the story, supernaturally or naturally.

The metaphysics of the divine ontology (Ogden) may or may not determine the acceptability of that divine being, but that being's ethics definitely will. And we do question Yahweh's ethics in the story, whether or not the liberationists "exclusively" concentrate on it. The liberation theology may develop its own metaphysics (Gudorf), but we would like to see it first straighten out the ethics of the "liberating" God in the exodus story.

---

118. Croatto, *Biblical Hermeneutics*, 16 (italics added).

119. For a good counterexample to this genre see H. Zinn, *A People's History of the United States* (New York: Harper and Row, 1980).

120. Knierim, *Task of Old Testament Theology*, 118.

121. See, for instance, M. Löwy, "Marxism and Liberation Theology," *Notebooks for Study and Research* 10 (1988). Löwy speaks of "the shortcomings of the 'classic' Marxist conception of religion [??] especially in its vulgarized version, reduced to the materialism and anti-clericalism of the eighteenth century bourgeois philosophers." He then asserts that "we can find in Marx's and Engel's writings — and in those of some modern Marxists — concepts and analysis that can help us understand today's rather surprising reality" (3).

Latin Americans may operate with mythological language and symbols (Gudorf), but mythology by virtue of being mythology does not offer a criterion for the validity of a truth claim. Their "lived reality of liberation" may offer such a criterion, but not if their "lived reality" obstructs from their view the cry of the six dispossessed peoples in the story. And I do not believe for a moment that we can assume that the members of the Latin American base communities are too self-engrossed to see the problem. That would be tantamount to patronizing.

We may "remythologize" our "modern" world (Gudorf), but "remythologization" does not guarantee an acceptable criterion for ethics. The theology of conquest is full of mythology. In fact, our "modern" society is not without its own share of mythologies (football stadiums, computerized technocracy, etc.), but we know all too well that the fact that they are mythologies does not automatically give us ethics. When we hear Gottwald speak of the Mono-Yahwist egalitarian society we experience *déjà vu* — Yoder's "counter-community" of "moral minority." Gottwald and Yoder operate, however, on two different methodological planes. And Yoder does not come anywhere close to Gottwald in clarifying what he means by "moral" minority when he cites these biblical texts. As we have seen, neither Israel's not lifting its own hand (but letting Yahweh do it) nor its other behaviors are motivated by morals. In whatever sense Israel may have been a countercommunity in Egypt, it proves a devastatingly "immoral" countercommunity to the six nations in their land.

As for Croatto, the theologian shows the enormous depth and breadth of his scholarship both in general hermeneutics and biblical studies. Although he does not always refer to them explicitly, he knows intimately the long-established elements of the discipline of Old Testament theology as they have developed and accumulated over the last several decades, from von Rad's categories of "history" and "credo" to Childs's "canon criticism"[122] and Sanders's "canonical criticism."[123] He skillfully weaves these elements along the Gadamer-Ricoeur axis of hermeneutics. But not content with the merely formal and descriptive nature of these categories and sciences, he supplies a normative criterion — the praxis of liberation — that allows him to find the kerygmatic axes of liberation in the Bible. In diametrical opposition to Stendahl's proposal that the task of biblical theology remain descriptive,[124] Croatto

---

122. Brevard S. Childs, *Biblical Theology in Crisis* (Philadelphia: Westminster Press, 1970); idem, *Old Testament Theology in Canonical Context* (Philadelphia: Fortress Press, 1986).

123. James A. Sanders, *From Sacred Story to Sacred Text* (Philadelphia: Fortress Press, 1987).

124. Cf. James Barr, "The Theological Case against Biblical Theology," in *Canon, Theol-*

unreservedly locates the Bible and its modern reader facing each other on a normative plane. It is here that the real beauty of his methodology shines.

Despite these merits, however, his methodology shows serious limitations in at least two respects. First, he seems to have imported the language of the "salvation-history" school too uncritically. It is one thing to say that the God of history is "not an object of study and of reason," or that "it was unnecessary to elaborate abstract terms and phrases" to describe this God, but it is another thing to treat this "God of history" and his people as if they are incapable of abstract thought or of reason. In fact, if "kerygmatic memory" "sheds light" on this God, some study and reason would be required to discern the God whom such "memory" and "light" describe. What does Croatto mean by the community's "reflection, pondering and exploration," if such activities do not imply study and rational thinking? And if the exodus is a "supreme act of divine love and grace" (Wright), this God of love and grace seems quite capable of conceptualized action. Yet, many modern interpreters allow this "God of history" little reason, study, or abstraction. They fail to see that Israel's history is in fact a reasoned, conceptualized history, and that their narrative therefore inevitably has a concept. Thus Croatto, as well as the other anticonceptual interpreters before him, such as von Hofmann, von Rad, and Wright, can scarcely render anything but conceptual, even systematic, interpretations even as they make anticonceptual and antisystematic disclaimers as their methodological presupposition.

With this methodological confusion these interpreters seem to act in denial and see Israel simply follow its God without reasoning with him. Yet, Israel did not just follow, but, by Croatto's own admission, followed programmatically. Did Israel do so from the beginning or retrospectively? Either would require a good deal of reasoning. But when we methodologically tune Israel and its God out of the range of reason, we cannot, it seems, make a call as to when their "history" follows the course that proper reason would not permit. We treat them as if they did not know what they were doing, and as if that is acceptable as long as they did what they did in "history." But the textual reality of the exodus story indicates, as Knierim's exegesis of its concepts shows, that they knew what they were doing in their history. And we know that what they did is unacceptable; and most importantly, the Old Testament, at least by implication, knows it too.[125] It is for this reason, and

---

ogy, and Old Testament Interpretation, ed. Gene M. Tucker, David L. Peterson, and Robert R. Wilson (Philadelphia: Fortress Press, 1988).

125. Knierim, Task of Old Testament Theology, 309–21.

at this point, that the need for a systematic comparison of Old Testament theologies becomes evident, because "the decision must be made concerning the Old Testament statements about Israel's relationship to her neighbors" and concerning "the understanding of Yahweh-God." Thus, "we must ask whether the understanding of the 'God of the conquest' and the 'God of Israel' is the only understanding of God in the Old Testament," and "the answer is obviously no."[126]

We cannot deny, of course, that the Old Testament is preoccupied with the question of Yahweh's relationship with Israel, but the plurality of Old Testament theologies includes the theologies that would have to render a sharp criticism of this major thrust of the election theology often characterized by a particularistic notion of Yahweh-God. The Old Testament "contains a significant variety of voices in which Yahweh-God is understood as the God of universal justice, righteousness, peace, and salvation" in all the genres of its literature.[127]

Thus, before we begin, with our "modern sensibilities," to express our discontent with the conquest theology, it already runs aground on the Old Testament's own strands. For instance, it conflicts with the notion that Israel's election serves as the channel for universal blessing:

> This question [of the validity of conquest theology] is raised with respect to a theological strand of the Old Testament itself, and not only with respect to our theology today in contradistinction to an Old Testament notion that is supposedly justifiable within the historical context of its own time. But just when we concede that the texts must be accepted in the light of their own time and culture, what about the witness of the same Old Testament that the same God who destroyed the nations for Israel's sake is a blessing to the nations through Israel?[128]

Conquest theology collides also with the Old Testament's concepts and stipulations about a fair and equal hearing in case of conflicting claims. Legal and prophetic genres both are keenly aware of this issue. Again, Knierim:

> What about the one-sided perspective from which the case is presented to us from Israel's vantage point, exclusive of and against the life of those nations? Their voice is not heard while their very existence was at stake! . . . Technically speaking, in terms of Old Testament genres, this conflict between two claims reflects the legal genre of litigation or trial in which two opposing parties meet in court before a judge. The Old Testament is very aware of this setting which was an essential part of Israel's own legal institutions. More importantly, the Old Testament — especially the prophetic tradition — knows of Yahweh as the judge who

---

126. Knierim, *Task of Old Testament Theology*, 319.
127. Knierim, *Task of Old Testament Theology*, 319–20.
128. Knierim, *Task of Old Testament Theology*, 317.

justly distributes justice. In the context both of Israel's legal institutions and of the understanding of Yahweh's just judgment, it would be inconceivable that someone who is attacked and deprived of freedom and life would not have the right to plead his or her case in court, and would not be heard and eventually rehabilitated and restored. Judges who listen only to one side are said to be corrupt! Even though they may be corrupt, and especially where they are in fact corrupt, Yahweh himself will see to it that equal justice, justice for all, is upheld. He hears the cries of the oppressed. Therefore, an interpretation of the conquest that ignores the cry of the Canaanites for help, a cry not represented by the Old Testament because it pleads only Israel's case, is in fundamental conflict with the Old Testament understanding of God as the just and merciful judge.[129]

Knierim argues that we cannot sidestep this conflict by insisting, as does von Rad, that Israel's holy wars were defensive wars,[130] or by arguing, as does G. Ernest Wright, that they are metaphors,[131] because these interpretations are simply inaccurate.[132]

The Old Testament does not, of course, systematize these conflicting views, which means that we must do it if we want to present a "biblical" case for a liberationist use of the exodus account. The result of the exegetical investigation of the text's theological concept, that is, "the programmatic justification for Israel's liberation from [homelessness] and oppression" serving simultaneously as "a programmatic justification for the oppression of free people by Israel,"[133] would have to be compared with the other theologies within the Old Testament. Then we would have to ask "if we should assume that God justifies our oppression of others for the sake of our liberation from oppression by others," and if so, if what we have is "at best, a particularistic and nationalistic God who is not the Savior of all" or "at most, we worship a God of oppression, a demon, which is the exact contrary of what the biblical tradition intends to say about God — even in the Old Testament."[134]

Gudorf defends liberation theology from the criticism that it relies on the lingo of the so-called northern theology, believing that the northern theology otherwise would not have taken it seriously.[135] We may

---

129. Knierim, *Task of Old Testament Theology*, 317–18.

130. G. von Rad, *Der heilige Krieg im alten Israel* (Göttingen: Vandenhoeck & Ruprecht, 1952).

131. G. E. Wright, *The Old Testament and Theology* (New York: Harper and Row, 1969).

132. Knierim, *Task of Old Testament Theology*, 318. See also M. C. Lind, *Yahweh Is a Warrior: The Theology of Warfare in Israel* (Scottdale, Pa.: Herald, 1980).

133. Knierim, *Task of Old Testament Theology*, 318.

134. Knierim, *Task of Old Testament Theology*, 318–19.

135. Gudorf, "Liberation Theology's Use of Scripture," 10–11.

agree with Gudorf on this point, but if we truly want to take liberation theology seriously, we would have to engage it critically. Likewise, if liberation theology were to engage the northern theology, it too would have to do so critically. Had Croatto applied his critical acumen to the salvation-history school, narratology, and semiotics (as he did to the other hermeneuticians — from Schleiermacher and Dilthey to the post-Bultmannians), his methodology would have been enhanced.

Croatto's semiotics approach does not prepare him for the conflict of theologies and their interpretations. It will enable him to find his texts and structure them into "a linguistically coded unity" along certain kerygmatic axes, but if someone comes up with a set of different axes with their structured and codified kerygma to oppose Croatto's kerygma, both theologically and hermeneutically, his semiotics will not help him.

Croatto can, of course, break his own rule at the exegetical level and try to detour around the opposing axes, as we have seen him do. But that will not get him very far. Ultimately he will have to go to his praxis as the norm and have the oppressed claim and "own" the Bible, but the other person will do the same with the people with whom he or she stands in solidarity in their "praxis." The Bible now becomes meaningless as "authority" because it does not have a guiding criterion that can adjudicate between the two. Semiotics will not do it; that is not its job. So the Bible becomes a mere warehouse of different and conflicting axes and kerygmas.

At this point we may wonder why Croatto and his imaginary opponent would go to the Bible to begin with. Why not simply confront each other with their separate praxes in the first place without resorting to the Bible? We might simply want to say that the Bible is where people go for authority. It is indeed! But we would not have said very much beyond this apparent tautology. Unless we are willing to consent to a notion, such as that of Gottwald, and admit that any attempt at systematic reflection on biblical faiths by biblical theology is doomed to failure, we need to move beyond the dialectics of semiotics and praxis. And wherever that "beyond" may be, if we ever get there, we should be prepared to do some serious comparing and prioritizing of different "biblical" theologies.

Such a task would in fact be only a logical extension of Croatto's semiotics. He insists that (1) the "closuring character" of narrative semiotics applies to the entire canon as a "single text"; (2) narrative semiotics demands that "the message of a text [be] not in a fragment of the account, but in its totality, as a structure codifying a meaning"; (3) "a text is not the cumulative sum of plurality... [but] the unification of a linguistically coded central kerygma"; (4) "the hermeneutic enterprise does not consist in *listing* relevant *themes*. It consists in the *structuration* of these themes in the total work that is the Bible."[136]

Croatto apparently means less than what he says. He has in mind different kerygmatic axes with their parallel trajectories throughout the Bible, but not the entire Bible itself as a "single text." He does not indicate how or if these different axes and kerygmas should be related to each other. Appropriation of the Bible as a "single text" has to involve more than selecting certain axes that will "own" the others. If we are going to speak sensibly of a "biblical" God for hermeneutical purposes, we need to delineate clearly that biblical God vis-à-vis the other equally "biblical" Gods. Otherwise, our use of the word "biblical" becomes chaotic and irresponsible. I believe we can and should make good the check Croatto wrote with insufficient amount, and apply these semiotic rules to the entire Bible "as a single text." Of course, I do not mean by this expression forcing the existing plurality into some artificial single structure. I simply submit that our modern aversion to the nomenclature of "a static, propositional doctrine of eternal truth" should hardly mean that the Bible is now scarcely more than a history book that simply records the trace of its faith communities as it was lived.

Therefore, the notion of a "single text" should not frighten to the periphery the varying voices within the canon. Every voice in the canon should always be guaranteed an equal hearing. We cannot, however, let the Bible say everything about everything. It must say something about something, if it is going to function at all. Such a hearing, therefore, should presuppose comparing, prioritizing, accepting, and rejecting the theological claims of the Bible. Without such a presupposition our reading of the Bible becomes an irresponsible behavior — unless we want to turn it into a mere history book. Without such a presupposition the Bible becomes an irresponsible book that forfeits its duty to clarify some of its age-old claims, if not to apologize for some of them before the world.

Comparing and prioritizing, when vigorously applied, also bear on such closely related notions as "liberation" and "justice," as Knierim has insisted elsewhere. We need to ask which serves which, which defines which, and which is the criterion for which. We find that justice defines liberation and liberation serves justice, not vice versa. For one thing, liberation is required only when justice breaks down. Justice is the goal, liberation a means. Also, liberation unchecked by justice can easily become corrupt and collapse into oppression, as we have seen.

---

136. Croatto, *Biblical Hermeneutics*, 9–10 (italics on *listing* in [4] added).

A biblical theology of liberation, therefore, must subject itself to the criterion of the biblical theology of justice.

Hermeneutically, this means that to the extent that the oppression caused the exodus, we should take the God of the exodus seriously. It should not, however, allow us to pietistically slur over the god of conquest and oppression in the name of "God's freedom,"[137] "God's covenant relationship," "God's initiative," "God's superiority,"[138] or even in the name of a recontextualized "new Exodus" in the Old Testament[139] or of the reconceptualized "new Exodus" in the New Testament.[140]

Comparing and prioritizing — that is, systematizing — the biblical theologies should presuppose, then, our unreserved right to choose which biblical God to reject, which biblical God to worship, and on what grounds. It also presupposes that we take the question of "on what grounds" seriously, with an abiding hope that we may find them in the Bible as we humbly search for the God beyond God. And whatever else we may want to say about that God, we must insist that God be just and universal, never only one or the other. God cannot be a god of one people, region, gender, or class more than of another and still expect to be God, no matter how just or justice-demanding God may be toward that particular people, region, gender, or class. While liberation subjects itself to justice as its criterion, justice, in turn, should subject itself to the universality of God as its criterion.

The world does not need to know Yahweh or Christ to understand the divine mandate of justice and liberation. Korean history (which I know best) alone already bears an ample testimony to this assertion. But if the biblical God wants to participate in and contribute to the world's agenda for liberation and justice, the world will want to know if it is the same God of the exodus. If we say yes, the "nations" of the world will want to know the whence and the whither of any other exoduses that might still be coming. They will want to know the precise "meaning of the departure" that "the entry deepens." And we, both our God and ourselves, should be prepared to answer with a matchless rigor of analysis and with a radical introspection and honesty. The world will expect nothing less. And as the world asks us and our biblical God these ques-

---

137. See A. A. Roder, "The Concept of the Poor in the Context of the Ecclesiology of Liberation Theology" (Th.D. diss., Andrews University, 1986) 333.

138. See A. R. Dupertuis, "Liberation Theology's Use of the Exodus as a Soteriological Model" (Th.D. diss., Andrews University, 1982) 234–58.

139. von Rad, *Old Testament Theology*, 2:238–50, 261.

140. See F. L. Fisher, "A New and Greater Exodus: The Exodus Pattern in the New Testament," *Southwestern Journal of Theology* 20 (1977) 67ff.; F. F. Bruce, *New Testament Development of Old Testament Themes* (Grand Rapids: Eerdmans, 1968) 32ff.

tions, we and our God may not be walking tall together around the world like we used to. That may teach us some humility, and it should. Micah will approve (6:8). The God hanging on the tree will approve. And they are in the Bible too.

BIBLIOGRAPHY

Cone, James. *A Black Theology of Liberation*. Philadelphia: Lippincott Co., 1970.

Croatto, J. Severino. *Biblical Hermeneutics: Toward a Theory of Reading as the Production of Meaning*. Maryknoll, N.Y.: Orbis Books, 1987.

———. *Exodus: A Hermeneutics of Freedom*. Trans. Salvador Attanasio. Maryknoll, N.Y.: Orbis Books, 1981.

Dussel, Enrique. *History and the Theology of Liberation*. Maryknoll, N.Y.: Orbis Books, 1976.

Gudorf, Christine E. "Liberation Theology's Use of Scripture: A Response to First World Critics." *Interpretation* 41, no. 1 (January 1987).

Gutiérrez, Gustavo. *A Theology of Liberation*. Maryknoll, N.Y.: Orbis Books, 1973.

Holub, Robert C. *Reception Theory*. London: Methuen, 1984.

Kirk, J. Andrew. *Liberation Theology: An Evangelical View from the Third World*. Atlanta: John Knox Press, 1979.

Knierim, Rolf P. "Israel and the Nations in the Land of Palestine in the Old Testament." *Bulletin 58* 4 (November 1978).

———. *The Task of Old Testament Theology: Substance, Method, and Cases*. Grand Rapids: Eerdmans, 1995.

Lohfink, Norbert F. *Option for the Poor: The Basic Principle of Liberation Theology in the Light of the Bible*. Trans. Linda M. Maloney. Berkeley: BIBAL Press, 1987.

Löwy, Michael. "Marxism and Liberation Theology." *Notebooks for Study and Research* 10 (1988).

McGovern, Arthur. "The Bible in Latin American Liberation Theology." In *The Bible and Liberation: Political and Social Hermeneutics*. Ed. Norman K. Gottwald. Maryknoll, N.Y.: Orbis Books, 1984.

McKnight, Edgar V. *Postmodern Use of the Bible: The Emergence of Reader-Oriented Criticism*. Nashville: Abingdon Press, 1988.

Nürnberger, Klaus. *Power and Beliefs in South Africa*. Pretoria: University of South Africa Press, 1988.

Randall, Margaret. *Christians in the Nicaraguan Revolution*. Trans. Mariana Velverde. Vancouver: New Star Books, 1983.

Ricoeur, Paul. *The Conflict of Interpretation: Essays in Hermeneutics*. Evanston, Ill.: Northwestern University Press, 1974.

———. *Interpretation Theory: Discourse and the Surplus of Meaning*. Fort Worth: Texas Christian University Press, 1976.

Wright, G. Ernest, and Reginald H. Fuller. *The Book of the Acts of God: Contemporary Scholarship Interprets the Bible*. Garden City, N.Y.: Doubleday, 1960.

Yoder, John Howard. "Exodus: Probing the Meaning of Liberation." *Sojourners* 5 (September 1976).

18

A New Approach to the Christian-Jewish Dialogue

Charles Mabee

HISTORICAL SKETCH

Those who know Rolf Knierim know of his abiding passion for Jewish-Christian dialogue. In fact, his decision to forego his primary love for the Methodist ministry in Germany for Old Testament scholarship and university teaching was partially due to his belief that he could make a better contribution to this dialogue through this alternative path. As a graduate student I studied under Rolf in the early 1970s, and this passion of his has never been far from my own theological quest through the succeeding decades. And when, some fifteen years ago, I discovered the revolutionary thought of Roman Catholic literary critic René Girard, my interests quickly ran to continuing this dialogue aided with Girardian insights. What follows in this essay is largely a result of the tools afforded me by Rolf Knierim and René Girard, the two great teachers in my life.

The thesis of my essay is that a new approach to Jewish-Christian dialogue is now possible with the application of the insights of Girard to the Jewish and Christian Scriptures. I understand this new possibility to be paradigmatic for interfaith religious dialogue on a wider scale, ultimately including the full cast of players on the world religious scene. The specifically Girardian insight that has arisen and provided reason for renewed optimism that a newly construed interfaith religious dialogue is possible with widespread implications, is based on the rise of prophetic consciousness in interfaith discussions of Judaism and Christianity. I need to state at the outset that for purposes of clarification, I am simply calling the Old Testament prophets the "Mosaic prophetic tradition."

The consciousness of this Mosaic prophetic tradition, as I understand it, was born and was initially embodied in the historical experience of preexilic ancient Israelite religion. While it undoubtedly existed on the periphery of preexilic ancient Israelite society, it moved into the mainstream of religious thinking within Israel only in the midst of the exilic experience. This exilic experience of ancient Israel is commonly viewed as the birthplace of the idea of textually based religion, an idea that may well have had its primary roots in those very same circles that had gathered around and maintained the words of prophetic figures dating back hundreds of years. The failure of these prophets previously to enter the mainstream of their tradition was the spark that ignited a kind of alternative religious tradition within ancient Israelite religion, a tradition that was maintained by circles of followers who believed them and their words to be efficacious for all subsequent generations.

It was, however, only during the time of the exile that a new community of faith was actually established around the peripheral traditions associated with the Mosaic prophetic tradition. The task for those who argued among the exiles themselves for the centrality of this alternative tradition had to contend with those still believing in — and even representing — royal, priestly, wisdom, and institutional prophetic traditions that had accompanied them into Babylon. Furthermore, it seems clear that the Mosaic prophetic tradition won out over other contending parties who would reconfigure Israel in exile according to some variation of the so-called Zion tradition that had characterized the Judahite religious and political establishment taken into exile. The strategy that the advocates of the Mosaic prophetic tradition adopted over the advocates of the various forms of the Zion tradition was one that is no stranger to religious discourse, namely co-option. The newly formed, textually based religion would win the hearts and minds of the exiles by turning the variations of Zion theology into text.

Now, for example, kingship would survive, but only in the form of a textually based institution subject to the newly formed texts and those who interpret them. The priesthood would survive, but only in the form of a priesthood of the text, that is, with text beginning the process of overcoming actual acts of sacrifice. The wisdom traditions would survive as well, only now they would be placed in the service of the entire textually grounded society, not simply the leisured upper classes. In fact, the national epics, those stories that explained the world and Israel's place within it, would likewise be subject to the new textually based religion built upon the Mosaic prophetic tradition.

The work of moving the peripheral prophets into the mainstream of exilic community formation was the work of the so-called Deuteronomists, or Deuteronomic school. No matter how we ultimately evaluate Deuteronomic theology (and I think that in this one instance "theology" is an appropriate word for a pre-Christian Israelite tradition), the achievement of its shapers was revolutionary in the only way that revolution makes sense: making peripheral in society what was central and making central what was peripheral. I propose that it was only because of their achievement that the world has been bequeathed the Hebrew

Scriptures, and ultimately the Christian Scriptures as well. I understand the basic formation of the Hebrew Scriptures, and the very idea of turning Zion into text, to be ultimately the achievement of the Deuteronomists. To them, in essence, we owe the debt of bequeathing the Mosaic prophetic tradition — first to Israel and then to the world. In that sense all Jews, Christians, and Muslims are Deuteronomists. And, I believe, the recapturing and reappreciation of their achievement is the beginning of the long road back to partnership in mission of these very same three Abrahamic religious traditions. (I believe that Islam could be fruitfully included in our discussions, but that exceeds the purpose of this essay.)

PROPOSAL

Against the historical sketch I have just outlined I propose that Judaism and Christianity represent variant forms of the Deuteronomic thought that successfully implemented the Mosaic prophetic tradition at the center of the postexilic Jewish community. And, in spite of significant and impenetrable differences that exist between them, a recapturing of their prophetic foundations would surely serve to minimalize the hostilities that have so frequently characterized their relationship. I believe that this common ground represented by the Mosaic prophetic tradition that exists between the Hebrew Scriptures and the New Testament offers an avenue of rapprochement that transcends their distinctive features — features that cannot be denied. Let me give the specifics of my case as a basis for continuing dialogue and engagement, in a series of four propositional statements — two each from the Hebrew Scriptures and the New Testament.

1. The Mosaic prophetic tradition represents the core of the Hebrew scriptural tradition. This means that the Pentateuch functions in its present position as a "prologue" to the Mosaic prophetic tradition, the core of which is normally termed the "classical prophets." The function of the Pentateuch is, so to say, to "institutionalize" those prophetic outsiders who had lived historically on the outside of established institutions of ancient Israel. With the death of those institutions at the time of the exile, however, the framers of Judaic thought seized what in essence turned out to be an historic window of opportunity and reframed their religious life in line with a group of prophetic outsiders who, in Girardian terms, dramatized the plight of the "scapegoated ones" of traditional society within the public domain. The Hebrew Scriptures are to be understood, thereby, as the imaginative religion of the silent ones now given significant public voice for (one of) the first times in human history.

2. The Deuteronomic tradition, which eventually emerges as the "Torah tradition," is the attempt to democratize the Mosaic prophetic tradition throughout the exilic and postexilic Jewish community. It becomes the core tradition of what comes to be called Judaism, a newly conceived central cultural tradition based on text rather than on king and sacrifice. The Deuteronomic tradition replaces the exhausted religious traditions of ancient Israel, which in effect came to an end in 586 B.C.E. This tradition had come to be built around what we might term the "Zion/Jerusalem traditions," that is, Davidic traditions, temple traditions, courtly wisdom traditions, and the like. From now on these traditions would participate in the mainstream of Judaic thought only in the form of imaginative texts.

3. The New Testament, with its central figures of Jesus and Paul, represents the continuation of the Deuteronomic Mosaic prophetic tradition into the heart of the Greek-speaking Gentile world. It represents the outreach of this prophetic consciousness into the non-Jewish world. This means that those things that ultimately separated the rabbinical Jewish tradition from Pauline Christianity were matters of spirit and strategy rather than fundamental orientation toward the world. By this I mean that at the core of both traditions the Mosaic prophetic tradition dominates. Both traditions represent variant readings of that tradition in light of historical circumstances, challenges, and matters of strategy.

4. The most important dispute between ancient Judaism and the emerging Christian church lay in the variant readings of this Mosaic prophetic tradition of Paul and his detractors within Judaism. That is, it is Paul who led the effort in understanding Jesus — quite correctly, it seems to me — in line with the Mosaic prophetic tradition. The core issue, simple and highly complex at the same time, revolved around the Judaic tradition of building a hedge around the Torah, or in our newly defined terms, around the Mosaic prophetic tradition. The hedge was designed to protect that prophetic tradition from contamination by the Gentile mythological, idolatrous, or polytheistic traditions. It was based on the long experience within the Jewish experience with those very same traditions within ancient Palestine and within the context of international relations. It had truly been a hard-fought battle of achieving the prophetic vision of the truth of the powerless and scapegoated ones against societies governed by small elites.

This experience had exacerbated the Judaic fear that this fragile prophetic voice would be lost upon extended contact with mainstream polytheism. It is all quite understandable, it seems to me, and not a cause for accusation — even on the part of those who would take a different track. In the face of this, Paul arose to proclaim a message that, seen against this background, seemed to risk the entire Mosaic prophetic tradition itself. His was a dangerous position because it potentially allowed polytheistic mythology to enter the core of the hard-won prophetic tradition. It was a gamble against the odds, really, and the Jewish religious establishment knew it. And, I think it is fair to say, Paul knew it himself. But make the gamble he did, and the rest, as they say, is history.

CENTRAL ISSUE

I wish to focus the remainder of this essay summarizing what I take to be the heart of the issue from the standpoint of Jewish and Christian self-understanding. The issue revolves around the problem of violence within each of the two traditions. I understand violence reduction within society to be the central work of religious thought and life. To put the matter differently, Does violence remain in one or both of the two traditions as well as the two traditions in relation to one another? And if so, does it remain in the same degree? The point here, of course, is to ask whether an evaluation of Judaism or Christianity can be made that leads to the superiority of one of the traditions over the other. I reject out of hand any kind of chronological framework for evaluating the respective worth of either tradition (this would also apply to Islam). Chronologically based arguments can work, of course, to the advantage of either of the parties. Judaism can claim superiority because it is the original, the parent of all Abrahamic religion. Christianity can claim superiority on supersessionist grounds, where it is viewed as the fulfillment or completion of Judaism. I reject both arguments because they bypass the real issue, namely, which, if either, of them does the better job of reducing violence in human society. All other questions, it seems to me, are rhetorical and bypass this central criterion.

When we ask the question of violence reduction or removal, it seems to me that we have a standoff with regard to the two traditions. In fact, more than a standoff — more accurately, we have a division of labor. I propose division of labor as a metaphor to describe their relationship, rather than the use of chronological arguments. Let me put the matter simply. Judaism as presently constituted is incapable of unmasking the many humanly construed gods within the context of, or on the basis of, the Gentile world itself. In order for that to happen, it is necessary to eliminate the hedge around the Torah that protects the prophetic tradition. From the standpoint of the Gentile mission the hedge itself was viewed by Pauline Judaism as an unnecessary *skandalon* around the prophetic Torah.

In an analogous sense, however, it seems to me that the cross of Jesus as such is incapable, in and of itself, of protecting the prophetic

tradition as it rushes across ethnic and cultural boundaries to "proclaim the gospel." In fact, it seems to me that the cross of Jesus and
his resurrection are proclaimed increasingly in our world in ways that
violate the prophetic consciousness that I am arguing was the fundamental identity of Jesus. The doctrine of the Trinity, as both Judaism
and Islam continually point out to Christians, at least has the appearance of crossing a line in which the prophetic tradition is either lost or
greatly in danger of extinction. Why? Because the absolute sovereignty
and independence of God from human manipulation lie at the foundation of this prophetic consciousness. The doctrine of the Trinity is
viewed by both Judaism and Islam as the return to a kind of polytheism — a move neither is willing to make. Of course, this doctrine as
such does not exist in the New Testament, and thus to cite it somewhat
begs the issue. Nonetheless, it is precisely the kind of subsequent theological move that confirms the worse fears and suspicions of the more
strictly monotheistic Judaism and Islam.

My basic point is this: simply to proclaim the cross of Jesus is not
enough. The passion of Jesus can be interpreted in complete error in
such a way that violence is maintained within Christianity, rather than
the passion producing the desired effect of Christianity becoming the
tool for the elimination of violence. Many of our most conservative television evangelists do this on a continual basis as they focus on the
traditional doctrine of vicarious atonement. They talk about the cross
continually, but they talk about it as if the world crucified Jesus rather
than admitting their own culpability. They obscure the God of love
with the god of vengeance. The corrective that Christianity needs at
this point is the ethical guideline provided by the Judaic Torah. I do not
believe that the ethical Torah of God (if I may speak in this way as a
Christian) is out of date. For example, the prohibition against covetousness — the tenth and culminating commandment — certainly retains its
firepower in the modern world as surely as in the ancient.

Yet, in the Jewish mind, as I understand it, there is no distinction to
be made between any of the 613 commandments that are laid out in the
Scriptures. That is the essence of the "hedge" theology that I mentioned
earlier. Once one takes the most insignificant of the commandments to
be as important as the most significant, then one has in effect built a
hedge around the Torah. Yet, for the Christian, only those parts of the
Torah that protect the meaning of the cross of Jesus have any ultimate
significance. The cross, in other words, becomes the lens through which
the Torah is viewed. For the Christian, the passion and resurrection of
Jesus represent a new act of God that does not deny as such anything
of the Judaic context of the prophetic tradition. Those aspects of the
Torah that maintain the integrity of the cross of Christ are universally

valid from a Christian standpoint. All the rest is rendered peripheral for the Christian as the prophetic tradition is proclaimed upon the distant shores of the world. To maintain them for the sake of the hedge becomes, in the mission to spread the universal gospel, a new act of violence because it provides an unnecessary secondary stumbling block beyond the stumbling block that is already built into the gospel itself.

CONCLUSION

The purpose of my essay is to give expression to my hope that the Jewish-Christian dialogue can advance meaningfully by appeal to the common presence within each tradition of what I am calling prophetic consciousness. As I see it, the disputes and frequently acrimonious nature of the historical relationship between these two religions have been a result of the inability of each to expel the violent religious nature that characterizes their imperfect actualization in human history. I do not believe that any fundamental issue stands as the cause of their antagonisms. My reason for believing that is not simply wishful thinking. The reason is that I believe both are grounded in the ancient Mosaic prophetic tradition that finally generated the conception of Holy Scripture, or textually based religion. This commonality is far more powerful than any specific points of faith that may separate us from one another.

That said, let me state clearly that I have no desire to collapse Judaism into Christianity. Rather, I find myself exclusively interested in the prophetic tradition not as Jewish or Christian but as a movement in its own right. And, since I as a Christian share this in common with Judaism, and to a largely underexplored degree with Islam, I increasingly find the differences that separate me from Jews to be of peripheral interest and importance. While I do not wish to become Jewish or Muslim, I am at the same time heartened by their lack of interest in being Christian. What I propose is that adherents of our respective faiths increasingly work out the consciousness of the prophetic tradition that unites us and move to the periphery those things that differentiate us that remain deeply embedded in our respective traditions. It is work that the world yearns to have accomplished.

19

Human Dominion over Animals

Stephen A. Reed

INTRODUCTION[1]

Ethicists and theologians have devoted considerable attention to ethical issues related to the treatment of animals. In a book on environmental ethics Charles Birch suggests that one may derive from the Bible three different attitudes toward animals: (1) exploitation, from Gen. 1:26–28 and Gen. 9:2–3; (2) stewardship, from Gen. 2:15; and (3) compassion, from Genesis 1 as a whole as well as some psalms.[2] He indicates that some have thought that Gen. 1:26–28 and Gen. 9:2–3 provided justification for the exploitation of animals. While he asserts that the dominant viewpoint of Western Christian thinking has been the "absolute rule over nature," he argues that compassion is the appropriate attitude.

In 1967 Lynn White wrote a classic article in which he argues that the "Judaeo-Christian dominance model" has led to our ecological crisis.[3] While numerous scholars have attempted to counter this thesis, the language of "dominion" remains problematic in today's world.[4] Larry Rasmussen argues that although "dominion theology" is hardly defended any more by ecologically concerned Christians as a valid view, it still reflects the practice of many people.[5]

It is not the intent of this essay to provide another critique of White's argument. It must be admitted that such dominion language can be used as a tool of oppression and as such does not provide "good news" for animals.[6] Yet even though historically these texts have contributed

1. An earlier and shorter version of this essay was presented at the AAR/SBL Upper Midwest Regional Meeting on April 4, 1997, at Luther Seminary in St. Paul, Minnesota. I thank the scholars who shared comments and suggestions at that time.

2. C. Birch, *Regaining Compassion for Humanity and Nature* (Saint Louis: Chalice, 1993) 92.

3. L. White Jr., "The Historical Roots of Our Ecological Crisis," *Science* 155 (March 10, 1967) 1203–7.

4. See B. Anderson, "Human Dominion over Nature," in *From Creation to New Creation: Old Testament Perspectives* (Minneapolis: Fortress, 1994) 111–31; J. Kay, "Concepts of Nature in the Hebrew Bible," *Environmental Ethics* 10 (1988) 309–27; R. Hiers, "Ecology, Biblical Theology, and Methodology: Biblical Perspectives on the Environment," *Zygon* 19 (1984) 43–59.

5. L. Rasmussen, *Earth Community, Earth Ethics* (Maryknoll, N.Y.: Orbis, 1996) 228–30.

6. For an interesting collection of essays see C. Pinches and J. McDaniel, eds., *Good News for Animals: Christian Approaches to Animal Well-Being* (Maryknoll, N.Y.: Orbis, 1993).

to the problem, they need not continue to do so. The Bible has been in-fluential in shaping peoples' attitudes toward and treatment of animals. It has been used to defend human freedom to use animals for human benefit and also to argue that animals should be treated with care and even respect.

This modern-day discussion is a hermeneutical issue that involves, in Rolf Knierim's words, "the critical comparison of the biblical world-views with our own worldviews."[7] What complicates the issue is that modern-day worldviews have been influenced at least in part by biblical worldviews. The present hermeneutical problem illustrates that a criti-cal comparison of biblical texts and modern-day attitudes is an ongoing reality in our contemporary world. Knierim's concern about critical comparisons of various vantage points is rooted in contemporary needs and concerns.

Before the modern-day hermeneutical problem can be resolved, it is essential that the meaning of "human dominion over animals" in the Hebrew Bible be explained exegetically and be evaluated theologically within the Hebrew Bible. To some degree this is what has been hap-pening as scholars using the Bible have been advocating a stewardship model that would replace the dominion model for understanding the relationship between humans and the world.[8]

Admittedly, it is this present-day hermeneutical concern that urges careful scrutiny of this particular topic. Although ideally one should proceed first exegetically, second theologically, and third hermeneuti-cally, it is often the case that special attention is given to those issues that engage us.[9] One must still read the texts honestly and carefully and give evidence for interpretations and critiques.

The present essay presents an analysis of the theme of "human do-minion over animals" as found in the Hebrew Bible and illustrates how one may engage in the exegetical, theological, and hermeneutical tasks as articulated in Knierim's proposals. The exegetical task involves a sur-vey of the relevant texts related to "human dominion over animals" and provides appropriate contexts for understanding this language. The theological task involves a critique of this theme in the light of other biblical modes of the relationship between humans and animals. The

---

7. R. Knierim, "Comments on The Task of Old Testament Theology," written version of an oral presentation at the annual meeting of the SBL, San Francisco, November 24, 1997.

8. See Rasmussen, *Earth Community, Earth Ethics*, 230–36.

9. See R. Knierim, *The Task of Old Testament Theology: Substance, Method, and Cases* (Grand Rapids: Eerdmans, 1995) 58–71. Knierim (481) indicates that one can begin either with a biblical concern or with one of our own.

hermeneutical task includes some reflections on the usage of these biblical texts for current ethical issues.

It might seem at first glance that the topic "human dominion over animals" is more ethical than theological. Still, in this case these texts indicate that it is God who grants this dominion over animals to humans. There are at least two separate issues involved here. First, what does the "universal dominion" of God mean as related to dominion over animals and humans and the nonliving parts of the world? It might seem rather odd to ask if God is anthropocentric or biocentric, but one at least would have to ask about relative priorities of values of the parts of the natural world. Is God more concerned about humans than animal life forms, or is God more concerned about living than nonliving parts of the natural world? Second, what is the nature and meaning of human dominion over animals in light of divine dominion? It is this second issue that I will analyze here. Even the issue of "human dominion over animals" is not just an ethical issue but must be interpreted within a theological context.

EXEGETICAL CONCERNS

Background of Dominion

The imagery of dominion is royal language. Several Hebrew verbs can be used for the exercise of dominion: *kbš* ("subdue");[10] *rdh* ("rule, govern");[11] *mlk* ("rule");[12] *mšl* ("rule, govern").[13] Such verbs refer in a literal sense to the exercise of the power of a king over his subjects. Such language can be used metaphorically for God as king who rules over all (1 Chron. 29:12; Bel.1:5). Such language can also be used metaphorically for the relationship between husbands and their wives and for the relationship between humans and animals. Our attention will be restricted to dominion over animals.

Human dominion over others is often seen as granted by God. The verb *ntn* ("give")[14] is used to indicate the granting of authority over animals (Jer. 27:6; 28:14). The Aramaic *yhb* ("give")[15] is used similarly in Dan. 2:37. Wagner indicates that the verb *kbš* is "one of several that ex-

---

10. S. Wagner, "*kābaš*," *TDOT*, 52.

11. W. Holladay, *A Concise Hebrew and Aramaic Lexicon of the Old Testament* (Grand Rapids: Eerdmans, 1971) 333.

12. Holladay, *Concise Hebrew and Aramaic Lexicon*, 198.

13. Holladay, *Concise Hebrew and Aramaic Lexicon*, 219.

14. Holladay, *Concise Hebrew and Aramaic Lexicon*, 249.

15. Holladay, *Concise Hebrew and Aramaic Lexicon*, 407.

press the exercise of force" and that "every exercise of force expressed" by this verb "is ultimately sent or at least permitted by God."[16]

In the Bible it is Nebuchadnezzar who is specifically depicted as having dominion over animals (Jer. 27:6; 28:14; Dan. 2:37–38; 4:20–22; Jdt. 11:7). Jeremiah indicates that God has given Nebuchadnezzar power over all nations and even over the wild animals (Jer. 27:6; 28:14). As Holladay indicates, this passage portrays the kings of the nations as having yokes on them like domestic animals. If even the wild animals are subject to Nebuchadnezzar, then it will be much easier for Nebuchadnezzar to control the domesticated kings.[17] Here, Jeremiah uses the language of dominion over wild animals to encourage the Judahites and members of other nations to submit to Nebuchadnezzar.

In Daniel the language of Nebuchadnezzar's dominion over the animals is again used (Dan. 2:37–38; 4:20–22). Chapter 4 has the allegory of the tree under which the birds and animals find dwelling places and food. Here the king's rule implies provision for the needs of subjects.

Even among Israelite and Judean kings power over both domestic and wild animals was a sign of their wealth and strength. Uzziah (2 Chron. 26:10), Hezekiah (2 Chron. 32:27–29), Solomon (2 Chron. 9:25), and David (1 Chron. 27:25–31) all had large herds. At Solomon's table there were both wild and domestic animals for food. Tribute often included livestock. King Mesha of Moab had to pay tribute to Israel of one hundred thousand lambs and wool of one hundred thousand rams (2 Kings 3:4). Arabs brought tribute to Jehoshaphat of seventy-seven hundred rams and seventy-seven hundred goats (2 Chron. 17:11). The most difficult animals to control were wild animals. Part of a king's responsibility was to control such animals. If wild animals were free, this could be a sign of chaos in the kingdom.

It is true that the language of dominion often is associated with harsh treatment of subjects. Mention is made in Isa. 14:6 of ruling with anger and persecution. The actual practice of dominion falls far short of the ideal of dominion. Dominion does not mean that one is free to do anything with what is ruled over. There are limitations to any power. One is not to rule over slaves with harshness (Lev. 25:43, 46). The parable of the shepherd ruling over his flock in Ezekiel 34 indicates that the shepherd has ruled with force and harshness (v. 4). This is not the kind of shepherd expected by Yahweh. The chapter makes a clear distinction between proper and improper dominion by a leader.

Almost all royal imagery has negative connotations today. In an egal-

---

16. Wagner, "*kābaš*," *TDOT*, 52.
17. W. Holladay, *Jeremiah 2: A Commentary on the Book of the Prophet Jeremiah, Chapters 26–52* (Hermeneia; Philadelphia: Fortress, 1989) 119.

itarian society such as ours such language is seen as inappropriate. Yet we should not read our own connotations into this biblical imagery. While the act of dominion rarely seemed to be questioned in the Hebrew Bible, the way one ruled often was. The Israelites could hardly imagine a world in which some humans did not have dominion over others — certainly not in the context of the Assyrian, Babylonian, and Persian Empires. If even humans are under the dominion of some king, it should be no surprise that animals too could be under the dominion of humans.[18]

Specific Texts

The major texts relating to the topic of "human dominion over animals" are Gen. 1:26, 28; 9:2–3; Ps. 8:6; Sir. 17:1–4; Wisd. 9:2–3.[19] All these texts deal with dominion over animals in the context of creation, and they indicate that God grants humans this status. These texts are concerned to articulate the relationship between humans and animals but also to indicate the relationship between humans and God. These texts help define the distinct nature of humans within the natural world that God has created. Creation is designed for life for living creatures and these creatures are valued as good.

The first three texts come from the Priestly source and must be interpreted within the system of the Priestly writer. The creation story represents a well-ordered world. The priests wish to maintain this order by living in an appropriate way. Primary concerns for priests related to animals included animal sacrifices and the eating of meat by humans. Humans — priests and lay people — exercise dominion by making distinctions among animals and treating various groups in different ways according to these distinctions.

Genesis 1

The deity gives humans dominion over animals, according to Gen. 1:26, 28. Dominion implies having authority and power and involves the exercise of that power. In Gen. 1:26 it is part of the divine decree and in 1:28 it is part of the blessing upon humans. Verse 1:28 can also be seen as a commission to the humans. The verb used is *rdh* ("rule").

---

18. Kay, "Concepts of Nature," 114–15.

19. Psalm 8:6 appears to be dependent upon Genesis 1, but there are different concerns here. The human dominion over animals seems to be a way of claiming human dignity and the potential of humans to influence the environment. Psalm 8 is a hymn, but because of its reflective nature it has sapiential concerns. Later sapiential books like Sirach and Wisdom, and other texts at Qumran (1QH 10:8; 1QS 3:17–18; 4Q423 2:2; 4Q422 1:9), continue to utilize such language of dominion. For further treatment of this topic in later sapiential texts see D. Jobling, "And Have Dominion...," *JSJ* 8, no. 1 (1977) 50–82. Primary attention is given here to the Priestly texts.

The language of dominion is linked to the fact that humans are in the "image of God," so it would seem that knowing how humans are in the image of God would illuminate "dominion."[20] Scholarly debate over the "image of God" has been extensive.[21] Gerhard von Rad's suggestion has been helpful:

> Just as powerful earthly beings, to indicate their claim to dominion, erect an image of themselves in the provinces of their empire where they do not personally appear, so man is placed upon earth in God's image as God's sovereign emblem. He is really only God's representative, summoned to maintain and enforce God's claim to dominion over the earth. The decisive thing about man's similarity to God, therefore, is his function in the non-human world.[22]

Similarly, Jon Levenson argues that God has appointed humanity to be his viceroy on earth. He "appoints the entire human race as God's royal stand-in."[23]

Language that is usually applied to a king and his relationship to his subjects is here applied to human beings in general and their relationship to animals. This metaphoric process has been called the democratization of an office — here, of the king. Levenson has suggested that this process of democratization of offices is found also in the text of the Egyptian Instruction of King Meri-Ka-Re and is also reflected in the promise to David applying to the whole nation in Isa. 55:3–5.[24]

H. Wildberger and W. H. Schmidt have suggested that this language comes from the royal court in Babylon and Egypt.[25] As Kraus has said, "The king alone is in the fullest sense human," and "the king stands in closest relationship to the gods."[26] To exalt the status of human beings to that of kingship was to bring great honor and dignity to the common person. Generally, in Mesopotamian cosmologies humans were "slaves created to maintain the universe for the gods," whereas here, humans have a more exalted destiny relative to the Creator.[27]

---

20. Terence Fretheim, commenting on my original oral presentation (see note 1), said that since humans are created in the image of God, God's relationship to animals needs to be considered for understanding how humans should treat animals.

21. See C. Westermann, *Genesis 1–11: A Commentary* (trans J. Scullion; Minneapolis: Augsburg, 1984) 147–58.

22. G. von Rad, *Genesis* (trans. J. Marks; Philadelphia: Westminster, 1972) 60.

23. J. Levenson, *Creation and the Persistence of Evil: The Jewish Drama of Divine Omnipotence* (San Francisco: Harper and Row, 1988) 116.

24. Levenson, *Creation and the Persistence of Evil*, 116.

25. Cited in Westermann, *Genesis 1–11*, 158.

26. H.-J. Kraus, *Psalms 1–59: A Commentary* (trans. H. Oswald; Minneapolis: Augsburg, 1988) 166.

27. R. Clifford, *Creation Accounts in the Ancient Near East and in the Bible* (Washington, D.C.: Catholic Biblical Association of America, 1994) 143.

Dominion over animals must be understood as metaphorical language somewhat analogous to the sun and moon "ruling" over the day and night. Clifford indicates that humans *rdh* ("rule," Gen. 1:26) over the life of three domains of sea, heaven, and earth, even as the sun and moon *mšl* ("govern") over the day and night.[28] While two different terms are used for dominion in Genesis 1, they are synonyms (*mšl*, *rdh*).[29] This means that the whole created realm is arranged into various hierarchies.

Some scholars view this royal language as mostly oppressive, while others view it in a more positive light. Phyllis Bird thinks the term *rdh* largely refers to "subordination."[30] She contends that a message of responsibility does not relate to the verb but "the action of God in setting Adam over the creatures in an ordered and sustaining world."[31] But she misleadingly suggests that *rdh* always has a negative connotation, when in fact it is the additional words in Biblical contexts that suggest negative aspects of particular kinds of rule.

Walter Houston argues that Isa. 11:1–9 is the most relevant passage for understanding dominion over animals in Genesis 1. In his words, "Here the rule of the messianic king creates justice and peace throughout the whole world, even in the animal kingdom — the lion no longer preys on the lamb, just as human oppressors are repressed."[32] He further states, "Creation as originally intended is a harmony inconceivable in the post-diluvian world — humanity as regents of God rule in peace over creatures who live in peace."[33] Hans Wildberger similarly says, "Where a legitimate king is in charge, as the representative of the deity and/or as the guarantor of world order in the righteousness appropriate to his office, the world can recover from its wretchedness."[34]

Ronald Simkins argues, "Human rule of the earth serves either to actively maintain the order of creation, or to cause its disintegration."[35] "Only when humans rule according to the created order is the world suitable for human habitation."[36] In this respect "dominion" itself does

28. Clifford, *Creation Accounts*, 144.

29. Clifford, *Creation Accounts*, 144.

30. P. Bird, " 'Male and Female He Created Them': Gen 1:27b in the Context of the Priestly Creation Account," *HTR* 74 (1981) 154.

31. Bird, " 'Male and Female He Created Them,' " 155.

32. W. Houston, *Purity and Monotheism: Clean and Unclean Animals in Biblical Law* (JSOTSup 140; Sheffield: JSOT Press, 1993) 255.

33. Houston, *Purity and Monotheism*, 255.

34. Hans Wildberger, *Isaiah 1–12: A Commentary* (trans. T. Trapp; Minneapolis: Fortress, 1991) 479.

35. R. Simkins, *Creator and Creation: Nature in the Worldview of Ancient Israel* (Peabody, Mass.: Hendrickson, 1994) 202.

36. Simkins, *Creator and Creation*, 202.

not indicate precisely how the humans will treat animals. What is certain is that they are in charge and in control of the animals.

Dominion does not mean that humans have the freedom to kill and exploit animals. According to Westermann, "The exercise of dominion does not begin with the use or exploitation of the animals for human ends."[37] Humans and animals are given permission to eat only plants (Gen. 1:29–30) until after the flood, when they are given permission to eat animals (Gen. 9:3). Westermann maintains that dominion may involve a personal relationship between the humans and animals and suggests, "Something of this too belongs to the rider, the horse trainer and even the hunter."[38]

There are several concluding points to make in relation to the dominion language in Genesis 1. First, most scholars agree that these texts are exilic or postexilic, when the Judahites had very little real power and dominion and were largely dominated by foreign powers. Such theology therefore presents an unrealized ideal for the people and not a kind of triumphalism derived from imperial power. Such a "dominion theology" is a means of giving people who are largely in submission to others hope for the future.

Second, while humans share much with animals, the humans are clearly differentiated from the other living creatures. Only they are considered to be in the image of God. They are created last and have a special place in creation. They have a special relationship with and responsibility toward other living creatures. This rules out some egalitarian ideal of humans and animals as equals.

Third, God grants humans dominion over creatures, but humans still stand under the authority of God and are held accountable. Creation is designed for life for living creatures, and these creatures are valued as good. Dominion over animals is linked to the image of God, which suggests that humans must act in accordance with God's desires. The killing of life would seem to violate the created order.

Dominion cannot simply be equated either with exploitation or with stewardship. Both alternatives are possibilities because humans are free to choose their own course. There was, however, a view of an ideal king and an ideal dominion that would result in peace and harmony. The divine granting of dominion over animals did not mean that humans were authorized to do whatever they pleased. Humans still stand under the authority of God and will be held accountable.

---

37. Westermann, *Genesis 1–11*, 228.
38. Westermann, *Genesis 1–11*, 228.

Flood

God sends a flood upon the earth because of the violence of "all flesh" (Gen. 6:11–12). Scholars are uncertain whether "all flesh" means humans or animals plus humans.[39] The issue relates to whether humans alone bring the catastrophe upon the earth or the animals share responsibility. In any case, this indicates that humans have failed in carrying out God's purposes on earth and that the flood destroys many individuals of the animal world, including humans.

Representatives of all living creatures are preserved on the ark so that a new beginning is possible. This indicates the importance of the preservation of the variety of species even though many individuals are killed in the flood. Richard Hiers has suggested that Noah's preservation of animals in the ark may represent the human dominion over animals for the Priestly writer.[40]

After the flood there is a new beginning, a new creation. While the language of dominion is not repeated here, specific instructions are given that indicate the relationship between humans and animals. God gives humans permission to eat animals, but they must not eat meat with the blood. Here we learn that the animals will fear and dread the humans (Gen. 9:2). The expression "fear and dread" is used for the inhabitants of Canaan in their reaction to the Israelites (Deut. 11:25; cf. 1:21, 29). God tells Noah and his sons that the animals "will be given into your hand," which, according to Westermann, is the language of holy war (cf. Lev. 26:25).[41]

After the flood God makes a covenant with humans and animals that the world would not be destroyed again by means of a flood (Gen. 9:8–17). Nevertheless, this did not bring peace among living things. In fact, as Anderson notes, there is a tragic dimension of this resolution because of the power of humans and their propensity to misuse this power.[42]

Further Priestly Concerns about Animals

The flood story does not yet bring us to the last word of the Priestly writer about the relationship between humans and animals. For the Israelites, further restrictions are given to Moses by God. In Leviticus 11 the criteria for clean and unclean animals are presented. A central issue relates to the perceived necessity of animal sacrifice. Lev. 17:11 is a programmatic text in which the means of atonement is blood. God gives people permission to use the blood of animals in sacrificial rites. Such

---

39. See Houston, *Purity and Monotheism*, 255–66 and footnote 1 on p. 255.
40. Hiers, "Ecology, Biblical Theology, and Methodology," 52.
41. Westermann, *Genesis 1–11*, 462.
42. Anderson, "Human Dominion over Nature," 148–49.

a theology makes the killing of animals mandatory as long as human sin exists.

Another issue relates to the eating of meat by humans. The eating of animals clearly represents the exercise of dominion over animals. Nick Fiddes argues that eating meat "tangibly represents human control of the natural world. Consuming the muscle flesh of other highly evolved animals is a potent statement of our supreme power."[43]

For the Priestly writer, there are three dietary regimes: (1) vegetarianism at creation; (2) eating of any animal but not with blood after the flood; and (3) eating of only some animals after the revelation at Mount Sinai.[44] For the Priestly writer, all humans are to honor the dietary regime after the flood but the Israelites are to restrict their behavior even more.

Houston argues that vegetarianism is the ideal at creation and that the eating of meat is granted only as a concession to human sinfulness. He contends that further restrictions are necessary for God to dwell with his people, who are sinful.[45] Edwin Firmage, on the other hand, argues that humans move progressively to the "diet" of God, who has been accustomed to animal sacrifice from the beginning.[46] Bernard Batto has argued that the movement from vegetarianism to meat eating in other creation stories from the ancient Near East sometimes is evaluated positively as moving from nature to culture. Thus, in the Gilgamesh Epic, Enkidu as a savage lives peacefully among the wild animals, but when he becomes civilized he eats them.[47]

Jacob Milgrom contends that many of the regulations regarding the dietary laws, the slaughter of animals, and other issues related to animals are humanitarian and teach the Israelites reverence for life. He argues that the purpose of the dietary laws is "to allow man to satiate his lust for animal flesh — and yet not be dehumanized in the process."[48] "Thus P's theory of anthropogenesis reveals its reservations

43. N. Fiddes, *Meat: A Natural Symbol* (London: Routledge, 1991) 196–97. For a more detailed discussion of meat eating in the Hebrew Bible see S. Reed, "Meat Eating and the Hebrew Bible," in H. Sun et al., eds., *Problems in Biblical Theology: Essays in Honor of Rolf Knierim* (Grand Rapids: Eerdmans, 1997) 281–94.

44. Houston, *Purity and Monotheism*, 256–58.

45. Houston, *Purity and Monotheism*, 257.

46. E. Firmage, "The Biblical Dietary Laws and the Concept of Holiness," in J. Emerton, ed., *Studies in the Pentateuch* (Leiden: Brill, 1990) 196–97. Sacrifices have at least been offered to Yahweh in the Yahwistic texts, which Firmage thinks did not offend the Priestly writer.

47. B. Batto, "Creation Theology in Genesis," in R. Clifford and J. Collins, eds., *Creation in the Biblical Traditions* (Washington, D.C.: Catholic Biblical Association of America, 1992) 20–22.

48. J. Milgrom, "The Biblical Diet Laws as an Ethical System," *Int* 17 (1963) 288. If Milgrom is correct about such laws as restraints upon human power, then the abolishing

and, indeed, its uneasiness regarding man's uncontrolled power over animal life."[49]

Psalm 8

Psalm 8 is a hymn in which scholars have recognized features of wisdom. The psalmist reflects upon the nature of humans and their place in the universe that God has created. The question "What are human beings?" in v. 4 reflects "the mystery of the greatness and the frailty of man."[50] Gerstenberger indicates that this question "is used in OT wisdom passages in the context of suffering, the quest for justice, and the fear of mortality and guilt (Job 7:17; 15:19; Ps. 144:3–4)."[51] When the psalmist reflects upon the created world, humans seem insignificant, and yet they have dignity within this world because of their position above the other creatures.

Humans are distinguished from God or divine beings and from animals. The psalm indicates an exalted status of humans in regard to their dominion over all other living creatures. While the word *mšl* ("rule, govern") is used instead of *rdh*, it is essentially synonymous to Genesis. Gerstenberger argues that this psalm arises out of the experience of "a general instability of life."[52] Furthermore, it relates to the problem of "human frailty and ambiguity within an overwhelmingly mysterious universe."[53]

In this hymn there is a sense of order and beauty that leads to worship and praise of the Creator. Unlike Genesis 1, humans are not given permission to have dominion, but instead, "dominion" is accepted and celebrated as a reality. The royal nature of humans is emphasized even more in Psalm 8 than in Genesis 1, because of the mention of coronation of humans in Ps. 8:5.[54] The human dominion over animals is a way of claiming human dignity and showing the importance of humans in the world. As Knierim notes, in Psalm 8 "humans stand on top of the pyramid of the order of creation."[55] This implies, however, not only a certain status but a responsibility to exercise this dominion appropriately.[56]

---

of dietary restrictions by Christians means that humans have been given a new freedom not found in Judaism. Any freedom, however, may be misused.

49. J. Milgrom, *Leviticus 1–16: A New Translation with Introduction and Commentary* (AB 3; New York: Doubleday, 1991) 712.

50. Kraus, *Psalms 1–59*, 179.

51. E. Gerstenberger, *Psalms, Part 1: With an Introduction to Cultic Poetry* (FOTL 14; Grand Rapids: Eerdmans, 1988) 69.

52. Gerstenberger, *Psalms*, 71.

53. Gerstenberger, *Psalms*, 70.

54. See Anderson, "Human Dominion over Nature," 121.

55. Knierim, *Task of Old Testament Theology*, 13 n. 10.

56. It has been argued that this psalm is a royal psalm referring to the king and

THEOLOGICAL CRITIQUE OF DOMINION

Anthropological Framework

Creation texts present cosmologies or worldviews. Cosmologies help people make sense of their world and their relationship to the world and also provide guidance concerning ethical issues. One of the common human problems that anthropologists identify is the relationship between humans and nature. Simkins refers to three solutions to the problem of human relationship with nature: (1) subjugation to nature; (2) harmony with nature; and (3) mastery over nature.[57] He contends that biblical texts can be found to support each of these possibilities and that some texts support more than one of these solutions. He does not see one solution as necessarily better than another.

These same three solutions can be applied to the relationship between humans and animals. One can speak of subjugation to animals, harmony with animals, and mastery over animals. One does not find a well-developed treatment of the relationship between humans and animals in the Hebrew Bible. Creation texts are an exception in that they sometimes include a comprehensive statement concerning humans and all animals. It would seem obvious at first that texts related to "dominion over animals" would fall into the category of mastery over animals. Curiously, however, Simkins argues that Priestly theology reflects harmony with nature much more than mastery over nature. Simkins draws upon the overall creation theology to arrive at this understanding.[58]

Ideal and Real Worlds

Biblical texts do not fall neatly into these three modes. Some creation texts speak programmatically about human dominion over all animals. These texts are prescriptive statements that propose ideals that are not necessarily realized and that often stand in tension with reality. Descriptive statements indicate actual human treatment of animals. One cannot and should not confuse these two kinds of statements.

---

that this dominion is royal dominion. Most scholars, however, see the psalm as referring to human dominion. The messianic interpretation of this psalm and its application to Christ in the New Testament follow in part from the royal nature of the language of the psalm. See Anderson, "Human Dominion over Nature," 123–35. Walter Houston offers interesting observations on the servant leadership of Jesus in the Gospels providing a model for dominion for humans ("'And Let Them Have Dominion...': Biblical Views of Man in Relation to the Environmental Crisis," in E. Livingston, ed., *Studia Biblica 1978: Papers on Old Testament and Related Themes* [JSOTSup 11; Sheffield: JSOT Press, 1978] 175–76). Further attention needs to be given to a biblical theology of human dominion over animals.

57. Simkins, *Creator and Creation*, 33.
58. Simkins, *Creator and Creation*, 205–6.

Descriptive statements about treatment of animals often refer to specific groups of animals and how they are treated in particular ways. Simkins notes that humans further classify animals "according to whether they belong to society (pets) or nature (wild animals)."[59] One does not often find in the Bible a universal ethic towards animals, but rather, different ways of treating different kinds of animals. Such texts may describe particulars about human and animal relationships, or prescriptive advice or regulations about particular relationships.

People related to different groups of animals in different ways. There were four different systems of classifications: (1) natural, in terms of location (land, sea, air); (2) natural, such as of diet (vegetarian, carnivorous); (3) cultural (domestic, wild); and (4) cultural (clean, unclean). Animals were domesticated for work, food, and, rarely, as pets. Some wild animals that were not dangerous to humans lived in close proximity to humans. Other wild animals, such as carnivores, were dangerous to humans.

Mary Douglas, Howard Eilberg-Schwartz, and Jacob Milgrom have shown how the animal world is understood to correspond to the human world.[60] Classifications of animals reflect classifications of humans. Thus, the Israelites are like domestic animals; specifically, they are sheep and Yahweh is the shepherd. Other nations that are in conflict with the Israelites are referred to as wild animals. While all animals can be eaten by the Gentiles, a restricted number of animals can be eaten by the Israelites, and an even more restricted number can be offered as sacrifices to God. These groups correspond to the basic human categories of the Gentiles, the Israelites, and the priests.[61]

Douglas has argued that distinctions between the clean and unclean animals are based on the creation story of Gen. 1:1–2:4a. Classification is based at least in part on physical traits or characteristics: land animals must chew the cud and have split hooves (Lev. 11:2–8), and sea animals must have fins and scales (Lev. 11:9–12). Only perfect animals without bodily blemishes can be used for sacrifices (Lev. 21:16–23; 22:20–24).[62] For the priests, according to Eilberg-Schwartz, "Carrying out the divine will involves keeping things in their proper categories."[63] "Israel is ex-

---

59. Simkins, *Creator and Creation*, 29.

60. M. Douglas, *Purity and Danger: An Analysis of the Concepts of Pollution and Taboo* (London: Routledge and Kegan Paul, 1966) 41–57; H. Eilberg-Schwartz, *The Savage in Judaism: An Anthropology of Israelite Religion and Ancient Judaism* (Bloomington: Indiana University Press, 1990) 115–40; J. Milgrom, "Ethics and Ritual: The Foundations of the Biblical Dietary Laws," in E. Firmage, B. Weiss, and J. Welch, eds., *Religion and Law: Biblical-Judaic and Islamic Perspectives* (Winona Lake, Ind.: Eisenbrauns, 1990) 177–86.

61. See diagrams 1 and 2 in Milgrom, "Ethics and Ritual," 179.

62. See Douglas, *Purity and Danger*, 55–57.

63. Eilberg-Schwartz, *The Savage in Judaism*, 219.

pected to affirm and uphold the distinction God implanted in the world at creation."[64] This helps to explain many aspects of Priestly legislation: one should not mate two different kinds of animals (Lev. 19:19); humans should not have sex with animals (Lev. 18:23).

Domestication of animals is never seriously questioned in the Bible. For the most part, too, there is little hesitation about eating meat when people can afford it. In the description of Solomon's peaceful reign the mention of the large amounts of meat eaten in a day includes both domesticated animals and wild animals (1 Kings 4:22–25). The power of a king could be seen in the large herds he had.

A mixture of agriculture and animal husbandry was a central way of life for many people living in the Mediterranean world. Domestication can be seen to represent the "mastery over animals." The domestication of some but by no means all animals of the ancient world had been accomplished long before the Priestly texts were written. In part, then, the language of dominion describes the present reality that humans do shape and modify their environment. Kay argues, "Indeed all societies, whether biocentric or homocentric in their world view, must extensively use nature in order to survive."[65]

Not all animals were domesticated. Domestication of certain animals is based partly on human choice and partly on human ability. The book of Job presents a series of several creatures that are outside of human control and knowledge in Job 38:39–39:30: lion, raven, mountain goat, wild ass, wild ox, ostrich, hawk, and eagle. The war horse (Job 39:19–25) is the only exception to wild animals in this section but even the war horse seems only partly domesticated. Behemoth, depicted in part as a hippopotamus, and Leviathan, depicted in part as a crocodile, clearly cannot be domesticated by humans (Job 40:15–41:34). While Behemoth and Leviathan can at times refer to symbolic/mythological creatures, their descriptions here contain some identifiable features of real creatures.[66]

There are a few texts in the Hebrew Bible that refer to the care of domestic animals. In Prov. 12:10 the righteous should care for the needs of their animals. Good shepherds should take good care of their flocks (Prov. 27:23–27). During a serious drought Ahab and Obadiah searched throughout the land to find grass to keep their animals alive (1 Kings

---

64. Eilberg-Schwartz, *The Savage in Judaism*, 220.

65. Kay, "Concepts of Nature," 325–26.

66. For a discussion of these passages of Job see G. Tucker, "Rain on a Land Where No one Lives: The Hebrew Bible on the Environment," *JBL* (1997) 12–16 and J. Crenshaw, "When Form and Content Clash: The Theology of Job 38:1–40:5," in R. Clifford and J. Collins, eds., *Creation in the Biblical Traditions* (Washington, D.C.: Catholic Biblical Association of America, 1992) 70–84.

18:5–6). Jacob tells Esau that he cannot travel with him but must travel slowly because of children and nursing flocks and herds. The concern is that if he travels too fast, they may die (Gen. 33:13). While this appears to be a ruse on Jacob's part, it was a believable excuse. Both David and Jacob are known to have cared for animals for which they were responsible. Stories of hospitality to strangers include the provision of food for animals (Gen. 24:31–33; 43:24; Judg. 19:19–21). Animals are to rest on the Sabbath just like the humans (Exod. 20:10; 23:12; Deut. 5:14). One should remove a burden from a donkey or an ass that has fallen down, whether it belongs to an enemy (Exod. 23:5) or not (Deut. 22:4). One should not muzzle an ox that is treading grain (Deut. 25:4). While one can argue that such an ethic sees not inherent but only instrumental value in animals, it is at least a start, and is not always a reality, even in today's world.

Some wild animals presented a threat to humans and their domestic animals. At times such animals actually subjugated the Israelites, and people are frightened of them (2 Kings 17:24–31). David protected his flock from lions and bears (1 Sam. 17:34–37). Amos 3:12 has the simile of a shepherd rescuing a few pieces of sheep from the mouth of a lion. Humans could be threatened by wild animals, such as snakes, bears, and lions (Amos 5:19; Eccl. 10:8, 11). A lion killed a prophet but, surprisingly, did not eat him (1 Kings 13:24–25, 28). The ruse of Joseph's brothers that Joseph was killed by a wild animal was readily believed by Jacob (Gen. 37:20, 33).

Yahweh sometimes punishes people by allowing wild animals to molest and eat them (Deut. 32:24).[67] He sent lions among the disobedient, which killed some of them (2 Kings 17:25–26). Depictions of disaster in prophetic literature include the presence of wild animals: "Therefore a lion from the forest shall kill them, a wolf from the desert shall destroy them. A leopard is watching against their cities; everyone who goes out of them shall be torn to pieces — because their transgressions are many, their apostasies are great" (Jer. 5:6 NRSV; cf. Ezek. 5:17). Another group of wild animals mentioned in judgment oracles is the scavengers, including birds of the air and animals of the land, which will feast on the dead corpses of the slain (Jer. 19:7; 34:20; Ezek. 32:4; 39:4).

Yahweh's care for the Israelites includes protection from wild animals. He drove out the Canaanites slowly from the promised land so that the wild animals would not multiply too quickly and pose a threat (Exod. 23:29; Deut. 7:22). This assumes that if humans are absent very long from the land, wild animals will take over. In fact, some judg-

---

67. Kay ("Concepts of Nature," 316–17) refers to examples of both animal and plant dominion over humans in the Hebrew Bible.

ment oracles depict cities inhabited only by wild animals (Isa. 13:21; Jer. 50:39; Zeph. 2:14–15).

Depictions of the future ideal life sometimes indicated that wild animals would no longer be a threat to humans (Ezek. 34:25–31). Hosea even speaks of a covenant made with the animals that will lead to peace between animals and humans (Hos. 2:18). In an ideal future there is no place for wild animals that may kill humans. Either the animals must be removed, as in Ezekiel and Leviticus (26:6), or they must be transformed into vegetarians, as in Isaiah 11.

There is less evidence concerning care for wild animals. Wild animals are allowed to eat in the fields during the seventh fallow year (Exod. 23:11). If one finds a bird in its nest, one should not take the eggs and mother together (Deut. 22:6–7). The reasons for such "care" are not certain. Job is reminded of the human inability to take care of many of the wild animals (38:39–39:30). God is the one who provides for these creatures. God is depicted as providing for all living creatures (Ps. 104:27–30). Wild animals, such as the lion (Job 38:39–40; Ps. 104:21) and young ravens (Job 38:41; Ps. 147:9), are fed. Wild animals are provided drink (Ps. 104:11).

Other Modes of Relating to Animals

Many scholars have thought that the naming of the animals by Adam in Genesis 2 is analogous to the dominion of Genesis 1. Von Rad notes, "Name-giving in the ancient Orient was primarily an exercise of sovereignty, of command."[68] George W. Ramsey argues, however, that naming signifies an act of discerning something about these creatures and not an act of domination.[69] Westermann states, "By naming the animals the man opens up, determines and orders his world and incorporates them into his life."[70] In this creation story the animals are brought to Adam as potentially suitable companions or helpers. This at least raises the possibility of a close relationship between Adam and the animals. But the animals prove inadequate, which leads to the creation of another human, Eve. The expulsion from the garden brings about a new relationship between the humans and the serpent, who may represent other animals as well. What remains is the reality of conflict between humans and animals.

Other biblical texts provide better models for harmony with animals than the language of "dominion over animals." In Psalm 104 humans are but one kind of God's creatures, not elevated above others. This

---

68. Von Rad, *Genesis*, 83.

69. G. Ramsey, "Is Name-Giving an Act of Domination in Genesis 2:23 and Elsewhere?" *CBQ* 50 (1988) 24–35.

70. Westermann, *Genesis 1–11*, 228.

may reflect harmony with animals. The food for humans listed is vegetarian (vv. 14–15) but God feeds the lion (v. 21), which is a predator. God's permission for predators to kill other creatures implies that some must die so that others will live. Sirach argues in a song related to creation that good things are for the benefit of the righteous and that bad things are for the punishment of the wicked (39:12–35). The fangs of the wild animals, and scorpions and vipers are for the punishment of the ungodly (v. 30).

Passages in Job encompass areas of the earth that are outside of the concerns of humans but still are part of the created world of Yahweh. As Tucker states concerning Job 38–39, "Although the first divine speech is not a direct critique of the commission to have dominion, it explicitly challenges the human instinct to control, especially to domesticate. Humanity does not understand all things, nor manage them, but God does."[71]

The passages in Job and Psalm 104 affirm the place and value of predators, since God feeds the lion (Ps. 104:21; cf. Job 38:39–41). This means that some must die so that others will live. Ideal descriptions of the future by some prophets assume that predators will no longer seek prey (Isaiah 11). The created world of God must be transformed before harmony and peace can be present. Harmony with animals appears in some creation stories and also in some idealized descriptions of the future. But daily reality shows that conflict exists between humans and animals. Humans at times are subjugated to some animals and also have mastery over some animals.

HERMENEUTICAL REFLECTIONS ON THE USAGE OF "HUMAN DOMINION OVER ANIMALS"

Conflict between Predators and Prey

There is a conflict between the intrinsic value of animals, even predators, and the fact that such predators are harmful to other animals that have intrinsic value. When predators kill other creatures, it does not seem that they can be held responsible for this. If anyone is responsible, it must be the Creator, who has made the predators what they are. God gives permission for predators to kill other creatures as their prey. This creates a theological problem. If God wants creatures to live, why does God create some creatures that must kill other creatures to survive?

Carnivores must have meat to survive. Omnivores like humans may live as vegetarians, but their digestive systems make it difficult to be herbivores. By their very nature humans are given permission to eat

---

71. Tucker, "Rain on a Land," 15.

animals. Even as God gave permission for the predators to eat, humans are given permission to eat other animals for their food. Humans, then, are allowed to be predators. Some humans have chosen to be vegetarian because they find being a predator morally problematic.

Threat of Dangerous Animals

Wild animals presented threats to humans in biblical times. In some areas of the world wild animals still present threats or are a potential food source for humans. They compete with humans for food and may even be a threat to the lives of humans. Farmers in Zimbabwe do not like elephants to trample their fields. Mothers do not like their children to be bitten by snakes. When animals become a threat to life, humans usually feel morally justified in protecting themselves.

While in urban America there may be few threats to life from dangerous animals, most people do not like vermin in their houses. How many people are willing to share their living spaces with rats, mice, wasps, mosquitoes, spiders? Much money and research is devoted to exterminating rodents. We spend much money dealing with disease-producing bacteria and viruses spread by animals. Certainly, we must be exercising dominion over these pests.

Much concern about animal rights pertains to large mammals, which receive much sympathy. How far does such concern extend? What about bacteria and viruses, which are a great threat to our lives? Do we have the right to exercise dominion over them? Does not the language of dominion accurately depict the desired kind of relationship over harmful bacteria and viruses?

Limits on Dominion over Animals

Humans attempted mastery of the world particularly through wisdom in biblical times, but this did not mean that they were optimistic about achieving total supremacy over creation. They assumed that there were limits to their wisdom. They did not assume that they knew all of God's purposes for creation. They did not have the power or means to exterminate large numbers of creatures. Since they knew of creatures which they could not tame, it is doubtful that they thought it even possible to control the world that God had created (Job 40–41).

For some biblical theologians the killing of animals posed problems. They envisioned a world in which animals and humans could live together in peace. They were primarily concerned about peace and security for humans. They could not imagine animals needing protection from humans. The present-day situation is quite different.

Although in biblical times there were important limitations on dominion, these have not continued to be operative. The language of dominion over animals has been historically problematic. It is not very helpful today, because it seems to legitimize and even accelerate misuse of the world. Language of stewardship and compassion seems more appropriate. Creation theology provides some justification for this.

Changing Contexts

Knierim argues that changing settings and contexts of texts from ancient times to the present must in turn shape our application of texts today. In regard to the language of "subdue" the earth in Genesis 1 he states, "Whatever this word does and does not mean, it must be considered in view of today's use of the earth by humans, but no longer in view of its use more than two millennia ago."[72]

Related to differences in contexts from antiquity to today is the fact that people also live in different contexts today. The reality of most people living during biblical times and the reality of many people in developing countries today is that they see themselves being in subjection to the world around them and in some cases to animals. In these contexts "dominion theology" provides hope for a better future. Such a message helps people to escape from a cycle of poverty, despair, and fatalism.

For people in the Western world who see themselves in control of nature and have shown in practice how destructive they can be toward nature and animals, such a message of "dominion theology" seems to legitimate their oppressive treatment of the world and simply reinforce a destructive ideology. Environmentalists are raising important questions related to such a false ideology. Yet while the corrective of such environmentalists is certainly appropriate to the Western world, it can be heavily oppressive, even imperialistic, toward people living in developing countries. Attention to the everyday and economic realities of people living in developing countries must be given more consideration. Even in the Western world it is those people who rely directly upon the natural world for their livelihoods, such as foresters and farmers, who often come into conflict with environmentalists.

Actions Affect the World

In the biblical worldview the actions of humans can affect other creatures in the world. We share living space with other creatures. A traditional scientific worldview sees humans pitted against nature. A holistic view sees that we belong to the world, depend upon the world, and are nourished by the world. If we damage the world, we in turn

---

72. Knierim, *Task of Old Testament Theology*, 466–67.

will suffer. Ecologists have shown how life forms are interdependent with one another.

Since all animals were created by God and declared by God to be good, they have intrinsic value to God. God cannot be pleased when these animals become extinct. Scientists are discovering the important role that all animals, even predators, play in the ecosystem. Even if humans cannot recognize the intrinsic value of predators, they need to recognize their instrumental value for the world in which we all live.

Animals as "Good to Think"[73]

In the Hebrew Bible animals were "good to think" as well as good to eat. Humans made analogies between the animal world and the human world. The ways that animals were treated reflected in some ways how humans of different groups were treated. Some of the logic for how humans treated particular groups of animals was related to how they were perceived.

Anthropologists indicate that humans understand themselves in part by how they are distinct and different from others. Humans often define themselves in opposition to animals. Humans try to distinguish themselves from animals. They may do this in many ways. As Fiddes in his book on meat eating suggests, one may do this either by eating animals or by refusing to eat animals. The irony here is that whether one eats animals or not, one still has power to do so and to choose to do so.[74] In this sense both options reflect a kind of dominion over animals.

BIBLIOGRAPHY

Anderson, B. "Human Dominion over Nature." In *From Creation to New Creation.* Minneapolis: Fortress, 1994.

Batto, B. "Creation Theology in Genesis." In *Creation in the Biblical Traditions.* Ed. R. Clifford and J. Collins. Washington, D.C.: Catholic Biblical Association of America, 1992.

Birch, C. *Regaining Compassion for Humanity and Nature.* St. Louis: Chalice, 1993.

Bird, Phyllis. " 'Male and Female He Created Them': Gen 1:27b in the Context of the Priestly Creation Account." HTR 74 (1981).

Clifford, R. *Creation Accounts in the Ancient Near East and in the Bible.* Washington, D.C.: Catholic Biblical Association of America, 1994.

Douglas, Mary. *Purity and Danger: An Analysis of the Concepts of Pollution and Taboo.* London: Routledge & Kegan Paul, 1966.

---

73. See Marvin Harris, *Good to Eat: Riddles of Food and Culture* (New York: Simon and Schuster, 1985). Harris identifies two approaches: one that sees food as a material reality ("good to eat") and one that sees food as symbolic ("good to think").

74. Fiddes, *Meat: A Natural Symbol*, 224–33.

Eilberg-Schwartz, Howard. *The Savage in Judaism: An Anthropology of Israelite Religion and Ancient Judaism.* Bloomington: Indiana University Press, 1990.

Fiddes, Nick. *Meat: A Natural Symbol.* London and New York: Routledge, 1991.

Firmage, E. "The Biblical Dietary Laws and the Concept of Holiness." In *Studies in the Pentateuch.* Ed. J. Emerton. Leiden: E. J. Brill, 1990.

Harris, Marvin. *Good to Eat: Riddles of Food and Culture.* New York: Simon and Schuster, 1985.

Hiers, Richard. "Ecology, Biblical Theology, and Methodology: Biblical Perspectives on the Environment." *Zygon* 19 (1984).

Houston, Walter. " 'And Let Them Have Dominion . . . ' Biblical Views of Man in Relation to the Environmental Crisis." In *Studia Biblica 1978. I. Papers on Old Testament and Related Themes.* Sheffield: Sheffield Academic Press, 1978.

――――. *Purity and Monotheism: Clean and Unclean Animals in Biblical Law.* Sheffield: JSOT Press, 1993.

Jobling, D. "And Have Dominion . . . ." *JSJ* 8: 1 (1977).

Kay, J. "Concepts of Nature in the Hebrew Bible." *Environmental Ethics* 10 (1988).

Knierim, Rolf. *The Task of Old Testament Theology: Substance, Method, and Cases.* Grand Rapids: Eerdmans, 1995.

Levenson, Jon. *Creation and the Persistence of Evil: The Jewish Drama of Divine Omnipotence.* San Francisco: Harper & Row, 1988.

Milgrom, Jacob. "The Biblical Diet Laws as an Ethical System." *Int* 17 (1963).

――――. "Ethics and Ritual: The Foundations of the Biblical Dietary Laws." In *Religion and Law: Biblical-Judaic and Islamic Perspectives.* Ed. E. Firmage, B. Weiss, and J. Welch. Winona Lake, Ind.: Eisenbrauns, 1990.

――――. *Leviticus 1–16.* New York: Doubleday, 1991.

Pinches, C. and J. McDaniel, eds. *Good News for Animals: Christian Approaches to Animal Well-Being.* Maryknoll, N.Y.: Orbis, 1993.

Ramsey, George. "Is Name-Giving an Act of Domination in Genesis 2:23 and Elsewhere?" *CBQ* 50 (1988).

Rasmussen, Larry. *Earth Community, Earth Ethics.* Maryknoll, N.Y.: Orbis, 1996.

Reed, Stephen. "Meat Eating and the Hebrew Bible." In *Problems in Biblical Theology.* Ed. H. Sun and K. Eades. Grand Rapids: Eerdmans, 1997.

Simkins, Ronald. *Creator and Creation: Nature in the Worldview of Ancient Israel.* Peabody, Mass.: Hendrickson Publishers Inc., 1994.

Tucker, G. "Rain on a Land Where No One Lives: The Hebrew Bible on the Environment." *JBL* (1997).

Westermann, C. *Genesis 1–11.* Trans. J. Scullion. Minneapolis: Augsburg, 1984.

White Jr., Lynn. "The Historical Roots of our Ecological Crisis." *Science* 155 (March 10, 1967).

20

The Value of Rolf Knierim's Old Testament Theology for Practical Theology

Janet L. Weathers

Rolf Knierim's approach to Old Testament theology is sparking lively conversations and important research in biblical studies.[1] As a practical theologian I am particularly interested in the contribution his work can make to the discipline of practical theology. The substance and method of his work in Old Testament theology can enrich and deepen our understanding of the Bible and inform preaching, pastoral care, and Christian education in important ways. His method for dealing with the diverse theological understandings in the Bible also models a form of discourse that is relevant to many of the philosophical issues practical theologians must grapple with today. The purpose of this essay is to encourage increased dialogue between biblical scholars and practical theologians, and to explore the contribution of Knierim's work to this dialogue.

Faculty in all of the subareas of practical theology engage the Bible in their work. As an example, there has been a long history of interest in the role of the Bible in Christian religious education.[2] Of particular concern has been the need to incorporate the insights of biblical scholarship into the educational program of the church. In Mary Boys's 1979 review of the contributions of contemporary biblical scholarship to religious education she begins by noting that "those who are both drawn to and overwhelmed by the vast amount of theological literature know the

---

1. See, for example, Rolf P. Knierim, *The Task of Old Testament Theology: Substance, Method, and Cases* (Grand Rapids: Eerdmans, 1995).

2. Texts that have been influential in considering the role of the Bible in Christian education include M. Boys, *Biblical Interpretation in Religious Education* (Birmingham, Ala.: Religious Education Press, 1980); I. V. Cully. *The Bible in Christian Education* (Minneapolis: Fortress, 1995); H. S. Elliott, *Can Religious Education Be Christian?* (New York: Macmillan, 1947); S. Little, *The Role of the Bible in Contemporary Christian Education* (Richmond: John Knox, 1961); J. S. Marino, ed., *Biblical Themes in Religious Education* (Birmingham, Ala.: Religious Education Press, 1983); C. E. Nelson, *Where Faith Begins* (Atlanta: John Knox, 1967); J. D. Smart, *The Strange Silence of the Bible in the Church: A Study in Hermeneutics* (Louisville: Westminster, 1969).

truth of the Jewish proverb that 'learning requires a talent for sitting.' "[3]
She believes that the problem of proliferating scholarship is most acute
in biblical scholarship.[4] Boys's comment is even truer today, after nearly
two decades of additional biblical scholarship has become available to
religious educators.

In 1987 Roland Murphy delivered an address at the Eastern Regional Conference of Religious Educators in Washington, D.C., in which
he reviewed current thinking on issues relating to historical criticism,
hermeneutics, and selected aspects of biblical theology, and identified
specific books and articles he thought would be helpful to religious educators.[5] Far more frequent participation by biblical scholars and practical
theologians in meetings of one another's guilds would be a helpful way
to increase discussion among the disciplines.

An example of an effort to encourage conversation among biblical
scholars and practical theologians in a more open, dialogical forum
occurred at Princeton Theological Seminary in the spring of 1997. Members of the Bible department asked to meet with the faculty of the
practical theology department. They asked the faculty in the areas of
Christian education, congregational studies, preaching and speech communication in ministry, and pastoral care and counseling what they
needed students to learn in their Bible courses to support the work
being done in practical theology. While it is difficult to add more
meetings to the load that faculty carry in any institution, it was clear
that the discussion was worthwhile and more conversations would be
valuable. Such interdisciplinary conversation can address critical pedagogical needs in theological education, but it also has the potential to
advance scholarship for both disciplines — biblical studies and practical
theology.

Practical theologians who frequently do extensive work with the
Bible in diverse contexts and with diverse groups of people gain rich
insights that can augment the work of biblical scholars. For example,
Charles Bartow, a scholar whose work focuses on performance theory,
rhetoric, and homiletics raises significant questions about biblical exegesis that occur as one prepares the oral performance of a text. Each line
in a text can be read with many different intonations, and each reading
changes the meaning conveyed. The different possibilities for reading
the text open up provocative exegetical questions. These insights may

---

3. M. C. Boys, "Religious Education and Contemporary Biblical Scholarship," *Religious Education* 74 (March–April 1979) 182.

4. Boys, "Religious Education," 182.

5. Roland Murphy, "Update on Scripture Studies," *Religious Education* 82 (fall 1987)
624–36.

be lost if the exegete does not consider possible *oral* interpretations of the text.[6]

New Testament scholar Donald Juel encourages all biblical scholars to pay attention to the insights gained from *hearing* the text through participation in its oral performance. He also acknowledges that participating in Bible study with youth and adults in the church has influenced his interpretation of texts. Once, a high school student challenged Juel's interpretation of Mark 1:9–11, arguing that when the heavens were torn open following Jesus' baptism, it was not so much that people now had access to God, but rather, God had access to us. "The protection is gone. God is here among us, on the loose."[7] Juel was struck by the significance of the youth's insight and later included it in his commentary on Mark.[8] Active participation in teaching, preaching, worship leadership, and pastoral care and counseling often involves scholars with texts in ways that can contribute to the enterprise of biblical scholarship, just as such participation contributes to scholarship in practical theology.

Scholarship and the church would benefit from reducing the distance that separates the disciplines in seminaries and divinity schools. Interdisciplinary work is increasingly valued in most fields, although the challenge of grappling responsibly with scholarship in multiple fields is daunting. For faculties committed to training pastors, the need for increased interdisciplinary work is particularly critical.

It is from this point of view that I am encouraged by the approach that Rolf Knierim is taking in his Old Testament theology.[9] Both the substantive results of his work thus far and the clarity of his method are important for scholarship and teaching in practical theology. There have been many Old Testament theologies written in the past several decades. The traditional approaches have assumed a unified whole in

---

6. See, for example, his extended analysis of Psalm 27 in Charles L. Bartow, *God's Human Speech: A Practical Theology of Proclamation* (Grand Rapids: Eerdmans, 1997) 79–93.

7. D. Juel, " 'Your Word is Truth': Some Reflections on a Hard Saying," inaugural address presented at Princeton Theological Seminary, fall 1995.

8. D. Juel, *Mark* (ΛCNT; Minneapolis: Augsburg, 1990) 34.

9. Knierim makes a strong case for recognizing the theological significance of the Christian Old Testament, the Jewish Bible, in its own right. See, for example, Knierim, *Task of Old Testament Theology*, 1; "On the Task of Old Testament Theology," in E. E. Carpenter, ed., *A Biblical Itinerary: In Search of Method, Form, and Content* (JSOTSup 240; Sheffield: Sheffield Academic Press, 1997) 157. From this point of view his perspective may be of special interest to practical theologians who are active in Christian-Jewish dialogue, because Knierim respects the integrity of the Old Testament and does not presuppose the superiority of texts in the New Testament. His approach allows the two Testaments to mutually inform one another. For Christians, this is important because it allows the Old Testament to address deficiencies in the New Testament in ways that are usually overlooked when we insist on reading the Old Testament only through New Testament lenses.

terms of which each of the parts can be seen as a facet that contributes
to the whole. Knierim's approach is different. He does not believe
that the diverse theological understandings in the Old Testament can
be brought into a harmonious whole. For not only are there different
voices, but also differing voices, voices making truth claims that are
contradictory.

THE REALITY AND CHALLENGE OF DIVERSITY
IN THE BIBLE AND IN THE WORLD

We live in a time in which pluralism and a diversity of perspectives
are major topics in the discourse of practical theology, as in other disciplines. But the issues of pluralism and diversity in the Bible are not
imported from contemporary discourse. Prior to issues raised by diverse
hermeneutical approaches to a single text, one is faced with the diversity of theological understandings inherent in the Bible itself. Knierim
believes that the task of Old Testament theology is to identify the diversity of theological understandings and explain the relationships among
them. Knierim makes clear what is at stake in this process:

> In the Bible we are not confronted with an individual biblical text in
> isolation from all others, but with all the texts at the same time. We
> are, therefore, confronted with the theologies of every text in the bibli-
> cal canon, rather than with the theology of only one text, biblical source,
> or book. This fact constitutes the basis for the theological problem of the
> canon and, in addition to the deficit of exegesis, the second reason for the
> need for biblical theology. The sum total of exegesis of the biblical texts
> has irreversibly demonstrated a considerable plurality and diversity of
> theological positions in and among the biblical texts. Because of this fact,
> no text considered in isolation from the others self-evidently assures us
> of its truth or of the degree of its truth. I am addressing the well-known
> problem of the "canon within the canon."[10]

One of the reasons that Knierim's work is helpful for practical theologians is that he takes the diversity of theological understandings in the
Bible seriously and does not create an external framework into which
he tries to make the diverse understandings fit. Although the diversity
is obvious to anyone who has read the Bible closely, it raises significant
pedagogical questions. The presence of conflicting theological understandings may contribute to the popularly espoused view that one can
prove anything using the Bible. If people believe this to be true, then
the credibility of the Bible is diminished. Biblical scholars who are committed to the significance of the Bible in the life of faith have reason to
join practical theologians in their concern about this.

10. Knierim, *Task of Old Testament Theology*, 67.

While it is important that Knierim acknowledges and clearly identifies the existence of diverse theological positions in the Bible, it is
equally important that he does not merely let the diversity stand.
Knierim insists that the task of Old Testament theology is to do the
hard work of thinking through the relationships among the diverse
theologies, making a case for which theological understanding is most
fundamental. Once this is established, it becomes the criterion with
which other theological perspectives must be evaluated. I will explain
more about the reasons and method behind Knierim's determination of
the most fundamental criterion later in this essay. At this point, however, let me indicate at this point that the result of Knierim's analysis
leads him to argue for the "universal dominion of Yahweh in justice
and righteousness" as the primary criterion of the Old Testament in
terms of which the truth claims of other theological perspectives and
concepts are to be evaluated.[11]

Knierim's approach to negotiating among the diverse theological
perspectives provides an excellent example of the kind of dialogue philosopher Richard Bernstein calls for in the wake of the postmodern
challenge to the possibility of objectivity.[12] Bernstein argues that rejecting objectivism does not necessarily lead to sheer relativism. Through
dialogue people of differing perspectives can engage one another in
ways that help us discern what is at stake in committing to one perspective rather than another. The knowledge that is generated from such a
perspective is contingent knowledge and not absolute truth. Nevertheless, it is not subjectivism and does not lead to sheer relativism.

Bernstein's approach is consistent with the turn to rhetoric that has
taken hold in many disciplines.[13] Rhetoric deals with contingent knowledge. We are engaged in the practice of rhetoric when we argue for
positions that could be otherwise. Knierim's approach to the diversity
found in the Bible is an example of such an approach. Knierim is not
suggesting that it would be possible to "prove" what the various relationships among the diverse theologies in the Bible are, thus making
possible a final, definitive biblical theology to which all would agree.
The careful study of biblical texts will continue to disclose new insights
that are likely to influence the substantive aspects of Old Testament
theology. Such changes, however, would not have any bearing on the
legitimacy of the theological method.

---

11. Knierim, *Task of Old Testament Theology*, 15.

12. R. J. Bernstein, *Beyond Objectivism and Relativism: Science, Hermeneutics, and Praxis*
(Philadelphia: University of Pennsylvania Press, 1983).

13. See, for example, C. O. Schrag, *The Resources of Rationality: A Response to the
Postmodern Challenge* (Bloomington: University of Indiana Press, 1990).

By engaging one another dialogically in our efforts to discern, as far as possible, the truth disclosed in the biblical texts and the relationships among them, we are engaged, at least in part, in a rhetorical process, a communal process of trying to discern where the fullest truth lies. This statement does not imply that there is no role for the Holy Spirit in our efforts to understand the Bible as people of faith. Knierim's essays, "The Spirituality of the Old Testament"[14] and "The Old Testament — The Letter and the Spirit"[15] provide fascinating insights into the Old Testament's own perspective on the relationship of the divine Spirit to the human spirit, and the concept of revelation. The Bible knows, and we confess, that the Holy Spirit plays a significant role in our relationship with the Bible as people of faith. But along with our confidence in the agency of the Spirit we must also recognize the nature of the human process we engage in in our joint efforts to understand what the Bible means.

Within the human aspect of the process there is always a rhetorical dimension. Kenneth Burke points out that rhetoric "is rooted in an essential function of language itself, a function that is wholly realistic, and is continually born anew; the use of language as a symbolic means of inducing cooperation in beings that by nature respond to symbols."[16]

When we are communicating with one another to discern the "better way" or "the better saying," we are seeking to induce cooperation from others in several ways simultaneously. In beginning the dialogue, we invite others to participate. They could do otherwise. In choosing certain forms of communication and avoiding others, we are influencing the ongoing participation of others and influencing the choice of the topic and the tone of the conversation. Our choice to use language that others will understand is part of the rhetorical process of seeking to induce others to communicate with us. If we choose to use language that others will not be able to understand, that choice is likely to influence others to drop out of the conversation or demand a change of language. Both the form in which we communicate and the substance of what we say function in ways that influence others. When influence is present, as it always is when two or more people communicate, there is a rhetorical dimension to what we are doing.[17]

---

14. Knierim, *Task of Old Testament Theology*, 269–97.

15. Knierim, *Task of Old Testament Theology*, 298–308.

16. K. Burke, *A Rhetoric of Motives* (Berkeley: University of California Press, 1950) 43.

17. From this understanding those who disparage the use of rhetoric are nevertheless engaged in a rhetorical process. We do not have the option of avoiding the process, if we are communicating. Failure to recognize the presence of rhetoric does not constitute its

THE INEVITABLE USE OF CRITERIA

Rhetorical analysis often focuses on ways in which we make a case for the superiority of one perspective over another.[18] The approach of claiming one perspective as "the better saying," as Knierim points out, is not foreign to the Bible itself. What we claim represents the better way rests on the criteria we apply to the evaluation of the available options. We often apply implicit criteria without conscious reflection. Criteria are always operative, however, whether we are aware of them or not.

If we are to describe the nature of the relationships among the diverse theologies in the Old Testament, we must have criteria to do so. One aspect of the task of Old Testament theology is to discern the criteria from the biblical texts themselves. These criteria then become the means of assessing the relative theological validity of competing perspectives. Assessment of the relative theological validity of biblical texts is not a new process. It has always been done. Regardless of how literally we understand the "Word of God,"

> all biblical "words" are never considered equally valid. Some are more important; others are less important.... The degree of importance results from the fact that the texts, just as the elements within them, are relative to each other. Such relativity does not mean irrelevance. However, it does mean that we should not strive for a truth that is absolute. The Bible, because of its knowledge of God, knew, long before modern science and philosophy established it, that there is no knowledge of absolute truth and that no knowledge of God is absolute. This insight must be a fundamental theological assertion (cf. 1 Cor 13:8–12).[19]

From a pedagogical point of view, it is important to acknowledge that we can never have knowledge of absolute truth, and that there are diverse theological perspectives in the Bible that make contradictory truth claims. If preachers and teachers simply ignore the texts that they think are of little importance, or with which they disagree, they miss the opportunity to give laypersons guidance in differentiating among texts. By

---

absence. It only means that those who refuse to acknowledge their own use of rhetoric have forfeited some degree of self-awareness in not recognizing the nature and function of their own communicative behavior.

18. For insight into the ways rhetoricians analyze these communicative processes see, for example, W. R. Fisher, *Human Communication as Narration: Toward a Philosophy of Reason, Value, and Action* (Columbia: University of South Carolina Press, 1987); S. Toulmin, R. Rieke, and A. Janik, *An Introduction to Reasoning* (New York: Macmillan, 1979).

19. Knierim, *Task of Old Testament Theology*, 72.

not addressing the process directly, they may send the message that we can simply pick and choose among the biblical texts, emphasizing those we agree with and ignoring those we disagree with. This is hardly the approach clergy intend to encourage.

Clergy need to be able to clarify for themselves the criteria they are using in emphasizing some biblical texts rather than others and help laypersons to understand the process. As Knierim points out, although we often do so without awareness, we are always applying criteria, at least implicitly, that lead us to lift up certain texts as more important than others. If we are not aware of what we are doing, we are more likely to deceive ourselves and others into thinking that we are treating all the texts of the Bible as equally valid. By insisting on the need to make our criteria explicit, Knierim helps us reduce the number of unreflected biases that influence not only our scholarship but also our preaching and teaching.

The diversity of theological perspectives in the Bible is of particular concern for preachers and religious educators in mainline denominations that take biblical scholarship seriously. As Knierim points out, however, the problem is not eliminated, even for those traditions that reject the legitimacy of a scholarly analysis of the Bible and hold to the most literal view of the Bible as the Word of God.

Recent discussions in the popular media highlight the inevitability of the use of criteria. On June 12, 1998, the president of the Southern Baptist Seminary, Dr. R. Albert Mohler Jr., and Rev. Jerry Falwell, president of Liberty University and a well-known spokesperson for the religious right, were interviewed on the CNN television show *Larry King Live*. The focus of the interview was the Southern Baptist Convention's recent adoption of the eighteenth article in the "Baptist Faith and Message," a significant theological text for Southern Baptists. The eighteenth article, which was just adopted, addresses issues of the family and emphasizes the biblically appropriate relationship between husbands and wives. It calls for wives to "submit...graciously" to their husbands.[20]

In questioning Mohler's interpretation of the text from Ephesians (5:22–33), Patricia Ireland, the president of the National Organization of Women, asked Mohler what he would say to people held in slavery. Ireland pointed out that Paul's admonition to slaves to be good slaves (Eph. 6:5–9) closely follows Paul's admonition to wives to submit to their husbands. Ireland asked if that passage would lead Mohler to condemn as sinful slaves in the United States who tried to run away using the underground railroad in the 1800s.

---

20. A brief discussion of the text appears in *Christian Century* (June 17–24, 1998) 602.

Mohler hesitated, but then proceeded in a way that probably surprised many. Based on his effort to treat every text in the Bible as an equally valid and literal Word of God, he said that the slaves should not have tried to run away. It would have been better if they had shown moral authority superior to that of their masters by remaining and being good slaves.

Falwell, who shares Mohler's view of the Bible, immediately jumped in following Mohler's answer. He said he would have no trouble at all blessing slaves who escaped via the underground railway. He thought that Harriet Tubman and those like her were doing the right thing.

The focus of the show was Paul's directives to wives to obey their husbands, but the fact that Patricia Ireland raised the question of what Mohler would say about Paul's directive to slaves in the same epistle highlights the issue that Knierim's work helps us to address. Both Falwell and Mohler believe in the Bible as the inerrant, literal Word of God. Yet the two men differed on the validity of a text that is not difficult to interpret.

Falwell may not value the kind of careful biblical scholarship Knierim engages in. Nevertheless, he exemplified Knierim's claim that whether or not we do so consciously, we all apply criteria that help us to discern among texts that hold varying degrees of validity for us. Falwell did not explain how he knew that slaves disobeying their masters and running away were to be applauded, not condemned, but neither did he hesitate in disagreeing with Mohler's commitment to the truthfulness of Paul's exhortation.

It would be easy to assume that Falwell made his statement because he was sensitive to the political fallout of claiming that slaves who were good Christians should not have run away, and therefore he made a point of disagreeing with his otherwise like-minded colleague. Their disagreement, however, undermined the issue they agreed on, which is that Paul's exhortation to wives to submit graciously to their husbands is a Word that means exactly what it says and applies to Christian women today. Since Falwell did not make explicit the criteria he was applying, it is not at all clear why one text is considered valid today while a text following it is not. Because we inevitably make such judgments, the failure to acknowledge what we do and to make explicit the criteria we use undermines the credibility of the speaker and is likely to diminish the credibility of the Bible itself for many who are listening.

Some preachers in the United States justified slavery as a proper relationship between two human beings according to God's Word. While this argument is totally unpersuasive today to any but those with a white supremacist mindset, it is nevertheless true that Paul's words remain in the Bible as part of the canon. This will be obvious to any thoughtful youth or adult who reads the Bible. And they will ask questions about what one is to do when the Bible takes a position that Christians today say is sinful. How does the case of Paul's exhortation to slaves relate to his exhortation to women to be silent in the church and submissive to their husbands in the family?

Scholars address the issues raised by these examples from various exegetical and hermeneutical perspectives. But perspectives that offer guidelines for sound exegetical and hermeneutical practices fail to make explicit the criteria we are to use to negotiate between texts that point in contradictory directions, texts that point to God's demand for just and loving relationships and a text like Paul's that encourages slaves to be content with their plight. It is at just this point in a senior high discussion or adult education class that someone may ask, "What good is the Bible as our guide anyway? How can it help us when it says slavery is acceptable?"

The problem raised by Paul's exhortation to slaves is that almost no one believes it should be used to guide Christian behavior today. We know in our gut that it is wrong, but we are discouraged from trusting our own subjectivity in making judgments that lead us to reject the position of a biblical text. What response can clergy and lay leaders offer instead? If we too quickly pass it off as something we all know is wrong, we miss the educational opportunity to think through how and why we reject the validity of certain texts.

Knierim's response is that this is just the point at which we need an explicit, articulated biblical theology to serve in place of the implicit criteria and implicit theology that guide all clergy and lay leaders, whether or not they are aware of it. The potential for deceiving not only ourselves but also others is a critical problem when our criteria remain implicit, and possibly even unconscious.

I emphasize Paul's text on slavery because there is a nearly unanimous rejection of the validity of that text today. Once we acknowledge that even one text is clearly not valid, however, we then must begin to question the criteria in terms of which we evaluate the more controversial texts regarding women.

The establishment of criteria for adjudicating among diverse theological understandings is part of the task of biblical theology, as Knierim understands it. I will return to these aspects of Knierim's approach to biblical theology later in this essay. At this point, however, to provide an overview of Knierim's approach to biblical theology, it is important to see how he understands the disciplines of exegesis and biblical hermeneutic, and their relationships to one another and to biblical theology.

THE RELATIONSHIPS AMONG BIBLICAL EXEGESIS, THEOLOGY, AND HERMENEUTIC

Biblical Exegesis

The task of exegesis involves our efforts "to interpret biblical texts in their own right, on their own terms, apart from us, by way of conscious distanciation. Exegesis focuses on each individual text, be it small or large, and includes attention to its literary context, to its tradition, and to extratextual factors such as anthropology, sociology, history, ontology, epistemology, etc."[21]

Knierim emphasizes the need to consider texts holistically. We cannot get at the meaning of the text as a whole by focusing on individual words or sentences. The meaning of the words and sentences can be found only by understanding their relationships to one another within the text as a whole. Exegetical efforts that focus on texts holistically are also important for the educational process. Encouraging participants in Bible study to consider whole texts rather than isolated verses can help laypersons learn to recognize the ways that meaning can be manipulated when individual verses are taken out of context.

In his insistence on dealing with texts holistically Knierim points to the ways in which ideas and concepts in biblical texts are related to one another in hierarchical semantic systems. For example, Knierim always considers the order in which issues are presented in a text to be semantically significant, not just the result of random chance. In considering the second set of petitions in the Lord's Prayer, for example, Knierim points to the significance of the prayer for daily bread prior to the petitions to be forgiven for sin and redeemed. What does it mean that of all the things humans might be told to pray for each day, the first petition we are to make for ourselves is for food? The order of the petitions does suggest a necessary hierarchy. Without food one's physical existence will end and one will no longer face the need for overcoming

---

21. Knierim, *Task of Old Testament Theology*, 60. It must be noted that Knierim continues to respect the text as an entity that is different from, and not fully constructed by, the interpretive community, as literary theorists such as Stanley Fish would argue. See, for example, S. Fish, *Is There a Text in This Class?* (Cambridge, Mass.: Harvard University Press, 1980). Knierim does not address the arguments that Fish makes against the existence of the text in its own right. While acknowledging that we can never be fully objective in our approach to a text, he argues, nevertheless, that we must strive to consciously distance ourselves from the text in an effort to let the text reveal its substantive content, regardless of our preconceived notions about it or our preferences in regard to its meaning. In striving to honor this process, students in biblical studies and practical theology can learn important lessons of listening to voices different from their own. Doing our best to allow ancient texts to speak for themselves may assist us in listening more openly and carefully to human beings whose life experiences are significantly different from ours.

guilt and seeking redemption. Knierim believes that we need to pay more attention to the theological significance of food.[22]

There is, of course, a wide range of exegetical methods available, any of which may be useful in the interpretation of a particular text. The deficit in exegesis, however, as Knierim sees it, is the inadequate attention given to the content of the text, in contrast to the attention given to the formal aspects of the text. Knierim emphasizes that "all texts say something. They express a subject matter in each element of their reality addressed by the exegetical methods. The neglect of these substantive statements, or their underrepresentation, in exegesis is certainly a major methodological error."[23]

In addition to stressing the need for more attention to the substantive content of texts, Knierim points out that because the biblical texts are theological in nature, exegesis is theological. Theological exegesis should not be considered a distinct method. Rather the theology of the text itself is rooted in the nature of the text. "We are not to theologize a text. We are to exegete its theology."[24] Interpreting the theology of the text is a necessary part of the exegetical process.

To gain insight into the fullest meaning that we can discover in the text, including the theology of the text, insights from the field of structural linguistics are particularly helpful. Structural linguists point to the ways in which a text functions as a semantic, linguistic totality. To exegete a text requires a consideration of the text as a whole, involving identification of all of its aspects and statements, an analysis of the relationships among the parts, and the definition of the whole that emerges from these two processes.

To gain depth of insight into what a text is saying, it is necessary to look beneath the surface expressions of the text to consider the presuppositions on which the more obvious, surface level of the text rests. Although this involves constructing hypotheses, the hypothetical nature of the task must be initiated and controlled by the signals that occur in the text itself. The presuppositions that function at the infratextual or subtextual level are operative in the text, even though we may overlook the signals of their presence.

An example of a textual signal that points to a subtextual concept is illustrated by the word "my" in the phrase "Let my people go!" (e.g., Exod. 5:1). The possessive pronoun plays a significant role conceptually in pointing to Yahweh's commitment to liberate this people

---

22. See, for example, "Food, Land, and Justice," in *Task of Old Testament Theology*, 225–43.

23. Knierim, *Task of Old Testament Theology*, 60.

24. Knierim, *Task of Old Testament Theology*, 61.

because they belong to Yahweh. There is nothing in this text that signals Yahweh's commitment to liberate all oppressed people, of whom God's own people are a part. The theology of liberation in this text is "controlled by the theological concept of Israel's exclusive election. Where this concept is overlooked in exegesis, the story and its concept of liberation are not correctly understood. The *concept* of a text controls its story, while the story actualizes its concept or idea."[25] The Exodus text is, of course, a particularly critical one in much contemporary theology. I will explore the implications of recognizing the underlying concept of exclusive election within it later in this essay.

In addition to describing the texts and their theologies, exegesis includes in its description

> the fact that the texts claim to be true, valid, and authoritative. The Bible does not understand itself as a lexicon of science, history, or sociology, but as a collection of books which may in any of these aspects refer to what it claims to be divine truth which is therefore valid and authoritative for the world and certainly its readers.
>
> Thus, we exegete the theologies and truth claims of the Pentateuch, the deuteronomistic and chronistic history works, of Job, each of the Psalms, the Proverbs, and so on, and of each of the prophets, just as we exegete the theologies and truth claims of the synoptic Gospels, of John, Paul, and the rest of the New Testament books. And the more we do careful exegesis, the more we learn that the Bible is a compendium: of many theological concepts and their stories; of theologies that sometimes agree, sometimes differ even as they complement each other, and sometimes disagree.[26]

The task of exegesis is to interpret the texts in their own right, which involves attention to the text as a whole unit, an analysis of the ways in which each of the formal and substantive aspects of the text relate, an exploration of the semantic concept functioning at the intra-textual or subtextual level that takes expression through the text, and an identification of the theology implicit in each text.

Biblical Theology

Careful exegesis leads to the identification of the diverse theological positions in the Bible. Exegesis itself, however, does not address the relationships among the diverse theological understandings. This is the task of biblical theology. Biblical theology is dependent on and works with the totality of exegetical scholarship, but it involves more than merely summarizing the results of exegesis.

Having identified the diverse theological positions, biblical theology must then do the hard work of establishing the nature of the rela-

---

25. Knierim, "On the Task of Old Testament Theology," 154.
26. Knierim, "On the Task of Old Testament Theology," 156.

tionships among them. Which concepts and understandings are most fundamental? How do the different theological understandings qualify one another? What are the criteria that will be used to evaluate the relative validity of each position?

A critical characteristic of Knierim's approach to Old Testament theology is his insistence on allowing the Old Testament to define its own criteria, thus setting its own agenda. In contrast to approaches that allow the Old Testament texts to define their position only in response to a predetermined Christian perspective, Knierim believes Christian faith can be served most fully by allowing the Old Testament to reveal its own self-understanding and commitments, apart from and prior to initiating a biblical theology that addresses the relationship between the two Testaments.

Thus, Knierim looks to the Old Testament texts themselves to discern criteria for evaluating the validity of any particular perspective. Knierim points to the need for both quantitative and qualitative criteria. Quantitative criteria deal with the extensiveness of God's relationship to the world. The most inclusive, and therefore fundamental, position of the Old Testament in this regard is the affirmation of Yahweh as the universal God of all realms of reality. Yahweh is not the local god of the Hebrews but the one God of all. Yahweh's concerns and involvements are not limited to specific realms of reality. Rather, all realms, all aspects of reality fall under the dominion of Yahweh. The universality of Yahweh's dominion over universal reality provides the most inclusive horizon of the Old Testament.

> It is most fundamental because it constitutes at the same time the ultimate criterion both for Yahweh's deity and for the dimension of his dominion.... Moreover, Yahweh's relationship to universal reality as expressed in the theology of creation, in the final analysis, can be discerned as what is at issue in the Old Testament. In this horizon, human history, Israel's election, and individual existence receive their meaning because they are all part of and have their place and function in Yahweh's dominion of his world.[27]

The quantitative aspect involves the extensiveness of God's relationship to the realms of reality. From the perspective of the Old Testament, there are three essential realms: "the cosmic and natural world; corporate human existence, including Israel's; and individual human existence. In our terminology: cosmos and nature, history and society, and existentiality."[28] The quantitative criteria must be coordinated with the qualitative criteria. The qualitative criteria reflect a hierarchy of the

---

27. Knierim, *Task of Old Testament Theology*, 15.
28. Knierim, *Task of Old Testament Theology*, 12.

ways in which Yahweh relates to each realm of existence. The ways in which Yahweh relates to reality "are found in words or word fields and concepts such as creation, sustenance, election, liberation, covenant, law, justice, righteousness, peace, atonement, forgiveness, judgment, mercy, and so on."[29] Old Testament theology must deal with the ways in which Yahweh relates to the world and the world to Yahweh through these various modalities.

In addition, biblical theology must address the nature of their relationships to one another. What, for example, is the relationship between liberation and justice? The notions are distinct and should not be used interchangeably. From the point of view of the Old Testament,

> liberation is neither the beginning nor the end of a process. It is always release from injustice, and it points toward the restoration or establishment of justice. It is itself an act of, and part of a process of, justice. The theology of liberation is not an independent theology in the Old Testament. It is a subchapter of a dominant theology in the service of which it stands: the theology of justice and righteousness.[30]

This distinction is critical. As previously noted, the Exodus text that is paradigmatic for many liberation theologians is nevertheless troublesome because it expresses a theology of exclusive election. God is not presented as freeing the Hebrew slaves because God stands over and against the oppression of all people. Rather, the text signals that God frees them because they are his people. The exclusivity of Yahweh's concern for one group and not all people is also expressed at the end of the text when it is made clear that the broad land of milk and honey, the land promised to the Hebrews, is the land of Canaan, the land of the "Canaanites, the Hittites, the Amorites, the Perizzites, the Hivites, and the Jebusites" (Exod. 3:8).

Because of the centuries of anti-Semitism, often fueled by Christian leaders, it is important to recognize the sensitivity of any Christian writer pointing to the problems within a text that is central to the theology of the land of Israel. Knierim addresses this issue directly and emphasizes his renunciation of anti-Semitism. He also points out that such renunciation does not mean Israel is beyond criticism. As the Old Testament makes clear, no one is beyond legitimate criticism. Knierim makes his point even more forcefully by stating that "the Christian community is not only unconditionally prohibited from being anti-Semitic but is also prohibited from criticizing Israel *without*

---

29. Knierim, *Task of Old Testament Theology*, 11.
30. Knierim, *Task of Old Testament Theology*, 11.

simultaneously speaking about its own streak of criminality, which runs throughout its entire history up to the present day."[31]

Some liberation theologians for whom the Exodus passage is paradigmatic have begun to address the incongruity of one group being liberated in a manner that leads to the oppression of others. Native American theologians have been especially sensitive to the incongruities of the text, recognizing the ways in which the text has been used against them, casting them in the role of the Canaanites, Hittites, Amorites, and others, whom Europeans justified displacing in their own process of liberation and journey to the promised land of North America.

A biblical theology that insists on addressing these issues within the Bible itself leads to a working out of the relationship between justice and liberation. Knierim's carefully nuanced analysis of justice in the Old Testament provides many insights that will be helpful to practical theologians who are working with the concepts of liberation and justice.[32]

The implications of dealing explicitly with the problems of texts, such as the Exodus text, within the context of biblical theology rather than through biblical hermeneutic only are significant.

> [T]he critical analysis of this or any other biblical text and the criticism of its theological conceptuality in terms of Old Testament theology, rather than on hermeneutical grounds, are inevitable as long as we, together with the Bible, affirm God as the God of universal justice and salvation. Either we may insist on this affirmation and discern where the Bible confirms or undercuts it, or we may accept the Bible's statements at face value (all is valid because the Bible says it) and forfeit our affirmation of the universality of God's justice and salvation. The choice between these two alternative approaches to biblical-theological interpretation is upon us.[33]

Biblical Hermeneutic

The task of biblical hermeneutic involves two aspects. The exegesis of biblical texts and comparable situations in the contemporary world is presupposed. Biblical hermeneutic deals with the encounter between the "validity of texts within the entire biblical theology and, on the other hand, the validity of today's situations within the totality of our own reality."[34] In this process biblical hermeneutic deals with the encounter of the system of meaning represented by the text and its place

---

31. Knierim, *Task of Old Testament Theology*, 135.

32. See, for example, in *Task of Old Testament Theology*, "Justice in Old Testament Theology" (86–122) and "Food, Land, and Justice" (225–43).

33. Knierim, *Task of Old Testament Theology*, 134.

34. Knierim, *Task of Old Testament Theology*, 69.

within the biblical theology, and the system of meaning represented by a particular life situation as it is exists as part of reality today.

Just as he points to the necessity of evaluating the relative truth claims of biblical texts within the task of biblical theology, Knierim likewise points to the necessity of evaluating the relative truth claims of particular life situations, and not settling for descriptions only. This issue is a critical one for practical theologians who struggle, along with scholars in many disciplines today, to understand how, or if, we can adjudicate among competing truth claims. As suggested previously, philosopher Richard Bernstein makes a strong case for recognizing that the successful postmodern challenge to our faith in objectivism does not necessarily leave us in a world of sheer relativism.[35] In a similar vein rhetorician Walter R. Fisher argues that we can and do judge between perspectives that compete for our adherence, and we can learn to discern more fully what is at stake in accepting one perspective while rejecting another.[36]

Knierim's method for establishing explicit criteria that allow us to adjudicate among the competing theologies in the Old Testament applies as we consider a specific life situation as it exists within the larger reality. We inevitably apply criteria that lead us not only to describe but also to evaluate individual situations. Making those criteria clear and reflecting on the source of the criteria are important aspects of interpreting the life situation that the biblical text encounters.

> Ultimately, biblical hermeneutic involves the encounter of two systems of meanings and their respective claims to truth. In this encounter, each speaks independently to the other; neither is the only one that speaks; and it is only through the comparison of the two systems, facilitated by their encounter, that the criteria appear for what is fundamental, guiding, and authoritative, and thus, for orientation, values, truth, and ethos today, and specifically for the authority of the biblical texts themselves for us.[37]

THE IMPORTANCE OF INTERDISCIPLINARY DIALOGUE

The proliferation of scholarship in all disciplines makes it increasingly important for scholars to develop regular ways of communicating with one another across disciplinary lines. As Thomas Kuhn pointed out years ago, specialization tends to lead to the requirement for specialized ears if one is to listen in on and understand what is happening in another field. For practical theologians and biblical scholars who are

---

35. Bernstein, *Beyond Objectivism and Relativism.*

36. Fisher, *Human Communication as Narration.*

37. Knierim, *Task of Old Testament Theology,* 71.

concerned about both the scholarly integrity of their work and the significance of their scholarship for the church, it is critical that dialogue increase. The kind of work represented by Rolf Knierim's Old Testament theology holds great promise for practical theologians. In his essays he explores topics such as justice, spirituality, and the significance of hope in the Bible, in addition to the much emphasized aspect of eschatological hope and the much neglected aspect of importance of food. The care with which he develops the biblical support for his understanding in each case provides rich material for educational programs and preaching. In grappling with the substantive insights of the essays, one can also see the value of his careful reflection on method.

This approach to the Old Testament, which, as Knierim points out, can be extended to the Bible as a whole, may be of particular value to theological educators who are training clergy and church leaders in traditions that honor the doctrine of *sola scriptura*. By learning how to discern criteria from within the Bible to adjudicate the diverse theologies, educators can help people to engage the Bible seriously, while still challenging texts that fail to embody Yahweh's universal dominion in justice and righteousness.

Knierim's approach to biblical theology is not a quick fix for the lack of biblical sophistication found in most churches today. Nevertheless, he provides a way forward that is well worth the time required to study and apply his method.

BIBLIOGRAPHY

Bartow, Charles L. *God's Human Speech: A Practical Theology of Proclamation.* Grand Rapids: Eerdmans, 1997.

Bernstein, Richard J. *Beyond Objectivism and Relativism: Science, Hermeneutics, and Praxis.* Philadelphia: University of Pennsylvania, 1983.

Boys, Mary C. *Biblical Interpretation in Religious Education.* Birmingham: Religious Education Press, 1980.

———. "Religious Education and Contemporary Biblical Scholarship." *Religious Education* 74 (March–April 1979).

Burke, Kenneth. *A Rhetoric of Motives.* Berkeley: University of California Press, 1950.

Cully, Iris V. *The Bible in Christian Education.* Minneapolis: Fortress, 1995.

Elliott, H. S. *Can Religious Education Be Christian?* New York: Macmillan, 1947.

Fish, Stanley. *Is There a Text in This Class?* Cambridge, Mass.: Harvard University Press, 1980.

Fisher, Walter R. *Human Communication as Narration: Toward a Philosophy of Reason, Value, and Action.* Columbia: University of South Carolina Press, 1987.

Juel, Donald. *Mark.* ACNT. Minneapolis: Augsburg, 1990.

————. " 'Your Word is Truth' : Some Reflections of a Hard Saying." Inaugural Address presented at Princeton Theological Seminary, fall 1995.

Knierim, Rolf P. "On the Task of Old Testament Theology." In *A Biblical Itinerary*. Ed. E. E. Carpenter. Sheffield: Sheffield Academic Press, 1997.

————. "On the Task of Old Testament Theology." *JSOTSup 240*. Sheffield: Sheffield Academic Press, 1997.

————. *The Task of Old Testament Theology: Substance, Method, and Cases*. Grand Rapids: Eerdmans Publishing, 1995.

Little, S. *The Role of the Bible in Contemporary Christian Education*. Richmond: John Knox Press, 1961.

Marino, J. S., ed. *Biblical Themes in Religious Education*. Birmingham: Religious Education Press, 1983.

Murphy, Roland. "Update on Scripture Studies." *Religious Education* 82 (fall 1987).

Nelson, C. E. *Where Faith Begins*. Atlanta: John Knox, 1967.

Schrag, Calvin O. *The Resources of Rationality: A Response to the Postmodern Challenge*. Bloomington: University of Indiana Press, 1990.

Smart, James D. *The Strange Silence of the Bible in the Church: A Study in Hermeneutics*. Louisville: Westminster, 1969.

Toulmin, S., R. Rieke, and A. Janik. *An Introduction to Reasoning*. New York: Macmillan, 1979.

Contributors

James E. Brenneman is Professor of Old Testament at Episcopal Theological School at Claremont, Claremont, California, and the pastor at Pasadena Mennonite Church, Pasadena, California.

Mary Katharine Deeley is Lecturer in Old Testament and Biblical Languages at Seabury-Western Theological Seminary, Evanston, Illinois.

Simon J. DeVries is Emeritus Professor of Old Testament at Methodist Theological School in Delaware, Ohio.

Michael H. Floyd is St. Michael and All Angels Professor of Old Testament at the Episcopal Theological Seminary of the Southwest, Austin, Texas.

John E. Goldingay is David Allan Hubbard Professor of Old Testament at Fuller Theological Seminary, Pasadena, California.

Robert L. Hubbard Jr. is Professor of Biblical Literature at North Park Theological Seminary, Chicago, Illinois.

Mignon R. Jacobs is Assistant Professor of Old Testament at Fuller Theological Seminary, Pasadena, California.

Isaac Kalimi is a Professor of Hebrew Bible and Judaic Studies. Currently he is Associate Member of Leiden Institute for the Study of Religions, Leiden University, Leiden, the Netherlands, and International Corresponding Fellow of Ingeborg Rennert Center for Jerusalem Studies, Bar-Ilan University, Tel Aviv, Israel.

Joel S. Kaminsky is Assistant Professor in the Department of Religion and Biblical Literature at Smith College, Northampton, Massachusetts.

Hyun Chul Paul Kim is Assistant Professor of Hebrew Bible at Methodist Theological School in Delaware, Ohio.

Wonil Kim is Assistant Professor of Hebrew Bible/Old Testament at La Sierra University, Riverside, California.

Rolf P. Knierim is Professor Emeritus of Old Testament at Claremont School of Theology and Avery Professor Emeritus of Religion at Claremont Graduate University, Claremont, California.

Charles Mabee is Professor of Old Testament and Director of the M.Div. Program at Ecumenical Theological Seminary, Detroit, Michigan.

Stephen A. Reed is Assistant Professor of Religion and Philosophy at Jamestown College, Jamestown, North Dakota.

Janet L. Weathers is Assistant Professor of Speech Communication in Ministry at Princeton Theological Seminary, Princeton, New Jersey.

Scripture Index

Author Index

Abrams, M. H., 105
Achtemeier, Elizabeth, 151–52,
  153–54, 156
Ahn, Sang Nim, 287n
Albrektson, B., 292
Albright, W. F., 239n
Alderman, H., 109
Allen, Ronald B., 222n
Alter, Robert, 259n
Anderson, Bernhard, 293, 328n, 336,
  338n, 339n
Aristotle, 109
Attridge, H., 96n, 201n
Augustine, 109

Bach, Alice, 263n
Baker-Fletcher, Karen, 286, 287n
Barclay, J. M. G., 183
Barr, James, 313n
Barr, R., 272n
Barrow, J. D., 148n
Barth, Karl, 14
Bartow, Charles, 350
Batto, Bernard, 337
Berger, Peter, 258n
Berlin, Adele, 89n
Bernstein, Richard, 353, 365
Betz, H. D., 200n
Birch, Charles, 328
Bird, Phyllis, 334
Boecker, Hans-Jochen, 215n, 221n
Borowitz, Eugene B., 178n
Botterweck, G. Johannes, 207n, 209n,
  210n, 211n
Bovati, Pietro, 212n, 221n
Boyarin, Daniel, 183n, 282n
Boyer, Edward J., 60
Boys, Mary, 349–50
Braulik, G., 222n, 224n
Brenneman, J. E., 103n
Brenner, Athalya, 278–80
Brett, Mark, 178
Brown, C., 189n, 197n
Bruce, F. F., 319n

Brueggemann, Walter, 89n, 161n,
  178, 206n
Bultmann, Rudolf, 14, 25
Burke, Kenneth, 354

Caird, G. B., 237n
Cannon, J. P., 306n
Cardellini, I., 190n
Cazelles, H., 189n
Charlesworth, J. H., 95n
Childs, Brevard, 14, 111, 161n, 188,
  205n, 214n, 236n, 237n, 238, 240,
  292, 313
Chirichigno, G. C., 189n, 190n
Chung, Hyun Kyung, 287
Clements, Ronald E., 115, 180n
Clifford, R., 333n
Clines, D. J. A., 189n, 263n, 307n
Coggins, Richard J., 207n, 213n,
  232–33, 248n
Collins, John J., 205–6n
Cone, James, 293
Coppes, Leonard J., 207n, 209n
Cox, J. Robert, 109–10
Craigie, P., 226n
Crenshaw, J., 341
Croatto, J. Severino, 292, 293, 294–301,
  303, 305, 308–9, 311–14, 317–18
Cross, Frank M., 273n
Crüsemann, F., 173n, 189n, 190n
Cullmann, O., 155n
Cully, Iris V., 349n

Dandamaev, M. A., 190n
Davies, E. W., 213n
Day, J., 152n
Deeley, Mary Katharine, 112n
Delling, G., 201n
Derrida, J., 309n
DeVries, Simon J., 90n, 129n
Dietrich, W., 248n
Dilthey, Wilhelm, 317
Douglas, Mary, 340
Duck, Ruth, 158, 159